Intellectual Growth

25. Observing the World Around Us: Social Studies, Science and the Beauty of the Earth — 130
26. Numbers in Everyday Living — 203
27. Reading — 210
28. Color — 212

Aesthetic Growth

29. Arts and Crafts — 214
30. Music and Dance — 225

The Grades

31. Nursery — 233
32. Kindergarten — 239
33. Primary — 247
34. Intermediate — 252
35. Senior — 258
36. Young Adults — Prevocational — 261

Bibliographies

General Bibliography — 263
Art Bibliography — 265
Music Bibliography — 266

Appendixes

I. Lesson Plans and Journals — 267
II. Forms Used in Various Procedures — 285
III. Balance Beam Exercises — 309
IV. Patterns for Tracing in Teaching Handwriting — 311

Performance Goals Record

Preface

The number of American and European educators of the retarded who pass each other in mid-Atlantic on their way to visit schools, institutions, and other professional centers is increasing each year. Comparing notes with colleagues who have visited in Europe has made it clear that there is no great consensus as to the merits of any given treatment matter excepting that which is concerned with the work and social abilities of mature retardates. On this point, most agree that the typical European sheltered workshop, for example, more often than not displays an array of work that is far more complex than what is usually found in most American centers. It seems that more of the moderately retarded Europeans engage in tasks that involve the high-level work skills often associated with the operation of machinery and other sensitive equipment than is usually found here. Many live in group domiciliary facilities such as hostels and "use" the commercial and recreational elements of the community in the ordinary course of events.

We could speculate about these differences in occupational and social competence between American and European retardates. They could be an outcome of staffing patterns and intensive supervision. Or it might be that we are seeing only a select segment of the moderately retarded population. Or both. However, when one studies the *total* program for these children and adults, it becomes obvious that what we are seeing in the sheltered workshop and in the community are the results of a long-term, intensive educational program—one that frequently accepts trainable children at the age of three or four and goes on from there, stressing learnings and behaviors relevant to the performance requirements on the way to and at maturity.

Children learn how to play and how to use the toilet and how to move within and about a group as part of the curriculum. And all the time, the essentials of adulthood are nurtured from their primitiveness through to whatever level of sophistication can be attained as a function of intensive and extensive classroom and individual work.

Here and there we have similar programs with similar results. As in the case of our European colleagues, the limited number that exist have derived from careful, but often intuitive, planning by a creative and diligent leadership and staff; intuitive because no extensive cogent groundwork has been laid as a foundation for anything near a universal educational program. Creativity has been in the direction of the synthesis of the literature and day-to-day experience into relevant activities that are consonant with the realistic objectives for trainable children.

Given time to germinate, many of these procedures and the thoughtfulness from which they emerge have to evolve into a document that can be shared by all who are involved and interested. This is what we have here: a book, because it looks like a book, but actually a comprehensive program. It is sectioned off because it is a book, and we all know very well what a book looks like. To the reader, however, the developmental aspects will emerge to some degree in just about every dimension, be it in, near, or about the pedagogic setting.

The reader will assume from the title that this is a book about trainable children. Once into the book, however, traditional concepts of trainability disappear, and the energies usually expended at holding to the "party line" soon become directed at a statesmanlike approach to the education of these children.

The reader can be assured that the content of this book, be it in the form of abstractions or activities, has been well synthesized out of research and experience. He should not equate the straightforward, sometimes homey, language of the authors with the usual speculations and ruminations of the well-intentioned but subjective educator. Instead, the reader should recognize that this book represents years of exploration and experience by an astute leadership and staff—exploration and experience that accounts in great part for the growth of the school from which the content has emerged.

Endeavors in the education of trainable children need the content and procedures contained in this book, if we are to approach the objectives for educating these children. The enhancement of their personal, social, and performance skills at maturity is among these objectives. We now have evidence that a sound educational program can reduce the distinctions between adult moderate retardates where education makes the difference. Hopefully, the users of this book will exploit its advantages in the spirit of its writers: to accumulate and to validate instructional programs for trainable children in the depth and scope such programs demand, so that they, too, can document their learnings as the next progressive step beyond this.

Herbert Goldstein
Chairman, Department of Special Education
Graduate School of Education
Yeshiva University
New York, N.Y.

Revised and Enlarged Edition

TRAINABLE CHILDREN
Curriculum and Procedures

Julia S. Molloy
Principal, Julia S. Molloy Education Center
Author, *Teaching the Retarded Child to Talk*

JOHN DAY BOOKS IN
S E
SPECIAL EDUCATION

THE JOHN DAY COMPANY   NEW YORK
An Intext Publisher

Third Impression, 1974
Copyright © 1963, 1972 by Julia S. Molloy

All rights reserved. No part of this book may be reprinted, or reproduced or utilized in any form or by any electronic, mechanical, or other means, now known or hereafter invented, including photocopying and recording, or in any information storage and retrieval system, without permission in writing from the publisher: The John Day Company, 257 Park Avenue South, New York, N.Y. 10010. Published on the same day in Canada by Longman Canada Limited.

Library of Congress Catalogue Card Number: 70-155017. Printed in the United States of America.

ISBN: 0-381-97028-0
ISBN: 0-381-97027 Paper

Note: The *Performance Goals Record* appearing at the end of this volume may also be purchased separately. Write to the Publisher for quantity prices.

CONTENTS

Preface by Herbert Goldstein ... 4
Introduction ... 5

The Trainable Child and His School

1. New Dimensions for Teaching Children with Retarded Development ... 9
2. "So This Is Your First Year in Special Ed!" ... 14
3. Planning a Day for the Trainable Retarded Child ... 20
4. Creating a Suitable Climate and Environment ... 26
5. Evaluation ... 28

Special People in a Special School

6. The Teacher ... 33
7. The Social Worker in Special Education ... 34
8. The School Nurse ... 39
9. The Psychological Assessment ... 43
10. Evaluating Language ... 45
11. The Multiply Handicapped Child ... 61
12. Prescriptive Teaching via the Illinois Test of Psycholinguistic Abilities ... 67
13. Parents ... 76
14. Volunteers ... 78
15. "Come Ride Our Bus" ... 79

The Five Growth Areas

Physical Growth

16. Body Image and Gross Motor Development ... 81
17. Fine Motor Development and the Grasp Function ... 90
18. Self-Care ... 97
19. Physical Education and Play ... 101
20. Handwriting ... 104

Emotional Growth

21. Behavior ... 110

Social Growth

22. Language and Communication ... 113
23. Child Care Training ... 125
24. Vocational Training ... 129

Introduction

The purpose of a training program for children with retarded development is to provide them with an opportunity to grow physically, socially, emotionally, intellectually, and spiritually, in order that adequate self-care, social adjustment, good planning of leisure time, and satisfying usefulness may be realized for living in comfort and contentment, at home or in an institution. A total program for the trainable child must include parent education, community and public relations, a volunteer program, understanding of teacher requirements, and counseling.

A curriculum is a compilation of experiences in developmental sequence from which useful, socially acceptable adult behavior can be realized.

The wide variety of mores and locale dictates that goals, both terminal and interim, must vary.

The child with severely retarded development living in a large metropolitan area faces adulthood with severe limitations for employment.

A similar child in an agricultutal area will be more readily absorbed in useful chores.

The curriculum presented here is general rather than specific, as it is intended to provide profitable experiences in basic essentials for acceptable adult behavior.

A feeling of worthwhileness and contentment is essential to good mental health. Being useful and busy are contingent upon finding satisfaction through a job well done and knowing that it contributes to a social milieu such as family or community. The job can be in competitive society, contract workshop, or institution.

Specific vocational training can be planned using the basic achievements of communication, particularly following directions, quantification, manipulation and mature social behavior.

Being busy includes good use of leisure time. We must prepare our young people to use leisure time appropriately and to enjoy the pleasures, excitement and beauty of the earth, its sights, sounds, and movements.

The material presented in this volume is intended to be an aid: (1) for planning a program for trainable children, (2) for presenting basic learning techniques in several areas, and (3) for evaluating the effectiveness of the curriculum and the progress of the children. The book is based on experiences and research at Orchard School for Special Education, Skokie, Illinois—a community school serving the "trainable" retarded and the multiply handicapped children of Niles Township. The findings are presented here in readable, practical language, rather than in the type of reporting that is based upon research design. Much of the material has been presented as papers at professional meetings (American Association on Mental Deficiency, Council for Exceptional Children, and the International Congress).

Orchard School was opened in 1950 as a licensed, private, community care center. It grew out of a need to teach children with retarded development the skills that would enable them to live and participate in activities at home, in a workshop, or in an institution. A few graduates have obtained jobs independent of a sheltered workshop. Our children range from 3 to 21 years of age.

In 1959, part of the school joined the public school program for special education. By July 1, 1969, the "part" had grown to 100 per cent public school administration. A new building was constructed in another village of Niles Township—Morton Grove—and was opened for the fall term in 1970. This building is the result of joint efforts of ten cooperating school districts in five villages and is named the Julia S. Molloy Education Center. I am deeply grateful to the community and my colleagues for this honor and for the support, opportunities, and confidence that have made it possible for our school to be what it is today. I have been truly blessed with a staff whose love for children and interest in "what makes them tick" makes many things possible.

The staff members are trained in nursery and kindergarten education (Merrill-Palmer and Pestalozzi Froebel); deaf-oral (Loyola, Chicago); home economics (Florida State College for Women); language pathology and/or communicative disorders (Northwestern University); psychiatric social work (University of Chicago); nursing (Winnipeg General Hospital); physical therapy (Harvard Medical School); occupational therapy (University of Illinois); music therapy (R.M.T., Roosevelt University); special education (Northwestern University); health education (University of Cincinnati), New York University, Illinois, Wisconsin, and Iowa universities.

Membership is held by staff members in the American Association on Mental Deficiency, Council for Exceptional Children, American Speech and Hearing Association (ASHA), American Psychological Association, American Education Research Association, Illinois Psychological Association, and the National Association for Music Therapy. Staff members have also participated in many conventions, workshops, and institutes in the United States, Canada, and Europe.

During my own previous work with physically handicapped children, I became concerned about their problems of communication. Graduate work at Harvard Medical School, the University of Wisconsin, and Northwestern University led to my interest in the problems of children with learning disorders and my association with the pioneering Orchard School. When Cook County Hospital in Chicago opened a clinic for retarded children (The Julian D. Levinson Research Foundation) in 1950, I became a member of the clinic team as a language pathologist and education consultant (part-time) for nine years, until the growing demands of Orchard School required my full-time attention.

Trainable Children was first published by The John Day Company in 1963. Several areas, notably self-care, were not covered in the 1963 edition. A four-year project to study the motor skills required for self-care was completed in 1967. The project, "The Development and Enhancement of the Grasp Function," was made possible by a grant from the Ben Levin Memorial for Retarded Children. The findings are reported herein. Another four-year project, "Prescriptive Teaching with Young Downs Syndrome Children," was supported by the Community Club of Jewish Women (Niles Township). The supportive data for both of these studies were published in 1970.

Current research is going on in two areas of major concern: visual functioning and evaluation techniques, with Dr. Lawrence Lawson, opthalmologist, as principal investigator and with the cooperation of Evanston Hospital. (This project is another tremendous contribution from the Ben Levin Memorial for Retarded Children.) A child care training program to train our teen-agers to work with young children with retarded development has led to a search for means to enhance social adequacy and communication (see chapter 23).

Staff members who have actively participated in these studies are: Stella Tabershaw Baer, Anne Blumenfeld, Calvin K. Claus, Edna M. Eby, Marie Forman, Eleanor M. Healy, Jeannie Johnson, Phyllis Kamin, Joan Kozub, Eleanor Lesak, Anita Bank Manchik, Arlene M. Matkin, Margaret C. Miller, Julia Molloy, Lillian Reed, Lucille R. Romanoff, and Rochelle Weinstein. Mary Stocker, of Toronto, Canada, has also taken an active part in these projects.

We are grateful to Calvin K. Claus, our psychological consultant, for his invaluable assistance in planning our evaluation procedures and for his tireless efforts in searching for potential in our children and interpreting data to parents and staff members.

We are greatly indebted to Maurice Dayan and Cecil Cowell for their invaluable assistance in working with our staff in behavior shaping and behavior modification techniques.

Education for all handicapped children in Illinois was mandated as of July 1, 1970. Dr. Vernon F. Frazee, presently the Director of our Niles Township Department of Special Education, was formerly Director, Department of Special Education, State of Illinois. During that time, Dr. Frazee proposed the mandatory legislation currently in effect and by his dedication to children and sincere convictions that our handicapped children have every right to a public school education, he guided the necessary bills into the School Code of Illinois.

He brought to Niles Township the same strength, courage and leadership that made possible the beautiful new Julia S. Molloy Education Center. Through his support and confidence, the staff and I have been able to explore, develop and refine teaching strategies and innovative procedures.

Abiding gratitude is expressed by the author to Vernon Frazee for his invaluable help and interest.

These words are etched in bronze in the foyer of this Center, and tell the story of the man and the community support he engenders.

Children — receive this Education Center as a living symbol of our love. Live here with joy and know the fullness of life. In this way, the cooperation of the 10 school districts of Niles Township will be justified and the contribution of countless board members will be recognized.

Unity in this project has made a permanent contribution to our sense of community; hence a gift to you, our children, has resulted in a better life for all of us.

Vernon F. Frazee Ed. D.

For hours of typing we extend sincere thanks to Anne Blumenfeld, Joan Potter, Ruth Kupferberg, and Sandy Grossman.

For confidence and encouragement to share our findings, we thank our many interested visitors and colleagues.

J. S. M.

The Trainable Child and His School

Philosophy

As each star differs in brightness, so do the children of man. Yet each serves its purpose in "One nation under God," and each is entitled to an opportunity to achieve his full potential—to adjust to his environment—to grow physically, emotionally, socially, intellectually, and spiritually.

Definition

"Trainable mentally handicapped children are those children who, because of retarded intellectual development, are incapable of being educated properly and efficiently through ordinary classroom instruction or special education facilities for educable mentally handicapped children, but who may be expected to benefit from training in a group setting designed to further their social adjustment and economic usefulness in their homes or in a sheltered workshop." This definition is quoted from the Illinois laws pertaining to special education for exceptional children (Article 2, Paragraph 20-30; Section 12-20; Item No. 4). In addition to the above definition, the Illinois law specifies: " . . . between the ages of 5 and 21." All children eligible by the above legal description and admissible by staff recommendation attend classes in Molloy Education Center instituted by the Niles Township Department of Special Education. This is a cooperative authority involving ten public-school districts, each of which reimburses expenditures for children residing in their school districts. Molloy Education Center is an outgrowth of the Orchard School which operated as a preschool program for children, aged 3 and up.

From this preschool experience a few children have had the opportunity to be transferred to a primary class for the educable mentally handicapped. Some have shown so little progress that the parents have been able to make early decisions about their children's future and to plan accordingly.

The children attending our school are divided into "grades"—nursery, kindergarten, primary, intermediate, senior, young adult (pre-vocational), and a multiply handicapped group. When the enrollment in a "grade" becomes too large, we divide it into junior and senior sections. Thus we may have junior intermediate, intermediate, and senior intermediate groups rather than just one intermediate group. Grouping is based on social and emotional maturity and on chronological age when feasible.

Identification and Procedures for Admission

1. *Referral from physician* stating the condition as retarded mental functioning—giving etiology if established—and noting that vision and hearing are usable.

2. *Recommendation by a qualified psychological examiner* stating that level of intellectual and social functioning is above that expected of a custodial child and below that of an educable child with competitive job potential.

3. *Indication* that the child can profit from a training program through:
   a. *history* and reports from previous agency contacts
   b. *observations*
      1. home visit
      2. parent conference
      3. social inventory indicating the child is amenable to a group situation and can make wants known
      4. expressed willingness of the parents to attend a preadmission study group.

Characteristics

The following characteristics are observable singly or in combination in our children:

1. Distractibility, manifest in:
   a. difficulty with foreground, background significance
   b. short attention span
2. Disinhibition, manifest in difficulty in controlling behavior

3. Sequellae of sensory impairments resulting in:
   a. difficulty in focusing on static material or the opposite—difficulty in focusing on material in motion
   b. difficulty in interpretation of auditory, tactile, or visual stimuli and its translation into appropriate organismic response (problems of perception and conception).

Purpose

Our purpose is to provide an opportunity to grow physically, socially, emotionally, intellectually, and spiritually, by means of a sequential curriculum, indicated by the residual sensory pathways and executed in a bland environment, by adjusted techniques such as described by Lehtinen, Kephart, and Myklebust (see Bibliography). The rationale for the employment of these methods and techniques is based upon the established organicity of the etiology.

The program is directed toward the goal of an adequately adjusted person, who is socially acceptable at home, in the school, in the community or institution, and who is capable of self-care, occupying leisure time purposefully, and being economically useful at home, school, in a sheltered workshop, or residential setting.

Operation

Our school is operated on a home-room, departmental system, with team teacning. Skilled direction is thereby provided in all areas contributing to the achievement of maximum potential of the trainable child for successful functioning at home, in a sheltered workshop, or in an institution.

To achieve the maximum potential for successful, contented living, we are concerned with:

1. Physical growth: to become independent in self-care, to develop good body mechanics, and to learn to practice good personal hygiene
2. Emotional growth: to learn self-control in work and play situations
3. Social growth: to learn to communicate purposefully and profitably, to respect the rights and property of others, and to consider oneself a part of a group with a common purpose
4. Intellectual growth: to learn those skills within the limits of mental capacity to permit the child to work and play safely, purposefully, usefully, and profitably
5. Aesthetic growth: to sustain and nurture an awareness of the beauty of the world about us and an abiding faith in God.

Many situations and experiences are necessary to allow the wide horizontal extensions of each step along the longitudinal program from nursery school to adulthood.

Parent cooperation is essential. This is gained by frequent conferences and evaluations. At our school, a study group for parents of young children holds monthly meetings, in addition to their regular parent-group meetings.

The community created by an attending age distribution from 3 to 21 presents an opportunity for the children to help others, to learn to control themselves in a group situation, to learn to share themselves and their efforts, to play together, and to work together.

1. NEW DIMENSIONS FOR TEACHING CHILDREN WITH RETARDED DEVELOPMENT

The Calf-Path

One day, through the primeval wood,
    A calf walked home, as good calves should;
But made a trail all bent askew,
    A crooked trail as all calves do.

Since then two hundred years have fled,
    And I infer, the calf is dead.
But still he left behind his trail,
    And thereby hangs my moral tale.

The trail was taken up next day
    By a lone dog that passed that way;
And then a wise bell-wether sheep
    Pursued the trail o'er vale and steep,
And drew the flock behind him, too,
    As good bell-wethers always do.

And from that day, o'er woods and glade,
    Through those old woods a path was made;
And many men wound in and out,
    And dodged, and turned, and bent about
And uttered words of righteous wrath
    Because 'twas such a crooked path.

But still they followed—do not laugh—
    The first migrations of that calf,
And through this winding wood-way stalked,
    Because he wobbled when he walked.

This forest path became a lane,
    That bent, and turned, and turned again.
This crooked lane became a road,
    Where many a poor horse with his load
Toiled on beneath the burning sun,
    And traveled some three miles in one.
And thus a century and a half
    They trod the footsteps of that calf.

The years passed on in swiftness fleet,
    The road became a village street;
And this, before men were aware,
    A city's crowded thoroughfare;
And soon the central street was this
    Of a renowned metropolis;
And men two centuries and a half
    Trod in the footsteps of that calf.

Each day a hundred thousand rout
    Followed the zigzag calf about;
And o'er his crooked journey went
    The traffic of a continent.
A hundred thousand men were led
    By one calf near three centuries dead.
They followed still his crooked way,
    And lost one hundred years a day;
For thus such reverence is lent
    To well-established precedent.

A moral lesson this might teach,
    Were I ordained and called to preach;
For men are prone to go it blind
    Along the calf-paths of the mind,
And work away from sun to sun
    To do what other men have done.

They follow in the beaten track,
    And out and in, and forth and back,
And still their devious course pursue,
    To keep the path that others do.

But how the wise old wood-gods laugh,
    Who saw the first primeval calf
Ah! many things this tale might teach—
    But I am not ordained to preach.

(via Norman Ellis)
Sam Walter Foss (1858-1911)

We have come a long way since the magnificent start given to us by Itard and Seguin. Somewhere we got lost on a calf-path. Until the mid-fifties, the American Speech and Hearing Association (ASHA) actually advocated *not* attempting to work with the child with an IQ below 70—and textbooks said (and some still do) that mongoloid children cannot learn to talk.

My introduction to children with retarded development was classically textbook plus a visit to an institution, so I too believed mongoloid children could not talk. Upon completion of my masters work at Northwestern University, I took a temporary job at a newly established (1950) school for retarded children. Being fresh from the Northwestern clinics I began my work by evaluating the communicating status of each child—and I met Pete. Pete, a 6-year-old mongoloid, the son of a truck farmer, and part of a loving large family, was strong and healthy. I was alone in the classroom, which was actually a field house in a park, with no recorder, no one to handle the auditory stimulation material, just Pete, myself, and some idealism. I held Pete in my lap in an effort to channel him and had a toy bus in my left hand and a pencil in my right hand to transcribe phonetically his expected utterances. I pushed the bus: "Say bus, Pete, say bus"; he said "bu—," which I eagerly entered into the record. Thinking I might have heard a trace of an "s" sound I tried again: "Bus, Pete, say bus." He turned his face toward me and said loud and clear, "I ted dat, yuh tupid jackass!" Thus I learned that mongoloids could talk.

Some people conceded that mongoloids could talk but thought they labeled and said words only, employed no syntax, and never could project in time. Then I met Marylou, a 7-year-old brightly smiling charmer, the oldest of a loving family of six. The day before we were to go to the Shrine Circus she entered her classroom and greeted her teacher with, "We can hardly wait until tomorrow, can we, Miss DeWose." Syntax, projection in time, and surely no paucity of ideas. But, that's the way it was...

"The traditional democratic invitation to teach the individual to achieve the best that is in him requires that we provide each youngster with the particular kind of education which will benefit him. This is the only sense in which equality of opportunity can mean anything. The good society is not one that ignores individual differences but one that deals with them wisely and humanely.

"... We must expect each student to strive for excellence in terms of the kind of excellence that is within his reach ... we must recognize that there may be excellence or shoddiness in every line of human endeavor. We must learn to honor excellence (indeed to demand it) in every socially accepted human activity, however humble the activity, and to scorn shoddiness, however exalted the activity ... The society that scorns excellence in plumbing because plumbing is a humble activity and tolerates shoddiness in philosophy because it is an exalted activity will have neither good plumbing nor good philosophy. Neither its pipes nor its theories will hold water." So stated John W. Gardner in *Excellence*.

We must pursue excellence in working with all children—the humble, the impoverished, the culturally or intellectually deprived, as well as the gifted.

We are concerned here with children with retarded development, as defined by Bijou in *A Factoral Analysis of Retarded Development*: " ... A retarded individual is one who has a limited ability to profit from experience. We therefore must create and manipulate opportunity for experience from which he can profit. This requires effective people and intriguing things."

The contributions from the old literature, such as works by Seguin and Descoeudres, gave us some basic material that somehow or other became lost around the turn of the century. We experienced some dark ages of institutionalizing rather than managing, of isolating or segregating rather than preparing a child to meet life realistically. Militant parents in the late 1940s rattled the cages in which they found themselves trapped with their children who were being kept away from society rather than prepared to live in it. By society here I mean any society appropriate and necessary in which a child must be prepared to function. This could be at home, in the community, in competitive society, or in an institution.

Recent literature is bright, daring, encouraging, and inspiring. No longer can we accept the equating of a group labeled "retarded children" as a bona fide sample; there actually is no such entity. If you accept the premise that retardation is a symptom rather than a disease you can readily understand this point. So much research cites the use of fifty retarded children in one sample and fifty in another, matched by sex, age, and IQ. If these children are broken down in etiological groups, research of course becomes very difficult, yet how much validity can we accord to results from such a nebulous entity as a group of "retarded children" or "retardates"? Today, Downs Syndrome cannot be considered an entity of oneness. Recent research indicates strong possibilities of differing disabilities between the mosaic and trisomy Downs Syndrome child.

True, we are still deluged with fragmented research that seldom becomes useful in the training and education of our children; however, each journal carries the excitement of the era. Surely it is a new day for our children. Our biggest task lies in the conversion of the trotters of the calf-path into thinkers and doers. No longer can we accept the premise of irreversibility. None of us is ready to proclaim that we can make normal children out of children with retarded development, but we can improve their functioning. Colwell and Dayan's work with behavior shaping of profoundly retarded patients at Pinecrest State School, Louisiana, demonstrated clearly that behavior changes can be made, reversing a child who is totally dependent to a toilet-trained, self-feeding, self-dressing, and receptive social human being. Communication shaping with this same group showed results far beyond anticipation.

We are very aware of the child who does not learn in the normal way, yet who, through proper diagnostic procedures, can develop strength through compensating manipulations or directly through remedial techniques. There are, I believe, thirty-four different terms describing these children: learning disabilities, minimal brain damage, etc. I am inclined to regard children with retarded development as children with learning disabilities in various degrees and patterns. The alternative to this theory seems to be the acceptance of the premise of irreversibility, and after my experiences at Pinecrest State School, where I was privileged to participate in the "J-1 project" with Cecil Colwell and Maurice Dayan, I am convinced that irreversibility applies to very few children and particularly to very few children attending public school programs.

We cannot deny that some descriptive material must be employed for legal purposes and definitions in the framework of laws, rules, and regulations. Actually such definitions are for the convenience of the lawmakers and the taxpayers. Such neat legal descriptions lose their neatness as you cross, not only from one school district to another, but also from one state to another. If you have an IQ of 32 you are not "trainable" in Illinois or Pennsylvania, but you are "trainable" in California and Indiana. If you have a 29 IQ you are "trainable" in Missouri. If you have an IQ of 59 you are not "educable" but you are "trainable" in many places. Can anyone honestly set a base line at this time that will predict the ultimate potential of children with retarded development?

Outline of the Behavioral and Medical Classification in Mental Retardation

Adapted with modifications (1960) from Rick F. Heber, *A Manual on Terminology and Classification in Mental Retardation*, Monograph Supplement to the *American Journal of Mental Deficiency*, September 1959, vol. 64, no. 2, 111 pages and available from the American Association on Mental Deficiency, P.O. Box 96, Willimantic, Connecticut—$2.00. The *Manual* was approved as the official terminology and classification in mental retardation of the American Association on Mental Deficiency at its annual meeting at Baltimore, Maryland, in May, 1960.

Mental retardation refers to subaverage general intellectual functioning which originates during the developmental period and is associated with impairment in adaptive behavior.

Subaverage refers to performance which is greater than one standard deviation below the population mean of the age group involved on measures of general intellectual functioning.

General intellectual functioning may be assessed by performance on one or more of the various objective tests which have been developed for that purpose.

Developmental period may be regarded for practical purposes as having an upper limit of approximately sixteen years.

Adaptive behavior refers primarily to the effectiveness of an individual in meeting the natural and social demands and expectations of his environment. Maturation, Learning, and Social Adjustment are of prime importance for the preschool, school, and postschool aged groups respectively.

Within the framework of the present definition mental retardation is a term descriptive of the *current* status of the individual with respect to intellectual functioning and adaptive behavior. An individual may meet the criteria of mental retardation at one time and not at another.

Patients must be classified on both Measured Intelligence and Adaptive Behavior in addition to supplementary specific impairments.

The Measured Intelligence dimension is intended for the classification of the current intellectual functioning of the individual as indicated by performance on objective tests designed for that purpose. It is not intended to reflect any inference of potential or absolute level of intelligence.

Level of Deviation in Measured Intelligence	Range in Standard Deviation Value	Range in IQ Scores for Revised Stanford-Binet, L.
Borderline	-1	-1.01 to -2.00	83-68
Mild	-2	-2.01 to -3.00	67-52
Moderate	-3	-3.01 to -4.00	51-36
Severe	-4	-4.01 to -5.00	35-20
Profound	-5	<-5.00	<20

The Adaptive Behavior dimension has two major facets: 1) the degree to which the individual is able to function and maintain himself independently, and 2) the degree to which he meets satisfactorily culturally-imposed demands of personal and social responsibility.

Level of Retardation in Adaptive Behavior

Mild	-1
Moderate	-2
Severe	-3
Profound	-4

Using the American Association on Mental Deficiency definition we are left with the question of how to measure adaptability. Leland's extensive work at Parsons State School in Parsons, Kansas, to develop an adaptability scale is most encouraging.

A brief overview of the current status of classes for children with retarded development reveals programs from the finest to the poorest: from excellent classroom situations to basement rooms; from truly charismatic teachers to discarded teachers with tenure; from stereotyped, repetitive curriculums, if you can call them that, to brilliant, experimental, lively programs, and all points in between. The bright new teachers coming along full of bright new ideas and energies to experiment will surely bring some changes long overdue.

The literature contains many surveys of the "graduates" of programs for the educable retarded child. The question that comes to mind is, How much use have these surveys been in effecting change in curriculum development? We need to bring together the fine ideas that are now too often lying dormant in bits and pieces.

If we analyze the success of the "graduates" of the programs for the educable, what kind of person has succeeded? It is usually the socially acceptable, adaptable person with a skill, and a good ability to follow directions. Gellman's studies of job analysis in vocational training have found much the same thing. Do we know how to teach our young people to be socially acceptable, to listen and follow directions, to be adaptable, and to have a marketable skill? Many people do know how to teach these skills, but not enough. The problem seems to lie in teacher training.

A genuine manpower shortage exists at the university level. Teachers are being trained by instructors who actually never taught in a classroom, who consistently rehash the literature and refuse to grow, refuse to change, and are prone to ridicule those who try to grow or effect changes. This is unfortunately too prevalent. They just cling to that calf-path. Many very fine university courses are offered for teacher training but not nearly enough. With mandatory legislation gradually spreading across the country, the growth of programs cannot be met by adequately trained teachers without some radical changes in current practices. Assigning student teachers to a top-flight master teacher would probably enable them to learn more of the practical teaching arts than they possibly could through the lecture rehash system.

If we could adopt Bijou's concept, a "Functional Analysis of Retardation," and sharpen our abilities to provide appropriate experiences, it would seem logical to propose a strongly integrated program for our so-called educable children. By this I mean integrated in the mainstream of life between those children who will stay in the competitive situation and those who need to be segregated and exposed to every device possible to realize their potential. Here is where we desperately need to study receptivity and adaptability.

The Vineland approach surely will not do this but perhaps Leland's material will. Language measures at the present time tell us only current output, and do not tell potential or predict success.

The severity of the learning disorder seems to be a predictor, but the word severity needs scrutiny. It is more the kind of learning disorder the child suffers that controls his behavior, which in turn dictates whether or not this child can be contained in a regular classroom. A child with a measured IQ of 90 could be non-containable while a tractable child with a measured IQ of 60 could manage very well in a classroom.

Can the Illinois Test of Psycholinguistic Abilities (ITPA) tell us what we need to know about cognitive potential? Many indications are that it will go a long way in helping us to plan for children with learning disabilities. It surely will provide some system for teaching children to follow directions, to "see and do", or to "listen and do."

Now let us look again at the program for integration of a child with a learning disorder, who functions in the mainstream of a public school. If the homeroom is a slower classroom and team teaching is available, if tutoring, language therapy, adaptive physical education, group counseling and diversified education can be made available via team teaching, the child should be able to grow socially and be better prepared to work in competitive society, because of long experience in the competitive society of his public school.

At this point, I would like to make it clear that I shall refer to children with retarded development and children with learning disabilities as one and the same group. It is a matter of degree of disability. I am fully aware that this is heresy to many people but I find I cannot subscribe to the old concept of irreversibility except in those cases where sensory and physical impairment have created an organism so far from neurological intactness that potential is hardly discernible.

Who, then, finds his way into a segregated school? In many places all special education classes (except for the gifted) are in segregated buildings. There is much to be said in favor of this method in that the expensive therapists and specialists in special education can serve more children. If the segregated school is large enough to allow competitive societies to exist in each level of a building, a strong case can be presented in defense of this arrangement. However, extreme caution should be used to allow each child to have his place in the sun. How many chores are to be done in any one school building? The trainable child or the non-ambulatory cerebral palsy child can easily be deprived of opportunities to complete a mission and gain a genuine feeling of worthwhileness. To manage such a situation is a strong challenge to the school administration.

The most effective team teaching can be programmed in this segregated school situation particularly if it houses only children with retarded development, or better stated, children with learning disabilities which preclude their containment in competitive "normal" school situations. The use of aides, ancillary personnel, can result in an all-out effort to enhance maximum growth. Social group therapy has long been neglected with our teen-agers with retarded development and becomes practical only when the population is large enough to justify the presence of a psychiatric social worker. The social worker is an extremely important staff member, as she is in a position to nurture parent support, parent understanding, and parent interest, and to provide supportive counseling with students and group discussions.

If we are to establish curriculum that is based upon what we know we must prepare our children for, we must try to state our goals clearly: we must ask the question, what are we going to try to produce? What is our guiding philosophy? We need objectives clearly stated, we need content to reach the objectives, we need methodology and techniques to get the content across. We must work with the child to prepare him to accept the inroads that must be made upon his disabilities. We must lead the child to be socially intact, to manage his behavior before we can attempt to get any content across to him. We must help the child to become motorically intact, developing his body image, his control of movements—what, where and how he moves. And we must strive for sensory intactness, training his receptive and his expressive abilities so that he may communicate profitably.

Self-realization is a beautiful objective. Only through the security of a feeling of success and worthwhileness can it be achieved.

At the present time building programs are being planned all over the country. Many of the concepts are magnificent. Unfortunately some of them are the minimal reflection of a "let's-get-it-over-with" attitude. There is one basic philosophy for building a facility as an education center—that is simply that it should provide space and equipment to do the job that must be done in a segregated school, and I mean the job that cannot be done in the integrated schools. There must be a place for social growth, for motor growth, for the development of skills for jobs.

We subscribe to the premises of Strauss, amply supported by Cruikshank and Bijou, that the environment must be as bland and as free as possible from distraction for the direct learning situation for the little children. There must be a place to be alone, either completely or with the therapist. It must be a happy, stimulating, comfortable place where effective people and intriguing things can happily find their way into maximum effectiveness.

2. SO THIS IS YOUR FIRST YEAR IN SPECIAL ED!

by Stella Tabershaw Baer

One must not rely on miracles.   Proverb

Special Education teachers are sensitive people. This is a very good thing to be. It is as though you have a special radar which allows you to pick up the subtle signals around you. Being sensitive enables you to tune in on the needs of others and helps you create effective ways for dealing with the many problems that are a part of each day.

You will be able to look past all the anomalies and see through to the child's own humanity, recognizing him as a person you respect. Every child in your room is worthy of your love. You may not feel it with each child all at once, but given time and the closeness of working and learning together, you will soon look for and find many lovable qualities in each child. You will begin to admire the unique way he responds to the life that was given to him.

As a sensitive person, you will want so much to help these children that you will experience an unbearable sense of failure unless you set realistic goals, not only for the children and their parents but for yourself as well.

How can you establish realistic goals for your class?   You will need:

1. *Knowledge* about the fields of mental retardation, child development, and learning disabilities. There is an excellent bibliography at the end of this book. If you have access to a library, read as much as you can. If there is no library, ask your principal to buy some books for you. If funds are limited try to borrow the books from another school, even if you have to sit there to read them because they can't be taken out. If you have no other alternative, buy some yourself. It is always a good idea to have your own library, anyway. Perhaps your school will reimburse you for part of the cost. Membership in professional organizations such as AAMD or CEC will bring you some excellent journals and periodicals to read and collect as part of your library.

    Visit other schools and talk with other people in the field and with those in related fields, psychologists, pediatricians, therapists, etc.

    Take advantage of any good courses, seminars, or institutes being given in your area. You will learn from them or, as sometimes happens, they will learn from you.

2. *Information* about the child. Good medical and psychological reports give you needed information. A social worker's report, reports from previous teachers and therapists, and an interview with the parents all help you to know the child.

3. *Observation.* Sharpen your senses and observe the child carefully. Notice the way he moves, the way he speaks, his successes, his failures, his frustrations, and his joys. Take your time and evaluate carefully. In the final analysis, an experienced teacher's observations about a child are probably the most valid indication of his functioning level.

4. *Faith.* Confidence that you and the child can work together is essential. You need to believe that there is a good chance that you can achieve what you set out to do.

5. *A Spirit of Adventure.* Curiosity and the courage to try something new and an open mind to explore and discover make your work exciting and meaningful for you and the class.

6. *Patience*—this above all. You will teach the same things many times in many different ways. It takes a long time for little movements to become great moments.

    The first time you have everyone's attention during a lesson, or your class lines up with partners and walks (no running or pushing) quietly through the halls; the first time a child flushes the toilet, hangs up a coat, zips a jacket, plays with another child, sits quietly in assembly, speaks in a sentence, hops, skips, writes his name, or reads an entire experience chart story—these are cherished rewards for patience—all great moments.

Don't be hasty in your evaluations. Often a child will show little evidence of learning. He may be absorbing many new things (reception or decoding) but not showing it (expressing or encoding). This can go on for days, months, or years until suddenly it seems he will blossom forth and surprise you.

Many factors contribute to great moments in teaching:

Many things contribute to this happening. Maturation is always a prime factor. Everyone, retarded or not, has his own developmental clock. You cannot take credit for maturation, but you can provide experiences for maturation to find its way.

These children often tend to repeat a learned response. If they are used to doing little, they continue to do little. It may be a change in grouping, a new technique, or a new friend that breaks the pattern and sets the child free to a more expansive repertoire of behavior.

Inner motivation is another factor. The child's needs change, and he expresses these needs. He wants to say more, do more, participate more fully in life. His image of himself is changing from passive and helpless to active and capable.

The child's awareness of outer motivation is also important. What is expected of this child? The functioning level of the class and the expectations at home should provide sufficient motivation for him to grow.

Dr. Edward Zigler, of Yale University, charts a philosophy that should point the way with precise clarity.

"Failure→expectation of failure→failure.
Success →expectation of success→success."

Plan and Overplan

Many of the children are either hyperactive or lethargic. In either case they have a short attention span, and you will need to be very positive about what you want to do if you are to keep order in the room.

It will be much easier for you if the day is planned ahead of time, so that you can go from one activity to the next without taking your attention from the children. In fact it is a good idea to overplan, at least at first. In that way, you can discard a lesson if it's going badly and go to the next one without worrying about ending up with a big piece of unused time at the end of the day. It would, however, be wise to have a collection of last minute fill-ins, bedlam breakers, and other similar activities that the class enjoys, to be used at crucial moments to save your sanity and put that beautiful smile back on your face.

Try to stay with your plan, making adjustments when necessary, until you feel comfortable in the classroom and know your children well enough to design a program more suited to their individual and collective needs. At the end of this chapter we have included a mini-curriculum which may help start you off. Please remember this guide is not to be followed religiously. It is intended not to limit you but rather to serve as a starter for your own ideas and those of the class.

Let's Face It

Contrary to popular belief, the child with retarded development does not remain a child all his life. He grows up to be an adult with retarded development. This distinction is very important to the teacher in establishing her long-range objectives. She will want to keep in mind those characteristics that are compatible with happy adult living and to find ways to help her children develop them. Whereas the child's primary concern is with himself and his own growth and adjustment, the adult must move away from this self-centered thinking toward concern for his loved ones, friends, the community, and all of mankind. The retarded adult will grow in these areas of concern too if he is encouraged to do so. He will gain in dignity and self-esteem if he can function as an adult with limited abilities rather than as a child. The law should recognize his status as an adult with special problems, for his needs are different from those of a child.

In former years the family of the retarded had been charged with the full responsibility for his care. This included the social, financial, educational, and medical needs for his entire life. The alternative for the most part was institutionalization. The growth of day schools, in recent years, has enabled many families to keep their children living at home during the school years. We face a tremendous challenge to prepare our children for adult life either at home, in the community, or in an institution.

Can the retarded adult live happily with his family and can the family live happily with the retarded adult? The American family is changing. Today each member of a family seeks to develop his own potential. We have an ever-increasing number of working mothers. We have a high incidence of divorce. We are a mobile population. Not only do individuals and families move, but whole communities seem to change from one generation to the next and often sooner. Change is becoming our way of life and making things particularly difficult for retarded people, because change means learning new routines, expectations, and challenges.

What can the teacher do to help the situation? She can prepare her children for adult living by not setting limits on their potentials, but by opening new avenues of experience and challenge for them.

By keeping her sights on the future, the teacher provides the broadest possible program to enable her children to find fulfillment as retarded adults.

As adults they have the right to:
1. An agreeable place to live
2. Meaningful employment, sheltered or competitive
3. Appropriate compensation
4. A satisfying social life
5. Continuing opportunity for learning
6. Interaction with the community
7. Respect as a warm and loving human being

One of our most respected contemporary artists has said, "The artist tries to draw a perfect circle. The imperfection in the circle is his humanity." The handicapped child tries to draw a perfect circle; the imperfection in the circle we call his disability. In special education, as we keep trying to draw that perfect circle, we would do well to keep in mind that it is human to be less than perfect. This means you, the teacher, as well as the child.

All too often a teacher is assigned to a class of children grouped as "trainable" with practically no warning, no preparation, and little or no cooperation from the administration. This is very unfortunate. This chapter is intended to be a quick help to a newly assigned teacher, to tide her over until she can accomplish some in-depth planning. Its main intent is to offer support for a valiant undertaking.

Enjoy your class. Be sure to include fun in your planning and remember the second year is always easier than the first.

A TYPICAL WEEK'S PROGRAM

9:00 to 9:30	*Routine of arrival* Put away coats and lunches. Go to washroom, check grooming, change to gym shoes. Encourage children to do as much for themselves as possible (self-care). Look at books or do puzzles.
9:30 to 10:00	*Morning circle* Arrange chairs in semi-circle around blackboard or bulletin board. Read job list (each child has a job which changes every week). Discuss date, weather; salute flag. Language development through Peabody Kit, Bereiter-Engelman Project Manual, teacher's pictures, *Sounds and Patterns of Language* series, etc. — or News Times and Show and Tell.
10:00 to 10:30	*Gym, outdoor play or physical ed. in your room* Balance boards, spatial orientation, explore movement-(directionality, flow, rhythm), calisthenics, stretch, bend, twist, pull, push, mat work, angels in the snow, gross motor games, races; use bean bags and ball, march, dance, jump, hop, crawl, creep, slide, gallop, skip, go over hurdles, under bridges, through tunnels, around obstacles, follow trails; and don't forget to pretend to be choo-choo trains, rabbits, turtles, ducks, bears; walk on tip-toes, walk backwards, run in place, and walk through the halls in line.
	Go to washroom if needed
10:30 to 11:00	*Three days a week* Handwriting Tracing Sequence, Frostig exercises, blackboard work, workbooks, writing, or simple eye-hand training such as string beads; use peg boards, pick up cotton balls with tongs. Plan carefully for individual work, depending on each child's level. *Two days a week* Cut, paste, color. Teach as skills, not as art lesson.
11:00 to 11:15	*Numbers and sequencing* Number work and number games to learn number concepts, count, recognize number symbols. *Time concepts and sequencing* When, now, later, tomorrow, yesterday, before, after, first, next, last. Listen, tell, compose sequence stories and play sequence games. Listen to and obey a sequence of commands — "jump up, touch the floor, touch the blackboard, and sit." *Quantity concepts* How much, not enough, enough, too much, a little, a lot, more, less, heavy, light, big, tall, small, short, tiny, teeney-weeney, gigantic, almost, one, alone, not alone, pair, many, group, crowd, close, touch, not touch, near, away, above.
11:15 to 11:30	*Prepare for lunch* Bathroom and wash up. Give out lunch boxes, clean and set table, if you eat in your room, or go to lunchroom.
11:30 to 12:00	*Serve and eat lunch* Clear table, stack and rinse dishes, wash table, sweep the floor. Stay with your class. This is a learning experience for them.

12:00 to 12:30	*Noontime recreation* *Part I (Quiet)* TV, quiet games, or rest. If the children are very young, you may want them to sleep on cots. Remember, poor spatial orientation makes it almost impossible for some of our children to lie still on a blanket on the floor. They need the definite boundaries of a cot to keep them from wiggling all over the floor.
12:30 to 1:00	*Noontime recreation* *Part II (Active)* In addition to the gross motor activities mentioned earlier, this is a good time for creative play and spontaneous socializing, such as playing house, school, cowboys, daddy, delivery boy, etc. Dolls, buggies, wooden horses, bicycles, wagons, etc. are all helpful in stimulating this kind of play. Creative play allows children to experiment with various roles and situations. It leads to social insights and resourceful thinking. You will learn a great deal about your children by watching this activity. Try to involve those who don't participate; hand them a toy, suggest things they might do, but don't force them. They may not be ready. Some children become bored or restless after a short while; be prepared to intercede with a more structured activity or game before this happens. For teen-agers or older youths, job assignments, group discussions, or dancing to current records would be appropriate.
1:00 to 1:30	*Afternoon circle* (or at seats) Reading, word recognition, reading words of protection. Science, the weather and what it means, experience charts using pictures and word stories, social studies (self-concepts, family living, community, self-control, responsibility and love and kindness). Health and safety.
1:30 to 2:00	*Art and music* Creative, expressive experiment with materials. Include tactile as well as visual sensory stimulation. *Tactile* *Visual* textures patterns soft colors hard lines flexible movement rigid mass cold area hot shapes rough bumpy smooth wet Also include easy craft projects. Easel painting and wood constructions are very satisfying to some children. If you feel hammer and nails are too dangerous, use a wood paste or glue. Encourage aesthetic responses. How does it make you feel? happy peaceful sad quick cold prickly summery feathery like a bird yummy scared hungry funny loving pretty mean wet windy *Music* Songs and dances, rhythm bands, pantomimes, records. Include all auditory sensory stimulation — sounds, rhythms, vibrations, etc. Vocal responses—sing, hum. Total body responses— clap, tap, snap fingers, dance.

| 2:00 to 2:30 | *Large group experiences*
Parties, assemblies. Invite another class into your room if assemblies are not scheduled at least once a week. Show filmstrips and slides; sing. Other days use eye-hand activities, manipulative toys, self-care projects, games and puzzles. |
| 2:30 to 3:00 | *Prepare for dismissal*
Clean up room, dress, wait for bus. |

Allow time for clean-up between activities; also remember that some children need time to shift gears from one activity to the next. Shorten or lengthen an activity time according to the needs of your class.

You really need a quiet place, the help of an aide, a volunteer or another teacher to do individual work. If you must work alone, try to teach your class to work at puzzles and games independently and quietly, so that you can work with each child individually as often as possible. It's difficult to do, but try.

Bedlam breakers

1. Train your children to sit when you count to 10. Don't say 10 until everyone sits. Lead them to their chairs if they won't go, and you sit too. Give a reward.

2. Change seats. Sometimes it helps to place a hyperactive child between two passive children or place him near you, or away from the stimulation of the class in a time-out room or in the corner. It's not punishment. It's just helping him calm down.

3. Turn off the lights. Lower your voice. Ask them to show you how quietly they can sit. Give reward.

4. If nothing else works, take them into the gym and let them run around for a while.

3. PLANNING A DAY FOR THE TRAINABLE RETARDED CHILD

by A. Mary Stocker

The world is so full of a number of things,
I'm sure we should all be as happy as kings.
—Robert Louis Stevenson

Introduction

The school life of the trainable retarded child must be very carefully planned in order to assure development of the whole child in all aspects of growth to the maximum of his potential. Daily activities must be organized, therefore, into stimulating learning experiences within the child's range of abilities.

The Teacher

Such planning of daily programs is the professional responsibility of the teacher. In modern concepts of education, the teacher is the key person in planning educational programs and evaluating each child's progress. She has achieved a much more significant role in designing educational goals for her pupils. She observes, plans, guides, and provides interesting experiences to integrate all activities into a total daily program.

The success of the day will depend upon the teacher's competency. The teacher has the following tasks:

1. setting educational goals and objectives;
2. planning individualized and group programs;
3. designing learning experiences in varied environmental settings;
4. providing opportunities for the pupils to explore the environment, experiment with materials, and experience learning through touching, moving, talking, listening, and creating;
5. organizing activities into interesting daily programs, including the organization of materials into sequential patterns, learning environments into interesting settings, learning tasks into sequential procedures; and
6. helping each child to his share of success in his daily efforts and achievements.

However, the most important task for the teacher is to understand the children she teaches. She must gain a close knowledge of each pupil and a deep understanding of his needs.

The Child

Every child follows the same general growth patterns of development. The retarded, like the normal, progresses through the same stages on the way to maturity, but at a much slower pace. The teacher will notice that the retarded children differ from one another in all the various aspects of growth and that each makes gains in his personal and social development according to his capabilities. Not all children in her class will reach the same level of development. Some learn at a faster pace than others. Children who learn at a very slow rate should not be forced to keep up with those who are faster. Each pupil will need a specially designed program in order to function meaningfully and purposefully at home and at school and to progress in his development.

Planning Groups for Learning

Because of the wide age range and wide range of differences in abilities among pupils in classes for retarded children, stress is on individualized programming based on developmental levels. It is important for every child to have success at his own level and within his own range of abilities for a positive sense of achievement. In a class for retarded children there are no artificial standards which are imposed by grades, and the grouping of children through which they will learn to live with others is flexible. There should be no pressure to conform to groups as this will only frustrate the children in their learning and thus hinder progress. The flexible grouping is in harmony with the social and emotional well-being of the pupils, and allows advancement in each child.

Groups are organized for various activities, such as music, physical activities, morning assembly, dancing, etc., so that the children may interact and develop socially, work or play together, and learn social skills. There are many valid reasons for teaching retarded children in groups: to develop attitudes, to increase the pupil's awareness of others, to awaken new interests, to stimulate verbal expression, and to develop an attitude of belonging and sharing with others in the group.

We must remember that the retarded child has great difficulty in adjusting to group situations. He will need time to relate to other people. He has to gain awareness of self before he will be able to relate to others individually and, later, in groups. It is important for the teacher to provide many opportunities for group experiences during the day to help the child to adjust gradually. Understanding each child's difficulties in social functioning and his needs for adjustment will help the teacher to group her pupils into class activities where they may best function and learn.

Planning Goals

The next step is the planning of educational goals. A group of trainable retarded children represents extreme individual differences. Educational goals consequently should be carefully considered by the teacher. Goals should form the foundation for the entire day at school. They provide direction and purpose for daily activities. Goals should be challenging to each child, and should lead to immediate success. Goals should lead to personal gains as well as approval. Daily educational goals should be derived from long-range aims and objectives so that continuous growth and development for each child can be assured.

The main objectives in the education of the retarded child are the development of: (1) *self-care skills*, (2) personal behavior, and *socialization* to help the retarded child to function acceptably in the community.

In the process of realizing these objectives, a teacher must establish favorable conditions for individual progress in terms of changes in the child's behavior. Goals should be an outgrowth of the retarded child's needs and within the range of his ability. Goals must be simple, clearly stated and meaningful so that the child will feel comfortable with the task and achieve success. Motivating the child into an activity that has meaning to him will always provide him with a greater sense of success.

Planning Space for Learning

Planning physical learning environments is another major task within the teacher's responsibility. Space where the child can experience freedom of movement and freely explore his whole surroundings in his own way is most essential to him.

In communities with a small school for the retarded, a home-like setting will provide a familiar environment for the trainable retarded child. The more natural atmosphere and learning climate encourages the development of self-care skills and acceptable social adjustment.

Learning environments for the retarded child include the classroom, gym or playroom, kitchen, washrooms, a playground, and the immediate school environment such as the street, stores, church, etc. In some communities where only few retarded children attend school, the teacher is provided with one spacious regular classroom in an elementary school and the use of washrooms, a kitchen, and a regular elementary school gym.

The Classroom

The classroom then becomes the teacher's main stage for planning learning experiences. This should not mean, however, that the teacher is confined to her room for the whole day or that she should not make use of all the other school facilities. Each teacher will approach the planning of learning environments according to her knowledge of the retarded child's needs.

Health conditions, such as the control of temperature, circulation of fresh air, and the ventilation system must be checked daily. Adequate lighting and cleanliness are of primary importance in all rooms used by the children. There should not be a speck of dust anywhere.

Safety is another aspect the teacher should take into consideration when planning learning facilities. Children should be trained regularly in fire drills and other safety measures.

The classroom should be a pleasant, attractive, inviting place for both the children and the teacher. A creative teacher will arrange many interesting classroom settings to stimulate learning. Children should be encouraged to keep the classroom neat and to plan with the teacher to make the classroom attractive.

First the teacher should make a careful study of how to arrange the classroom as a functional setting for the different developmental levels of her pupils which will interest each group. Both young and older pupils need to be able to move around freely, to be heard easily, to sit on the floor or bench, and to feel at ease. The classroom arrangement must be simple and consistent. The simpler the environment is, the easier it is for the child to control and experience success; the more elaborate and complicated, the more confusing it is to him.

Learning centers or resource areas facilitate independent learning. In small confined resource areas, each pupil is on his own. He is given freedom to use materials of his own choice, to set his own goals, and to work out his own procedures. The materials or equipment are carefully planned by the teacher and strategically placed to stimulate learning and to allow the child to proceed at his own rate of learning. Materials placed on shelves or in cupboards must be easily accessible. Ideally, it should be possible quickly to convert the classroom into a large area for dancing, dramatization, free movement to music, and other group activities.

Equipment

The learning environment and the equipment and learning materials should be planned well in advance and placed in readiness before the children arrive at school. The teacher then can devote her full attention to the children and be with them when they need her. Equipment and materials that are thoughtfully arranged and replaced by the children after use develop good working habits and encourage independence.

Movable equipment is recommended. The trapezoidal shaped tables should replace traditional desks to enhance flexibility. Cupboards with sliding doors allow access to materials on shelves visible to the children. Sink and counter space facilitate household activities, cleaning up and washing dishes, and training in practical skills.

Materials

Materials should be carefully selected for the various developmental levels in a class. They should be distributed in learning areas for the children to use in individual activities. The equipment and materials should be geared for concrete learning experiences, and for training in skills, as well as for providing the opportunity for a child to use his own time allotment purposefully. Such training is needed in preparation for sheltered workshops.

Planning Activities

In planning for the day, the teacher should establish a framework of activities within the child's range of abilities. Activities should be in accordance with the child's present stage of development and should proceed to well-defined goals. Two major types of activity should be planned by the teacher: routine activities for individual children to develop personal skills in self-care; and group activities to develop social skills and self-expression.

The balancing of these activities is very important for the overall program. The children must not be overtaxed with too many stimulating group activities. A daily program of routine and non-routine activities should counterbalance activities of an active and passive nature. For example, sitting and moving should be scattered among the various areas of development—social, physical, intellectual and emotional, and individual or group. The total daily program in a school for retarded children should go far beyond the conventional program of routines and correction of defects. A creative teacher will extend the daily activities and provide opportunities for the child to express himself in movement, in expressive language and in creative arts. Events of interest to the children will often provide meaningful themes for daily unit lessons and integrated learning.

Planning Time for Learning

The establishment of blocks of time for activities should be recognized as the structure for planning daily activities. To plan a daily schedule does not imply rigidly adhering to the timetable allotment for every activity. Scheduling a day means planning the time carefully for learning, planning both in space and in time, to help the child to do certain things at appropriate times, to use the time allotted for a task purposefully, and to differentiate between working time and playtime. Finishing a task in time gives a sense of accomplishment and teaches responsibility. Finishing a task which has been started the day before is important for a child who forgets easily. It provides training in good working habits and in reliance. In a school for retarded children, there can be no rigid timetable, fixed curriculum, or rows of seats. Rigid scheduling and static settings cause frustrations and negative behavior. In a well-planned environment free from rigid conformity to groups or daily schedules, but following his own pace of learning, a child feels much happier.

The establishment of large blocks to time for various routine activities performed by children during the day develops self-direction and provides opportunity for self-control and for acquiring a time perspective.

Following daily routines is important and most essential in the present and future life of the retarded child. Individual learning tasks help him to progress not only in the acquisition of personal skills but also in establishing a pattern of daily life at school and in the transferring from the school situation to his home.

In all routine activities at school, such as dressing, washing, eating, tidying, each child is taught to attend to his own basic needs. Special attention is given to skills which will prepare the child for the everyday life situations that he will meet at home and at school. Planned, sequential, routine procedures and situations provide opportunity for consistent, repetitive experiences which lead to the acquisition of skills in personal care and to the feeling of success and accomplishment.

Sequence of Daily Activities

The scheduled day at school begins with the arrival of children and the activities performed in the cloakroom. Learning to dress and undress is a serious activity. Well-prescribed procedures are essential for the child to proceed in his development of skills and independence.

For the retarded child, this is a long and complicated learning process involving the ability to recognize his own clothes, to know how to take off or put on his coat, to know which article to put on first and how to manipulate buttons, zippers, or belts. The most complicated process is learning on which foot to put which shoe and how to tie shoe laces.

Assembly

In some schools, the teacher starts the day with group activities of the whole class (this assembly is called circle time or morning circle in many schools). Participation in a large group situation will help the child to develop a sense of belonging and build attitudes and patterns of behavior acceptable in the community, at church services, or other community events to which his parents may take him.

Routines in Groups

This activity is performed daily around weather charts, a calendar, or a large thermometer and develops abilities in observing changes in the environment by marking changes in weather on weather charts, or by noting special events of the day on the calendar. The child becomes aware of his own environment and develops language for everyday living, such as dates, seasons, and common phrases. This is the time when the group discusses daily news and plans daily duties. Acceptance of assigned daily or weekly jobs and the sight of his own name on the duty chart develops the child's sense of responsibility and teaches self-reliance.

Unit of Interest

The unit approach provides the children with integrated experiences related to real life situations and centered around one theme. A unit consists of varied

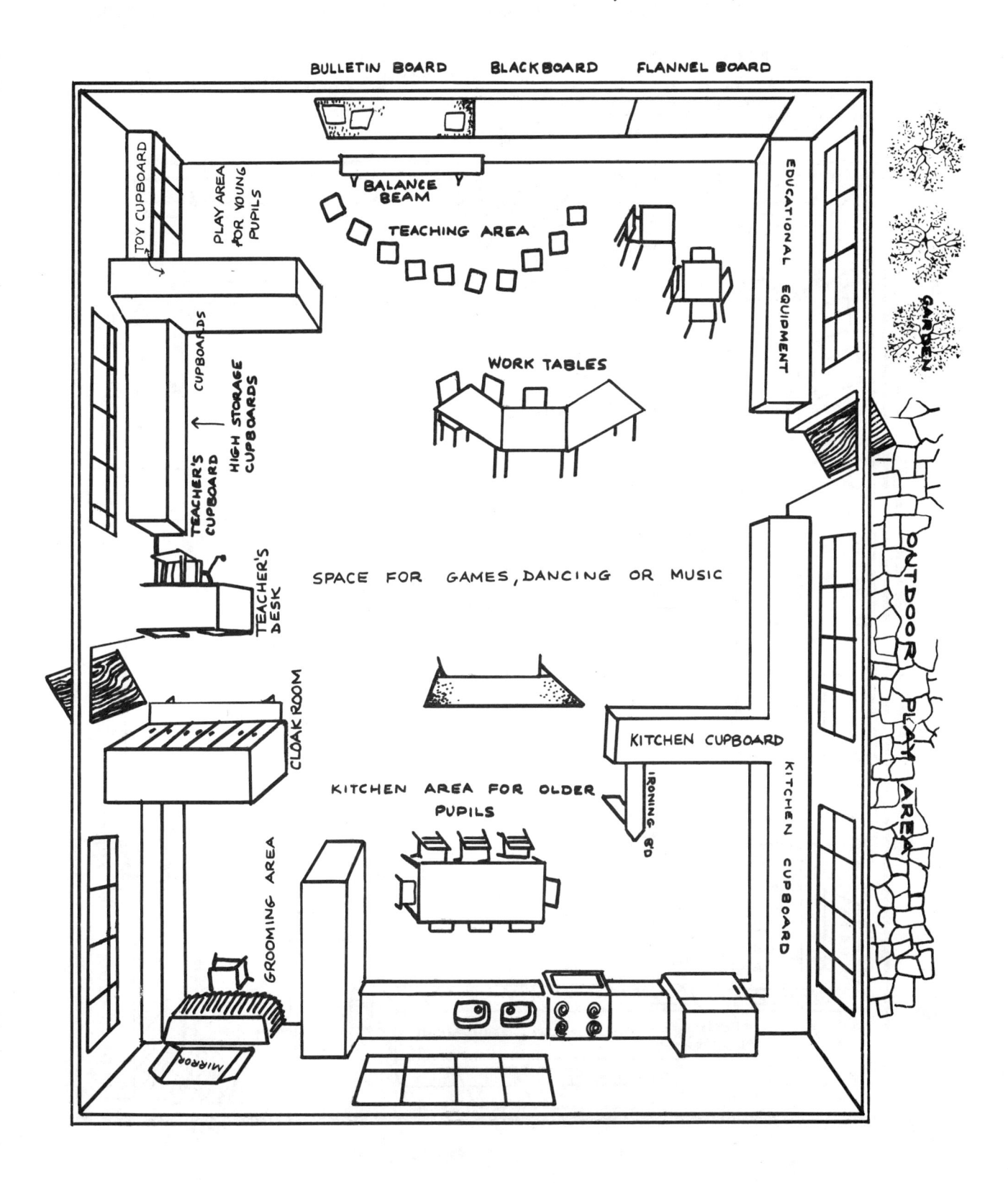

SELF-CONTAINED CLASSROOM – PLANNED FOR TRAINABLE RETARDED CHILDREN
MOUNT FOREST, ONTARIO, CANADA

CLASSROOM ARRANGEMENT

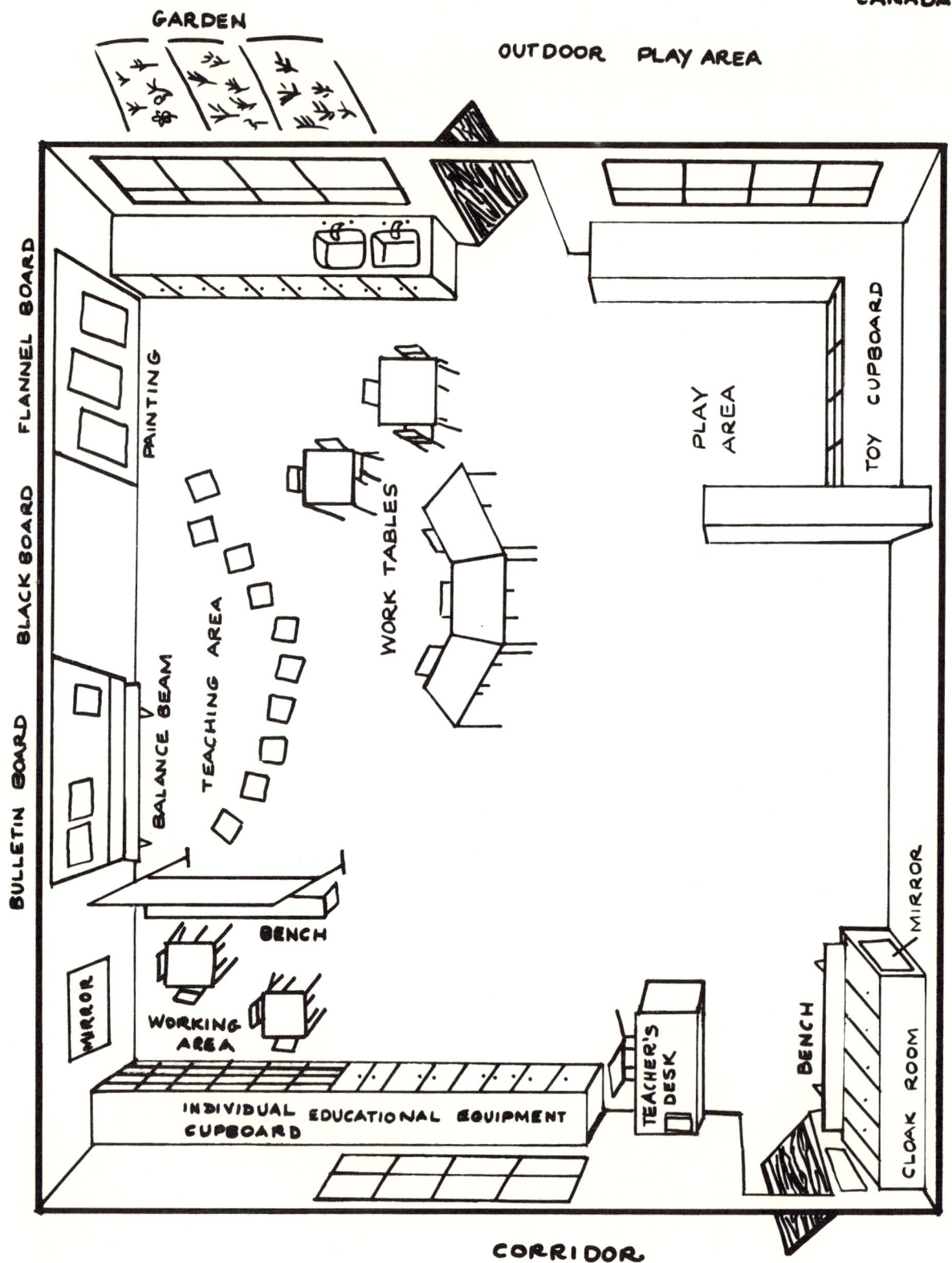

PLANNED IN SCHOOLS FOR TRAINABLE RETARDED CHILDREN, ONTARIO, CANADA

activities through which the child may gain simple knowledge of his own environment; it develops number concepts, language—by verbalizing his own observation, which stimulates thinking processes—and alertness. The practice of printing his own name and creatively expressing himself through arts and crafts are experiences for reinforcing concept formation.

Physical Activities

To develop physical and social skills, motor coordination and posture, awareness of the body and its function, and control of body movements is essential. Included are agility activities; game action emphasizing bean bag, hoop, or target action; rhythmic activities or dancing with piano or other music. Outdoor and indoor activities should be provided daily by the teacher.

Lunch Time

Preparation for lunch will include simple tasks such as setting the table, either acting as helpers or performing the whole task independently. Usually older pupils are able to handle this task well, following prescribed procedures prepared by the teacher on charts. During the lunch period, the children develop good eating habits, table manners, and habits of politeness. This training is closely supervised by the teacher to help the children establish personal behavior patterns acceptable in the community. Some children assigned to kitchen duties follow prescribed procedures in washing dishes, sweeping, mopping, polishing; these are all simple yet essential and meaningful activities in the training of household tasks. The same well-learned practical skills can be transferred and performed in the child's home.

Grooming Activities

To develop habits of personal cleanliness and health, teeth, face, hands, hair, clothes, and shoes should be attended to immediately after lunch. Each child should follow his own grooming procedures, based on his needs and prescribed by the teacher on individual charts for the children to follow and observe their own progress.

Music Activities

Music affords an opportunity to enjoy participation in group activities, to develop initiative and creativity in movements and self-expressions through listening, singing, percussion band, dancing, games, and dramatization.

Individual Activities

Individual programming is based on each child's level of development and diagnostic results. Training in specific skills is carefully planned and prescriptive teaching applied. Time is taken in directing experiences of individual children in order to develop sensory-motor perception (visual, tactile, auditory, kinaesthetic training).

For gross and fine motor control, fine muscular development, speech and language games, each child has his own prescribed program prepared by the diagnostic team or teacher for the child's own progress.

Practical Activities

These activities are usually performed in the afternoon individually or in small groups. For example, one child may be ironing clothes, another child may be polishing silver (six spoons or six forks), and the rest of the group may be involved in crafts or in sorting, matching, cutting, stapling, etc. There should be a balance between sitting and moving activities and individual and group activities during the morning and afternoon. It is also desirable that each child experience more than one kind of activity during the afternoon, and that all children not be engaged in the same activity at the same time.

Throughout the whole day the teacher provides meaningful learning experiences for all developmental levels with specific guidance for each child in mastering skills of everyday life.

Through the teacher's constant efforts, more realistic goals for the children are being developed, and trainable retarded children are able to function more purposefully in the community, and living at home with their parents and family, and attending a school of their own.

4. CREATING A SUITABLE CLIMATE AND ENVIRONMENT

*There's many a life of sweet content
Whose virtue is environment.*

—Walter Learned

A good teacher for young retarded children will work in a bland environment, creating a series of structured situations saturated with a genuine attitude of empathy, worthwhileness, confidence, and love.

A bland environment is achieved by avoiding the inclusion of any and all extraneous material, bright colors, shiny or shimmering surfaces, or moving things. Chalkboards should be steel-backed to accommodate magnets. A large cork-board surface is desirable.

The room should be painted in pleasant pastels, with *no* decorations, decals, pictures, printed materials, murals. Hardware should be satin finish, if possible. Lighting should be indirect, shielded fluorescents.

Draw draperies should cover all views during work time. Draperies are opened on purpose to watch a fire engine, birds, clouds, swaying trees—to watch for the station wagon and learn to wait patiently.

The goldfish should spend most of their leisure hours in another room and come in only "to work." In this way they draw complete attention as an event of the day and assume real importance, rather than being a part of the scenery all the time and serving more as a transfixor than a direct stimulant.

Primary colors—red, bright blue, bright green, or deep yellow—are reserved for teaching devices.

Furniture should be pastel, gray or beige, with unpatterned, undecorated formica tops on tables.

Teachers should wear pretty pastels or plain-colored dark clothing. Smocks should not be gaily patterned.

Dangly bangly jewelry, bracelets, and earrings should be avoided. Bright-colored fingernail enamel is very distracting. The effect of red nail polish is notable when the retarded child is older and learning to direct attention to flat surfaces, pictures in a series, or printed material. With these older children, having a red-enameled index fingernail on the target will draw attention readily. This technique is valuable at the appropriate time. The nursery and kindergarten children are learning to direct attention toward a gross target, an object, or person, and must not be distracted to attend to fascinating details of a teacher's appearance.

All materials—toys, books, etc.—must be kept out of sight at the nursery and kindergarten level. The task at hand must have all the attention. Record players should be closed. The moving turntable is often more compelling than the sounds we are using for learning.

As the children move along and their attention becomes more readily captured and sustained, "things" may be a part of the environment. Open shelves, books and toys, are a part of the junior intermediate class. These children have had learning experiences in the nursery, kindergarten, and primary groups. More color and extraneous material is permitted through the intermediate years. The older children work in rooms very much like any other classrooms—pleasant, uncluttered, with materials for independent projects and pursuits accessible.

Habitual tidiness—a place for everything, and pride in having a comfortable, happy, and beautiful place in which to work—contributes to the achievement of a mature, socially acceptable individual.

The Playground

Outside play areas should be fenced completely for maximum safety; learning to stay out of streets can be worked on elsewhere. Peace of mind for both teacher and child will permit a happier and more profitable outdoor playtime. Learning to get along with others, to share, take turns, is of equal importance to the opportunity for physical growth through playground activities.

Let the balls not the children fly into the street. Actually the restraining fence contributes to the concept that the street is off limits.

A blacktop area is necessary. Two concentric circles, 14' and 16' in diameter, should be painted in two colors on the blacktop. These circles are used for many games and provide a wonderful track for wagons, tricycles, etc.

Guardrails fore and aft the tanbarked swing area will prevent accidents.

Rubber swing seats are strongly recommended in place of the rigid wooden seats usually provided in stock-ordered equipment. The rubber swing seats cost very little more and are less hazardous.

Colored tracks painted on a path of blacktop around the play area, possibly winding around among trees or bushes, make a fascinating course for a trip. By interwinding and varying the paths, routes laid out by the color-tracks provide a structured experience to complete a mission. All the tracks start from one central point near the storage area for the tricycles, wagons, etc. A child may take a red trip, a yellow trip, a blue trip, or a green trip. "Rules of the road" include being courteous at intersections, and sharing—and it is a lot of fun.

Outside sandboxes should be provided with some sort of "animal-proof" covering when not in use.

The Gym or Multipurpose Room

The gym or multipurpose room, well lighted and well ventilated, should be large enough to play volleyball in comfortably. Severely retarded children do not seem to be comfortable in too large or too-high-ceilinged spaces. This space will accommodate three square-dance sets, a shuffleboard court inset in floor tile, and provide ample space for a physical education class of twenty-four or a free play group of ten or twelve young children.

Sturdy benches, built in along the walls, are very convenient and should be provided if at all possible.

Basketball goals, adjustable in height, can be used for many games.

Stall bars, balance beams, pescolite mats for tumbling, rough-textured 9" inflated balls (Voigt), volleyballs, bean bags, a variety of devised targets, a few Indian clubs for games, shuffleboard cues and discs, jump ropes, a volleyball net, a sturdy, covered record player, a movable piano (with a cover, please), will equip a gymnasium adequately for trainable children.

A Teaching Bathroom

A hand-controlled (and thermocontrolled) spray attachment in the shower will help the teacher, child, and school nurse immeasurably.

A special shower stall that will serve as a teaching shower can be made at very little cost. It is an adaptation of the shower used in some physical-therapy departments to help handicapped children to more independence.

A 4'-square Terrazzo shower base is set in the corner of the bathroom. A wall 27" high is built of 4" concrete block on the two open sides. An opening 15" wide is left in the right side, over a 6" rise. All of the concrete block and exposed wall is covered with ceramic tile. A shower curtain hangs from a suspended rail.

This arrangement allows the teacher or nurse to stay dry while helping a child in the shower.

A young child who is very frightened of water, and particularly of showers, can play in a few inches of water by putting the rubber stopper over the drain in the floor of the shower. Being gradually introduced to the hand-controlled spray will usually overcome this fear.

Juvenile-height toilets are essential in the lavatory serving the preschool rooms.

The Teacher

Creating an appropriate school environment for trainable children is the subject of this section. The most important factor in creating this environment is the teacher. What kind of a factor is this person?

She must have a deep interest in children and like them, regardless of their shortcomings. She must be sensitive to human relationships. She must be mature in self-control, instant in service, and have a gentle sense of humor. She must have the strength of David, the wisdom of Solomon, and the patience of Job.

5. EVALUATION

A pinch of probability is worth a pound of perhaps.

—James Thurber

Evaluation is the process by which we judge and thereby learn what a thing or act is worth at the time the judgment is made. Evaluation in education serves the important purpose of providing evidence to suggest whether an existing curriculum does or does not do the job it is intended to do. This serves several purposes.

The effectiveness of a curriculum must be evaluated to test the hypothesis upon which the curriculum was established. Thus needed improvement can be made. Evaluation provides security to the school staff, and to the parents. It produces sound information for public relations.

If evaluation is to be meaningful, its purposes must be kept in mind. As objectives change and crystallize, the techniques for evaluation, the results of evaluation, the interpretation of the results should change accordingly.

We evaluate students in order to learn what they *can do* so we may plan an appropriate placement and program. We evaluate what students *do* so that we can record evidence of progress, plateauing, or regression, and report to parents.

Tyler's classic statement on evaluation* defines six basic assumptions germane to planning evaluation.

First assumption: Education is a process which seeks to change behavior patterns in human beings. Through education we seek to develop certain skills, to recall and use ideas not used before, and to modify students' reactions to aesthetic experiences such as music and the arts.

Second assumption: The kinds of changes in behavior in human beings which the school seeks to bring about are its educational objectives.

Third assumption: Evaluation of the educational program is a process by which we find out to what degree these changes in the students are actually taking place.

Fourth assumption: The way the student organizes his behavior patterns is an important aspect to be appraised.

Fifth assumption: Any device which provides valid evidence regarding a student's progress toward the stated educational objectives is appropriate.

Sixth assumption: Participation of teachers, students, and parents in the process of evaluation is essential to derive the maximum values from a program of evaluation. Development of an increasing degree of *self-evaluation* is in itself a major goal of education.

These six basic assumptions lead us to recognize the necessity of basing any evaluation program upon educational objectives and clearly show that educational objectives must be stated in terms of desired changes in the behavior of students.

The evaluation procedure suggested by Tyler and based upon his six basic assumptions requires that: *First* we formulate the statement of educational objectives. These statements are then classified into major categories or types. The categories must not be too many in number for practical organization.

Second, we define each of these types of objectives in terms of desired behavior change. The statement or definition must be very clear and direct. Claus suggests that objectives be so stated that the student do something (using the imperative mood) with some tool or medium, about some content, according to a criterion. ("Verbs and Imperative Sentences as a Basis for Stating Educational Objectives," Calvin K. Claus).

Third, we identify situations in which students can be expected to display these types of behavior so we may know where to obtain evidence regarding the objective.

Fourth, we select and experiment with any promising method of obtaining evidence, regarding each type of objective.

Fifth, we may very well want to construct new instruments for a specific need.

Sixth, we select the most promising instruments for further development and refinement, for ease of use and clarity of results.

Seventh, we devise means for interpreting and using the results of the evaluation instruments. Tyler suggests the development of norms. This is hardly possible with trainable children because of the wide variety of etiologies and disabilities. He also suggests year-to-year comparisons, use of profiles, studying the inter-relationship of several scores to identify or note patterns in individual children and in the group as a whole.

---

* Ralph W. Tyler, "General Statement on Evaluation." *Journal of Educational Research*, Vol. 35, March 1942.

The important purpose of evaluation, Tyler reiterates, is to provide evidence which suggests hypotheses for modification and improvement of the curriculum. We are always faced with recurring demands for the formulation and clarification of objectives.

Tyler refers to the effective teacher as "an artist who creates situations, conscious of purpose, aware of conditions and able with creative ingenuity to work in many ways to stimulate students and guide them toward their goals."

We must evaluate the impact of the events in a child's history, the sequellae, and residual pathways for learning, to plan for and effect desirable changes in behavior.

Evaluation of Curriculum

When we look back at the fuzzy so-called curriculum we labored with in 1950, it seems almost impossible that we expected to accomplish so little. No criteria existed for day schools and those brave enough to put some ideas together under the title of "curriculum" or "plan" operated upon the inheritance of experiences in institutions. About the only so-called school or training experiences in institutions were with educable children. The groups in institutions labeled "educable" were truly a hodge-podge of patients who were ambulatory, could communicate in some way, and were tractable in their behavior.

In the new day school classes in the early 1950s, working with the children labeled "trainable" was confined to self-care with heavy emphasis on nose-blowing and shoe-tying. Children were not admitted unless they were completely toilet-trained and could communicate, so the parents had a major training job to do on their own, and many children never did find admission to classes or were not admitted until they were 7 or 8 years of age.

Early intervention, parent education, the admission of children close to 3 years of age, toilet-trained or not (and toilet training can usually be accomplished very quickly in a nursery class situation, with parent cooperation), has proved to be very profitable. Holding class size down to a workable unit, ideally four, but no more than six, *with* an aide, in a nursery or preschool class, with a teacher trained in nursery school methods, has shown profitable results which have demanded constant revision of curriculum as objectives were being readily realized.

Preschool means different things in various school systems. Preschool to us means nursery school age— *under* 5. Preschool in some systems is any class *before* admission to public school classes with rigid admission criteria.

Monthly lesson plan reports and a skeleton outline of curriculum organization have been used annually to review what was actually going on in each classroom, to note successes and failures in productivity of various experiences. These annual reviews resulted in constant upgrading of objectives.

If our performance goals or objectives are in the imperative mood and say that a child *does something, with some tools or media, about some content, according to criteria*, no subjective guessing is needed in evaluation; it becomes merely a question of, does this child do this or doesn't he do it? Stating objectives according to this model is very strenuous but very gratifying.

All subject areas can be arranged in sequence of difficulty. The *criteria* set the level of difficulty. The levels or sub-objectives can follow developmental scales against which each individual may compete at his own pace.

For example, an objective in one curriculum organization is *social adequacy*. Using Claus' formula:

do something	acquire social adequacy
media or tools	structured experience
content	self-care, social adaptability, and work habits
criteria	function with independence and maturity within the framework of individual limitations

Here is an example of stating the objective for a definite task. The objective is, in this case, a part of the objective of social adequacy.

do something	wash hands
media or tools	mixing water, soap, and towels
content	dirty hands
criteria	end results to be:
	clean, dry hands
	water turned off
	soap clean, towel placed in proper place.

The nursery child can't do all that, so objectives must be stated using the same formula for each level and you have a sequence of difficulty. At all costs avoid stating an objective thus:

"to learn how to———"
"to be able to———"
"to understand———"

Claus disparages such constructs as "fuzzy, frightful and foggy." These all involve value judgments and can never be measured objectively. (The February 1969 edition of *Education and Training of the Mentally Retarded* carries an article about teacher education, "An Undergraduate Course in Organization of Programs for the Mentally Retarded," by Florence Chirstoplos and Peter Valletutti. The students actively practice stating educational objectives according to a formula.)

Program evaluation is essential if you believe in the worthwhileness of what you are doing. This information can be shared with parents and the community of taxpayers. It challenges us to state our objectives clearly as we move toward the realization of the maximum potential of each child as we prepare him for the life he will lead as far as it is within our power to predict.

As we became (1) more knowledgeable in the management of language development, (2) more constructive and knowledgeable in the enhancement and therapeutic approach to motor growth, (3) aware of the needs dictated by the individual differences of our children, many events were recorded which could be translated into restatements of objectives.

For many years we have held a series of parent education workshops for parents of children new to the school. More need and more ways to incorporate the parents in one team effort enfold each year. It is always sad when we are faced with disinterested and rejective parents. Fortunately this does not happen very often. We know that this is an area for constant study—to establish better communication with, and participation by the parents.

The organization of a curriculum takes many forms. Hudson's excellent survey in the mid'50s (see General Bibliography) reported what was going on then and which areas of blocked-out time were emphasized in some existing programs.

This material became the basis for curriculum planning in many instances. The ensuing years have brought considerable constructive research and indications for many new avenues of investigation.

Mandatory legislation has forced program development with some results that are quite staggering.

Sitting with the committee assembled by Dr. Margaret Moss of George Washington University, and chaired by Dr. Samuel Kirk, to study and ponder the problem of objectives in programs for TMR children, it became evident that no basis existed for planning a curriculum when we did not really know what we were preparing our children for.

Upon returning from the conference we decided that we should look back and try to find out just how well we had been doing with the children entrusted to us. We assembled a questionnaire that we sent to every family with whom we had contact since Orchard School opened in 1950. The response was most gratifying. One hundred eighty-four of 207 questionnaires sent out were returned. As we studied the data, these questions came to mind: Are we satisfied? What could we have done better to prepare these children for the lives they are now living? What could we have done differently that would have possibly precluded some of the institution placements? What can we do now with more information, more research findings, and more willingness on the part of administrators? Our data showed clearly that we must either devote more time to preparation for institutional living *or* find better ways to prevent institution commitments.

The survey directed our attention to search into the possible future occupation of our graduates. Employment in competitive society seemed unlikely. To find space for all our graduates in contract workshops requires complete optimism and a little ostrich-playing. Retaining all our students in the community would be highly desirable if security were available. Kitchen, laundry and yard jobs, and jobs in the contract shop can all transfer to an institution life. Three years ago, we began to incorporate child care training in our curriculum with most gratifying results. Our young people learned eagerly and were very anxious to please. A reward system was set up—the girls receiving pink smocks and the boys blue jackets (marked Orchard School Child Care Worker) —when they completed a course of study as well as a certain number of practice hours, and demonstrated that they could perform the tasks satisfactorily as judged by reports from staff members.

One of our graduates now has a full time job in a local nursery school. Another, whose parents had died, leads a very busy life in a private institution working with young children. Presently we have two recent graduates working with us as aides, and we hope to find jobs for them in nursery schools.

A bonus from this program has been a whole new field of investigation in the language we use in communicating with our students.

Evaluation for Planning

As we plan for each child who enters a special school, information is needed to establish a base line in several growth areas. We cannot use pencil and paper tests for readiness or achievement.

The psychologist can tell us about the measured intelligence. This legally establishes eligibility if the score is tidily within the extremes. The decision about the placement of a child scoring between 50 and 60 or slightly below 35 must depend upon much more information.

A thorough study by a speech and language pathologist is a very important part of evaluating the child's current behavior. As communication is germane to the entire educational process, this area must be carefully evaluated. The speech and language report should include both objective and subjective results from the testing of inner, receptive, and expressive language skills. The Illinois Test of Psycholinquistic Abilities is a part of our evaluation of communication processes. The occupational therapist evaluates the motor developmental level, including the child's visual-motor abilities as well as gross and fine motor functions.

Before a child enters school, one or more interviews are scheduled with our psychiatric social worker. The social worker uses a Record of Performance Goals very much as the Vineland Social Maturity Scale is used. She does not use it as a checklist in front of the parents, but enters information after the interview is concluded. Through conversation she tries to learn from the parents as much as possible about what the child does or does not do at home. This covers ambulation, self-care, communication, emotional control, social adequacy, use of leisure time at home and in the neighborhood. She tries to learn what the child does in household tasks. Most of our new students are very young, but we frequently receive children transferring from other areas or from classes for "educable" children.

The social worker or nurse also takes a history that helps us receive a medical report more quickly from the child's attending physician.

Reports from other agencies acquainted with the child and family are gathered.

All this material, the reports from the psychologist, the speech and language pathologist, and the social worker, the Performance Goals Record, and information from other agencies, is then reviewed by the possible receiving teachers, the principal, the OTR, the special education coordinator, in addition to those staff members submitting the reports;

Careful interpretation of the raw data from a Merrill-Palmer, Binet, or Wechsler Intelligence Scale for

Children, plus an Illinois Test of Psycholinquistic Abilities profile adds the needed information about strengths and weaknesses in cognitive ability.

This information, plus the achievements noted by the social worker, should provide enough material to establish base lines for planning.

The material is discussed and a decision made for appropriate placement on a trial basis. During the last six weeks of school each spring we try to have all possible new students expected for fall enrollment come in for a few hours so that we can observe them in a group setting. We also try to have new students attend our six-week summer session. This gives us more information than we can ever get from more formal procedures.

Prescriptive teaching means that uniqueness dictates what procedures and experiences will provide the most profitable remediation for the learning disabilities revealed in evaluation. We regard all children with retarded development as children with learning disabilities of varying degrees of severity.

The employment of the ITPA is an evaluation device for prescriptive teaching, which was suggested (and urged) by Dr. Jeanne McCarthy as a follow-up of the implication of her doctoral study. We had a unique population of the Downs Syndrome children enrolled. This group was used as a part of Dr. McCarthy's sample. This evaluation for planning via the ITPA has shown very exciting results so far. (See Chapter 12.)

Evaluation for Reporting to Parents

As mentioned in the general overview of the purpose of evaluation, the parents are of vital importance not only to us in working with their child, but also to the actual progress their child may or may not be making.

"A Handbook for Parents" is re-edited and issued on check-in day each fall. The objectives of each age group are stated as clearly as possible so parents can be knowledgeable about what is expected of the children in each peer group.

Since children described as "trainable" do not produce pencil-and-paper test results and daily grades upon which some factual reporting could be done, we must rely upon material that has been carefully collected to yield tangible evidence of the child's progress, both as an individual competing against himself as he moves along a sequence of tasks, and as a member of a peer group which moves toward objectives realistically stated as appropriate for an age group such as nursery, CA-3-4, kindergarten, CA-5-6-7, junior intermediate, and so on, as groups are scheduled to age 21.

The Performance Goals Record will show how well the child is moving ahead in the sequenced tasks in the five areas we have found to be workable divisions for stating objectives. With objectives so stated, the child either does or does not do the tasks planned and no subjective opinion can change the evaluation of notable progress, plateauing, or regression.

Some actual "testing" is necessary. In a group of eight to ten children, aged approximately 10 to 14, without frequent review (or "testing") on a one-to-one basis, for example, it is impossible for a teacher to keep account of just where a child might be in quantification skills. It is necessary to know just where each child is in the development of number concepts (see chapter 26).

Daily journals should record observations of general behavior and unusual events. The teacher should confer with all staff members working with each child—the language and speech therapist, music therapist, occupational therapist, social worker, bus driver—and incorporate reports from this team in her anecdotal report for parent conferences. The anecdotal report is written with an evaluation guide to assure coverage of all areas, gross objectives and sub-objectives.

In writing a report for parents of children with retarded development, the teacher should tell the story the way she herself would like to hear it if she were the parent. Use language that is clear and understandable and that reflects a feeling of warm interest in the child. It is very easy and seems to mean so much to parents to hear their child referred to with more than casual reference. "This lovable little fellow," "this little rascal," or "this very well-mannered young lady" can help parents feel much better about accepting your report about their child.

Parent conferences are scheduled in late January and mid-May, in the evening so the father can come. A half-hour appointment is made with each family.

Reports are typed and usually no longer than one page or one and one-half pages at the most, and copies are available for each parent to read along with the teacher. The report is read aloud by the teacher and a general discussion follows. Any questions the parents ask that are not covered in the report should be noted on the teacher's copy as a record of something of concern to the parents.

If it has been necessary to report, for example, that John refuses to put things away, or some other negative item, at the end of the reading before the parents can ask a question, it helps immediately to refer to the item by saying, "He's a real scamp about putting things away. We try not to ask him to do something he does not understand or would be unable to do—but tell me, how do you manage this at home?" The answer could be very revealing and could help you to pinpoint the source of the undesirable behavior. The words the mother or father use are revealing. Do they say, "He won't; he doesn't; he can't"? This reflects some feelings about their child.

At the end of the conference, one parent should sign the copy of the report that will be kept in the permanent record. The parents may keep a copy. The rationale for signing the report is one familiar to all teachers who work with handicapped children. Should that sad day of termination ever come, the parents are apt to say, "We had no warning. You never told us he was that rough," etc. The reports should always be completely honest and in words you could understand if you were the parent. (Even with this system, parents have been known to deny ever having seen "*that report.*")

At conference time be prepared to share any little gems you might have—some art work or some good work in the writing sequence. If you are using the ITPA and doing any prescriptive teaching, you can show the accumulated profiles to the parents and explain the implications.

The speech and language therapist and the occupational therapist should be available on conference nights. They may request a conference if it is necessary.

We debated about using the Performance Goals Record directly during the conferences, but found it did not prove satisfactory. The parents wanted copies of it, tried to copy items, and seemed almost frantic to "try to teach him those things at home."

We have enjoyed good acceptance by the parents of this system of reporting the periodic evaluations of the status of their child. The reports comprise a longitudinal survey of progress.

Evaluation for Permanent Records

Entries of data into permanent records should clearly show substantiated evidence that certain objectives of the program have brought about changes in behavior and that, because of these changes, the child does do certain things with some media or tools, about some content, according to a criterion.

This is a reiteration of the system for stating objectives. If the objectives have been so stated, the evaluation is merely a record of whether the child does or does not do the tasks expected of his age level with *full* consideration of his unique individual differences.

The Performance Goals Record kept by the teacher as long as the student is in school should become a part of the permanent record. This record, plus the copies of all parent conference reports and the annual reports of the social worker, give a clear picture of what the student was doing in relation to the total objectives of the school curriculum.

Permanent records are used for information needed in transferring students to other schools or residential placement. Data for longitudinal studies should also be available in the permanent records.

Legal requirements vary all over the country. Consequent reports of Qualified Psychological Examiners are required in Illinois and become a part of each student's permanent record.

Special People in a Special School

6. THE TEACHER

To teach is to learn twice.
Joseph Joubert

Every contribution to this book and every area covered by the author touch upon the kind of person our successful teacher really is. She is a very special person.

She—is knowledgeable about child development.
    understands the psychology of young children and handicapped children.
    knows basic techniques via task analysis, and sequencing of difficulty.
    is creative and highly imaginative and resourceful.
    has a light touch and a firm grip.
    has pride in her work and her appearance.
    has infinite patience and durability.
    truly loves children.
    can see through the eyes and hear through the ears of parents.
    is a clam in confidentiality.
    respects the rights and opinions of all people, particularly of
        colleagues and parents.
    is instant in service.
    is not squeamish.
And she has a genuine sense of humor.

7. THE SOCIAL WORKER IN SPECIAL EDUCATION

by Marie Forman

Be pliable like a reed, not rigid like a cedar.
—The Talmud

What Is Social Work?

Social work is a method of professional practice which helps individuals to function better by learning to cope more effectively with personal, family, and community relationships. From the beginning social work has stressed the interaction of the individual and his environment. Through their education and training, social workers gain an organized body of knowledge and skills which enables them to understand human behavior and its malfunctioning. As the social worker's fundamental purpose is to help individuals deal effectively with difficulties in relating to others, they are uniquely fitted for practice in a school setting. To quote from the Policies and Procedures Manual on School Social Work in Illinois: "School social work, using its unique methods, integrates into this setting additional and different knowledge and skills, which supplement the basic function of the educational institution."

Goals of the Social Worker

The primary goal of the social worker in the school is service to the individual student, based on the principle of educating the whole child. This goal is achieved through *evaluative services* aimed at early detection of incipient conflicts and maladaptive behavior and analysis of longstanding difficulties which impede the child's growth or cause conflict between the individual and others in the environment. Through *consultation* and *interdisciplinary collaboration*, the social worker contributes to an understanding of the child and increases the self-awareness of the teacher and other persons in the child's milieu. Interaction involves one or any combination of the three basic social work methods—casework, group work, and community organization.

Social Work Methods

The three methods mentioned above are briefly described as follows:

Case work uses a psychodynamically based, one-to-one relationship to help the student make maximum use of himself in his environment.

Group work enhances individual functioning "through purposeful group experience."

Community organization involves providing leadership in greater utilization of existing services, in interpreting school programs to the civic organizations in the community upon request, and in serving on community boards as a resource member.

Intake

Intake begins with the first inquiry about service for a given child. At this point the social worker focuses on clarifying the appropriateness to him of the school. The importance of family involement is recognized from the beginning and we ask that contact be intiated by the parent or by another responsible relative if the parent is unable to act. Parents are seen together for the initial in-person interview in order for them to share, in each other's presence, their individual perception of their special child, and in order to allow them in this context an opportunity to ventilate feelings. Experience has established the need for this.

We view the parents' request for help, the working out of their own feelings, and the acceptance of their child's real individuality as a process toward which they work over a period of time. Parents give at least verbal recognition of their child's need when they ask for his admission to a special school. Expectations may range from the simple beginning one of placement for training to concern about the child's capacity for development over the years. What can he learn to do? Will he ever become self-supporting? What care will he need in the future and who will provide it? Parents who have not been able to face such typical concerns are encouraged to think about and to express them.

During this interview the social worker learns from the parents what experiences the child has had in self-care and play activities, what his reactions are to events of emotional and social impact, and what evidence of learning difficulties exists. Afterward the interview notes are entered on the Performance Goals Record (see chapter 5). This information is given to the teacher and becomes part of the base line for program planning.

Information about the home and family environment and climate as it pertains to the child is recorded as part of the intake interview and is retained by the social worker.

From the child's developmental history, the social worker obtains an account of all agencies, schools, etc., where the child was known in the past and, with the parents' consent, requests reports. A comprehensive medical history is secured, beginning with the prenatal period and covering all contacts to the present time.

After the history-taking the child is scheduled for evaluation by our psychologist. The psychologist must possess personal capacity and professional skill for relating to and getting responses from very limited children. The Merrill-Palmer Scale of Mental Tests is the one most frequently used. An Educational Objective Form based upon the Haeussermann material is also completed. During the testing of the child, the parents sit in an adjoining room equipped with a two-way mirror so they can see, hear, and share their child's experience. Because the parents are emotionally stirred, the social worker is present to offer support and to answer questions.

No test can give a complete picture of the child and his capabilities. Observation in the classroom or within the school building reveals a number of things that do not, and probably could not, show up in a structured testing situation. As they watch the testing and note that their child fails to respond to some of the psychologist's questions or commands, parents may say, "But she does that at home!" Finally all information is shared and integrated in a meeting including the principal of the school, the teacher, psychologist, social worker, language pathologist, occupational therapist, and any other relevant staff member. Thus, the groundwork is laid for the child's individualized placement in our school. Following the meeting, recommendations are carried out by the social worker or another member of the staff.

Orientation

As part of the extended intake process, parents of children who will enter our school and parents of children recently admitted meet in a series of orientation meetings. Other close relatives, such as siblings, grandparents, etc., are encouraged to attend. Information is given about our program and curriculum. Information also is given about the broad range of needs of the retarded child, including such diverse aspects as recreation, leisure-time activities, guardianship, and religious education. The group discusses the question of retardation as it affects the child and the family. Typically, parents are concerned about telling other people about their retarded child and through the group process it becomes clear that they must first "tell" themselves. One parent said, "I knew it with my head but not with my heart." When the mother of a mongoloid child was asked how he was, she said, "He's fine but you know he is a mongoloid."

The social worker brings relevant literature to the attention of the group.

An entire orientation session is given to plan for the child's future. Despite the assistance offered by our own or another school, we recognize that most of our children will have lifelong needs for service and protection. We work with parents toward plans for physical and psychological care, financial support, and fulfilling the totality of needs which the individual will have in the years to come. Where it is indicated, we encourage parents to place their child on waiting lists for private or state residential schools. Workshop training is a future resource for some retarded children. In such a program the individual can develop work skills and earn money while he continues to live at home. Provision needs to be made for the individual who is able to move into employment in industry where he can earn more and function in a less restricted environment. For optimum development the retarded person should be given as much independence as he can realistically handle. Guardianship of the individual's person or property or both is a basic issue which needs to be anticipated. The parents are not automatically guardians of retarded children over 21 unless they are so appointed by the court. Many states are developing Guardianship Plans. The need for such programs will increase as retarded individuals are enabled to leave large institutions for return to community life. Parents can safeguard their child's future material security by including them in insurance policies, trust funds, or wills. In making such plans a specialist should be consulted regarding the best and safest coverage. A lawyer should explore future planning for a retarded person to offer him maximum protection. Social Security also provides some benefits for the mentally retarded person.

Discussion Groups

The response of parents asked to participate in discussion groups indicated that such groups have a very important function in a special education school. The meetings are left unstructured as to content so the members can bring up their individual concerns. The strong bond which develops within the group is a source of emotional support. In dealing with their own feelings, parents become more comfortable with themselves and with their child. They exchange viewpoints, share experiences, and make new discoveries. It is important to move away from "Why did this happen to me?" to "What shall I do next?" Acceptance of the problem comes first. After acceptance, the next step is what can be done about it. In families where members are treated as individuals, the retarded child is regarded as an individual with some special needs but like all children in his need for love.

Leisure-time Activities for Students

Bowling. For trainable children, bowling is a major physical and recreational activity throughout much of the country. Older boys and girls (ages 14-21) bowl once a week in our Bowing League.

Park programs. After-school and summer recreation programs for our children are provided by the local park district. With courage and conviction, community understanding and willingness to experiment, many such programs can become realities.

Camp programs. There are many summer camps, both day and residential, throughout the country, some costly and some managed by parents' groups or service organizations. The social worker keeps an up-to-date file of such camps and assists in arranging for camping experiences.

Swimming. Swimming is highly recommended as part of a recreational program for trainable children. Many area YMCAs have swim programs for the handicapped on a private membership basis, and many of our children participate.

Social clubs. One of the needs of the TMH young adult is for socialization with his peers. For several years, parents at our school have sponsored a monthly social club, where dancing, entertainment, and refreshments create a party atmosphere. Currently, two facilities have joined together in this endeavor, which has added a new dimension to the program and enlarged the social contacts of students.

Religion classes. Religious training expands the horizon of the trainable child. Classes are conducted in the area of the Molloy Education Center for children of the Catholic, Protestant, and Jewish faiths. Innovative teaching methods are used by teachers of religion. Religious education of the mentally retarded is a comparatively new field. As in any new undertaking, there will be success and failure, trial and error, until realistic methods can be found to teach old values in new ways.

Application to a Residential School

Parents are encouraged to consider such an eventuality and seek information about residential schools. Application under stress of emergency is very difficult and long periods of waiting are encountered.

Application to a State School

Application to a state school is urged, even if serious consideration for such placement is not imminent. Placing the child's name on a waiting list can save time in the eventuality of having to find care away from home. The waiting lists for state schools are long and one can wait as long as five years in many states before admission.

In some states if the child is on the waiting list, and in need of emergency placement in a residential school, parents may, after placing him in a private setting, request funds from the state to help defray the expenses of the private school. This is an important consideration as such placements are costly.

Application to a Workshop

In Illinois, a trainable student, under law, is eligible for public schooling from age 3 to age 21. Application for community workshop placement should be made several months before the terminal public school age.

Workshops are becoming more available and will no doubt continue to increase in number. Here a person can earn money for work produced. Such a facility is usually a contract workshop, where orders from companies supply the basis of the jobs. In this setup, the person can continue living at home, and go to the workshop each day. If he cannot continue to live at home, foster home care, supervised homes with housemothers, apartments with supervisors or social workers, recreational facilities, or self-contained community living plans may answer his needs.

Such community involvement will be a greater need as the retarded person moves out of the contract workshop into employment in industry where he can earn more and have greater freedom to live in a less restricted environment. This is all within the realm of reality. The retarded person should be given as much independence as he can handle.

Draft Registration

Prior to age 18, a boy should go to the local draft board accompanied by a parent or other responsible relative. To register, he needs only to state his name, address, and birth date. Later, he will be sent an eight-page Classification Questionnaire with questions to determine his eligibility for deferment. Parents may help fill out the questionnaire and state that they have done so. A parent can state the condition of the boy and also enclose letters from doctors, teachers, or other professionals who know his condition. When a boy is in an institution, the director of the institution may register him. Draft boards usually grant immediate deferment if proof of the disabling condition is adequate.

Crisis Care

Emergencies do arise: serious illness in a family, death, family crises, serious changes in behavior, progression of a deteriorating condition. Placement of a child out of the home in a crisis situation is very difficult. It is a nagging source of worry and concern to parents that such a situation could arise.

The parents' organization of the Molloy Center has developed plans for a small homelike residence to house no more than 12 children on a short-term basis. This can serve crisis situations, be available for parents' vacations, or facilitate trial separations and give the child an opportunity to be away from home for a short stay to "practice independence." Emergency placement in state institutions has been accomplished but is not always desirable.

Liaison

Liaison between such different disciplines as psychology, psychiatry, social work, occupational therapy, and speech pathology is essential, as is the liaison between school and home.

When all staff members working with a child have the opportunity for thoughtful consideration of all material concerning a student, everyone is better equipped not only to understand all facets of the material, but to consider the most appropriate way of working with the student.

A conference opens up new areas, gives members of the staff an opportunity to express their feelings about the student and how they may have contributed to negative rather than positive thinking about him.

Everyone involved with the student is interested in him and has a wish to make his class placement as beneficial as possible. The larger the facility the more complicated and essential is the communication among disciplines.

A second type of liaison, the link between school and home, is carried out by the social worker, who can on many occasions serve as a buffer. For a parent to deal directly with the teacher in problem areas can become difficult, with the teacher having to absorb the hostility of the parent. With the social worker acting as an intermediary and absorbing this hostility, the teacher is left to her main function of teaching. The social worker makes all parent contacts regarding any misunderstandings about matters such as transportation schedules and bus drivers. The social worker can involve the parents in a cooperative effort in the best interests of the student.

The Social Worker's Jobs

Recommending Agencies

In metropolitan areas, there are a great variety of agencies—public, community, and private. Some are more appropriate than others to meet the needs of the student and his family. The social worker has up-to-date information and can suggest selecting agency resources to meet a specific need. If this groundwork is not done by the social worker, the family is left to flounder with the nearly insurmountable task of numerous calls and frustrations in trying to find what is needed. When an agency is located, the worker offers the information to the parents, who can then follow through with the agency if they wish. If more than one agency can handle the particular request, the names of all agencies to contact are given to the family.

Nothing is more discouraging for a parent than to call an agency, be rejected, and to be given no help in finding the proper one.

Locating Other Resources

Many special resources are needed for the mentally retarded student. To meet the needs of parents, lists of babysitters, dentists, orthopedic surgeons, and others have been compiled. Some parents, in an effort to find babysitters for students, contact student nurses' residences, high schools, and colleges in the area to locate the names of young people who are willing to babysit with a retarded child. This proves very successful and babysitters secured in this way have been most satisfactory. To be of value, it is necessary to renew the contacts yearly to find out if the sitters are still available or, if they are not, to recruit new ones.

As an interesting sidelight connected with this project, a teacher in one of the area high schools gathered all the potential babysitters together and talked to them about retardation and what things they might expect in babysitting for a retarded child.

To compile a list of qualified pedodontists in the area, one of the university dental schools shared its list of interested and qualified graduates, enabling us to pass on names to parents as they requested them. At least three alternatives are given to them if possible.

Many students had not had dental work done because it had been impossible for a dentist to work on their teeth. Some had to go into the hospital so they could be anaesthetized in order to have necessary dental work done. The school nurse plays "going to the dentist" with most gratifying results. Students who had never allowed a dentist to work on them surprised even their parents by being able to sit quietly in the dentist's chair.

A careful survey of dentists in the area became especially necessary when in 1969 the state required that each school child have a dental examination yearly.

These are just some of the services that are offered to parents, as it has been recognized that special efforts are needed to provide maximum service for the student.

Attending Meetings

Attending meetings of welfare councils, family service agencies, and youth groups in the area keeps the social worker abreast of what is going on and of any new programs which might serve the retarded student. This is also a way to become more closely involved with other social workers and others in the community who are interested in the field.

Serving as a Board Member

Social workers as board members in mental health agencies and other social welfare agencies serve a most useful purpose, as they can present school needs to other board members and play a part in showing the public gaps in services and pointing out priorities from a school standpoint.

Acting as a Resource Person

At community meetings, such as those of the YMCA or PTA, the social worker is a valuable resource person who can explain the special school program to the wider community, by speaking when asked and by working with various organized groups to further their understanding of the retarded child as part of the community.

Participating in Research

The social worker is a member of the team of educators, psychologists, and others engaged in research projects. As parents must be involved in projects if cooperation is to be gained, the social worker maintains their involvement. The aim of the research is to discover new facts about the retarded or to verify present knowledge.

Performing Other Assigned Social Work Duties

Special duties assigned by a principal are, for example, interviewing and training volunteers, conducting visitors, and explaining the school program to them.

The volunteers are interviewed to determine their background, special interests, and reasons for wishing to volunteer and also to evaluate their ability to function in a special school.

Visitors from various universities, other special schools, and community groups are seen throughout the year. After they have had an opportunity to observe the classrooms, they gather together in a common meeting room, where they may ask questions, discuss programs, and learn more about the philosophy of the school and team teaching, research projects, or special interest areas.

Projections for the Future

New laws in many states make it mandatory for trainable mentally retarded children to receive a public school education from age 5 to age 21, and, if they are multiply handicapped, from age 3 to age 21. Mandatory legislation is being considered in other states. Such legislation is provocative of careful assessment.

Many questions will be raised regarding the law. Will it apply across the wide spectrum of mental retardation? Will interpretation of the law be relaxed or rigid? Will the law be used to find ways to reject students rather than accept them? What happens if a student is rejected? Or admitted and then dismissed? What recourse do parents have? What financial responsibility do school districts have to provide for a student rejected from a school program? What constitutes a valid reason to reject a student? Who determines the reasons for rejection? These and many other questions need asking as new laws are implemented. What will be the effect of the new law on students, parents, and school personnel?

As with any new program, there will be students who "fall in the cracks." In other words, there will be children who cannot meet the exact letter of the law. The social worker will need specific information on any student who does not meet the school's criteria. Although this is essentially a school administrative problem, the social worker may be called upon to deal with it in relation to the parents.

The competent social worker can deal with parents' feelings and anxieties related to school decisions when the reasons are clear. The social worker may or may not be in complete agreement regarding the decision but is charged with handling it in a professional, objective, factual manner.

Does Social Work in a Special School Differ from that in Other Schools?

Social work is generic. It rests on relationships between individuals, and its goal is to help individuals to function more adequately in their day-to-day living. School social work is generic social work, practiced in a school setting, and therefore the focus is on the student in relation to the educational process.

The main difference we see in social work in the special school is the need for added understanding of the retarded and a willingness on the part of the social worker to try a variety of approaches to the individual problems and needs of the student.

Social workers in special education schools need to find innovative ways to break down old ideas about the retarded child. One way to do this is by stressing their similarities to other children, rather than the differences. For instance, Johnny is first a little boy with feelings and fears, strengths and weaknesses just like any other child. He has to be considered as Johnny with a distinct personality first and then as Johnny with his distinct personality who has also been diagnosed as retarded.

In a special school, there can be a dozen children with the diagnosis of brain injury, but this diagnosis is superimposed upon a dozen totally different children with their distinct individualities. One danger to be avoided is lumping children together in a particular diagnostic category without taking into consideration all of the individual differences. Often, in thinking of the retarded child, one gets a particular mind set and concentrates on the retardation rather than on the total picture the child presents.

Are There Limitations to the Practice of Social Work in a Special School?

Limitations to the practice of social work in the special school are man-made ones. Administrative limitations may exist. However, one usually is free to try new approaches to social work in the special school, as the field is relatively new. The social worker has few guidelines to follow and can try many things as long as they are in the best interests of the student.

Time is also a limiting factor. Priorities have to be established. What is most urgent? The focus needs to be kept constantly on the education of the whole child in the school setting. Is the social work service appropriate in the school setting, or should the student be referred to some other community agency? How far should the social worker go in furnishing overall service to the student and his parents?

These are just some of the things to be considered in offering services to the retarded student.

The social worker has a mandate—to safeguard the rights of the retarded student, to treat him with dignity and respect, and to consider his individual needs.

8. THE SCHOOL NURSE

by Margaret C. Miller, R.N.

"Health is Wealth"

The health program for our school has been planned through the combined efforts of the teachers, the occupational therapist, the social worker, and the nurse. Many sessions were held to determine what was needed to attain the goal of maintaining good health and independence in self-care.

A complete medical history of the child prior to admission is of great importance in understanding and facilitating future plans for him. The nurse works with the intake evaluation team. The physician attempts to pinpoint the etiology of the retarded development. He explores thoroughly the history of the mother's pregnancy—during the pregnancy, during the birth, and immediately after birth. The events of the first two years are very important. The family histories of both the mother and father are studied and any anomalies are so discovered.

In Appendix II the complete medical report which must be filled out and signed by the physician is presented. This medical history form was complied by the physicians on our board of advisers. The nurse takes the medical history before sending the complete form to the physician. This saves time for the busy doctor and assures detailed reporting.

An annual checkup is requested before school opens in September to alert school personnel to any changes which might occur from the medical standpoint, and to bring them up to date on the well-being of the child, present medications given for control of convulsions, behavior, or whatever the case may be. The annual medical and dental checkup forms are sent to all parents with an explanatory letter in July, to allow plenty of time. The June issue of our school newspaper carries a story urging parents to make appointments "now," as August is a very busy month for dentists and physicians. (These forms follow the initial medical form in the appendix.)

Within the first two weeks of school, the height and weight of every child are recorded and at mid-term the measuring is repeated. Any abnormal gain or loss in weight is reported to the parents at once. Frequently, too much gain in weight is found as our children tend to be sitters rather than doers. In conference with the parents we urge them to encourage some form of exercise for their child at home.

A review of the child's diet with the parents, indicating all the extra snacks, will make them aware of the reason for the extra pounds, and with suggestions as to a proper diet they are willing and eager to cooperate.

An emergency card is kept for each child for quick and easy reference. It contains a record of home phone number; father's business phone; a neighbor or relative who has agreed to come and take the child if the parents cannot be located in case of an emergency; physician's name and phone number; current medication dosage and time; and known allergies; immunizations; contagious diseases.

When a contagious disease is reported to the school, the sick child's name is given to the local health department. The emergency cards are then used to prepare a list of all the children who have never had the particular contagious disease and a note is sent home with each of these children informing the parents that their child has been exposed to *"the disease"* on *"date."* The incubation period is given and the signs and symptoms to watch for. This form is in Appendix II. To be readmitted to school, a child must have a note from the doctor stating that he is free of contagion and ready to be readmitted to school.

If medication is to be given during school hours, which very often is the case, a signed and dated Rx. from the doctor must accompany the medicine, stating the name of the medication, dosage to be given, the time to be administered, as well as permission for the nurse or teacher to dispense it. Under no consideration should medicines be given without the doctor's orders, and this applies to the acetysalicylic acid compounds and the many cough syrups prescribed or taken at home without prescriptions from a physician.

A yearly dental examination is required in Illinois and many other states. To allay the fears the child may have of his visit to the dentist, much time is spent in role playing. One child sits on a chair, while another one dresses in a white gown (one of father's shirts on backward with ties sewn on to keep it secure), puts a towel under the chin, and directs the patient to open his mouth. A tongue depressor may be used to explore and water is given the child with instructions on how to rinse his mouth as he would at the dentist's office. A book entitled "A Visit to the Dentist," published by Whitman (Tell-a-Tale Books), is excellent and is used during morning circle time. Pictures of the various machines are carefully observed and talked about—what they are, how they are used, and what kind of noise they make as well as why they are used. The book also explains the necessity for seeing the dentist at regular intervals as well as the importance of dental care at home. Most of our little ones are very ready when dental examinations are made, and the experience mother and father are dreading is a surprisingly pleasant one.

The same role playing is used to make a trip to the doctor less traumatic. As a rule, this visit entails "getting a shot." Again, one child puts on the white shirt and, with another child acting as the patient, he cleans an area on the patient's arm and with a plastic play hypodermic syringe (obtained at the local variety store) administers the shot; the teacher at the same time explains how it will prick and hurt a little but not for long. Children use tongue depressors to practice looking at each other's throats, a rolled piece of paper to look into the ears and nose, and a play stethoscope (also from the variety store) to check heart and lungs. The first few times the teacher will have to be the doctor; however, very soon there are many volunteers to carry on.

When a child is scheduled for surgery, such as a tonsillectomy, some time is spent each morning showing pictures of a hospital—a bed with the curtains around it, the bell to summon the nurse, the bedside table, the operating room (how white and bright it is) and the masked doctors and nurses. By the time the operation is scheduled, all facets of the hospital and its personnel have been thoroughly studied and are familiar to the child. He is also aware that it may "hurt" but that it will "hurt" less each day.

Teaching self-care begins on the first day the child enters school. The objectives in self-care for each group can be found in chapters 31-35.

As the girls reach puberty, many mothers do an excellent job preparing their daughters for the onset of menstruation. Our mothers meet in groups over coffee with the nurse and social worker and share their experiences in dealing with their daughters at this time. The school nurse should help the girls to understand and accept without fear this "monthly period." She explains that "the first sign of growing up" may be a red stain on the panties or pajamas or a red flow as they go to the toilet, which is perfectly natural and nothing to fear. Sometimes with this, cramps in the stomach, a backache, and an overall feeling of misery occur. These too are not at all unusual. The little lady must be assured constantly that all this is part of growing up; though certainly not pampered, she should be comforted. For discomforts, the nurse may have her lie down for a time and, with the doctor's permission, she could administer an aspirin or such. Before all this happens it is wise to familiarize the girl with pads and set aside time to go over and over and over the application of the sanitary napkin, its removal, and proper disposal, with emphasis placed on careful wrapping in either waste paper or a paper towel and disposal in a special bag provided in the girls' lavatory. That pads should never be flushed down the toilet is also a point to be stressed strongly. Much emphasis is put on the need for cleanliness at this time, and girls should be assured that bathing is safe and no different from bathing at any other time. If the use of the sanitary belt and the pad proves too difficult, we suggest using the Santy Panty which has the built-in "safti-grip." These are put out by Belten Corporation, SPB, Box 807, St. Louis, Missouri, 63101, and usually can be found in local department stores.

Kimberly-Clark Corporation, Education Department, Neenah, Wisconsin, 54957, has printed a pamphlet called "How to Tell the Retarded Girl About Menstruation" which is a help to apprehensive mothers.

Masturbation often starts very early and is of great concern to the parents. Punishment for masturbation only draws more attention to a behavior that is experienced at one time or another by practically all adolescents. It is wiser to concentrate on providing the child with comfortable loose clothing, plenty of exercise via physical education and numerous interesting activities.

A weekly period is set aside for each age group for discussions as well as individual instruction and participation in care of teeth, bathing, shampooing the hair, and nail care. A bathing chart is kept which includes preparation for bath:

        check for towel, soap, washcloth
        undress—discard dirty clothes, fold others
        adjust water
        body care in shower or tub
        turn off water
        clean tub
        dry thoroughly
        use deodorant
        dress and groom hair.

The cooperation of the parents is essential in keeping this record up to date.

The older groups are given special instructions in folding towels, sheets, pillow cases for putting away; caring for clothing; proper bed making, from the correct way to strip the soiled bed and place the dirty linen in the pillow case (if no other container is used) to making up the bed completely.

Caring for dishes is part of this area—scraping dirty dishes, rinsing them for the dishwasher or washing by hand. It is essential to constantly remind those on dish-drying detail of the importance of washing their hands before beginning; should it be necessary for them to scratch their heads, wipe their noses or such, washing again is necessary.

The health of the student is important to his development. Cooperation of the parents once again is all-important. We request that a child be kept home with any of the following symptoms: eye infection (except sties); inflammation or watery eyes; sneezing and runny nose; cough associated with a cold; skin rash; fever (remain home 48 hours after the temperature is normal); sore throat; earache; extreme fatigue; or nausea and vomiting.

Children who develop any of the above symptoms during school hours are sent home at the discretion of the school nurse or the principal. On return to school, a note from the parent must accompany the child. Upon arrival, he is checked by the nurse, who records his temperature.

When vomiting or diarrhea occur, a generous sprinkling of Steriloid completely covers up the mess and stops the odor. This is similar to the consistency of sawdust and is easily swept up and disposed of. It can be safely sprinkled on the clothing of the child also and is easily brushed off with no trace of odor. Steriloid is available in quart containers or bulk from the Madison Chemical Corporation. Each classroom and all of our buses have Steriloid and a small brush and dust pan (ordered from the same company) readily available.

If a child has ever had seizures of any sort, a request is made that the parents give the school a complete description of the episodes—the aura, duration, and aftermath—in writing. Medications which are to be administered at a warning signal or during the seizure (these are always given rectally) *must* be given to the nurse or teacher and *must* be accompanied by a signed note from the doctor permitting the medication to be administered as prescribed. Some seizure patterns show a definite type of behavior prior to the episode itself. In such cases, it is very helpful to have the cooperation of the physician so the school personnel may know when inappropriate behavior is the product of seizure activity.

The vision of our children has always been a matter of concern and many times we believe their learning is deterred because of poor vision. So few ophthalmologists will take the time to understand and work with these children. Examination with standard methods, for most of the children, is almost an impossibility. Our concern about the visual problems experienced by our children and the number of C.N.T. ("Could Not Test") reports that came to us led us to discuss the problem with our medical advisory board. Through the efforts of Doctor Noel Shaw, a pediatrician on our board, we enlisted the services of Dr. Lawrence Lawson, an ophthalmologist who was part of the team headed by Dr. Helmer Myklebust, of Northwestern University, that was investigating the factors contributing to a definitive procedure for the management of children with learning disabilities. Dr. Lawson explored possibilities for developing a procedure and defining techniques for evaluating the visual functioning of children with retarded development. The standard method (Snellen Chart) was applied in testing those children who were able to recognize and name the letters of the alphabet. Much discussion followed as to how to reach the remainder of the children. The teacher, speech pathologist, occupational therapist, principal, and nurse were involved in this discussion. What child isn't interested in food? A banana, a hot dog, an apple, and an ice-cream cone were selected from the pictures in the Peabody Language Development Kit. After many, many hours of study and work with a photographer, Dr. Lawson produced a set of these familiar pictures that can be projected to the same proportion as the standard lettering. Each teacher in the individual classroom works with each child to familiarize him with these pictures so even the non-verbal children can identify them in their own particular way—for example, the ice-cream cone, a licking motion; the hot dog, patting the stomach; the banana, a peeling motion; and the apple, a biting pretense. As long as the response is consistent for each picture, the problem is solved. The same play-acting goes on in the classroom. The teacher with the white coat plays the doctor and uses the stick found in the bottle for blowing bubbles to pretend to look into the child's eyes. The children are very comfortable and cooperative on the day it is their turn to have their eyes tested professionally. Out of eighty children only four were not able to tolerate the situation. Dr Lawson's study—"A Technique for Visual Appraisal of Mentally Retarded Children" by Lawrence J. Lawson Jr. M.D. and Greg Schoofs, M.D.—has been reported in the *Journal of Ophthalmology* and is available, as are the charts, from: Medical Contact Lenses, 1225 Circle Tower, Indianapolis, Ind. 46204.

The need to evaluate a child's hearing sensitivity in order to rule out a hearing impairment as a contributing factor in the child's delayed development has continued to be a concern to the evaluating team and the staff members. Two factors are apparent in the literature: (1) the reported high incidence of hearing loss among the mentally retarded population, (2) the difficulty in obtaining accurate and valid formal tests for these children. Chapter 10 discusses these points in detail. However, the medical implications and the role of the nurse in acting as an agent of follow-up are of extreme importance.

Where a hearing impairment is suspected, particularly in children with a history of chronic respiratory infection, a thorough otological examination (prior to formal testing) should be carried out to rule out organic involvement. Many of our children have fluctuating hearing due to their susceptibility to colds or allergies. Encouraging parents to obtain medical clearance for such testing is the responsibility of the nurse. The teacher must be alert constantly and report symptoms to the nurse. Some nurses are able to obtain training in the screening of hearing sensitivity and so fill an additional role when the services of a speech and hearing specialist are not available. The nurse must realize that hearing impairment can and does exist with retardation. This added handicap can limit the training and the child's potential greatly.

Annually, all personnel—including teachers, office workers, custodians, food handlers, and bus drivers, as well as volunteers—must have negative chest X-ray reports before they are permitted to work in the school or be in contact with the children. It is the responsibility of the nurse to enforce this safeguard to health. Health control regulations vary in different areas. Immunizations for smallpox, German measles, and poliomyelitis are usually required. In some states, complete annual physical examinations are required of all personnel. Food handlers and custodians are usually required to have annual complete physical examinations.

The nurse checks the sanitary conditions in the bathrooms and kitchen and makes a report to the principal periodically. The toys and manipulative educational materials must be washed frequently with Zepherin, Bactine concentrate, Amphyl spray or equally effective disinfectants. Our older boys and girls take turns washing and rinsing (with supervision). It is a learning experience for them and part of their child-care training program.

Children should feel free to speak with the nurse at any time about any problem, no matter how small. She is their friend and their problems are hers also and between them they can be solved.

In a small unit, where there is no full-time nurse on

the staff, any help the teachers may need can be obtained from the local Visiting Nurses' Association. Should the community not have such an organization, the one nurse usually assigned to a number of schools will probably be willing to aid the teacher.

Good health, good health habits, and control of sanitation are all important in any school. Healthy children as a rule are happy children and happy children are eager, cooperative, and willing to work to the extent of their capabilities.

9. THE PSYCHOLOGICAL ASSESSMENT

by Calvin K. Claus

> *Let not the strong*
> *Be cozened*
> *By* Is *and* Isn't,
> Was *and* Wasn't,
> *Truth's to be sought*
> *In* Does *and* Doesn't.

—B. F. Skinner (quoted by kind permission of *Encounter*)

Psychological assessment—the *do's* and *don'ts* of can't, won't and *Does* or *Dosen't*.

In the assessment of children suspected of showing retarded development, the procedures generally used today continue to have a close tie to the original work of Binet and Simon, begun over sixty years ago. I would like to take a new look at some old ideas and describe another point of view and approach to the psychological assessment of children with retarded development.

When looking at a translation of the 1908 published work of Binet and Simon (Jenkins and Paterson 1961) we find items such as the following classified at particular age levels, on the average:

> give [own] last name
> name key, knife and penny
> give [own] age
> distinguish morning and evening

Jenkins and Paterson also include, in translation, the 1905 Binet-Simon listing of items arranged in an order going from simple to complex. The wording in the text uses "ing" endings on the verbs, but for purposes of exposition, this ending is dropped. Some of the items, thus, are:

> Grasp a small object which is touched
> Find and eat a square of chocolate wrapped in paper
> Name objects in pictures

Although each such statement occurs in the context of a so-called "intelligence" test, each has relevance outside of this context. They describe everyday, functional behaviors. By what could be called societal sanction, they are declared to be essential parts of any person's behavioral repertoire.

A more up-to-date example is taken from the Illinois Test of Psycholinguistic Abilities (Kirk, 1966). The wording used below is a paraphrase of the task descriptions found in this test. Here are two samples:

Select, from groupings of four different pictures, the one which has a functional relationship to each of several given pictures.

Describe, orally, real common objects in terms of multiple characteristics such as name, color, shape, composition, function, parts, numerosity, simile, metaphor, or relationship to other things, places or persons.

Without too much difficulty, it is possible to show that these behaviors also have relevance to everyday life.

This brief look at the "old" and the "new" in tests suggests a basic question which should be asked by anyone involved in the task of psychological assessment. Does the testing instrument being used incorporate behaviors called for in everyday life? Greenspoon and Gersten (1967) say that the answer to this question should be in the affirmative. If the test items are, indeed, directly related to real-life situations, and if the educational objectives or performance goals outlined in the special education curriculum are also real-life oriented, the following conclusion is warranted: test tasks and curriculum objectives or performance goals should be identical. The close relationship between the test examples cited earlier and the performance goals given at the end of this curriculum guide is too obvious to be overlooked. With this as background, then, a partial definition of the process of psychological assessment would run something like this: *Psychological assessment is the systematic recording of the behaviors and behavior changes shown by a person which are considered desirable in relation to previously stated performance goals.*

A psychologist following this approach would then record information something like the following:

> Bill *does*:
>   give own last name.
>   name key, knife, etc.
>   give own age.
>   distinguish morning and evening.
>   grasp a small object, etc.
>   find and eat, etc.
>   name these pictured objects, etc.
>   select from groupings of four different
>   pictures, the one which has a func-
>   tional relationship to each of these
>   pictures, etc.
>   describe, orally, these objects . . . in terms
>   of . . .

On the face of it, this procedure appears to be little different from traditional testing. One rather subtle difference, however, is the use of the periphrastic word DOES and, by extension, DOESN'T, in the negative case where the behavior is not shown. It is very easy—indeed, too easy—for the psychologist as well as the teacher to say that a child "can't" do something. Furthermore, there are occasions when the inference of "won't" is also attached to the statements of performance. It should be noted with emphasis that words such as "can't" and "won't" seem to carry excess baggage of meaning when talking about children showing retarded development. The suggestion made here is to avoid, whenever possible, any prejudicial remarks about assumed, inferential inner qualities of capacity, willingness or intention to perform a task. Always refer to the child in terms of what he DOES or DOESN'T do.

Another difference between traditional psychological assessment procedures and those being discussed here is in terms of a technical distinction. Glaser (1963) and, more recently, Popham and Husek (1969) have drawn a contrast between norm-referenced measurement and criterion-referenced measurement (see General Bibliography for full references). When the average performance of some norm population is the basis for comparing a child's individual performance, there is a strong tendency to say that a ten-year-old, for example, "can't" do what the average ten-year-old "can" do. Comparing what a particular child does with what is done by a statistical fiction called the average child is but one method of psychological assessment. It is here proposed that criterion-referenced measurement be the basis of psychological assessment of children with retarded development as well as others. The prime requisite for this approach is that the detailed educational objectives or performance goals be stated beforehand. As pointed out earlier, using the examples of Binet and Simon, along with those from the ITPA, this type of assessment becomes possible if the criterion for each performance is specified sufficiently. The performance goals serve as a kind of checklist for making an assessment.

The psychologist may function in two different ways, depending upon the point in time when an assessment is made. If a child is being assessed on an initial intake basis, the psychologist's role is to record those behaviors the child currently DOES perform. The child's readiness, in terms of entering behaviors in his repertoire, is one bit of data the teacher uses in determining where, in the list of performance goals, the training process should begin. If the child is being assessed on an annual, biennial, or triennial basis during the training process, the psychological assessment serves merely as an abbreviated check on the child's change in behavior. This supplements and is independent of the more complete assessment of day-to-day, week-to-week changes in performance recorded by the teacher.

Psychological Assessment: Considerations Other Than What the Child DOES or DOESN'T do.

The definition above seems to fall somewhat short of the mark for a complete statement of the psychologist's role in assessment. This partial definition says nothing about assessing the antecedent as well as the consequent conditions that may have effected the behaviors and behavior changes recorded. A basic assumption must be made before proceeding in this direction, however. Except where clear-cut medical evidence is to the contrary, it is assumed that all the manifest behavior of a child is learned. Thus, to say that a child has a short "attention span" says nothing about a particular stimulus or the range of stimuli that may exert stimulus control as a focus of activity. What things or events has the child learned to focus on? Which of these stimuli might be used positively and constructively to assist in the training process? This is one aspect of the assessment—i.e., to answer such questions about stimulus control variables.

It helps not one bit merely to say that a child perseverates. If, for example, a child claps his hands from moment to moment during an activity, it may well be that people in his environment perseverate in using only one type of nonverbal reward or reinforcement, namely, hand clapping. Perseveration may be a function of environmental perseverating, and the psychological assessment may highlight the necessity of varying reinforcers or help to locate new reinforcers. Thus, another facet of psychological assessment is identifying particular reinforcers or types of reinforcers to assist in the process of training children to achieve specified performance goals.

To summarize, psychological assessment has been defined as systematic:

1. recording of behaviors and behavior changes shown by a person which are considered desirable in relation to previously stated performance goals, and
2. identifying of relevant reinforcers and stimulus control variables which have produced or which should be expected to produce desirable behavior changes.

There should be a close alignment between a school's specified curriculum performance goals and the items in the psychologist's assessment instruments. Under these circumstances the psychologist no longer functions in a rarefied environment, with esoteric tools, but rather becomes an extension of the teacher as a recorder and identifier. The key is to specify the positive DOES DO performance goals.

10. EVALUATING LANGUAGE

by Arlene M. Matkin

"When I use a word," Humpty Dumpty said, "It means just what I choose it to mean— Neither more nor less . . . When I make a word do a lot of work like that, I always pay it extra."

—Lewis Carroll

Language Development

"Delayed Language" is a term commonly associated with mental retardation. However, "delayed language" has also been used as a generic term to describe numerous types of communicative disorders associated with other handicapping conditions found among children. In this chapter, language delay as it specifically relates to a child with retarded development will be discussed. The implications of multiple handicaps, that is, mental retardation in association with other sensory and emotional deficits, are also considered.

The ability to communicate is one of the most important but difficult skills that a child has to master. The acquisition of language—the ability to understand and to express—is a critical part of a child's development. In this context, language is viewed as a complex, symbolic process, which includes both learning to understand gestures, the spoken word, and the printed word, and learning to express thoughts, ideas, and emotions through gestures, speech, and writing.

The capacity to communicate is dependent upon psychological, neurological, and physiological integrities. If these integrities are present, the sequential development of language can be predicted in children of different ages. Factors related to learning and maturation are primary considerations in the acquisition of communicative skills.

Learning has been defined as bringing about a change in behavior as the result of experience. In other words, experience is the foundation for learning. Learning includes a very wide range of changes in behavior, from mastering a simple task such as drinking from a straw to adding words to one's vocabulary. It is important to realize that the learning of any skill does not just happen, but occurs in a step-by-step procedure. Language learning refers to the acquisition of an arbitrary symbol system that has developed over centuries by which human beings communicate. As a child, one first learns receptive language (encoding), that is, learns to understand gestures, the spoken word, and then the printed word.

Although language acquisition has been explained in many ways, specific terms reoccur in defining this learning process. The learning of language can be broken into the following sequential steps:

1. The child must be aware that a stimulus (something that causes action) is present (*awareness* and *attention*). This stimulus may be visual, auditory, olfactory, tactile, or haptic.

2. To be aware or to pay attention, one of the senses (ear, eye, nose, or touch) must be functioning in order to receive or pick up the stimulus. The stimulation of the ear, eye, nose, or sense of touch is called *sensation*.

3. These impressions on the senses must then be organized into meaningful units (*perception*). Initially, it appears that an infant hears, sees, feels, and smells his environment in a confused and unrelated way. However, as he grows, he is able to pick out common characteristics (percepts) of those things that he experiences. In other words, in attaching specific meaning to a variety of stimuli, a child begins to differentiate or discover differences as well as likenesses between things, felt, heard or seen.

4. The most complex step (*conceptualization*) involves discovering and defining the outstanding features found in a group of objects or events which make them alike or different. The young child's concepts are at first concrete, that is, he is able to learn only from things that he can see, hear, touch, feel, or smell. Later he can associate percepts or characteristics from all his senses and formulate a meaningful idea. For example, the word "chair" to the child refers only to the chair visible in the environment. After the initial and repeated experiences, "chair" refers to a piece of furniture with a back, made in a variety of materials and used primarily to sit on.

An example of learning through the sense of hearing involves the child's awareness of the simultaneous presence of several different sounds. The presence of normal hearing is assumed. Once these sounds have been received or "heard" the child must separate (*discriminate*) one sound from another. The infant initially responds to gross environmental sounds such as loud noises or a voice. At first he reacts to these sounds by some type of startle reflex. However, very soon the response becomes more refined; that is, he will quiet at the sound of his mother's voice.

The next step in development is to associate a voice or sound with a particular object or event (this process may involve sight and hearing or hearing plus another sensory modality). By having the same experience with the same sound many times the child then learns to listen for certain characteristics and to associate them with the source of the sound. He soon learns to recognize that mother's voice is different from dad's voice or to distinguish between a pleasant voice and a stern voice. Conceptualization occurs when the child is able to associate a common stimulus to many different sources; to know, for example, that barking sounds come from all dogs and not just from a pet or to associate the word "Daddy" with his father rather than with all men.

Another way of showing these ideas is by the following outline:

EXPERIENCE→SENSATION→PERCEPTION AND DISCRIMINATION→CONCEPTUALIZATION= LEARNING

To acquire language, the child must complete the following process:

1. Recognize, identify, and understand the world around him.
2. Learn to understand the speech he hears from others around him; and
3. Develop the ability to produce many speech sounds and then put various speech sounds together so that they simulate adult words.

Early in the developmental process, the child begins to babble and experiment with his voice, tongue, and lips. Such experimentation appears to lay the foundation for later use of speech. Also at this very early age, an infant starts to recognize that many sounds in his life are different. In other words, both receptive and expressive prelinguistic skills are developing simultaneously. In a remarkably short time, a normal child begins to obey very simple verbal commands such as "No, no" and "Come." As he continues to listen to speech and other sounds about him, he then begins to produce speech himself. Thus, a key concept is:

Understanding comes first, then speech develops.

Receptive language, in the broadest sense, includes not only speech, but understanding other nonverbal concepts that a child must process before he is able to use verbal language. As an infant develops to the toddler stage he not only learns motor skills, but is able to experience and identify many aspects of his total environment.

Learning language seems to develop very rapidly, but a youngster must listen, imitate, and experiment with simple words before he moves to the more difficult level of putting two or three words together. So each new word, phrase, or sentence represents another step in a very complex developmental process. Although a great deal of research has been undertaken, it is still not known exactly either how a small child develops a vocabulary of many thousands of words or how he learns to form the idea of a sentence and then to use the parts of speech in the correct way. From normal developmental studies, it is recognized that speech develops before a child learns to read and that reading precedes writing.

In summary, language should be viewed as a complex learning process which includes both receptive and expressive functions. The input function or decoding includes understanding of gestures, the spoken word, and the printed word, which are all symbols for the objects or ideas they represent. The output function or encoding includes expressing thoughts and ideas through gestures, facial expressions, speech and/or writing in an appropriate way. This means that language develops from hearing and/or seeing, then thinking and responding in an appropriate nonverbal way. Later, the appropriate response may involve saying or writing something about what occurred as a result of the thinking, associating, and action.

$$\text{STIMULUS} \rightarrow \left\{ \begin{array}{c} \text{HEAR} \\ \text{SEE} \\ \text{FEEL} \end{array} \right\} \rightarrow \text{DO} \rightarrow \text{SAY}$$

Finally, it should be kept in mind that language, both receptive and expressive, develops from simple to complex and from concrete to abstract.

The Language Evaluation

Although a child is functioning at a retarded level of development, a program of language training based only on information from psychological tests leaves much to be desired. It should be remembered that most intelligence tests are used as tools for general classification.

The level of a child's language development can be estimated by a psychologist, physician, or parent familiar with the normal developmental language sequence. However, a rough estimate of the child's ability to understand and to communicate verbally may be misleading. A thorough evaluation of delayed language development, both receptive and expressive, is of utmost importance. An adequate language program can be designed only if specific, rather than general, information is available regarding various components of language skills.

The evaluation of a child's intellectual ability as well as of his motor, social, and language development is most adequately completed by a diagnostic team. Typically the family physician is contacted first when a child fails to develop at the expected rate for his chronological age. Most frequently the parents' chief complaint is that the youngster has little or no speech. Too often the diagnosis is attempted by one professional worker rather than by a diagnostic team. Thus, attention may be focused upon some limited aspects of the child's total development, such as his failure to acquire speech, rather than upon the language function.

A speech and language therapist should be a member of any diagnostic team which evaluates retarded children. This professional worker's training includes a background in child development as well as in diagnostic and remedial techniques for communicative disorders. The role of the speech and language clinician working with trainable children differs from that of the public school speech correctionist, who has focused primarily on one aspect of speech production, that is, articulation. In contrast, the language therapist is concerned with the development of receptive as well as expressive communication.

As has been stated, language is learned and the development of input skills precedes output. Therefore the failure of a child to develop speech may occur at any of the steps underlying the language learning process. A lag in development of receptive language can occur as a result of a breakdown at any of the following levels:

1. Development of attention.
2. Sensation, as the result of a hearing loss or a visual impairment, for example.
3. Perception which results in an inability to find or learn specific meanings and pick out common characteristics of experiences.
4. Conception, the association of experience with a set of symbols—gestural, spoken, or written—and generalizing this information to similar experiences. Several possible defects may be considered. Problems in storing or in recalling past experiences are only two of the possible breakdowns in the conceptualization process.

Although the preceding is a very limited and overly simplified description of the receptive language function, it highlights two important considerations. First, there are many types of problems which may disrupt language development. Secondly, an evaluation of a child's receptive language function is an involved procedure requiring an adequate understanding of the language acquisition sequence.

Informal Evaluation of Receptive Language

Useful information regarding a child's receptive language skills can initially be obtained through the use of selected items from developmental scales during informal observations. Normative data regarding language development from several scales can provide a sequential guide to receptive communication behavior which increases in difficulty with maturation. The obstacle in using such normative data for determining the level of a youngster's receptive language function is that the items included in these scales are limited to only a few specific milestones for each age level.

In attempting to establish a language program for the trainable mentally retarded child, a compilation of items from several developmental scales has been found to be more useful than any one particular scale. Table I provides not only a tool for evaluation, but also a guide for designing a meaningful program for the enhancement of communication development. However, it must be kept in mind that speech will not be forthcoming until the child develops adequate understanding and begins to attach meaning to our complex set of symbols which comprises language.

You will note that a chronological age has not been placed on any of the items in Table I. The concept of "developmental delay" is based on the premise that although there is a lag in language performance the sequence of development as observed in the normal child will unfold through training and maturation.

TABLE I

Observed Receptive Language Behaviors
(Full references appear in the General Bibliography)

Behavior	Source
Activity diminishes as sound is made close to child	Gesell
Responds to social approach by smiling	Gesell
Looks directly at examiner's face	Gesell
Turns when a voice is heard, without other stimulation	Cattell
Responds appropriately to friendly or angry tone	Van Riper
Locates source of sound	Gesell
Responds by raising arms when mother says "Come up" and reaches toward child	Gesell
Moves toward or looks at family member or pet when he is named, e.g., "Where's daddy"	Gesell
Activity stops when he hears "no,no" or his name	Gesell
Waves bye-bye or patty-cakes in response to verbal request alone	Gesell
Gives toy on request accompanied by gesture	Gesell
Gives object on command ("Give it to me")	Cattell
Pats pictures in book	Gesell
Finds "the baby" in picture when requested	Cattell
Obeys simple commands: "Give me the pencil." "Put the key on the chair." "Bring me the ball."	Cattell
Follows directions: "Put on your hat." "Put on your coat."	Cattell
Recognizes and points to parts of body of doll. "Show me dolly's mouth . . . eyes . . . ear . . . hands . . . feet . . . hair."	Cattell
Points out objects in picture (one to four pictures). "Where is the dog?"	Cattell
Responds to command. "Throw the ball."	Gesell
Responds to three directions with ball.	Gesell
Responds to four directions with ball or other object. "Put it on the chair." "Put it on the table." "Give it to me." "And then sit down."	Gesell
Comprehends prepositions. "Put the block on the chair." "Put it under the chair." "Put it in front of me on the floor."	Cattell
Understands "just one block." Selects one block from group in response to command.	Cattell
Responds to information about things from picture. "Show me the one that is up in the sky." "Show me the one that is good to eat." "Show me the one that you wear." "Show me the one that flies."	Cattell
Understands taking turns.	Gesell
Carries out two commands involving prepositions, e.g., "Put the ball on the chair, then in the box."	Gesell
Responds to information about things. "Show me the one that can run the fastest." "Show me the one that you eat most often." "Show me the one that can swim the best." "Show me the one that will be biggest and heaviest when it is grown up." "Show me the one that is heaviest to lift."	Gesell
Understands and replies appropriately with word or gesture to questions. "What do you do when you are sleepy?"	Gesell
Points to a penny, nickle, and dime.	Gesell
Identifies four colors.	Gesell
Knows right and left.	Terman & Merill
Understands number concepts to ten.	Terman & Merrill

Additional diagnostic information can be obtained through informal observations. The way in which a child responds to the sounds and speech around him is a useful indicator of his ability to hear. However, only through the use of standardized tests and measures can an appropriate evaluation of hearing function be determined. The use of pediatric hearing tests will be discussed later in this chapter.

Formal Tests of Receptive Language

Another approach for determining receptive language skills is the use of receptive vocabulary tests such as the Peabody Picture Vocabulary Test and the Ammons Full Range Picture Vocabulary Test. These two tests consist of single word items and can be used with any child who is capable of pointing to selected pictures upon command. However, it is suggested that test scores be reported in terms of *receptive language quotient* rather than as intelligence quotient, which is the usual procedure. Otherwise, the test score may be quite misleading in some instances.

Receptive language items can also be found within subtests of the Merrill-Palmer, the Stanford-Binet, and the Illinois Test of Psycholinquistic Abilities, to name only a few. Language items from the Stanford-Binet for example are scattered throughout the test. Unless each test item is analyzed from the standpoint of the stimulus and the required response, one is unable to determine the specific abilities or limitations of the child whose communicative process is being measured.

The Illinois Test of Psycholinquistic Abilities was specifically designed as a tool to investigate abilities and deficits in perception and language areas. Although the clinical utility of the ITPA has been well documented through research with children, its use with young trainable children has been questioned. The routine evaluation of many trainable children through the utilization of the ITPA leaves much to be desired since most subtests require a verbal response. However, if a particular child has even limited speech this language test can provide helpful information regarding strengths and weaknesses in learning through specific sensory modalities, such as the visual or the auditory channel. At the present time, prescriptive language training based on the results of this particular test can provide a useful guide in both the classroom and the language training program.

In summary, receptive language develops in a sequential pattern. Further, the development of receptive language skills precedes the acquisition of speech. However, receptive language does continue to develop concurrently with expressive language. In order to develop a therapeutic language program, it is not only necessary to understand normal developmental patterns, but also imperative to analyze a child's performance on selected subtests from standardized tests. Further, the examiner must have a clear understanding of the stimulus being used and the type of response required for the successful completion of the language task.

Informal Evaluation of Expressive Language

The acquisition of expressive verbal communication proceeds from simple differentiated crying to the formulation of complex sentences. The trainable child should be guided carefully through each developmental stage if he is to realize his maximum potential. Expressive language is more observable and thus appears to be less difficult to evaluate than is receptive language. Understanding receptive language development is confusing since it is difficult to comprehend how information is transferred from one sensory modality to another. For example, if a child sees and feels a ball, it does not necessarily follow that he will be able to grasp the auditory symbols associated with the object. The step from nonverbally identifying an object when asked to "put your finger on the ball" or "give me the ball" may occur months or even years before the child can actually label or say the word, "ball." After this, the child must store, recall, and generalize this verbal symbol to all ball-like objects or their pictorial representations.

The evaluation of expressive language has been the focus of attention since the beginning of the profession of speech correction. The idea that speech represented only a functioning larynx, tongue, and lips neglected to consider the many components involved in oral output. Tongue clipping for tongue-tied children is not yet past history. Perhaps this lack of consideration of psychological, neurological, and physiological integrities is due to an analysis of the gestalt of speech rather than a consideration of the dimensions that constitute speech development. Some of the considerations when evaluating verbal language are:

1. phonemes—speech sounds of the language basic to the word
2. vocabulary—the word
3. grammar—the arrangement of words into acceptable sequence.

Although there is a lack of agreement as to how each of these parameters of speech develops, there is a need to consider each of these aspects during an examination of oral communication.

Phonemes generally refer to the sounds of speech that comprise a word. A recent publication refers to speech sounds which a child uses during the babbling stages as vocal utterances. In contrast, when the infant's speech productions are considered to have symbolic meaning by an adult listener, they are referred to as verbal utterances. As the child imitates longer and more complex phoneme combinations, he acquires expressive vocabulary.

It has been thought that a sequential hierarchy or order could be applied to vocabulary growth. For example, use of nouns is thought to precede use of verbs, adverbs, etc. Contemporary writings by psycholinguists are de-emphasizing the classic analysis based on parts of speech and are attempting to explain expressive language development in terms of transformational grammar.

In an analysis of syntax, a branch of grammar, one is concerned primarily with the manner in which a child sequences words to formulate a phrase or a sentence. Early development of syntax consists of the use of a noun phrase and a verb phrase. This is referred to as a kernel sentence. However, there are other combinations of words which psycholinguists have illustrated and which may indicate that a child has a receptive knowledge of sentence structure.

The rules for creating acceptable phrases and sentence construction must be learned before the child speaks in sentences. Children do not merely repeat verbatim previously heard or learned sentences, but express their thoughts, ideas, and feelings in unique but acceptable form. The expressive language development of children with diagnosed intellectual impairment indicates that the sequential use of sounds, words, phrases, and sentences does occur with maturation. However, each step occurs later and perhaps more erratically than in the unimpaired child.

At this time, research in the expressive language development of retarded children is not extensive enough to indicate whether their development follows the same patterns as that seen in the normal child. However, until more information is accumulated the language evaluation consists of utilizing normal developmental data relative to each of these linguistic systems. Table II presents a compilation of items from different language scales which have been developmentally sequenced. While the information in Table II has been found to be useful, a more inclusive analysis of the sequence of speech development must be available for optimal programming during language habilitation.

TABLE II

(Full references appear in the General Bibliography)

Vocalizes only involuntarily—throaty noises	Gesell
Vocalizes mainly during crying	Van Riper
Vocalizes in play when alone or when he is talked to	Cattell
Cries differently for pain, hunger, etc.	Van Riper
Chuckles	Gesell
Responds vocally to social approach	Gessell
Laughs aloud	Gesell
Babbles, using series of syllables, e.g., ba/ba/ba	Van Riper
Uses variety of sounds, such as squeals, grunts, etc.	Gesell
Vocalizes displeasure, e.g., when toy is removed	Van Riper
Increases babbling occasionally if parent uses same sound while child is babbling	Van Riper
Initiates social approach vocally	Gesell
Vocalizes to toys	Gesell
Vocalizes to his image in the mirror	Gesell
Combines several vowel sounds	Gesell
Occasionally repeats same sound for several days	Van Riper
Says "dada" or "papa" or "mama" during babbling, but not in relation to parents	Van Riper
Babbles with inflection similar to intonation he has heard from adults	Van Riper
Says "dada" or equivalent word appropriately	Gesell
Imitates sounds such as cough, tongue click, etc.	Gesell
Says "dada" and "mama" or two equivalent words and one additional word	Gesell
Imitates number of syllables as well as words	Van Riper
Says two words besides "dada" and "mama"	Gesell
Accompanies gestures by vocalization, e.g., babbles while pointing	Van Riper
Spontaneously tries to imitate sounds such as adult exclamations	Van Riper
Combines two or more syllables	Cattell
Imitates sounds	Cattell
Says four or five words including names	Gesell
Uses jargon or inflected flow of connected sounds that seem like a sentence	Gesell
Says "tata" or equivalent for "thank you"	Gesell
Indicates wants by pointing and/or vocalizing	Gesell
Says approximately ten words	Gesell
Asks for wants by naming object	Cattell
Names objects, e.g., block, watch, cup, key, doll	Gesell
Says approximately twenty words	Gesell
Joins two words, e.g., "Daddy go," "Bye Mama"	Gesell
Asks for food, toilet, or drink by gestures or words	Gesell
Echoes some speech of adults	Gesell
Names familiar objects in pictures	Gesell
Uses sentences of three words	Gesell
Refers to self by name	Gesell
Uses pronouns (not always correctly) I, me, you	Gesell
Verbalizes immediate experiences; uses some parallel play	Gesell
Discards jargon in favor of specific meaningful phrases	Gesell
Uses sentences of four or more words	Gesell
Gives full name	Gesell
Refers to self by pronoun (may confuse "me" and "I")	Gesell
Can repeat two digits	Terman & Merrill
Repeats sentence containing six syllables: "John has a little dog"	Gesell
Uses some plurals	Gesell
Gives own sex in response to question, "Are you a boy or a girl?"	Gesell
Answers a few questions correctly	Gesell
Responds to action pictures and questions regarding pictures	Gesell
On request, names what he has drawn after scribbling	Gesell
Repeats one series of three random digits correctly out of three trials	Gesell
Knows a few rhymes or songs	Gesell
Repeats a sentence composed of 12-14 syllables, "I am going with Mommy when we are through talking"	Gesell
Counts three objects, pointing to each in turn	Gesell
Counts ten objects, pointing to each in turn	Gesell
Gives a descriptive comment while naming objects in a composite picture	Gesell
Recites numbers to thirty	Gesell
Knows number of fingers on one hand, and also total number on both hands	Gesell

Initially, a speech program may involve only stimulating voluntary vocalizations before expecting imitation of phonemes or words by a child. A six-year-old trainable child may not have developed even to the level of babbling. Each trainable child may have a unique communication development and thus present a challenge to the diagnostic teacher or language therapist.

Phoneme Development

A standarized articulation test will reveal information concerning the child's ability to imitate and to spontaneously produce consonants and vowels in isolation or in words. The shortcomings of using standardized tests and their stimulus pictures with the trainable mentally retarded should be realized by the speech and language clinician. For some of the children any of a number of articulation tests may produce adequate information. In other instances the use of selected objects to evoke speech production will prove to be a more meaningful approach. In the past, focus upon articulation or phoneme development was stressed to the point of excluding investigation of the other aspects of expressive verbal language.

As an adjunct to an investigation of articulation skills, an examination of the child's oral mechanism as well as the function of his tongue, lips, jaws, and velopharyngeal closure must be undertaken. A formal oral evaluation may not be possible with many children; therefore, observing the child as he sucks from a straw, swallows, and chews may provide a gross estimate of oral function. A brief discussion of additional problems such as neurological impairment as well as organic involvement of the palate, teeth, and lips which interfere with the ability to voluntarily produce speech sounds will be presented later in this chapter.

Vocabulary

The most effective indicator of a child's expressive language is the speech or speech-like utterances he uses during the day. The child's parents and classroom teacher can contribute to the evaluation by recording a vocabulary list of words the child uses in his spontaneous speech. Parental reports of gestures and speech used at home may differ markedly from the expressive language that the child uses in the school or therapy environments.

Spontaneous communication may include gestures used to satisfy the child's wants just as jargon and intelligible words are used in a meaningful and consistent way. Although vocabulary tests are available, observation and informal reporting may prove to be more useful tools than a standardized battery, since a lag in development of all aspects of expressive language is an apparent deficit among the retarded. By gaining information concerning what the child is able to do rather than what he is *not* able to do, we can help him use his abilities as a stepping stone to build on already existing communication skills.

Syntax

The use of different sentence structures by children is a relatively recent addition to our knowledge as to how speech is acquired. An effective analysis of sentence structure and grammar can be carried out by taping spontaneous speech samples. A more common procedure consists of showing the child a series of pictures which have been judged as being effective in stimulating speech. The child's task is to tell a story about the pictures. More verbal responses may be obtained to objects, such as a favorite toy, with some subjects. Other children may speak more freely in a less structured environment such as during free play. The goal, however, is to obtain a realistic appraisal of the child's speech development. It may be noted here that a question/answer interview is often the least effective method of obtaining a speech sample.

The most effective method of analyzing a speech sample is a subject for controversy. The practice of finding mean length of response from a designated number of verbal responses is only one of the considerations in a language evaluation. Knowledge and use of syntax and grammar should be analyzed not only quantitatively but qualitatively. In other words, the ability to formulate different types of sentences, the use of nouns, verb tense, pronouns, adjectives, and adverbs is a more meaningful consideration than the number of words a child uses.

Appropriateness of response as well as complexity of the sentences are considerations in the establishment of a training program designed to enhance the development of communication skills.

Formal Tests of Expressive Language

The verbal portions of several psychological tests can be used to evaluate expressive language abilities. Again, such tests fail to provide an index of many language skills. In contrast, the Illinois Test of Psycholinguistic Abilities is purposefully designed to assess specific language skills. Test items which require a verbal response to an oral stimulus are in the subtest "Verbal Expression" in which a child describes objects and in "Grammatic Closure" which evaluates a child's ability to handle syntax and grammatic inflections. Other information relative to expressive abilities can be obtained from the "Auditory Association" and "Auditory Receptive" subtests of the ITPA, both of which require an understanding of speech and an ability to give a verbal response.

The recently published Northwestern Syntax Screening Test provides a method for estimating a child's ability not only to understand (receptive portion) but also to reproduce sentences which have been verbally presented by the examiner in association with appropriate pictures (expressive portion). If the child is able to formulate a sentence and has developed the basic rules of grammar, this task may provide information as to his specific abilities and disabilities. Considerations in using this screening tool for children with deficits in auditory recall and memory may preclude the standardized method of administration; however, this aspect of the test has not been researched.

It should be stressed again that while a language age can be estimated with any of the formal tests, few have been standardized for use with retarded children. Expressive communication skills of children with delayed and atypical development can be evaluated on the basis of normal developmental scales. Standardized psychological tests as well as language tests can also be effective indicators of existing language abilities. Utilization of information provided from these tools can serve as a base for an individually planned language program. This is a more meaningful approach than focusing upon test scores which may only indicate the child's developmental age.

Additional Handicaps

The child who has been diagnosed as "developmentally delayed" or mentally retarded may be expected to follow a somewhat logical sequential development in all areas. The steps in this sequence, however, will appear more slowly than the gains made by the child who is not handicapped by intellectual impairment. However, the need to evaluate the neurological and physiological integrities of mentally retarded youngsters cannot be overstated.

The imposition of an additional handicap, such as hearing loss, can delay the learning of language to a much greater degree than intellectual limitations alone. A battery of screening tests including the evaluation of hearing, vision, and motor skills should be completed by qualified professional workers who then can initiate meaningful referrals for full exploration of the suspected problem. While it is important to keep in mind that many mentally retarded children are multiply handicapped early in life, it must also be realized that an additional handicap may be imposed at any period during childhood. Thus, the initial diagnosis of "retardation" does not preclude the possibility that other organic or emotional deficits may be present or may develop at a later date. For this reason, periodic reevaluation must be completed as the child grows.

Audiological Tests

Whether a child hears or does not hear can usually be detemined in the hospital following birth. However, at the present time, neonatal hearing screening is not a routine procedure. The child who does not respond appropriately to sound during infancy should be followed closely at frequent intervals. Testing techniques have been developed for children of all ages. For example, observations of the startle reflex in the very young; techniques implementing behavior modification; visual-auditory conditioning and the more traditional play audiometry can be utilized by a certified audiologist to obtain specific information relative to the child's capacity to hear soft sounds.

The literature reports a relatively high incidence of hearing impairment among the intellectually impaired population. The frequency of upper respiratory infections prevalent among many of the children, especially those with Downs Syndrome, highlights the need for medical intervention and careful observation on the part of the parent and teacher when frequent colds or nasal congestion are present. The need for otologic examination is apparent in such cases. Little information is available relative to the effects of fluctuating hearing sensitivity on the acquisition of language in any population of children. However, the child who is delayed in developing cognitive skills may be jeopardized to a greater degree since he is less able to compensate for erratic shifts in his auditory threshold. The distortion of an auditory signal may be much more detrimental to the development of listening skills for a child with learning disorders than previously considered.

Motor Skill Evaluation

The child who exhibits a mild to severe motor delay may not only have difficulty in ambulation, but may also lag in the development of self-help skills. Because the development of speech sounds and words requires very fine motor movements of the jaws, lips, tongue, and larynx, a cerebral-palsied mentally retarded child, for example, is far more handicapped than is the mentally retarded child who is able to carry out gross and fine muscle control of these parts of the body. For these reasons, the full potential of the physically handicapped child may be underestimated.

The initial manifestation of motor problems in the multiply handicapped child may be apparent on the vegetative level, that is, the lack of development of adequate chewing, sucking, and swallowing patterns. The delayed development of the use of the oral muscles further delays speech sound production. The child may have difficulty in controlling drooling, he may not be able to open and close his jaws without difficulty, there may be inability to vocalize volitionally, and movements of the lips and tongue may be laborious. The lack of oral experimentation by the child which is basic to developing a repertoire of speech sounds should be one of the initial concerns of the speech and language therapist.

Another important factor in the development of language is the ability to learn through motor experience. The motorically handicapped child who is unable to move about independently will not have the same experience as the child who is able to explore his environment through crawling or walking. Thus, limiting the basic receptive language learning provided through motor experiences will impose an additional handicap on such children.

Another related aspect of development, important to learning, is an ability to learn through visual-motor experiences. The neurologically impaired child may have difficulty in processing visual stimuli or he may be unable to move quickly enough to form associations related to visual-motor and language skills. Of couse, the same may be true in perceiving auditory stimuli. The child who is unable to turn quickly toward the source of sound may eventually ignore auditory cues which are valuable in learning.

These examples can be duplicated and paralleled to other learning experiences such as the processing of tactile information which the multiply handicapped child may be unable to associate with its source when learning about the world about him.

The need to analyze the child's motor development, whether minimally or severely impaired, is an important diagnostic consideration when establishing an adequate educational program for any child. The team effort of the neurologist, orthopedist, occupational or physical therapist, school nurse, language therapist, and classroom teacher will ideally assure insightful evaluations and recommendations regarding ongoing therapy and education for the motor-handicapped child.

Organic Anomalies of the Speech Mechanism

Retardation is frequently encountered among those children born with cleft palate and/or cleft lip. Early difficulty in sucking and swallowing may delay or prohibit experimentation with speech sounds during the pre-language stage. Surgical management is being instituted earlier in life and procedures are becoming more refined for repair of such organic anomalies. However, stimulation of better use of the tongue, lips, and jaw, as well as development of adequate closure of the oral-nasal cavity, should begin very early in the life of the child even though surgical procedures have been successfully carried out.

Early "speech correction" should be curtailed until the child has achieved success in basic language skills. However, stimulation of the muscles for chewing, sucking, and swallowing, with an emphasis on developing listening skills, should be provided in addition to classroom activities. This child also should be observed and tested frequently for fluctuating hearing sensitivity since upper respiratory infections may be more common among those with organic anomalies of the speech mechanism.

Another indication of neurological deficit may be observed when the child has no apparent gross motor problems but continues to drool, is unable to hold his lips closed, or carries out chewing, sucking, and swallowing only with great difficulty. In the testing situation this child may be unable to imitate movements of the tongue. A word of caution here: the traditional methods for evaluating oral activities may not truly indicate gross neurological deficits, but may reveal symptoms of the overall delayed development. In other words, the failure of a child to respond to such commands as, "Do as I do" or, "Place your tongue on the roof of your mouth" may be due to a lack of understanding of the command rather than to a motor deficit.

When difficulty with the involuntary movements of the tongue, lips, and jaws in activities such as eating is observed, the prognosis for developing intelligible speech is not favorable. A structured program to stimulate movements of the oral mechanism should be considered as an integral part of the language therapy program. Shaping techniques initially utilizing tangible reinforcers, such as ice cream for tongue movements and Kool-Aide to stimulate sucking through a straw, can bring about the most effective results. With these techniques the stimulus is also being used as the reinforcer.

Brain Damage

It is generally accepted that "brain damage" and mental retardation are not mutually exclusive or inclusive. Damage to brain tissue may cause developmental delay. However, the brain-damaged child may exhibit different developmental patterns than a child with Downs Syndrome, for example. The child with diagnosed brain damage may show adequate development in some areas such as motor skills, but his understanding and use of speech may be delayed. One of the more common observations in the language development of such children is the inappropriateness of their responses. Many times, quantity of speech is present but quality is marked by errors in syntax as well as in word usage. The traditional educational procedures for the mentally retarded may not meet the needs of these children. Reduction of stimulation, structuring a learning situation, designing activities on the basis of strengths and weaknesses will provide more meaningful experiences.

Frequent evaluation by the diagnostic team should begin early. A neurologist should attempt to determine the extent and areas of brain damage. The results of the evaluation should be interpreted by the neurologist to those working with the child; this will help to provide insights into both the child's deficits and his unobservable potentials.

The results of the psychological battery will also provide more information relative to the child's learning disorder. The classroom teacher should not expect to have the expertise of the neurologist, psychologist, or language pathologist, and therefore, must rely on their reports.

The brain-damaged child must be taught to organize stimuli and cannot be expected to learn only through repetition. Individualized language therapy may provide the best environment to meet his needs. Rejection of these children by speech clinics is hopefully occurring less frequently. If the brain-damaged mentally retarded child is not given direction early in his life, development in all areas will only be further delayed.

Emotional Problems

Pseudo-retardation is a condition which may be encountered, especially among the emotionally disturbed pediatric population. The child who does not develop language skills in a sequential order due to emotional disturbance may respond to his environment in a bizarre way and may be misdiagnosed as retarded. However, a child with delayed development may, in addition, have developed emotional problems which will require professional attention. An inability to communicate through either gestures or speech may lead to severe frustration and can be one of the major contributing factors in the development of emotional problems in the trainable child. Early diagnosis of learning disorders may be a preventive step if, through parental counseling, an environment of understanding and acceptance is established in which a child can develop emotional stability.

If parents can accept a child's developmental delay, their expectations for speech, mature motor control, and behavior will be more realistic. Emphasis during parent education should be placed on the dangers of undue stress caused by unrealistic goals for their child. There is little research concerning the emotionally disturbed developmentally delayed child and therapeutic techniques for establishing a meaningful training program.

Table III has been prepared as a guide for professional workers. The major additional handicaps encountered among mentally retarded children, as well as their manifestations and the preferred management are presented in this Table.

TABLE III

MENTAL RETARDATION PLUS:	WILL CAUSE:	AND MUST BE TREATED BY:
Hearing Impairment	Partial or total loss of ability to acquire language and learning through the sense of hearing	Medical management and hearing aids where possible; teaching language and communication skills using residual hearing and/or developing speech-reading and/or gestural communications
Cerebral Palsy	Partial or total loss of gross and fine motor control; impaired ability to develop speech and language using body and facial gestures, mouth, and lips, and tongue	Medical and physical therapy to develop motor control from gross to fine; speech and language therapy to develop the use of fine muscle control for speech and/or gestural language skills
Cleft Palate or Cleft Lip and Palate	Mechanical difficulty in chewing, sucking, blowing, swallowing; inability to produce many speech sounds	Surgery and/or special prosthetic devices to seal the abnormal opening from the roof of the mouth to the nasal passages and throat; speech therapy to develop correct use of oral structures
Brain Damage	Bizarre learning and behavior patterns that interfere with learning; erratic understanding and use of speech and language for communication	Therapy techniques and material designed to compensate for particular learning problems
Mental Illness	Unrealistic and threatening relations between the child and his environment; speech and language growth may be impeded by the child's emotional problems	Psychotherapeutically oriented social and educational experiences designed to stimulate language learning and emotional stability.

Gestural Language

Any discussion of programs for language remediation is inadequate if the nonverbal child is not considered. The older child who may have had individual training, as well as group experiences, for developing communicative skills but has not used speech meaningfully may still evidence a significant level of receptive language potential. A combination of factors may preclude the use of oral expression, such as level of retardation, severe physiological and/or psychological deficits. A means for communicating with gestures may make it possible for such children to develop a degree of independence and to develop more fully their maximal communication potential. If integrities are present at the receptive level, some children may learn to communicate spontaneously through informal gestures. A system of formal gestures which has been used in the past with young children with impaired hearing and with some aphasic adults may provide an expressive communication system for the retarded youngster who fails to develop speech after training.

If a child's language delay is more marked in the expressive area and if he has already developed his own gestural system which his parents and teachers can interpret, a trial period of training with a more universally known gestural system may be well worth investigating. This does *not* refer to a manual alaphabet or finger spelling, but to a system of hand symbols which can represent common objects and actions.

Natural gestures which are used with or without speech are generally recognized and understood. Using the index finger to beckon someone— "Come here" —raising and lowering the hand for "up" and "down," and the simplest gesture of pointing to what one wants are only a few gestures used every day. The deaf nonverbal child usually develops a method of signing without being able to finger-spell words very early in life. Training in manual expressive language is based initially on gross imitative motor skills. A manual, *The ABC'S of Sign Language*, was published recently in order to provide a text of standardized gestures for common nouns (see the General Bibliography). It is desirable to have a more extensive signing vocabulary than is presented in this manual. However, if realistic goals are established for some trainable children, especially those whose hearing sensitivity or physical handicaps of the lips, tongue, or palate preclude the use of speech, an extension of this manual may be forthcoming.

A word of caution: successful development of any expressive language is based on the ability to associate the symbol with the experience and respond in a meaningful way. Thus, spontaneous use of gestures may not be feasible for those children who are severely handicapped intellectually or physically. A reasonable trial period of training in gestural communication should be attempted, however.

Summary

A significant delay in both receptive and expressive language is characteristic in the development of the trainable mentally retarded child. Guides for evaluating the level of development of language skills through both informal observations and formal testing have been presented in the preceding discussion. Of particular concern to the language therapist or speech and hearing specialist is the multiply handicapped child who is mentally retarded and may have one or more organic or functional impairments complicating the learning process. The difficulty in diagnosing these additional problems as well as planning a realistic therapeutic communication program has been pointed out. A need to develop and utilize a "team approach" involving all specialists and teachers to evaluate a child's potential as well as to further diagnostic teaching is of utmost importance.

Although most trainable children develop speech with varying degrees of facility, a portion of this population of children will not acquire usable verbal language. Training the nonverbal child to use natural gestures and signs as well as a formal signing system may provide a useful tool of communication for some children.

Language Stimulation Record for the Classroom Teacher

The word lists below have been accumulated from two sources:

1) A paper, "A Basic Picturable Vocabulary List as Stimulus Material for Mentally Retarded Children," by Ed Leach, Parsons Training School, Parsons, Kansas, 1966

2) "The Spontaneous Speaking Vocabulary of Children in Primary Grades," by Helen Murphy, *Journal of Education*, 1957.

The intent of this compliation is to provide a basic vocabulary list to use as a guide in language training in the classroom. Marking, when appropriate, the R (receptive comprehension) and the E (expressive usage) following each word, can provide a record of an individual child's or a class's language development. A secondary function of these lists is to provide a uniformity in vocabulary stimulation among those individuals who come in contact with the children.

Words preceded by an asterisk (*) are found in the Murphy study.

HOME AND RELATED ITEMS

Furniture | R | E

- bed
- bench
- bookcase
- *chair
- clock
- dresser
- fan
- ironing board
- lamp
- picture
- radio
- rug
- sewing machine
- sink
- stool
- stove
- *table
- *telephone
- television (TV)
- wastebasket

Desk Items | R | E

- book
- calendar
- desk
- crayons
- envelope
- eraser
- glue
- letter
- package
- paper
- paste
- pen
- pencil
- pin
- ruler
- scissors
- shelf
- stamp
- typewriter

Rooms | R | E

- *bathroom
- bedroom
- closet
- den
- dining room
- kitchen
- laundry room
- living room
- recreation room

Personal Items | R | E

- bracelet
- comb
- earring
- hairbrush
- hairpins
- hair rollers
- Kleenex
- lipstick
- necklace
- perfume
- pocket knife
- powder
- ring
- shoepolish
- suitcase
- toothbrush
- toothpaste
- watch

Tools | R | E

- hammer
- nail
- pliers
- rake
- sandpaper
- saw
- screwdriver
- shovel

Musical Instruments | R | E

- bell
- bugle
- drum
- guitar
- horn
- piano
- violin

Clothing | R | E

- apron
- bathrobe
- belt
- billfold
- blouse
- boot
- button
- cap
- *coat
- *dress
- glove
- handkerchief
- *hat
- jeans
- jacket
- nightgown
- mittens
- pajamas

Clothing (cont.) | R | E

- pants
- purse
- pocketbook
- raincoat
- robe
- scarf
- shirt
- shoes
- shorts
- skirt
- snowsuit
- socks
- *sweater
- swimsuit
- suit
- tie
- umbrella
- zipper

Household | R | E

- blanket
- banister
- broom
- bucket
- can
- chimney
- door
- fence
- fire
- floor
- garbage
- gate
- key
- home
- house
- lamp
- light
- mop
- porch
- roof
- soap
- stairs
- towel
- wall
- washcloth
- window
- yard

Transportation | R | E

- *airplane
- bicycle
- bus
- *car
- *choo choo
- *train
- *tricycle
- *truck
- *fire engine

Materials | R | E

- *board
- cardboard
- clay
- cloth
- cotton
- glass
- leather
- paper
- rubber
- steel
- wood
- wool

Money | R | E

- dime
- dollar
- fifty cents
- nickel
- penny
- quarter

Colors | R | E

- black
- blue
- brown
- green
- orange
- purple
- red
- yellow

Numbers | R | E

- one
- two
- three
- four
- five
- six
- seven
- eight
- nine
- ten

Miscellaneous | R | E

- chalk
- circus
- flag
- hole
- map
- moon
- movie
- music
- party
- rock
- star
- stick
- story
- string
- sun
- wheel

FOOD AND RELATED ITEMS

Meats | R | E

- bacon
- cheese
- *chicken
- egg
- fish
- ham
- hamburger
- hot dog
- roast
- steak
- turkey

Vegetables | R | E

- beans
- *carrot
- celery
- corn
- lettuce
- peas
- potato
- pumpkin
- radish
- squash
- sweet potato
- tomato

Fruits | R | E

- apple
- banana
- cherry
- grape

Fruits (cont.) | R | E

- grapefruit
- orange
- peach
- pear
- pineapple
- plum
- strawberry

Drinks | R | E

- chocolate milk
- coffee
- coke
- lemonade
- Kool Aide
- milk
- orange juice
- juice
- soda pop
- tea
- water

Eating Utensils | R | E

- bowl
- cup
- dish
- fork
- glass
- knife
- napkin
- pan
- plate
- spoon
- tray

Candy | R | E

- candy bar
- gum
- gum drops
- lemon drops
- mints
- M & Ms
- sucker
- lollipop

Other Food Items | R | E

- bread
- butter
- cake
- cookie
- *cracker
- doughnut
- ice cream
- Jello
- jelly
- pancakes
- peanut butter
- pepper
- pickle
- pie
- popcorn
- potato chip
- pudding
- pretzel
- salt
- sandwich
- soup
- sugar
- waffle

LOCATIONS AND CONDITIONS

Town | R | E

- barber shop
- bowling alley
- *church
- downtown
- drugstore
- fire station
- garage
- *grocery store
- home
- hospital
- house
- movie theater
- park
- post office
- restaurant
- *school
- shoe store
- sidewalk
- *store
- street
- zoo

Country | R | E

- *barn
- farm
- field
- highway
- hill
- woods

Seasons | R | E

- spring
- summer
- fall
- winter

Directions | R | E

- front
- back
- right
- left
- start
- stop
- top
- under
- up
- down

Weather | R | E

- cloud(y)
- *cold
- fog
- hail
- *hot
- *ice
- lightning

Weather (cont.) | R | E

- rain
- sleet
- *snow
- snowball
- snowman
- sun
- wind
- tornado

Holidays | R | E

- birthday
- Christmas
- Easter
- Halloween
- Fourth of July
- Thanksgiving
- vacation
- Valentine's Day
- Yom Kippur

Family | R | E

- aunt
- brother
- daddy
- father
- grandmother
- grandfather
- mama
- mother
- sister
- uncle

Insects | R | E

- bee
- bug
- fly
- grasshopper
- roach
- spider
- wasp
- worm

Plants, Trees, Etc. | R | E

- branch
- bush
- corn
- flower
- garden
- grass
- leaf
- nest
- seed
- shrub
- tree
- trunk
- wheat

Daily Conditions | R | E

- afternoon
- breakfast
- dinner
- evening
- lunch
- morning
- night
- noon
- now
- supper
- today
- tomorrow
- yesterday

Body Parts | R | E

- arm
- bone
- cheek
- chest
- chin
- ear
- elbow
- eye
- feet
- finger
- fingernail
- foot
- hair
- hand
- head
- knee
- leg
- mouth
- neck
- nose
- shoulder
- skin
- teeth
- toe
- toenail
- tongue
- tooth
- waist

People | R | E

- baby
- boy
- clown
- cook
- cowboy
- doctor
- farmer
- fireman
- girl
- grocer
- Indian
- man
- milkman

57

People (cont.) | R | E

- Negro
- nurse
- paper boy
- pilot
- policeman
- teacher
- waitress
- waiter
- woman

Animals | R | E

- bear
- bird
- butterfly
- cat
- chicken
- cow
- dog
- duck
- eagle
- elephant
- fish
- fox
- frog
- giraffe
- goat
- goose
- horse
- lion
- monkey
- mouse
- owl
- parrot
- pig
- rabbit
- reindeer
- robin
- seal
- sheep
- snake
- squirrel
- tiger
- turkey
- turtle
- wolf
- zebra

Sport Equipment | R | E

- baseball
- baseball bat
- baseball glove
- basketball
- football
- golf club
- ice skate
- *jungle gym
- roller skate
- sandpile
- sled
- slide

Sport Equip. (cont.) | R | E

- swing
- tennis ball
- tennis racket

Toys | R | E

- *box
- *ball
- balloon
- *blocks
- *cards
- crayon
- doll
- doll bed
- doll buggy
- doll house
- drum
- gun
- horn
- jumping rope
- kite
- marble
- *puzzle
- *sand
- scooter
- top
- wagon
- whistle

Verbs | R | E

- *am
- *ate
- *be
- *bark
- *beat
- *been
- bite
- blow
- bounce
- break
- *bring
- brush
- build
- burn
- button
- buy
- *call
- *can
- carry
- catch
- chase
- clap
- *clean
- *climb
- close
- comb
- *come
- cook
- cough
- *could
- count

Verbs (cont.) | R | E

- cover
- crawl
- cry
- *cut
- dance
- *did
- dig
- *do
- *don't
- draw
- dream
- *dress
- *drink
- drive
- drop
- *eat
- excuse (me)
- fall
- *feed
- fill
- *find
- *finish
- fly
- fold
- found
- *get
- give
- *go
- *had
- hang
- *have
- hear
- *help
- hide
- hit
- hold
- hunt
- hurry
- hurt
- iron
- *is
- *isn't
- jump
- *keep
- kick
- kiss
- *know
- laugh
- lick
- lift
- like
- listen
- lock
- *look
- made
- may
- measure
- melt
- move
- need
- open
- paint

Verbs (cont.)	R	E
*pass		
paste		
peel		
pet		
pin		
pinch		
*play		
*pour		
print		
pull		
push		
*put		
race		
rake		
*read		
*rest		
*ride		
roll		
rub		
*run		
*sail		
*saw		
scratch		
scrub		
*see		
sew		
shake		
shine		
shovel		
*show		
shut		
*sing		
sit		
skate		
slap		
*sleep		
*slide		
smell		
smile		
sneeze		
spank		
spend		
spill		
splash		
stand		
*stay		
*surprise		
sweep		
swim		
swing		
take		
talk		
tear		
*thank		
*think		
throw		
tie		
*told		
*took		
*touch		
*turn		
unbutton		

Verbs (cont.)	R	E
*undress		
*use		
*wait		
*walk		
*want		
*was		
*wash		
wave		
wear		
*weigh		
*were		
*wet		
whip		
*will		
wipe		
*won't		
work		
would		
wrap		
*write		
yawn		

Adjectives	R	E
*all		
*any		
awake		
bad		
*big		
broken		
clean		
cold		
cool		
crippled		
curly		
different		
*dirty		
dry		
*every		
fast		
fat		
*fine		
first		
full		
*good		
*happy		
*hard		
*heavy		
*hot		
hungry		
large		
*last		
lazy		
*light		
*little		
long		
loud		
more		
neat		
*new		
*nice		

Adjectives (cont.)	R	E
noisy		
old		
other		
quick		
quiet		
rough		
round		
sad		
sharp		
short		
sick		
sleepy		
slow		
small		
smooth		
soft		
square		
stormy		
straight		
surprised		
tall		
thirsty		
tired		
town		
warm		
wet		

Pronouns	R	E
*he		
*her		
*him		
*his		
*I		
*it		
*me		
*mine		
*my		
*our		
*she		
*that		
*them		
*they		
*this		
*we		
*what		
*who		
*whose		
*you		
*your		

Prepositions	R	E
*about		
*as		
*at		
*before		
*for		
*in		
*into		

Prepositions (cont.)	R	E
*of		
*on		
*to		
*with		

Adverbs	R	E
after		
again		
ago		

Adverbs (cont.)	R	E
already		
away		
down		
here		
just		
next		
no		
not		
*so		
*there		

Adverbs (cont.)	R	E
*too		
very		

Miscellaneous	R	E
*fun		
*thing		
because		
if		

11. THE MULTIPLY HANDICAPPED CHILD

by Jeannie Johnson

*Beautiful faces are they that wear
The light of a pleasant spirit there;
Beautiful hands are they that do
Deeds that are noble, good and true;
Beautiful feet are they that go
Swiftly to lighten another's woe.*

—McGuffey's Second Reader

You and I are teachers of exceptional children who are special and unique even in schools where all students are labeled "exceptional." Each individual in our class is either totally or partially dependent physically and intellectually, but each is a whole human being who functions in a fragmentary manner. Our personal challenge is to know each child, recognize his strengths and weaknesses, and work with him through his growth and developmental periods to achieve successful learning experiences within his capacities.

We integrate recommended therapeutic techniques into all classroom activities; our goal for all of our children is the attainment of as high a level of physical independence as possible. Our little ones have even greater emotional and social needs throughout their maturational periods; they must accept themselves and each other and find acceptance in their environment, in their homes, school, and community. Their self-acceptance must be positive; we are their guides as they expand their self-concepts from an awareness of their limitations to recognition of their achievements. With a positive approach many of our children will accept the challenge of their own limitations as temporary blocks to progress while viewing their achievements as ongoing and limitless. We face our challenge by examining the needs of each child, planning a program to meet those needs with specific objectives and goals for the individual child, the class, and as a part of the total school program.

Composition of a Multiply Handicapped Class

I have seven multiply handicapped children in my primary class; five are wheelchair children, two are ambulatory; six of them are cerebral palsied children; and the seventh has severe physical anomalies. The wheelchair children are quadriplegic (all four limbs involved); one is blind; two have varying degrees of perceptual handicaps; one is also deaf. One very beautiful little girl is a battered child. Of these children, one child has no expressive language abilities; one repeats songs and poems, mainly; one has a babbling form of speech; two children have excellent receptive language skills and are now developing and overcoming motor problems for gains in expressive language. Two of the girls have mature language abilities and are now functioning close to the normal IQ range. They will be transferred to a class for orthopedically handicapped children.

Illinois laws and codes impose no IQ limitations for children accepted into this class; these children are not acceptable in a normal school situation, nor could they function in a class for the physically handicapped due to the extent of their involvements. The Illinois code is mandatory: Multiply handicapped children from 3 to 21 years of age ". . .shall be regarded as eligible for special education facilities only as long as benefit [to them] from the program can be determined to exist . . . and if they do not . . . endanger the health or safety of [themselves] or other pupils . . . [and are not] disruptive of class activities as to prevent other pupils from benefiting . . ." The benefits dervied from our program must be evaluated for each child individually based upon the objectives and goals established for our group and the school. We admit children at 3 years of age to our class and move them to more appropriate placement when indicated.

Our school utilizes the team approach for evaluating the child and his problems and prescribing teaching and therapy techniques for remediation. The "team" for my multiply handicapped children includes our school principal, the occupational, language, and music therapists, a psychiatric social worker, a nurse, my teacher's aide, and myself, all full-time personnel. All these people work directly or indirectly with our children. Frequent reviews of progress are scheduled with the entire team involved in seeking ideas from experiences with the group and reviewing the educational prescription.

Contributions of the Evaluating Team for Multiply Handicapped Children

Specific functions of each member of the evaluating team are discussed in separate chapters in this book. The psychiatric social worker is our liaison between home and school, working individually and in groups with parents, staff, and children. Through observation of each child in physical therapy and group instructional periods, the language therapist points up areas of weakness and methods of implementing instruction and development within our classroom. She meets with certain children individually on a regularly scheduled basis. Music therapy is a scheduled group activity, and the therapist suggests classroom music sessions such as holiday songs, rhythm exercises, and rhythm instruments with accompanying records. Our school nurse's office adjoins our classroom and is equipped to meet the special needs of our children.

The Role of the Occupational Therapist

Of the evaluating team members who work directly with these physically handicapped children, the role of the occupational therapist is stressed; her work is of primary importance for children between the ages of 3 and 10, years when physical development is augmented through therapy techniques. Gross motor movements and fine motor skills are promoted through the patient application of these techniques throughout the daily program, beginning with individual therapy sessions with the O.T. and continuing with specific methods of handling the children and positioning them during instructional and recreational periods. The O.T. makes recommendations for carrying through prescribed techniques for each child. Manipulative skills for fine motor development apply to self-care areas—self-feeding, the use of bathroom facilities, dressing and undressing with independence; gross motor stimulation is directed toward the objective of walking, in some cases, with or without mechanical supports as braces, crutches, and canes. In other cases therapy objectives are toward self-propelling in a wheelchair, or maintenance of adequate postures for sitting or standing for learning experiences and recreation periods.

Individual therapy is provided by our O.T. for one or two children per day in our room, and on one day each week she supervises a recreational group program for one period in the gym. We have a large, double room with a sink; half the room is used for therapy, mainly, and the other half has tables and chairs, blackboards, and cupboards for instructional periods. In the therapy area, one large 18' x 6' mat extends along one wall with bolsters and pillows for support for the children during their work-therapy period. At one end of the mat is a full-length movable mirror intended to motivate the children. Heads are held up and backs are straighter as the children look at their own images and see themselves through the therapist's instructions. Next to the mat is a rigid pole extending from ceiling to floor with a trapeze-like attachment; we have exciting progress in several of our youngsters who developed the strength in hands and arms to grip the trapeze and support and swing their bodies on it. Broom handles held by the therapist are also used to strengthen the children's grasp and grip as they pull themselves upward from the mat. To the children this is great fun, and it is fine preparation for strengthening arms and hands to manage crutches or canes when they are ready for walking.

Other items for the therapy program include: smaller mats for individual work, parallel bars installed along one wall, a walker on wheels (the latter two items for those children who are ready for walking practice with artificial support and under adult supervision); two "Swiss" therapy balls, each large enough to hold a child with arms and legs extended, lying on his stomach. This position stimulates more extension of spastic arms when manipulative toys such as bean bags, puzzles, and blocks are placed on chairs or on the floor in front of the balls. A child can sit on the ball while supported and roll in all directions.

A large stand-up table with two box-like structures attached at either end supports two children at a time in a standing position while they play games, write, and color in workbooks or on work sheets, or read. The table top is chalk-board surfaced steel, cut from a wall partition. This allows the use of wrist or arm magnets to hold a hand in a functioning position. Other furnishings are supporting bars in the bathroom to stimulate self-help; low benches on which the children lie down, sit without supports, and do therapy exercises such as sit-ups and push-ups, with adults providing additional body support; smaller stools used for sitting or supporting legs; a variety of shapes and textures to stimulate grasp, holding and release activities, and manipulations. Items to intrigue and fascinate our youngsters for attention-getting purposes are from time to time: toys and dolls with movable parts, blocks with unexpected noise-making qualities, friction toys and puzzles. One giant floor puzzle contains all the parts of a child's body and is particularly effective for teaching body image and learning the parts of the body.

The O.T. supervises us in handling the children in a therapeutic manner: side-sitting and ring-sitting on the mats at low benches; postural support for kneeling and standing positions for some of the children; methods of easing tense or cramped muscles; methods of carrying a child, as, with legs straddled over a hip, or with the child completely flexed with legs and knees brought up in front under the child's chin; use of braces (when prescribed by doctors) with periodic checks on their mechanism and proper fit. Wheelchairs are checked for appropriate size and possible adjustments, or for additional supports, padding, restraining belts, or straps.

After observing our children in their activities other than therapy, the O.T. will suggest positioning of the children for activities, such as blanket or pillow supports while sitting in small schoolroom chairs with block or stool support for feet when they do not reach the floor.

Rubber bands or molded plastic around pencils or crayons induce a firmer grasp; magnets strapped to wrists or elbows with velco bands are attracted to steel table surfaces and stabilize arms and hands for writing work, drawing, and eating. An electric typewriter is used for those children who have started reading; they do some phonics work and spelling with large blocks and large magnetic block letters, but they will probably never use a pencil sufficiently well for written expression.

The O.T. constructs special handles on spoons with wax and tape and bends them appropriately for right- and left-handed children; suction plates provide the athetoid child the opportunity to eat without help and with a minimum amount of spillage.

Special periods of positioning for children with braces are prescribed by doctors. The O.T. contacts children's doctors for specific therapy instructions, and works with a physical therapist who handles individual children. Some recommendations go to the home when necessary or when requested. Suggestions from parents are essential for us in handling each child; in most instances a very close relationship exists between the parents and our immediate staff, enabling the O.T. to assist the home in carrying out therapeutic measures and exercises. She participates in parent conferences, at which time she reports on each child's progress in therapy and answers pertinent questions from the parents.

A Teacher's Aide Is Essential

An aide is indispensable in the management of a room in which five of the seven children are totally dependent in their physical functioning abilities; two pairs of strong arms and hands are busy throughout the day lifting children from wheelchairs to therapy mats, changing their positions on the mats, lifting them back to the wheelchairs, positioning them in the small table chairs for academic work and for lunch periods, lifting and carrying them for toileting and training for the use of bathroom facilities, and assisting those children who walk with support to utilize parallel bars, walkers, and other wheelchairs for their practice sessions. Braces are put on some children each day, requiring additional handling for dressing and undressing children for therapy.

My aide and I are both occupied with these varied activities; one individual's strength would be taxed beyond limits in meeting just the physical needs of these children, and there would be little time left for instructional and learning activities. An aide for a teacher of multiply handicapped children must be a physically strong person and one who loves children and is gentle with them. Matrons are used in many school situations in rooms for the handicapped children. Our aides are much more involved in our daily work than the title "matron" implies. They are trained, and through observation and participation in all areas of our school program, they become acquainted with our teaching materials and methods and are truly a "third dimension."

With the diversity of ability levels, individual work periods are blocked out for each child, and my aide and I alternate our work activities with individual children and in group instructional periods, and in the "circle time," according to daily plans. The aide lays out appropriate materials for instructions and discussion during circle time, prepares tagboard cards, organizes the pictures the children collect, and assists in making experience charts and stories. The children join with her in short recreation periods with songs, games, poetry and stories.

Room maintenance is a particularly important and ongoing task for the aide; wheelchairs not in use must be placed out of the way to avoid interference with therapy and other work areas; benches, small chairs, bolsters, work bins, movable mats and large balls must be stored after therapy is completed; and the day's array of other teaching materials and manipulative items must be promptly replaced in cupboards and closets. She shares with me the duties of preparing the children for lunch in our room and serving them, giving special assistance to those more seriously handicapped. We relieve each other for half-hour lunch periods in the teacher's lunchroom.

Other duties performed by my aide include operating some of our audio-visual material: record player and appropriate records for my instruction program, filmstrip projector and filmstrips with records, the tape recorder and Language Master. She participates in parent-teacher conference discussions and all school staff meetings. Her fine rapport with our children is a solid base for her work with them; she observes them closely for any signs of physical or emotional problems which may arise, and discusses any difficulties with me. Special learning achievements as well as problems which she encounters in her individual work sessions with the children are also reported to me and become part of the students' anecdotal records. A good aide is indispensable in our special class.

Senior students in our school receive part of their training to be child-care helpers in our room: the boys riding on the special bus with the chair children, carrying them to and from the bus, securing them in their seats with seat belts and being responsible for their braces and lunchboxes. Senior girls learn child care in the mornings; removing children's outer clothing, hanging them on hangers, and working with one or two children with peg boards and puzzles. These older students love our young dependent children; they learn the meaning of the words "gentle," "kind," "careful," and "responsibility"; they gain self-esteem in the knowledge that they are useful human beings, accomplishing meaningful worthwhile tasks.

The Teacher's Responsibilities and Functions

Integrating, organizing, planning, teaching, and evaluating comprise my role as teacher of a class of multiply handicapped children. I am acting director and stage manager within the room, manipulating pupils and staff members, materials and techniques to be used with each child, and the time periods appropriate for all activities. I have the closest contact with the children in my class, direct lines of communication with all the members of the team who contribute diagnostic, remedial, and therapeutic techniques, and I plan the programs for each child, making full use of staff recommendations and all school resources. All therapy schedules are established with the occupational, language, and music therapists and integrated into my total daily program. My daily plans must include group teaching experiences, as in the circle period, but for maximum learning as much time as possible is devoted to each individual child by a staff member, aide, or volunteer. Some of our children require more individual work periods both in physical therapy and in academic areas because they have a greater developmental potential than others in the class. The younger children often have periods of growth "spurts" during which they seem to progress rapidly and profit from accelerated efforts in all areas.

A study of each child's history, tests, and personal and medical records provides information for prescriptive planning by the evaluation team. Ongoing observations are reviewed frequently, and new plans are developed as the children change. Half-day school attendance and/or limited participation in academic and therapy activities are recommended in some cases. Some children require their own periods of observation within the classroom before participating in the group; this quiet period may be a day or a week, but gradually they are drawn into the room activities and schedules.

The social and emotional climate of our room must establish a setting for learning. Our small group thrives on the intimacy of an atmosphere of warmth and acceptance in which each child is acknowledged and recognized for himself. Each child is helped to know that his own rate of progress is measured without comparison or competition with other children in the class. These children need a sense of humor, a "games" approach to attacking their problems; when one child pulls himself to a kneeling position, maintains his balance for a few seconds and then topples down again, the laughter which accompanies the fall serves as a spur to renewed efforts for that child and motivation for another to attempt some feat of her own. A boy or girl will crow with delight at the climax of every achievement, but will join the giggles of the other children and the staff to make light of failures. Repetition and variations on the theme are part of the game until the task is accomplished. Combined with good humor is freedom of expression; what our children say and do is important to all of us and is recognized by all.

During "mat time," for instance, everyone joins with Barbara when she sings "Eensie-Beensie Spider" or "Humpty-Dumpty," since singing is recognized as her only contribution to the group at this time. Within such an atmosphere each child learns self-acceptance and then grows in awareness and acceptance of his classmates.

Regardless of the vast spread in physical and intellectual functioning, our children develop a group cohesiveness. Each is called upon to achieve at his or her own rate, and all learn to share their experiences in turn during "circle" periods.

Informality in a relaxed atmosphere, humor, understanding, and a planned individualized program promote achievement for our multiply handicapped children, and, hopefully, self-fulfillment at each level of their maturation. Our children expect to achieve and they reflect the joys of successful learning experiences. A close relationship exists between the homes of our children and the school; we enjoy a mutually profitable association with parents, sharing with them the accomplishments and the common problems which arise, accepting and offering suggestions which may solve many of these problems, and maintaining realistic expectations for each child.

Daily journals are kept for each child; my aide or volunteer or the therapists discuss with me areas of progress with the children with whom they work each day. Specific problems in the day's individual work are also brought to my attention, and we plan methods of attacking these problems. Materials and teaching techniques for group instruction and for individual work periods are demonstrated for my aide and volunteers. Monthly plans and daily plans for a unit approach to group teaching are part of my record-keeping chores. I review these plans with my aide, who assists me in preparing teaching materials for each day's work.

The Daily Program

Mat time	8:45 to 10:30
Circle time	10:30 to 11:15
Lunch time	11:30 to 12:45
Afternoon circle time	1:00 to 1:30
Practice time	1:30 to 2:00
Going home preparations	2:00 to 2:15

Planning the program for my class requires the setting of schedules within blocks of time divided into four major periods each day. Within these periods, activities for the group and for individuals in the group are planned. There are fewer blocks of time in a class of primary multiply handicapped children than in other classes in our school, due to the physical dependence of the children, and the time required in handling them, toileting, and changing from one activity to another. The wheelchairs are used as little as possible during the day, and then mainly for transporting the children to and from our room, to the multi-purpose room gym, music room, or on special errands to other parts of the school.

Mat Time—The Day Begins

The chair children are positioned on our large floor mats for the first period of the day; this is the informal period, truly a "social hour," during which the children prepare for therapy, learn some self-care tasks such as lacing and unlacing shoes and removing shoes and socks. A general period of socializing occurs at this time when the higher level children "show and tell" about pictures and toys from home, news items and special happenings in their lives, and some special project or achievement pertaining to their therapy program or academic work. In addition to pleasure they derive from sharing these experiences, spontaneous language development is a benefit of this procedure.

The occupational therapist, my aide, and I motivate the children to participate in various gross motor activities; small competitions include a race on the floor in any manner which suits the child to reach a favorite game or puzzle, a wheelbarrow race in which staff members hold children's feet while their arms, hands (and even noses) support their bodies, and knee-balancing feats with or without support from adults. This can be a very hilarious and exhilarating time. All of these activities are designed to stretch and strengthen larger body muscles.

During mat time our occupational therapist works with one or two children either on the large mat or on smaller ones; she will direct our handling of the other children as we loosen taut muscles through extension on the mats, a roll over the therapy balls, or a bounce and "jiggle" on our laps. The children lie on the mats on backs, stomachs, or sides supported by pillows, blankets, and bolsters to relieve the tensions of their spasticity; numerous manipulative skills are stimulated in these positions through play. Arms stretch out and fingers and hands are occupied with wood puzzles, form boards, peg boards, and building and parquetry blocks. The more advanced children work with heavy-duty games, such as chutes and ladders, picture lotto, tic-tac-toe and a pin-ball machine, in addition to some teacher-made games, such as word-and-number flash cards and picture-and-word matching games. In a small group, some reading readiness work is accomplished with rhyming pictures and by constructing rhyming words with magnetized wood or plastic letters on a large metal chalkboard or on small individual metal boards.

Several of our children are profoundly involved physically; they are observers during most of the activities, but they smile, laugh, and reach out toward the other children or to an adult who is with them. Our aide, child care helper, or volunteer works with these children with tactile objects to stimulate grasp and gain their attention and some response. Large blocks are placed in a wooden basket, large round pegs are taken from a peg board and placed in a container, balls of various sizes and textures are rolled between the children, who are further tempted with furry kittens and bears and dolls. This tactile stimulation is particularly appealing to the blind child; short poems or songs are repeated by her during play. Ambulatory youngsters work at low tables in a separate section of our room on similar manipulative materials.

Learning to be with a group of children, the give-and-take of being with other people and being cared for by someone other than one's own mother, is essential for social readiness for continuing day care or institution life. Observe the growing social awareness, the smiles of pleasure from being with other children, as learning to listen and participate becomes a part of daily living; each element of their growth justifies the investment of time, love, and energy in these very limited children.

Mat Time—Individual Work Periods

Included in the mat time period are individual work sessions scheduled for each child. While some of the children work on the mats and in therapy, we divide our time among four children who have started a reading program and are at the pre-primer and primer levels in standard readers and reading workbooks. Each child has a bin with his own materials, flash cards, and other special aids, and I mark the day's lesson and the method for proceeding with it; the volunteers participate in these special work periods. There is an 8′ x 12′ time-out room adjoining our therapy area, free of the distracting activities of the other children. This room is used as the instructional area for private sessions. The children sit at a low table in the special room where they read and write in their workbooks; a low chair or rocker is often used for a reading session behind a screen, or a child sits on the mat at a low bench, side-sitting with knees and legs together and bent to one side, or ring-sitting with the soles of the feet together and knees bent to opposite sides in front of the child, both therapy positions suggested by the occupational therapist. A low stool, chair, or the mat serves as a seat for the staff member working with a child.

Circle Time

After mat time the children are seated in their wheel-chairs or on low chairs for a morning circle period. On two mornings each week, instead of circle the children have music with the music therapist and enjoy movie time which is an all-school assembly period. The circle includes the entire group in a pleasant routine geared to a language development program similar to the one conducted in the primary classes in our school. The "Pledge," flag songs, attendance, calendar work, room work charts, and a "good morning" story begin the period. Pictures and activities from the primary Peabody Language Development Kit are keyed to the developmental level at which each child is functioning.

Poems, songs, finger-plays, and games are interspersed with the instructional program to stimulate both gross and fine motor responses and include a multi-sensory approach to learning. Guessing games may require tactile response in the "feely" bags, auditory response to common sounds and special recordings, and olfactory stimulants. Holiday units are also part of this instructional and communication period.

Lunch Time

Lunch is served in our own room with the children sitting on chairs at a table instead of in wheelchairs. A longer period is required than that provided for the other children in the school. The process of eating is more involved and each child requires assistance to a different degree. Lunch time is another instructional period during which some children are learning to handle food independently, to use special appliances in some cases, to manage eating utensils, and to use appropriate table manners. The socialization process is part of their sharing of "goodies" and relaxed communication. Setting the table, handling lunch boxes, and then cleaning up are all areas of work shared by some of the children; one child eats more rapidly now for the privilege of washing the dishes while standing at the sink; one girl enjoys pushing a wheelchair with another child in it, carrying the room lunch tray back to the kitchen. The dishwasher, wheelchair pusher and the tray carrier all feel their usefulness and growing independence doing jobs that had not been possible for them previously. All of these activities are time-consuming and require much patience. We enjoy the relative peace and quiet of lunch time in our room.

Some of our children are able to learn self-care in toileting procedures. Special bars are installed in our bathroom to assist the children in steadying themselves while standing, sitting, and supporting themselves to adjust their clothing. They stand with support whenever possible, and at the washstand they learn to manipulate the hot and cold water taps, soaping their hands, rinsing and drying them.

Afternoon Circle Time

An arithmetic period is usually included in this block of time, from 1:00 P.M. to 1:30 P.M., during which the children learn time concepts: o'clock and half past the hour; rote counting, grouping of numbers and number facts, addition and subtraction, and money concepts—pennies, nickels, and dimes. I utilize magnetic wooden numbers and animals for counting and building arithmetic sentences on our metal chalkboard; from these sentences number-fact cards using raised dots (Denison) are made up. Later we use flash cards with the number symbols.

From 1:30 P.M. to 2:00 P.M. the children practice the writing sequence and tracing work, for those who have progressed this far. Work sheets from the Marianne Frostig Visual Motor Development Sequences are also used during this period.

Filmstrips, special afternoon programs, and outdoor activities vary the afternoon routine. Unit materials are planned involving holidays, seasons, family and community, foods, animals, and some simple science concepts. These materials and discussions are part of the morning or afternoon circle periods. From 2:00 P.M. to 2:15 P.M. a story or a special record provides a quiet note on which to finish our very active days.

Hints for Room Management

Keep your room as clear of teaching and therapy materials as possible by providing ample storage space. Store those items which are not currently being used. Keep wheelchairs out of the way but handy enough for emergency use, as in a fire drill. Provide for these emergencies by having sufficient staff members oriented to report to your room to handle each wheelchair for removal from the building. Crutches and canes should be close to the children and can be supported off the floor by empty coffee cans attached to chairs. Try to convince your custodian that waxed floors are really detrimental to our children who are learning to walk. Non-slipping floor finishes can be used.

Our class is far from a baby-sitting service. It is a busy place. Our objectives are specific in working with our children, but our objectivity is often overwhelmed by very personal but honest emotional responses to the children and the progress made by them in all areas of their development. Each child sparkles with his own light, and the whole school responds when Barbara smiles and laughs spontaneously because she recognizes her classmates and teachers and loves the activity around her; she gave us no response or reaction of any kind last year. The children love to remember how William used to say La, La, La, La, La, but now he says real words like, "elephant," "telephone," "lunch box." And as they progress physically a few of the children are so close to walking that they feel as though they are ready to fly out of our arms. As they walk through the school halls in walkers, they are spurred on by each child and staff member they meet. There are no set limits for our children; they are little surprise packages, and it is our reward to watch their unfolding and opening, and to feel some small share in the total process.

12. PRESCRIPTIVE TEACHING VIA THE ILLINOIS TEST OF PSYCHOLINGUISTIC ABILITIES

by Lucille R. Romanoff

> Seal the dignity of a child. Do not feel superior to him, for you are not.
>
> —Robert Henri

In order to meet the specific needs of a handicapped child it is necessary to modify individual instructions and to develop a structured program which will yield techniques that a classroom teacher can utilize. We must have a definitive picture of the individual child which can be broken down into its component parts or areas. Within these areas we can then establish our prescriptive teaching.

The Illinois Test of Psycholinguistic Abilities is a test which reveals strengths and weaknesses in cognitive functioning. It encompasses defined areas of language function, in any one or more of which a child may show a severe deficit. The two stages of communication (which are included in the areas) are, basically, decoding and encoding. Decoding refers to the process of receiving, and encoding to the process of expressing. In addition to these, the ITPA includes a memory component.

Through specially designed activities based on the ITPA it is hoped that the children can achieve more profitable and useful communication skills, which will be retained throughout life and help them to become more independent and useful as adults.

Keeping in mind that our actual goal is for the child to have usable language to the best of his ability, we must be careful to structure the program to include the lows and well as the highs of the individual differences of each child. Realistic short-term goals for each child should be set, and whereas one child's goal might be to label five newly introduced objects, another's might be to use the past tense correctly, or to use proper pronouns.

It is important to find the child's interest in order to stimulate language development. This can be done from the social inventory, observation, and discussion with parents. It might be food or toys that interest one child the most. Another might be extremely concerned about accidents, fires, or other things of this nature. Whatever it might be, this can be the beginning. Use the actual food or toy. Tell the child about it. Have him tell you about it. You can expand upon this indefinitely, if it holds the interest of the child.

In communicating with a child, ask questions that require a motor response such as a nod or a verbal response. Accept any answer given initially. However, it may sometimes help to supply another answer that is more appropriate. Whenever possible, give clues that can be picked up in the child's strongest area—visual, tactile, motor or auditory, whichever it might be for that individual child.

When giving directions, give them briefly, only expanding when you are sure that the child is decoding auditorily on a higher level. Use appropriate gestures for visual cues as added support when necessary. Gradually withdraw such support to enhance the demand to the target channel.

Although the majority of our language development program takes place in the morning circle, it is extremely important that it be reinforced in all other activities and classes. All school personnel must be aware of the stress put upon syntax and expect and demand of the child the same expressive language that the teacher expects and demands.

Encourage verbal and social interaction between children, giving them ample time to display spontaneity in verbalizations. Using a structured play situation with hand puppets, for instance, can evoke some extremely illuminating conversation which can pinpoint weak areas in the auditory-vocal automatic areas. Often you will not get this type of conversation in a teacher-child relationship.

Children cannot communicate about experiences that they have never had. Their environment must be stimulating, particularly in institutional settings. It is up to us to supply the stimulation. As many outside activities and trips as possible must be experienced by the children. Visiting nearby airports, zoos, farms, orchards, and different kinds of stores will help them to relate to the verbal substitutes, the sound symbol for the real thing. It is all very well to show pictures of an airplane and to tell the child that it flies, but to see a plane up close, taking off, or to board it and sit in the seats will give the word "airplane" an impact that cannot be realized any other way. Make as many experiences available to the child as you possibly can. Then encourage him to talk about his experience immediately — what he did, what he saw, who went with him, where he went.

Give the child an opportunity to express his ideas. Asking each child to tell you something that he did over the weekend, or after he left school, starts verbal interchange. This is an extremely important function in the life of children, particularly retarded children where the "listening ear" and the "helping hand" are not always extended at home or in the community. With the teacher's syntactically correct repetition of the child's conversation, a process of imitation is set up for the use of future grammatically correct language. Never make the child feel that you are criticizing his use of language. Do not correct to the extent of inhibiting language flow because the child is apt to withdraw from social intercourse. Go slowly and accept whatever he says. You may have difficulty in the beginning distinguishing between what has happened and what is going to happen, this being the result of improper use of tenses. But with the proper type of questioning you can usually sort out the future from the past and thus help the child to clarify his own sense of time.

Often in a verbal child you will get the parents' incorrect patterns of speech. Have the child repeat the phrase correctly, listen to you, or hear a story read aloud; use any device to overcome an incorrect speech pattern. Changing a speech pattern heard at home is very difficult. You may not always succeed.

The following chart is set up to cover activities in the nine areas of the original ITPA design and to include children with M.A. from 2.0 through 9.0. After studying these activities you will find that many variations can be devised and new activities can be added.

Although we have tried to keep the various activities strictly within their individual areas, you will notice some overlapping. This is generally on a higher level. It is necessary, when starting out with a very young child, that you do not demand too much of him. Try to keep the areas separate, as you cannot expect a child to decode visually (understand what he sees), associate, and then respond verbally (encode) or manually until you are positive that he can do all three. The receptive or decoding functions must be working before meaningful encoding takes place.

In programming these activities we have started as low as possible, working sequentially to the more complex activities. Our ultimate goal has not been determined. One cannot possible predict, at this time, the gains a child can make with prescriptive teaching.

Resources

My Weekly Reader — Kindergarten level and level 1

Frostig Materials—Visual Perception. Worksheets and workbooks 1 and 2 (See General Bibliography)

Peabody Language Development Kits—Levels 0, 1, and 2

Discovering Opposites—Instructo

Classification game—Instructo

Let's Learn Sequence—Instructo

Designs in Perspective — Developmental Learning Materials, Chicago

Scott, Foresman Workbooks
  We Read Pictures
  We Read More Pictures
  Before We Read

Sounds and Patterns of Language by Martin, Weil, and Kohan (Holt, Rinehart & Winston)

Lite-Brite — Hasbro Co.

Association Picture Cards — Developmental Learning Materials

Counting Picture Cards — Developmental Learning Materials.

Continental Press Work Sheets—Continental Press, Elizabethtown, N.J.

Reading Readiness Cards, Tell (Sequencing)—Beckley-Cardy, Chicago

Reading Readiness Cards, See (Likes and Differences)—Beckley-Cardy, Chicago

Objects that Rhyme—Ideal, Oak Lawn, Ill.

Objectives	Preschool	Primary	Jr. Intermediate
Auditory Decoding Understanding spoken word with no visual clues.	Responding to gesture such as nod or smile Responding to own name Responding to simple commands, such as "Come," "Sit," "No"	Responding to commands, e.g., "Put your coat in the closet," "Bring me my book" Responding to absurdities—e.g.: "Do children wear clothes?" "Do babies talk?" Stay within the experiences of the child	Answering (yes or no) oral questions about school or home activities Responding to absurdities e.g., "Do cows fly?" "Do animals talk?" "Does furniture sleep?" Give child statement, such as "John is going swimming tomorrow." Then ask, "Who, where, and when," to strengthen recall
Visual Decoding Understanding or interpreting what he sees Verbal response not necessary	Interpreting social cues such as smile, frown, nod Ask "Show me your chair, desk, door, window, flag" and other items from his environment Use miniature objects with same format as above Use three-dimensional objects Recognizing own name (with color cues)	Picture identification of common objects Discriminating among objects by size, e.g., "Show me big chair, little car," etc. Recognizing own name and names of peers Indicating understanding of job list Specify action such as running, jumping; then ask "What did I do?" Child can either show or give verbal response Lotto games using geometric forms in color and black and white	Identifying shaped objects: round, square, etc. Identifying colored objects Identifying by function: "Give me what we eat with." "Show me what we cut with." Finding other objects in room that are round, red, etc. Recognizing names of peers, first and last Knowing words of protection Knowing weather words such as hot, cool, warm, cloudy, rain, snow, windy Show pictures depicting scenes of a farm, city street, accident, etc. (can be cut from magazines); have child describe what he sees, pointing out the various things Reading

Objectives	Preschool	Primary	Jr. Intermediate
Auditory-Vocal Association Relating spoken word in a meaningful way	Categorizing or classifying Ask questions such as "Where do you sit?" "Where do you put your lunch box?" On nonverbal level, accept motor response (child points to chair or bin). As child points, say "chair" or "on the chair" Forming concepts of same and different Use miniature objects, e.g., two chairs. Point out that chairs are alike because we sit in them. Have child find another one in the room Simple riddles, e.g., "I am an animal who barks and wags my tail. Who am I?" "Dog." If nonverbal, have three pictures that they can select from	Naming things we wear Naming things we eat Naming things we play with Forming concepts of same and different. Use pictures for classifying. Have children identify pictures of fruits, toys, furniture, animals, birds, transportation, clothing, and explain each category so they will understand why they are alike Introduce simple opposites that can be illustrated, such as "hot" (light bulb), "cold" (water or ice cubes), "wet" (water), "dry" (sand), "boy," "girl," etc. Always use a demonstration when possible. "Up" - "Down" "In - out" "Stop" - "Go" Riddles, e.g., "I'm round, red, and you can eat me." (apple, cherry) Lotto games	Naming as many fruits as possible Naming transportation methods Reverse above and say, "An apple is —" (could be fruit, round, red); all are classifications "A hammer, pliers, etc. are all —." (Expect word, tool.) This can be done in all categories "How are things alike?" e.g., an apple, a pear, and a banana are alike because "they are fruit," "they are sweet," "they grow," "we eat them," etc. Answering riddles — more complicated ones than level one or two Problem solving. "What would you do if: you were lost, it were raining outside, you fell and hurt your knee?" Supply the child with alternatives, if appropriate Opposites: Teach them by illustration or demonstration as much as possible, e.g., high-low, in-out, tall-short, woman-man, wife-husband, white-black, morning-night Analogies Lotto games—discovering opposites Classification game. Give each child two minutes to name as many toys, animals, foods, etc. as he can. Mark on blackboard as he says them. The winner gets to pick the next circle activity.

Objectives	Preschool	Primary	Jr. Intermediate
Visual Motor Association Relating meaningful visual symbols	Ask child, "*Show* me what you sit on, where you hang your coat, where you eat your lunch," etc. Use objects in child's own environment Use common objects such as pair of scissors or key; ask, "What do you cut with?" Expand to selection from three or four objects. Lotto games; make own with pictures of fish and water, mother and baby, cup and saucer, shoe and sock, etc.	Use pictures of two or three common objects, such as brush, bed, etc. Ask child questions such as, "What do you do with your hair?" "On what do you sleep?" Lotto games Use common objects in the room and say, "Show me what goes with this": chalk, pencil, cup, sock, etc.	Use five to ten pictures. Have the child show you: Which one flies? Which one can we ride on? Which one can we wear? Lotto games Ask, "Why do a sock and shoe go together?" "Why do a cow and barn go together?" etc.
Motor Encoding Expressing ideas in gestures.	Follow the leader songs such as "Two little hands go clap"—"Put your finger in the air" Have child imitate activity of animals, TV characters, other children. Gross motor activity — crawling, jumping, hopping, running, etc.	"Follow the Leader" "Simon Says" Use action pictures and have child *show* you what is happening in the picture: running, dancing, jumping, etc.	Without pictures have child role play: Show me what a soldier does; a ballet dancer; a gardener and others Act out such records as "A Visit to My Little Friend," "My Playful Scarf," "Train to the Zoo" Have children move about in spaces in as many different ways as they can Do not tell them how. Let them improvise the various means of locomotion (crawl, jump, hop, skip, run). Ask child to show you how he would use a hammer, pencil, flute, etc.

Objectives	Preschool	Primary	Jr. Intermediate

Vocal Encoding
 	
Expressing ideas in spoken words
	Naming objects in environment such as, ball, doll, cup, etc.
	
	Have child discriminate among simple shapes such as a square or round object, ball or block
	
	Ask what color it is. Expect *one*-word answers. If child does not know, tell him
	
	Transfer to pictures of *one* object. Ask name, color (if he knows color) and shape
		Give child simple object and ask him to tell you about it
		
		"Ball": it bounces, is red, etc. Help him with description by adding to his
		
		Show child a simple picture and ask him to tell you about it. If he misses anything point it out and tell *him* about it.
		
		Have children talk about weekend activities, holidays, weather, seasons, etc.
			Give child a more complex object such as a tool and ask him to tell you about it.
			    What size is it?
			    What shape?
			    What color?
			    What is it used for?
			    What is it made of?
			
			Ask questions: "What is the girl doing?" "Where are they going?" "What is this?"
			
			Start a simple story using names of children in class. Have each child add an idea and then put it into sentences
			
			Have children talk about what they did after school, on weekends, on vacations, etc.
			
			Have one child be the teacher for morning circle. Let him go through routine: role call, job list, calendar, weather. Be sure child is using complete sentences. Correct where necessary, but unobtrusively
			
			Have children take turns organizing games and being the leader. Leader must explain rules of game such as "Duck, duck, goose," or "Doggy, Where's your bone?"

Objectives	Preschool	Primary	Jr. Intermediates
Auditory-vocal automatic Responding in automatic or grammatical terms	Responding to roll call with "here" or "I am here." If nonverbal, raises hand *Simple* jobs changed weekly. Ask child, "What is your job?" (messenger, etc.) Nursery rhymes, simple poems, and rhyming stories. Have children start by supplying last word in each line; "Baa baa black sheep, have you any——". Finger plays Have children imitate what teacher says in simple sentences	Responding to roll call: "I am here" Job list: child gives job in simple sentences: "I take the message" Nursery rhymes, simple songs, and poems using rhyming words Teach plurals, emphasizing "*s*" sound Choral readings Language Master cards with one idea sentences; child repeats	Weekly job list. Responding in complete sentences and describing the job simply. Ask, "What do you do in your job?" "Put books in bin" or "Turn on and off the lights." Build up gradually to more complex sentences Start past and future tenses using same jobs. "What did you do?" "What will you do?" Rhyming stories such as the Dr. Seuss books. Have children supply last rhyming word in each line; gradually leave out more and more words Teach plurals, emphasize *s*. Show examples: "Here is a boy"; "Here are two boy*s*" Teach irregular plurals: mouse, man, woman, child Give children a chance to talk and express their own ideas. Correct grammar as they go, but do not interrupt their train of thought Imitation: use a two-idea sentence and have children repeat Language Master cards. One- and two-idea sentences; child repeats Dramatic play using children and hand puppets

Objectives	Preschool	Primary	Jr. Intermediate

Auditory-vocal sequential
 	
Developing auditory sequential memory
	Repeat finger plays and simple nursery rhymes (the combination of rhyming words plus the visual-tactile reinforcement helps child to retain rhyme and increase memory, non-meaningful patterns as well as meaningful ones)
	
	Counting to five (rote)
		Two digit repetition. Repeat Pledge of Allegiance
		
		Repeat rhythm patterns, using child's name. Stress letters by clapping hands or beating a drum P-A-T-T-Y. Child repeats pattern, saying it and doing it
		
		Simple three-card picture stories. Have child arrange in correct sequence
		
		Rote counting to ten
			Three or more digit repetition. At first use number symbols on cards; show them as you say them, then take them away
			
			Pledge allegiance
			
			Days of the week (use visual clues, repeat in beginning)
			
			Alphabet; sing it first (use visual clues at first)
			
			Nonsense poems and songs:
			    Tabu
			    Moon don't go
			
			Cut out and mount picture stories from Scott, Foresman Pre-Primer Workbooks. Place pictures in pocket chart in correct order. Tell the story. Change order and have the child rearrange correctly and then tell the story
			
			The game "Let's go Shopping." The teacher starts "I am going to the store and I will buy ——." Each child adds an item

Objectives	Preschool	Primary	Jr. Intermediate
Visual motor sequential Developing memory for sequential visual symbols	"What's missing?" Use two items, cover and take one away. Have children tell you what's missing. Use related objects in child's environment Have child copy simple peg pattern using one color and very few pegs Have child copy simple bead stringing pattern and simple designs in color with 1″ cubes	"What's missing," using three or four articles related, e.g., cup, saucer, spoon Put three articles in certain order, cover and rearrange. Have child put back in original order Reinforce by naming each article Make a simple one-colored straight line peg pattern. Have child produce Tracing name Copying simple patterns on Lite-Brite Arrange three-picture story sequence (Reading Readiness cards)	"What's missing," using five or more articles unrelated. Name them first. Then take one away and ask, "What's missing?" Put three or four pictures in certain order; change order and have child put them back in the original order Reproducing peg patterns in color Solving mazes. Complete the incomplete pictures (Frostig Material) Reproducing name and other meaningful words Reproducing numbers Copying designs with blocks (1″ cubes-Milton Bradley) and designing in perspective (Developmental Learning Materials); copying patterns on Lite-Brite

Resources

Auditory Training: Familiar Sounds; Rhythm Band—Developmental Learning Materials—Chicago.
Barnyard Animals—Droll Yankees, Inc.—Providence, R.I.
Call and Response Rhythmic Group Singing—Folkways—New York
Can Be Fun series, by Munro Leaf—J.B. Lippincott—Philadelphia
Counting Games and Rhythms for the Little Ones—Folkways—New York
DLM Perception Material—Developmental Learning Materials—Chicago.
Dubnoff School Program 1, Level 1: Sequential Perceptual–Motor Exercises—Teaching Systems and Resources Corp.—Boston.
Fearon Teacher—Aid Books—Fearon—Palo Alto, Cal.
The Fitzhugh Plus Program: Perceptual Learning and Understanding Skills, by Kathleen and Loren Fitzhugh—Allied Education Council—Galien, Mich.
The New Frostig Program for the Development of Visual Perception—by Marianne Frostig and David Horne—Follett—Chicago.

Listening Skills for Pre-readers, vols. 1 and 2—Educational Activities, Inc.—Freeport, N.Y.
Lite Brite-Developmental Learning Materials—Chicago.
Now I Look; Now I Read: workbooks accompanying *Readiness and Reading for the Retarded Child*, by Bebe Bernstein—John Day—New York.
Peabody Language Development Kits, by Lloyd M. Dunn and James O. Smith—American Guidance Service—Circle Pines, Minn.
Physical Fitness for Pre-school Children; Physical Fitness for Primary Children—Rhythm Record Co.—Oklahoma City, Okla.
Songs for Children with Special Needs—Bowmar—Glendale, Cal.
Sounds I Can Hear—Scott, Foresman—Glenview, Ill.
Teaching Children Good Manners; Teaching Children Safety, by Dorothy B. Carr and Ernest P. Willenberg—Educational Activities, Inc.—Freeport, N.Y.
Visual-Motor Perception Materials—Teaching Systems and Resources Corp.—Boston.
What's Its Name? by Jean Utley—University of Illinois and the Maico Company of Minneapolis, Minn.—Urbana, Ill.

13. PARENTS

> But let not him who longs much say to him who longs little, "Wherefore are you slow and halting?" For the truly good ask not the naked, "Where is your garment?" nor the houseless, "What has befallen your house?"
> —Kahlil Gibran

The parents of our children are the most important players on our team. It is to them we must turn to learn how each child solves his own problems in daily living. The child's solutions may not be economical in time and energy or appropriate for group living, but they are our key to opening new and perhaps easier pathways for him.

Our task is to plan experiences and opportunities which will enable each child to achieve his maximum potential. Only through mutual sharing of observation, with parents and teachers working together, can we move ahead toward realizing that potential.

During a parent conference you can learn a good deal if you ask the parents, "How do you manage this rough behavior at home?" or "Tell me how Tom plays at home" instead of complaining, "Tom's entirely too rough at school." Most parents welcome a chance to help solve a problem.

Many parents are apprehensive about placing a little one in a special school. Some parents are so grateful and relieved to find a place that offers help and interest that they become almost maudlin in their efforts to please the school staff. Some are so relieved they practically say, "It's your baby now!" Some parents withhold information in their effort to fulfill a hope that the problem really isn't there or that it will go away tomorrow. Most parents are valiant and very cooperative. The excellent attendance at our Parent Education Workshops is evidence of the parents' interest in learning all we can offer so we can work together.

When a child enters our nursery class, it is usually after we have had considerable contact with his parents. We frequently start to work very early with a family, particularly when a child's condition, such as Downs Syndrome, is recognized at birth. Early intervention, planned stimulation, and knowledgeable parents combine to produce a child ready for a nursery group experience.

Children transferred to our school from higher level classes—"educable" or "slow learners,"—sometimes have difficulty adjusting to the "new" school because their parents find it so hard to accept the change. But the child who failed time and again in classes for "slow learners" may very well achieve success after success in our special school. Through honest reporting and conferences, parents can be prepared to accept and perhaps even welcome reclassification of their child. When parents are a part of the team, they can share the teacher's apprehensions for the future and can prepare for a probable change with full knowledge of all the ramifications. The involvement of a social worker in helping the parents understand is a tremendous help.

Parents of young retarded children need a great deal of help in understanding and coping with the problems they face.

It is all well and good to say "These parents need counseling," but where are they going to get it? A few private schools have counseling services. Most public-school counselors and public-health nurses are not trained in problems of mental deficiency and are quick to admit it. They find it difficult to do the kind of counseling that is required to help parents face life with a retarded child.

A physician or examining psychologist cannot take time to discuss adequately all of the problems that should be clarified. It is usually the daily job of the teacher to try to answer the questions of bewildered parents.

Pamphlets and books are available and are very helpful. However, group discussion with some resource leadership is needed. Misinterpretation of printed material, failure to understand, only one parent reading pertinent material—these can create more confusion than existed earlier.

An opportunity for studying their problems, together with good leadership, should be available to all parents of young retarded children. Participation in six workshop sessions should be required—both parents attending—before a child is admitted to school.

Informed parents who have had an opportunity to discuss the problems facing all parents of retarded children will be cooperative and better able to carry on their share of the training program in the home.

The workshop topics offered here have been derived from many workshop sessions held over several years. These topics seem to be what parents ask about the most.

Appropriate reading material for parents and possible resource people are suggested.

A director of special education should conduct some of these workshops or help locate good resource people.

Topics for Workshop Sessions

1. "What is Retardation?" and "How do You Find Out Whether Your Child is Retarded?" A physician, pediatrician, neurologist, or psychiatrist could be a resource person for this session.

2. "What Does it Mean When You Find that Your Child is Retarded?" and "What Can You Do About It?" A psychologist could be helpful in this session.

3. "How Do You Tell Brothers and Sisters, Grandparents, Relatives, and Neighbors about Your Retarded Child?" A social worker would be able to discuss such findings as the Farber reports or other appropriate resources.

4. "How Will Your Child be Educated for His Own Particular Future?" "How Will He Learn?" "How Will Your Child Learn to Talk?" A good nursery school teacher or a language therapist could be helpful for this discussion.

5. "How Do We Toilet Train a Retarded Child?" and "How Do We Discipline a Retarded Child?" The teacher or a school nurse should be able to help with this discussion.

6. Discussion of submitted questions arising from all the previous sessions should occupy the time of this last session. The teacher should summarize at the end of this session.

Good reading for parents may be found in the many pamphlets available through the National Association for Retarded Children, 420 Lexington Ave., New York, N.Y. 10017.

14. VOLUNTEERS

by Suzanne C. Callner

> The best kept secret in America today is that people would rather work hard for something they believe in than enjoy a pampered idleness. They would rather give up their comfort for an honored objective than bask in extravagant leisure. It is a *mistake to speak of dedication as a sacrifice.*
>
> John W. Gardner

Most schools have discovered the critical need for a volunteer service of some kind. Planning for such a service entails much more than a set of techniques. It involves a commitment to the idea that volunteer help is a way of life; it involves understanding that we need some of our best people committed, devoted, and genuinely trying to understand the particular environment.

Upon becoming a member of the Molloy Education Center Volunteers, you join forces with a fine group of people who are there because they want to be and who want to share their strength and love with our children.

Disciplining the children is based on patience, empathy, tolerance, and quiet perseverance. Problems in management are discussed in Volunteer Workshops which guide you to understand our philosophy. A quiet voice, a few well chosen words that deliver the message, and a smile of anticipation and assurance—these are signs of an effective volunteer. A smile, or a pat after each or any success by a child will lead to more success. Patience and understanding is our guiding principle.

The pace is slow! When you drive your car in normal traffic at 30 mph and slow down to 15 mph or half speed, you feel you are scarcely moving. You become impatient. Our children all move at half speed or less. There will be times when you feel you are scarcely moving ahead but when you become accustomed to our pace, you will take it in stride. You must always remember that the tiniest gain is tremendous because it *is* a gain.

Just sitting beside a little one who is disturbed helps him to learn to sit still and is an important job. You must never become discouraged because you feel you are not doing anything. Your presence as an adult lends security to the children.

Volunteers want to know what is expected of them. Volunteers want to be informed Our volunteer handbook contains a scheduled study program for the school volunteers, a listing of the school staff, a school calendar, and pertinent questions and answers relating directly to communication between volunteer and child and volunteer and teacher.

> A true volunteer is she
>   who accepts authority
>   who resolutely and firmly acts
>   but only when she has the facts
>   who speaks well, writes a splendid letter
>   but also listens even better
>   who works as long as anyone
>   and leaves her desk clear, tasks all done
>   who even on the darkest days
>   can summon up a word of praise
>   and bravely smiles amidst disaster
>   who goes to church and knows the pastor
>   who chairmans P.T.A. and Chest
>   who, hale and hearty, needs no rest
>   resourceful, charming woman of talents
>   possessed of perfect poise and balance
>   her words and deeds and aims all mesh
>   we'll never see her in the flesh

Postscript by Julia S. Molloy

An extra pair of hands, extended with willingness, warmth, and love—these hands belong to the sixty women who proudly wear the blue smock and the golden apple of the Molloy Education Center Volunteers, devoting a half day to three full days per week, sharing their time and energies so that our children may have more individual attention.

These are not fund raisers. These are nose-wipers, bathroom-takers, hand-washers, spoon-and-cup steerers, swing-pushers, tricycle-steerers, tear-driers, "tranquilizers," story-readers, game partners, listeners, trained speech aides, light-touch-behaviorists, loom warpers, typists, hand-holders, and laugh-sharers. They provide life experiences by allaying fears, building confidence and faith in adults, enhancing a sense of humor, sharing love and strength—the tools for making life worthwhile.

Our volunteers are true believers that *retarded children can be helped*, true believers in the worthwhileness of each child and in his right to achieve the excellence that is within his reach.

Their services, bringing them into direct contact with our children, staff, and families, qualify them to present an enlightened and enthusiastic picture of our school to the community and to participate with almost evangelical zeal, and marked success, in teacher recruitment.

15. "COME RIDE OUR BUS"

by Joan Kozub

"and leave the driving to us"

"Beep Beep" — and a wild scurry for lunch box, note, mittens, or swim suit, show and tell treasure, a kiss — and a sigh of relief: "we made it!" Or maybe a serene little package is all put together and waiting primly on the front steps or perhaps there is a king-size void with a little one hiding shyly in the bushes, lunch box where?! But the driver is a friend waiting with a smile to whisk the child away to his own wonderful world, his special place in the sun, his school.

And that smile is just about the most important thing that will happen all day. "I'm welcome, I'm wanted, I'm loved" is what that smile should make the child feel. That smile plus a few comfortably spoken words can set the theme, timbre, and tempo for the whole day: "Good morning, Jodie; aren't your shoes shiny today!" to "Hi, fellow, mighty snazzy shirt you're sporting today."

Driving a school bus is very much like being an actor or a public servant. Being in the public eye, you must put your best foot forward. The bus driver is usually the rider's first contact with the outside world away from the comforting faces at home. No matter what the driver feels physically or mentally, it must not show through the smile and warm friendly greeting that the riders need and want.

Some transportation systems provide paid aides to ride in buses carrying handicapped children. This is essential for some types of handicapped children. Students attending schools for trainable children should behave well enough to require no more than a trained "senior" student as a helper on the bus.

The upper teen-age students at the Molloy Education Center receive training in child care. (See Chapter 23). The training includes the tasks required in helping in the buses. Not all students are able to be bus helpers, but those who can be trained become good conscientious helpers and make things much more comfortable for the other students and the driver. The title "bus helper" is a real status symbol.

The most trying experience for any driver, new or old, is the new rider, who is, of course, having a most trying experience himself. That stranger behind the wheel of this strange vehicle, the new faces of the other students! At times like this, the driver must be parent, baby sitter, counselor, adviser, and all the other things it takes to maintain calm and order.

Until calm has been restored—this may take several days in some cases—the driver herself must remember to keep her cool. One of the most frustrating moments, for any driver, is when a new student learns how to unfasten the seat belt. Most of the older children can be trained to watch for this and other danger signs, and to respond accordingly. They may also help calm the younger children and assist in making them comfortable for the ride to school.

All the children must be made to understand that they are all to be on their best behavior. Here again, we depend on the older children to assist in maintaining order. Some of the younger children will attempt to eat their lunches on the bus while others may try to take off items of clothing. Many sit quietly during the bus ride, but some of the older children have interests of their own such as music, sports, or allergies. The driver should be versatile and converse with these children; it may help to keep up on current sports events and weather reports.

Giving some of the older children little chores to do while on the bus gives them a feeling of importance and helps build a sense of responsibility. Showing an interest in their problems or ideas gives them a sense of belonging. The younger children are more prone to accepting a hug and a squeeze. What it all amounts to is establishing a rapport with the children and making the bus ride to school or back home an enjoyable experience.

The children come to recognize the bus as their own and the driver as their friend. At times it is necessary to have a substitute driver and the children recognize this. Some of them will question this and accept an explanation, while others will resent the substitution. The substitute driver will have to establish her own form of acceptance by the children. Once accepted this driver can substitute at any time. The children can be of great assistance to any driver; many times the driver may be unfamiliar with a particular street or the route taken by the regular driver and the students are quick to offer advice. There are times the regular drivers will deliberately take another route just for fun and to test the children's ability. It also causes some excitement and the children get a chance to laugh and tease the driver. These children are individuals and must be ministered to accordingly. They are subject to home problems, physical pain, and pleasures, good days and bad days.

Each bus is equipped with a radio (great for a quiet ride), a first aid kit (drivers must pass the Red Cross First Aid Course), a blanket, a few folded brown paper bags, a carton of Stereloid, fire extinguisher, and a supply of wrapped candy. The candy is used as reward for good behavior or a thoughtful helping hand.

Insist that the children do not litter the bus. The older students can help keep the inside of the bus clean. They can wash and shine the windows and sills, keep the chrome work shiny and vacuum the carpet or floor covering. If your school has more than one vehicle, a competition for the cleanest bus is very productive. The winner each week can display a small flag (if legal) or a sign of merit devised by some creative staff person. Be very sure the teams are of equal strength. It would hardly be fair to expect a passenger list of less able children to compete with the big guys.

Saying goodbye is just as important as saying good morning. Part with a smile and a good word. If the mother meets the bus, have a pleasant word for her too—especially if you are late!

We transport our bowling league each Monday, take the children to a park field house for recreation each Thursday after school, and go on field trips.

Every other Thursday morning, right after the last bus arrives, the drivers have coffee with the principal and sometimes the social worker. We talk over problems of mutual concern and exchange some of the gems of the week. Problems requiring contact with the parents are put in writing and discussed, then followed up by the social worker or principal as the situation indicates.

Drivers should avoid altercations with parents by pleasantly saying, "You had better call the school and discuss this with......" Try always to be aware that the parents of our children have had a profound shock in their lives. Try always to put yourself in their place as you hang onto your cool.

Driving a school bus full of special children can be a very rewarding experience.

Postscript. Successful bus drivers are real treasures. The drivers can make or break the school day. They are very special people.

J.S.M.

The Five Growth Areas: Physical Growth

16. BODY IMAGE AND GROSS MOTOR DEVELOPMENT

by Phyllis Kamin, O.T.R.

I met a little Elf-man once,
  Down where the lilies grow.
I asked him why he was so small
  And why he didn't grow.

He slightly frowned, and with his eye
  He looked me through and through.
"I'm quite as big for me," said he,
  "As you are big for you."

John Kendrick Bangs

Suppose we are viewing a group of children of approximately the same age who have been asked to move around the gym floor. There is no sound communication between us and the group, and we have not been given any information on abilities. None of the children has obvious physical handicaps, such as cerebral palsy, etc. The children move around for a while, and as we watch, we become aware of some real differences. Some move about the room exploring with their eyes, occasionally touching or feeling objects, some interact with each other; some remain quite isolated from the group. We begin to focus on one child who is clumsy and awkward in his movements, on another who pushes and bumps and touches others, on one who walks slowly and stiffly with a toe-heel shuffle, and on yet another whose overactivity spills into a butterflying motion of the arms. The children are asked to remove their shoes, and then to put them on again. The performance of some of these children in contrast to the others is quite revealing. They may appear to be quite inept although apparently putting forth much effort to complete the assigned task. Even with such a cursory observation period, we may "tag" some of the children as "developmentally retarded."

In a cross-section of children with retarded development, we would generally observe the following motor behaviors:

1. Gross, uncoordinated movements that appear as "clumsy." Walking is often flatfooted, or is accomplished by a toe-heel shuffle. Arms hang at sides, or are held stiffly with elbows bent.
2. Generally well-developed gross movements, but with deficits in control of these movements. The child may run rapidly around the gym, but does not stop or change directions to avoid collisions. He perseverates with the same kind of movement often, avoiding equipment or situations that require changes in posture or balance or tempo.
3. Movements requiring fine motor-coordination that appear as awkward or inept. The child may attempt to zip his jacket by trying to manipulate the zipper pull with almost a full fist—two or three fingers opposed to his thumb. Efficient manipulation of a zipper pull would be accomplished with forefinger and thumb opposition.
4. Gross or fine movements used inappropriately or used only in the performance of trained tasks. (These tasks are akin to the "splinter skills" which Dr. Kephart describes.) The child may zip his jacket with finger-thumb opposition but not transfer this manipulative ability appropriately. He may then attempt to use the same pincer grasp in pulling on boots, a task requiring several fingers in opposition to the thumb.

Independence in self-care is essential for all children, and no less so in children with retarded development. A child who requires much help in caring for his own clothing, in managing personal needs such as toileting, is hampered in the development of his self-image. His potential for acceptance in the everyday world is considerably lessened.

The Learning Process

Normal learning processes are the basis for all rationale in education, and we must consider the physiology of learning as well as the psychology of learning. There are some primary factors involved in the learning process: first, we are constantly receiving "input" or stimuli through many sensory channels, which we may or may not be aware of; and second, all input brings forth some kind of motor response. If that motor response is repeated and reinforced often enough, that particular behavior becomes a part of a repertoire of behaviors that are more easily elicited or automatic.

In an oversimplified but graphic way, learning occurs in this way:

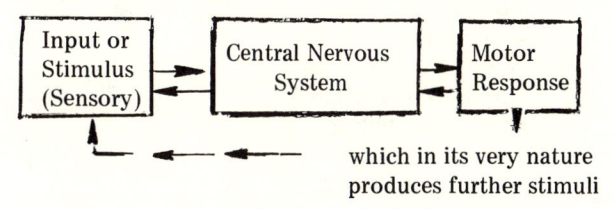

| Input or Stimulus (Sensory) | → ← | Central Nervous System | → ← | Motor Response |

which in its very nature produces further stimuli

Since input is essential and precedes all motor output, an analysis of the many avenues for stimulation should be of prime interest. We must be aware of the multitude of ways to stimulate the nervous system. Motor responses will occur when there is stimulation through *vision*, through *hearing*, through *taste* and *smell*. Cutaneous (*skin*) receptors may be stimulated by means of lightly *touching* the skin, by *contact of the body* or *parts of the body* with various substances which offer differences in texture or in temperature. Sensory input occurs in each *change of body position* which affects *muscles*, *tendons*, and *joints*. Such primary needs as *hunger*, *thirst*, or *discomfort* act as sensory input, the motor response being crying or other irritable behavior.

When do children "start" to learn, and what do they learn about? We, as educators, child-care workers, or therapists, are concerned with children in the post-natal stage. An infant starts to learn, on a motor level, on his first day in the world. In his crib, he experiences stimuli in the nature of hunger, thirst, or discomfort, all coming from within himself, and generally resulting in crying behavior. His motor response brings about a change of behavior in those caring for him, a chain of stimuli and motor responses that may be illustrated in this way:

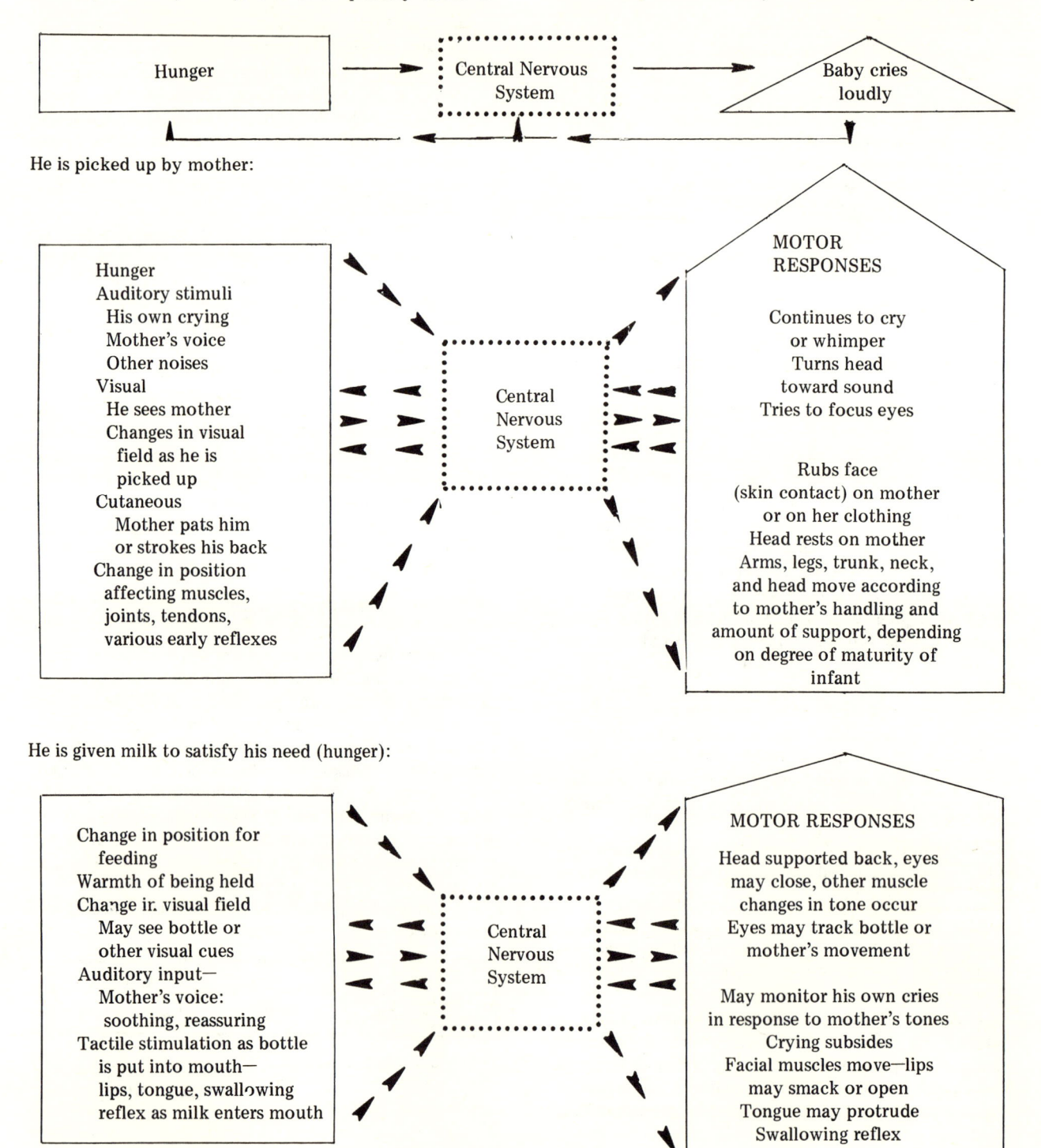

Hunger → Central Nervous System → Baby cries loudly

He is picked up by mother:

Stimuli:
- Hunger
- Auditory stimuli
  - His own crying
  - Mother's voice
  - Other noises
- Visual
  - He sees mother
  - Changes in visual field as he is picked up
- Cutaneous
  - Mother pats him or strokes his back
- Change in position affecting muscles, joints, tendons, various early reflexes

→ Central Nervous System →

MOTOR RESPONSES
- Continues to cry or whimper
- Turns head toward sound
- Tries to focus eyes
- Rubs face (skin contact) on mother or on her clothing
- Head rests on mother
- Arms, legs, trunk, neck, and head move according to mother's handling and amount of support, depending on degree of maturity of infant

He is given milk to satisfy his need (hunger):

Stimuli:
- Change in position for feeding
- Warmth of being held
- Change in visual field
  - May see bottle or other visual cues
- Auditory input—
  - Mother's voice: soothing, reassuring
- Tactile stimulation as bottle is put into mouth—lips, tongue, swallowing reflex as milk enters mouth

→ Central Nervous System →

MOTOR RESPONSES
- Head supported back, eyes may close, other muscle changes in tone occur
- Eyes may track bottle or mother's movement
- May monitor his own cries in response to mother's tones
- Crying subsides
- Facial muscles move—lips may smack or open
- Tongue may protrude
- Swallowing reflex

With this chain of events occurring time after time, the infant learns. He begins to attach meaning to some of the input and to the resulting developments. He learns some of the signaling necessary to satisfy his primary need for food. This may be the first of many steps in perceptual processes. With growing maturity, the infant begins to attach meaning to the signals he is giving, as well as to gain meaning from what he is receiving.

Physiologically some of the deterrents to learning are improper diet, lack of sleep, and fear. The nervous system reacts best to the familiar, and anyone who has panicked or "blocked" has experienced the fear of thinking. This might be overcome by conscious relaxation, by walking away—having a "time-out," a tool used in behavior shaping with success.

We learn through observation; we learn more easily when we are not tired, or hungry, or fearful; we learn when there is *fun* involved; we learn through stimulation of all of our senses, a combination of visual, auditory, tactile, proprioceptive stimuli.

We learn what we do. Repetition is essential.

The use of multi-sensory stimulation is beneficial, if all stimuli are directed and appropriate to producing the same goal or behavior. In other words, background music in a classroom, unless specifically tied to the activity offered, is not helpful; the nervous system can react to only one thing at a time. On the other hand, in teaching a child body parts, you may play a record or sing a song that identifies the body parts, you may stroke or touch his arm or leg, move that limb, focus your eyes and direct his attention to that part of his body, verbally reinforcing each motor response or visually reinforcing his response with a nod or smile. And for real success, don't ever forget to add that very important ingredient: *fun!*

Body Image

As the infant learns about satisfying a basic need such as hunger, he is also learning a great deal about himself and his environment. He rolls about his crib, touching the soft bumpers or the hard rails; he feels the smoothness of the sheet, the roughness of a terry cloth coverlet; he rubs his fingers on the cold hard surface of a rattle or the warmth and softness of a stuffed toy.

At this infantile level, however, the most meaningful input comes from within himself, hunger, thirst or discomfort, all of which result in crying behavior. The immediate response of those caring for him reinforces this behavior, and the signaling for this need becomes learned and part of his repertoire of motor behaviors. No wonder his world begins with himself, and he must build upon that "self" first. He must learn how to move that "self" around in his world in the crib. As he matures and develops, reflexive behavior permits him to roll over, to play with his own fingers and hands, and eventually to direct his hands to a desired object. As he reaches out and touches and explores, new sensations are experienced, new motor behaviors occur, and he begins to formulate an image of a "self" which has arms, hands, and fingers as an extension of his eyes to the visual world.

The point of reference from which he organizes his impressions of the world around him is his own "self"—his body image—and the position of things around him must be judged from the position of his own body. If he is always on his back, looking up, his perception of his own size and the size of things around him will certainly be different than if he were viewing the world from a sitting or standing position. Shape and distance would also be so influenced. If he sits or stands, but his head flops forward or to a side, his visual field will be distorted. If he never moves around independently, he will not experience the sensory input and the consequent motor behaviors that a freely ambulating child experiences. His world becomes limited, his concept of body image and body schema (what his body is, and how it moves) in relation to the world around him, is distorted.

If he reaches but does not grasp, his knowledge of the shape, size, texture, temperature, and use of objects is limited; his manipulative ability may remain gross and ineffectual, his potential for self-care is minimized.

Growth and Development

There is a sequence of reflex development and development of skeletal function through which we all progress, if development is normal. As maturation takes place, certain postures become characteristic of age levels. Such postures might be referred to as developmental milestones. While a baby progresses from one posture or pattern to another, however, each step along the way may *not* be performed par excellence before proceeding to the next. As one observes any normally developing baby, he may pull to standing, revert to crawling or rolling, assume a sitting position, etc. He draws on a continually expanding repertoire of motor behaviors and postures. The substitution of one for the other comes with gradations of skill and experience that lead to the discriminative use of one means of locomotion or ambulation, the adaptation of behavioral responses as maturation occurs.

It has not been established that a child must crawl in order to reach the next level of development. Therefore, when we suggest offering activities that reinforce crawling behavior, it is with the idea of expanding a repertoire of position-moving activities which call in postural readjustment, and which are not an end in themselves, but rather a means for the child to become more aware of the function and potential of his body, a means for exploring the environment.

Motor skills develop only with repetition and reinforcement of desired motor behavior. Body schema develop within the child as he becomes aware of:

1. WHAT he is moving (body parts identification)

2. WHERE he is moving (space)

   Personal space: the space required by his own body in terms of size and shape

   General space: the space that can be utilized by moving the body, in all directions: forward, backward, sideways, up, down. Different levels may be reached by moving in different ways; one may stretch to move "higher," or curl up or lie down to move to a "lower" level

3. HOW he is moving:
time factors such as quick, slow;
flow factors such as sudden, sustained, rhythmic;
weight factors such as strength, lightness.

The gross motor activity program which is developing at the Molloy Education Center is based on a three-laned structure, stemming from philosophies of Rood, Kephart, Bobath, and the British movement exploration approach.

The first lane stresses the reinforcement of the sequential milestones that mark motor development. The second lane has to do with the use of a multi-sensory approach, stimulation via as many channels as appropriate to the desired motor response. The third track, running parallel with the other two, but with the potential of vertical extension, incorporates the use of the British movement exploration approach.

Characteristic Posture or Developmental Milestone	Sensory Input	Movement Exploration
Withdrawal pattern Total flexion of trunk, arms, and legs while supine (lying on back). Early childhood posture which we have tendency to assume throughout life as a "defense system." We curl up when we are cold, or not feeling well or feeling insecure or defeated.	Tactile stimulation is of extreme importance since security can be communicated in this way. Example: at the early infant stage, a blanket wrapped around the baby prevents the "startle reaction," the extension and flailing of arms and legs an infant shows in response to his fear of falling or of loud noises. Passively roll the child in a large towel or blanket, with arms folded across body, legs curled up. Give him a large pillow or large cuddly toy to hold. Have him stretched out on the mat, then put his right hand on his left shoulder, his left hand on his right shoulder, flex his hips and knees, and roll him gently back and forth on the mat "like a ball".	Verbally direct him, and/or demonstrate: 1. Curl yourself up as *small* as you can. Stretch out into a long shape, and then curl into a small shape. (Alternate stretching and curling so the difference is felt in body tone.) 2. Hug yourself, and roll around the floor; hold yourself very tight. What shape are you? Are you round? 3. Can you fit into this laundry basket? How? What size must you be? Big? Or little? What shape? 4. From this curled position on the floor, we might do some "tumbling": curl up, but with hands on floor in front of us; we might do a "frog-hop," or a forward roll, or with hands at the sides of head, elbows up, we may do a back-roll.
Roll-over Rolling from prone to supine (stomach to back) and from supine to prone.	Tactile stimulation as well as proprioceptive stimulation are extremely important. As he rolls, large areas of his body are in contact with various surfaces, giving him sensory input. Changes occur in visual field as child rolls over. Roll the child from supine to prone, with arm and leg flexed on under side, arm and leg extended on side to which he is rolling. Roll him down an incline (raise one end of mat to give him the feeling of the pull of gravity). Roll him over a pillow, or large bolster.	Verbally direct him, and/or demonstrate: 1. Roll under an obstacle. 2. Stretch yourself into a long shape while lying on the floor. Now, you are long, and low to the ground (little), like a log. Can you roll over and over like a log? Keep your arms stretched over your head, and roll over and over. 3. What parts of your body are touching the floor as you roll? Your back, your left side and left arm and left leg, your stomach and the front of your legs, now your right side and right arm and right leg.

Characteristic Posture or Developmental Milestone	Sensory Input	Movement Exploration
	On the auditory level, talk about changes in the visual field; point out landmarks for him to watch. Use different tactile surfaces: smooth or roughly textured cloth. Have him notice differences in the speed when he is rolling downhill, of the softness, smoothness, etc. of a mat, a carpet, the grass, a tiled floor, etc.	
Pivot Prone The child lies on his stomach. At the infant stage, his head is raised as the body is in complete extension. Later, weight is placed on shoulder girdle and elbows and forearms, eliminating the rocking of trunk; the legs are extended but feet are in contact with the floor.	The shift of weight from one side to the other provides proprioceptive input, stimulates balance reflexes. As head is raised, visual field expands. As the child begins to shift weight from side to side, and he is able to support himself on either side, one arm and hand become free to reach—the extension of his expanded visual field. Cutaneous stimulation is accomplished by means of varying textures in the supporting surfaces that the child is in contact with—a mat, a terry towel, a wooly blanket, the cold hard surface of a floor, the warmth and softness of a pillow, etc.	Verbally direct him and/or demonstrate: 1. Wiggle through a tunnel or wiggle under an obstacle or 2. Slide down a sliding board on your stomach, feet first or Slide down the sliding board on a part of the body other than your seat or back or Is there another way to slide down the sliding board?(after the child has come down in the conventional fashion). 3. Ride on a scooter on your stomach or Can you move around on the scooter in some other way-on a different part of your body?(after the child has used the scooter in the conventional way). 4. Move around the floor like a snake (or wiggle like a worm). 5. Play a circle game, like rolling a ball, passing a bean bag, patting out various rhythms on the floor with the flat of your hand, while all players are on the floor lying prone.
All-Fours Hands and knees position with weight being assumed equally, or weight being shifted to knees, hands, or either side.	Tactile stimulation can be achieved by crawling on different surfaces. Kinesthetic reinforcement may be added by having the child crawl with	Verbally direct him and/or demonstrate: 1. Crawl over, under, through, in, out, on, off, in front of, in back of or

Characteristic Posture or Developmental Milestone	Sensory Input	Movement Exploration
	weighted sandbags, pony express style, or by having bean bags on different parts of the body (back, head, backs of hands). If the space into which the child crawls is just large enough for him, there will be body contact with the sides or top of the tunnel, box, etc. which will provide further sensory input. Crawling uphill or downhill (sliding board) offers an added dimension to maintaining balance against the pull of gravity.	behind various set-ups in equipment or Direct him to "Come to me" and place yourself so that he must adapt his body position and method of movement to surmount a certain obstacle. 2. Keep your right knee and right hand on the mat, your left knee and left hand off the mat (or line) as you crawl. (This will help separate out body sides as he moves). 3. Crawling relay races; any added dimension or direction will add fun and wider experience in the possibilities of exploring the environment.
Two-point kneeling Balance is established to the extent that the child can "heel-sit," or sit on knees, with hands somewhat free to explore and manipulate.	As balance is shifted from side to side and body adjusts to shifting weight, muscles, tendons and joints receive input. Tactile stimulation may be added by kneeling on varying textured surfaces.	Verbally direct him and/or demonstrate: 1. Move around on a part of your body other than your feet. Do not use your hands. (The child may find parts other than the knees to move on—the back, stomach, etc., but eventually will probably bring crawling into the picture.) 2. Circle games with children "heel-sitting." 3. Relay races, with children carrying bean bags in their hands. 4. Knee-drops on a mat or trampoline. 5. "Heel-sitting" at low benches or tables will free the child's hands for manipulative tasks.
Sitting There are many postures classified as sitting. A firm sitting "base" must be established to really free a child's hands for manipulative activities. One-level sitting (on the floor or on a mat) may be accomplished by Side-sitting	As child moves body parts while in the sitting position, his balance and overall posture-changes provide stimulation to muscles, joints, tendons, and balance reflexes. As he touches various parts of his body he is providing cutaneous and kinesthetic input. Visual and auditory input are ongoing in any of these activities. Make sure these are directly related to the motor responses desired.	Verbally direct him and/or demonstrate: 1. Play "Simon Says" or "Do As I Do": imitative movements touching body parts, following a clapping or tapping rhythm, or playing other musical games appropriate to this position. 2. Circle games, such as pass the bean bag or ball around from one child to the next, will necessitate constant shifting of balance.

Characteristic Posture or Developmental Milestone	Sensory Input	Movement Exploration
Ring-sitting  Tailor-fashion  Sitting with extended knees  Sitting with flexed knees  Two-level sitting is accomplished either with support (on a chair with a back) or without support (on a bench).		3. Ball rolling, catching, throwing, or bouncing from sitting position alters equilibrium, forces many small changes in posture. 4. Direct children to sit on small colored mats and match primary colored bean bags to the mats. Play "Simon Says"; "Put the bean bag on your head, etc." 5. Have child sit in as many sitting postures as he can think of. "Can you sit another way?" 6. A mobile toy such as Marx's "Krazy Kar" necessitates sitting with extended legs. A seesaw or a toy such as the "Swervy-Curvy-Topsy-Turvy" brings in other sitting postures. Sitting on a small scooter or dolly gives the child a chance to be mobile, uses leg muscles. A tricycle enhances that motor ability.
Standing balance Static motor development may be assessed with such tasks as the ability to: stand on one foot assisted, stand on one foot unassisted, stand and walk on tiptoes, stand heel-to-toe ten seconds, stand on one foot and maintain balance five to nine seconds, then ten to fourteen seconds.	Proprioceptive stimuli are primary at this stage of development. Any activities that call for a shift in weight and balance and posture provide more input. Standing on surfaces with different textures, such as the smooth cool surface of a tiled floor, the wooly scratchy surface of carpeting, the cool damp surface outside, warm gritty sand—all should be experienced with the bare feet. Balance itself is affected by the differences in the firmness of the surface. With the children standing in designated "spaces"—which may be on a small individual mat (carpet sample), on a line or mark on the floor, inside of a hoop on the floor—play many kinds of games: "Simon Says"; "Head, shoulders, knees and toes"; "Did you ever see a lassie?"; imitative movements. Play catch and throw with a ball or bean bag.	Verbally direct him and/or demonstrate: 1. Stand in your space, and move your arms in different ways. 2. Stand on your toes in the space, move as many parts of your body as you can, but NOT your feet. 3. Stand on your heels. Stand on your toes. Stand on your feet and bend your knees. Stand with your feet apart. Stand with your feet together. Stand on a line, one foot in front of the other. 4. Place a low obstacle like a cardboard block about three inches high in front of the child. Have him hold one foot over it (knee should be bent). This might be a first step in balancing on one foot. 5. Stand on an incline: facing upward; facing downward. 6. Stand on a balance beam.

Characteristic Postures or Developmental Milestones	Sensory Input	Movement Exploration
Walking Walking becomes a means for the child to experience the use of his body in many ways. Walking may be achieved functionally but be characterized by different patterns: The child may: a. be ataxic, but gain objective b. have a bizarre gait, without rhythm c. touch heel to the floor first, with toes extending for thrust forward, and without rhythm d. walk rhythmically, but with slappage or steppage gait e. walk with rhythmic gait, heel touching the floor first, toes extending for thrust forward.	Input through proprioceptive channels would be constant with changes in muscles, joints, and tendons with each varying movement. Kinesthetic reinforcement will occur in any activity where the child carries objects, walks uphill against gravity or downhill toward gravity; walks on surfaces that offer resistance to movement such as sand or water. The visual field expands with the enlargement of his world—a child who is walking is able to come in contact with many experiences that provide visual input. Walking around a room with bare feet provides a different kind of stimulation than walking around the same room wearing hard-soled shoes, or wearing gym shoes. Each of these activities has merit; our objectives should be to provide variation in kinds of experiences.	Concepts of time: fast or quick 　　　　　　　　　slow Concepts of flow: sustained movement 　　　　　　　　　sudden movement Concepts of force: hard (marching) 　　　　　　　　　soft (tiptoeing) all can be experienced through movement of the child. Verbally direct and/or demonstrate: 1. Walk around the room; do not touch anyone with your arms or hands as you walk. Walk in a different way. Faster? Slower? Quietly? Walk with your knees straight. Walk with your knees bending. Walk with your arms out; or up; or on your head; or on your waist. Walk with your hands on your knees; do you have to bend part of your body to reach your knees with your hands? 2. Walk . . . walk . . . walk . . . until I say "Freeze" (or "Stop"). Then, do NOT move. Stand perfectly still until I say "Walk!" (Vary rhythm of walk, vary tempo.) 3. If we tiptoe around the room, we are walking softly. Now, let us walk and put our feet down HARD. You must bend your knees and raise your knees up high in order to put your feet down hard. That is like *marching*. 4. Walk on a balance beam. See Appendix III for balance beam exercises.)

Summary

We have discussed the components of the physical education program, the necessity for reinforcing developmental milestones by using varied stimuli, and for creating situations which provide the children with opportunities to move and explore the environment. The structure of the program should vary with the number and kind of children, the physical set-up of the facility, other programs or services offered by the facility, and the amount of help available.

Some very general objectives for the children being served in a physical education program might include the following behaviors:

1. Identifying all body parts, by gesture, touch, or verbal response.
2. Assuming characteristic postures or developmental milestones, when verbally directed or by demonstration.
3. Moving with flexibility and coordination necessary for using specific equipment.
4. Changing body position to perform activities or tasks.
5. Maintaining balance as body position changes.
6. Moving body parts and maintaining balance while performing self-care tasks.

7. Following directions pertaining to spatial factors: in-out, over-under, up-down, in back of—in front of, to the side, around, through, between, etc.
8. Following directions pertaining to how he is moving: fast-slow; sudden-sustained; continuous-stopped; with lightness-with strength

Children who are enrolled in a school will probably have experienced in a limited way most of the developmental milestones. We must try to enrich each of those steps, by using variations and combinations of sensory input, by offering many kinds of pleasurable experiences during which the child can move his body in different ways; by guiding him through the whole gamut of motor behaviors which may eventually result in an ease of performance and greater opportunities for him to explore and become involved in the world around him.

17. FINE MOTOR DEVELOPMENT AND THE GRASP FUNCTION

by Phyllis Kamin, O.T.R.

Work while you work
Play while you play;
One thing each time,
That is the way.
All that you do,
Do with your might;
Things done by halves
Are not done right.

(McGuffey's Reader)

Just as we notice differences in gross motor behaviors in children with retarded development, so might we notice differences in their fine motor skills. These, in all likelihood, will show up particularly in the performance of self-care tasks.

The grasp function is as much an exploratory way of finding out about the world around us as is walking. If a child does not experience holding objects in his hands, he will have great difficulty in learning to discriminate certain characteristics in his environment such as: *size*—does an object fit into his hand, is it small enough to hold easily in one hand, or are both hands needed; *weight*—does the object feel light, or is it too heavy for easy handling; *shape*—does the object with smooth rounded edges feel comfortable in his hand, or does it have sharp edges and points; *texture*—does it feel furry, scratchy, smooth, rough, pebbly, sticky, ribbed, coarse, leathery, silky, etc.; *resiliency*—does it feel soft and "squeezy," or is it hard and tough?

Experience in all areas of handling behaviors contributes to the child's perceptual and conceptual development, and to his ability to handle his own clothing and eating utensils, and to manage his own personal needs.

The kind of grasp a child uses is affected by all of the things that make up a child's history: his chronological age, his mental age, the cause of his handicapping condition, the establishment of hand preference, the degree to which his bone structure has matured, the gross motor behaviors that may indicate a certain level of development and maturity, the very experiences he has been given an opportunity to participate in, and the kinds of stimuli that appeal to him.

The ability to reach, grasp, hold, manipulate, and release develops in a certain sequence, just as gross motor abilities follow a pattern of development. An understanding of the sequential development is helpful to all who are concerned with program planning and working with developmentally retarded children.

The infant spontaneously grasps items in a tightly clenched fist, which is part of the whole flexion pattern. He is at birth a curled-up individual, with arms and legs held in the fetal position, described as the "withdrawal pattern," the fingers too, tightly curled or flexed. As he grows and develops, his whole body position becomes more open, and the reflexive grasp he initially uses gives way to a more open hand position. This somewhat extended hand becomes even more open as the infant begins to roll over. As the total body begins to turn, the baby gets the feel of pushing against the surface on which he is lying in order to get some leverage, which affords tactile and kinesthetic input to the muscles of the hand and arm. The same kind of input occurs as the infant lifts his head from a prone position, and begins to support himself on his hands and forearms.

When on his back, he often reverts to the more dominant flexion pattern. With elbows and shoulders flexed, his hands wave first in a line even with the body, but gradually start to approach his midline, and he becomes aware of them. His visual field becomes quite focused on those two fists, and he engages in finger play, adding kinesthetic and tactual input to the visual input.

Hand to mouth activity occurs about this time, and this is pleasurable in terms of sucking on fists or fingers; as he gains control and direction in guiding his hand to his mouth, this act becomes a useful lifetime behavior.

Grasping behaviors then begin to develop, with objects being clutched by the whole hand closing. Reaching for objects is generally accomplished with both hands approaching, when the infant is on his back. Reaching directly for an object with one hand does not occur until the child has fairly good balance. Reaching for objects directly, holding them with various levels of grasp, transferring items from one hand to another, releasing them at will are all behaviors that emerge in normal developmental sequence.

In a study at our school, children with retarded development were observed and grasp levels were categorized (based on Halverson's work with normal infants):

Palmar Grasp

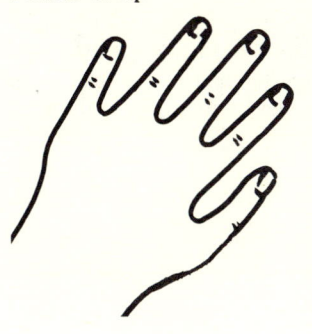

There is more palming than use of leverage at the distal metacarpals. Proximal phalanges are flexed and distal phalanges extended or flexed depending on the size of the object. The child approaches material desired with flat hand, fingers extended and lightly spread.

Dagger Grasp

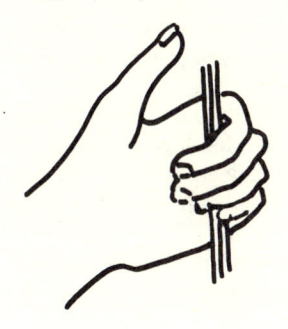

The manipulandum extends from the ulnar side of the hand in almost a vertical position. The thumb varies in its position:
Fingers flexed around object, thumb over fingers. Thumb enclosed by the fist.
Thumb used as leverage or assist.
Thumb extended alongside fingers and not in play.

Shovel Grasp

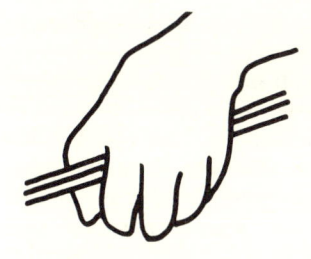

The manipulandum extends from the radial side of the hand. The wrist is radially pronated. The fingers and thumb are as described in dagger grasp.

Scissors Grasp

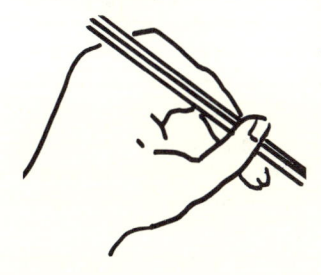

The manipulandum is held by the thumb adducted against the side of the index finger.

Pincer Grasp

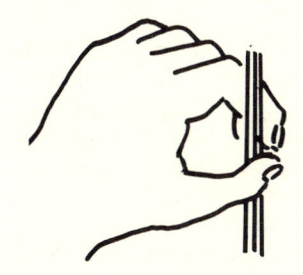

With finger-thumb opposition, the manipulandum is held against the thumb and tip of index finger (and/or middle finger).

Each kind of grasp serves a different purpose, and the ability to draw on a repertoire of grasp behaviors is essential in performing all the activities of daily living. One cannot effectively pull on boots, hold heavy objects, throw or catch a large ball, or turn a doorknob using a pincer grasp; nor is a palmar grasp effective to pull up a zipper, hold a pencil, use a light switch, or press a button.

We encourage children to acquire certain academic and self-help skills from the day they enter a classroom. Judgments on whether or not the child is ready to learn these skills are difficult. If he is not ready, the teacher, child, and parents may become increasingly frustrated and impatient with repeated failures. (Keep in mind that repetition of any behavior yields learned behavior and, therefore, failure itself becomes a learned behavior.)

Professor Viktor Lowenfeld (*Creative and Mental Growth*) found that there is a close correlation between the level of scribbling and other motor performances. Molloy Center studies found similar correlations. The sequence of motor activity described by Lowenfeld is as follows:

1. Random scribbling:

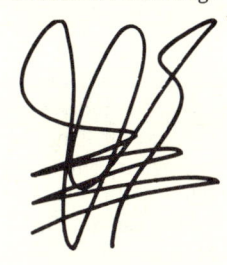

A "disorderly scribbling, bold or dainty in its lines, depending on the personality of the child." The child may hold the crayon in the palm, and will draw by moving the shoulder, raising the elbow up, down, and out. Children who are at this level are not yet ready to learn skills requiring fine motor coordination, such as dressing, buttoning, using scissors, tying laces, etc.

2. Push—pull:

Lines begin to show an up-and-down motion. The grasp of the crayon may be at about the dagger-shovel stage, with little control stemming from any wrist or finger movement.

3. Circling:

Many lines show a circular motion. The crayon or pencil may be handled with the same shovel-or-dagger grasp, but the fingers are beginning to exercise a little control.

4. Named scribbling:

The child begins to attach meaning to what he is "drawing," and goes about rather purposefully making lines and patterns. There is increased use of fingers and the wrist, less movement stemming from the shoulder and elbow.

5. *Emergence of schema:* The drawing becomes an obvious product to the observer. Clues to the child's own body image may be found in his reproduction of a human figure. The pencil or crayon may be held in the fingers, as in the scissors grasp; the pincer grasp is probably observable in at least some tasks, if not in this one.

The classroom teacher might find it beneficial in planning to observe closely what each child produces with crayon or pencil, and how each handles these implements. If the child is at scribbling stage #4-5, and is using a scissors grasp at least, then it is logical to start working on self-help skills, on using a pair of scissors, or on pre-writing skills. If he is handling the writing implements with a dagger or shovel grasp and is producing scribbling stages #1-2-3, then he will only be frustrated with repeated efforts to teach him to tie shoelaces, or reproduce symbols.

Differences in size, shape, texture, weight, and resiliency in objects result in variations in grasping behavior. The purpose of the object, and how the individual intends to use it, may also change his way of handling it. That means that *motivation* is important, and motivation is an elusive psychological factor that is difficult to pinpoint, and certainly difficult to generalize. What motivates one child may not motivate another. Or what motivates one child at a given time may not bring the same response at another time.

For instance, a child may use a pincer grasp to pick up a small piece of candy or sugar-coated cereal to put in his mouth. When buttoning his coat, however, he may attempt to pull the button through the buttonhole with almost a palmar squeezing of the fabric and the button. Put a small piece of candy through the buttonhole so that he sees it emerge just as a button would. Watch him carefully extract it, using a pincer grasp—plus "Motivation." Now put the button through the hole, same position; follow it with the candy. He will eventually get the idea that the dainty pincer grasp might be used for more than finger-food. The motivation has been a primary reward, and learning takes place as the result of repetition and reinforcement of a behavior.

As an adult, consider the activities in which you engage each day, and note the kinds of grasp you are using.

Palmar

Brushing your hair? The brush will probably have a fairly substantial handle, and you will find it necessary to hold it securely in your palm. Movement in your shoulder, arm, and wrist will direct the brush.

Shovel

Brushing your teeth? The toothbrush will often be held with three or four fingers, with the thumb for leverage. The wrist will be pronated and movement will stem from the raised elbow, the shoulder, and the wrist.

Dagger

Using a bottle brush? A small hammer? Or a knife to loosen a cake or jello mold from the edges of a pan? All of these implements may be held in the dagger-like position, with jabbing motions stemming from the wrist and elbow.

Scissors

Holding some papers in your hand to read? A scissors grasp is comfortably used and keeps the pages secure and wrinkle-free.

Pincer

Using a pencil, a needle, a zipper-pull? The more precise pincer grasp is the most convenient.

We must offer a variety of motor activities to each child, so that his experiences in reach, grasp, and release are constantly reinforced, and his grasp experiences are enriched on every developmental level.

There has been frequent reference to "normal development." Children with retarded development generally lag in motor behaviors, just as they are slow in acquiring other behaviors. However, normal sequences should be the basis for evaluating and planning for retarded children. A teacher needs to assess what the child *does* in order to give him added experiences in using those motor acts, and to introduce other activities and new opportunities for him to experience new motor behaviors. Growth and development is a continuous process, occurring in many aspects of an individual's life at any given time. The process should never be segmented by teaching to only one unit or step.

The choice of materials and activities is unending. Each of us has individual aptitudes, skills, training, and background experience that affords uniqueness to teaching. The selection of materials and activities in the following outline is only a *sampling* of possibilities. Consider the grasp level, the scribbling stage, the gross motor development, the individual child's own background and social experience, his chronological and mental age. These will all give clues to the selection of appropriate materials.

When a child first enters your classroom, provide him with crayon and paper (shirt cardboards are excellent). Observe the way he holds the crayon and what he produces. Frustration and failure can be avoided by planning a program for him that will involve the use of materials and activities with which he can be successful. Wait until he has shown some degree of abduction and/or opposition of the thumb and forefinger before introducing fine manipulative skills.

The use of scissors is often expected on a primary level. However, success in this area cannot be expected unless the child has developed at least to the scissors grasp.

Instruction in using a pair of scissors would begin with "open-shut" hand activities. Have the student play with a child's tongs, picking up cotton balls, once he has achieved the open-shut movements. When thumb movement has developed to the point where he is able to separate thumb movement from total hand movement, then he should be able to manipulate the tongs well enough to pick up cotton balls and release them. Then control will improve so that he may be able to pick up other small items, such as ping-pong balls.

The scissors may be attempted then, and these should be held with the thumb and middle finger inserted in the handles, with the forefinger adding leverage to the blade held by the middle finger. The child's wrist and forearm should rest on the desk with the side of the hand and the thumb perpendicular to the desk. By moving the thumb up and down, "open-shut" cutting action is achieved.

The teacher should sit opposite the child and hold the paper securely so that the child can make single cuts along the edge. Very narrow strips of paper held tautly by the teacher enable the child to cut "pieces." Often when the teacher stops holding the strips of paper with two hands, the child will automatically reach to hold on with his other hand. When he is able to make several cuts consecutively, have him cut a triangle, with the base of the triangle being the edge of the paper. A rectangle is the next geometric form that may be cut, with the circle being the most difficult. Use a magic marker to outline what is to be cut, as this affords him a wide definite line to follow.

A word of caution relating to manipulative skills requiring considerable coordination and finger dexterity: it is extremely difficult for anyone to perform such activities if "off-balance." One must feel secure in sitting or standing when engaged in fine motor activity. Until balance is well-established, or complete security is offered to the ataxic or impaired child by seating him in a chair with his feet on the floor or on a foot-rest, performance of fine motor activity will be extremely difficult.

Questions on hand dominance are also correlated to gross motor development and the establishment of balance. When a child feels insecure and must constantly "rescue" himself from falling over to one side or the other, he has little opportunity to use one hand more than the other. Both arms will be going into protective extension at any time. Therefore, when you are working with a child who seems to use both hands equally often, concentrate on improving his balance rather than imposing a dominance on him. Balance beams, kept in each classroom, are used at circle time, recess time, etc., and are accessible to the children during the school day.

Motor Behaviors

    Grasp reflexively

    Watch own hands while supine in crib

    Touch, scratch on contact

    Push

    Palmar grasp

    Hand to mouth activity

    Squeeze and release

    Shovel grasp

Materials and Activities

Crib mobiles

Stuffed toys, textured items

Roly-poly rattles, balls

Depending on child's age, size, etc., use various textures, resiliencies, shapes, sizes in beanbags, stuffed toys, blocks, pegs, bells with handles, etc.

Use water play
   sand play
   silly putty (Thera-plast) for pulling
Hair brushing
Pulling on hats, boots, pulling up slacks
"Tug-of-war" with towel

Plastic rings
Rattles
Food
Horns to blow

Squeaky toys
Flexible toys with different degrees of hardness
  and softness
Meat baster, in water play (add food coloring
  to the water to increase interest)

Large plastic spoons, pounding or stirring
  or mixing
Cubes
Balls
Winding toys that have large handles or knobs
Spoon to feed self (if old enough)

Motor Behaviors	Materials and Activities
Slap, push against	Suction toys that bounce back Water play Balloons, balls Dangling toys
Reach (with open hand)	Suction toys Dangling objects Toys offered at varying heights and distances from the child
Grasp and shake (dagger or shovel grasp)	Bells Rattles Dangling, noise making toys Plastic "hourglass" Containers with water, beads, marbles, seeds, etc. securely stored inside Containers for cubes or large items (that cannot be swallowed)
Hold with both hands	Large stuffed animals or dolls Large balls or balloons Pillows or bolsters Bars, as on a "cradle-gym" Water play (use an egg beater) Broom or mop Pulling on hat, boots, pulling up slacks Holding hoop or jumprope
Reach, grasp, and release	Blocks and pegs Rattles, small toys with various textures, shapes, sizes Bean bags and balls Pegs (eventually precise release into formboard) Puzzles Small items into containers Never ending list involving self-care tasks
Grasp and transfer from hand to hand	Cubes and pegs, etc. Feeding procedures Passing a ball or bean bag around in a circle (Until balance is thoroughly established, dominance of one hand over the other is difficult. Until that time, the infantile behavior of transfer from one hand to the other is a much used behavior.) Shoe tying Buttoning Shoelacing Bead stringing
Poking	Small pellets, beads, sugar-coated cereals, etc. Toys with openings, forms, etc. for small fingers to poke through

Motor Behaviors   *Materials and Activities*

    Scissors grasp

                                           Toys and implements small enough to handle with
                                               this finer grasp
                                           Water play with eyedropper and vegetable color, etc.
                                           Bead stringing
                                           Handling of papers, small books
                                           Adjusting clothes
                                           Unrolling toilet tissue
                                           Using a scissors

    Pincer grasp

                                             Picking up small bits of finger food
                                           Using medicine droppers in water play
                                           Finger cymbals, or buttons attached to rings of elastic
                                              to fit on thumb and tip of forefinger
                                           Holding lace for bead stringing
                                           Zipping, buttoning

Other Movements to Observe and Encourage:

    Pulling motions

                                           Pulling down on strings, items hung in cribs, etc.
                                           Pulling toys toward self by means of cord or string
                                           Using pull toys correctly

    Two-handed activities
       with same movement bilaterally

                                           Catching or rolling a ball
                                           Dumping pail of sand or water
                                           Pushing self up from prone position to rest on
                                           both forearms and elbows
                                              (This is an excellent position to do reach,
                                              grasp, and release activities; when body weight
                                              is supported on the shoulders and upper arms,
                                              the forearms, wrist, and fingers function
                                              with greater differentiation.)

                                              Hand clapping
                                              Dressing activities

    Two-handed activities with
       different movement on each
       side

                                              Toys or activities demanding that one hand hold
                                              down an object and the other manipulate such as:
                                                 Wind-up toys
                                                 Egg beater in water play
                                                 Shovel and pail in sand play
                                              Pouring water from one container into another
                                              Drawing or writing, with one hand as support
                                              Bead stringing

    Wrist movements

                                            Rotation of wrist—swishing water with hand,
                                            using a doorknob
                                           Pronation of wrist—pushing against toys with
                                            open hand, bouncing a ball,
                                            shoveling sand
                                            Supination of wrist—carrying object in open hand,
                                            balancing balloon on fingertips gently,
                                            using eating utensils (spoon and fork) correctly

    Finger movements

                                            Extension—clapping, fingerpainting, pushing
                                            on surfaces
                                            Flexion—squeezing sponges in water play,
                                           holding tightly to slim objects
                                            Separation of each finger—typing, piano playing,
                                            "counting down on fingers"

Summary

Objects to be handled have varying characteristics, making it necessary for all levels of grasping behavior to be used. Reach, grasp, and release are motor behaviors that develop in a sequential order. Grasp behaviors are at first accomplished in a gross way and become more refined and precise as normal development occurs. A pincer grasp is normally observable in a one-year-old child, with grasp becoming more differentiated and refined as the child grows and develops in other areas of motor activity and physical maturity.

All types of grasp are desirable, if each is used appropriately for given tasks. Substitution of one for another comes with successful experiences in using each grasp type in many situations. Provide opportunities that are correlated to each child's developmental stage, challenging in content and variety. Exploit each step of motor behavior the child has demonstrated, opening the door gradually to new motor behaviors. Be aware of the complexity of motor planning and motor acts involved in seemingly simple activities and motor behaviors that we do "automatically." Repetition and reinforcement of each successful performance is the only way the motor behavior is learned. Success breeds success.

18. SELF-CARE

"I can do it myself!"

The tasks involved in learning self-care are listed in sequential order of difficulty and necessity (as far as can be determined) in the Performance Goals Record.

Each group's lesson plans and curriculum outlines include the tasks and criteria that can be expected at its particular level.

Maturation, both physical and social, is basic. One can hardly expect a child to manage clothing for toileting if his grasp function has not matured past the dagger level. Buttoning and zippering are very difficult if the focal point of manipulation is on the ulnar side of the hand and still difficult without good opposition, either scissors or pincer, as described in Chapter 17.

Motivation is a positive factor in manipulation skills. Some of our children, using a dagger grasp rather consistently, suddenly employ a pincer or scissors grasp to retrieve sugar-coated cereal or M & M's. It must be determined if a child *can or cannot, does or does not*, use a grasp that enables him to manipulate clothing, utensils, and necessary gadgets such as water faucets, drain closures, and toothpaste tubes. Frustrations have been heaped upon our children through demands that they tie their shoes or button a shirt when their hands are not ready.

A four-year study, "The Development and Enhancement of the Grasp Function in Young Retarded Children," statistically supports a significant correlation between grasp level and basic manipulation required in dressing, toileting, and feeding.

The child care training program has revealed some very interesting observations. As we teach our teen-agers to "teach" the little ones such tasks as washing hands, their own skills seem to improve, truly giving meaning to the parable "To teach is to learn twice."

The target tasks should be reported to parents to enlist their cooperation. Their involvement is essential, as it does little good to teach a child to feed himself or wash his own hands, only to have these jobs done for him at home. Demonstrating techniques for groups of parents will usually arouse sufficient interest to assure cooperation.

With the gracious permission of Mr. Cecil Colwell, superintendent of Columbia State School, Columbia, Louisiana, we are privileged to reprint his paper, "Teaching the Profoundly Retarded Child through Behavior Shaping Techniques." Although this material is concerned with the profoundly retarded child, the techniques are applicable to all children for whom self-care is a frustrating challenge. The minutely detailed task analysis of any clothing or feeding manipulation gives the necessary steps in learning a skill such as pulling pants down to use the toilet. The control of language, the stimulus-reward, using bridging signals appropriately, combine to motivate a child to complete a self-care task without any feelings of failure or frustration. As a one-to-one situation is necessary for shaping procedures, someone other than the classroom teacher must do this training. We arranged to have one of our most able aides be in residence at Pinecrest State School, Pineville, Louisiana, to learn shaping techniques. This has been a very profitable investment.

Behavior Shaping Techniques

Cecil N. Colwell

Background Information

Research in the last few years has cast doubt on many widely held concepts regarding the limitations of the mentally retarded. In teaching complex skills to retarded youngsters many have used a S-R reinforcement paradigm. Such an approach to teaching is the foundation for programmed learning and the teaching machine.

Ayllon and Michael (1959) found that nurses who used social reinforcement were able to teach desirable social skills to the mentally retarded. Zigler and Williams (1963) found social reinforcement to be more effective in motivating learning with the retarded who came from an environment which was not socially deprived. This illustrates the importance of first having to teach the child to respond to praise and other forms of social reinforcement.

Horowitz (1963) utilized a variety of physical and social rewards to stimulate language development among the retarded. She found that a combination of both was more effective than either type utilized by itself.

Girardeau and Spradlin (1964) used a program based on positive reinforcement to manage and train a group of moderately and severely retarded girls. Tokens were established as generalized reinforcers by making them redeemable in food, soft drinks, jewelry, clothing, and novelties. These tokens were given to the retarded whenever they were engaged in constructive and socially acceptable activities. They found that this method was effective in teaching skills such as bed-making as well as in improving social adjustment.

Ellis (1963) presented a theoretical analysis of this approach and suggested how it might be applied to teach toilet training.

Dayan (1964) applied this method of teaching to a group of profoundly retarded children in the area of toilet training. Many of the boys, age six to twelve years with IQs below 30, were able to learn to use the toilet independently and to remain dry at night.

Bensberg, Cassel, and Colwell (1965) applied this method to teach self-help skills, dressing, toileting, and feeding with six profoundly retarded children. These boys, age seven to fifteen years with an average mental age of one year, could not dress or undress themselves and could feed themselves only with their fingers. After three months of training, they were completely toilet-trained, could feed themselves with forks and spoons, and could dress themselves with only minor help. Their social behavior changed even more dramatically. Prior to the training project, the children frequently had to be controlled through physical or chemical restraint. They were unresponsive to verbal commands and had to be controlled through physical force or gestures. After they were in the training cottage for two months, they became more relaxed, more interested in their surroundings, and were anxious to please their cottage parents. Stereotyped behavior tended to disappear, and their level of frustration tolerance was raised. Several boys were taught to complete simple chores, such as hanging up clothing, making their beds, and sweeping.

Basic Principles

This method of training involves two major principles. First, it is based upon positive reinforcement or reward. It has been demonstrated that people tend to repeat behavior which is followed by something pleasant or desirable. Behavior which is not accompanied by positive reinforcement tends to disappear or extinguish. How many people would continue to fish if they never caught a fish? How many comedians would we have if they never got a laugh? How many bowlers would we have if one never were reinforced with a strike?

Unfortunately, most retarded children experience little success in life. The result is that most have just stopped trying!! Neither their environment nor the people around them give them much pleasure, because they have not been able to make things work and thus earn from other people a social reward. They do not receive, as do normal children, praise or approval for small things learned. Long sequences of behavior ending in the pleasure of accomplishment are impossible for these children.

The exact, precise use of rewards changed the outlook on life of the retarded with whom we worked. They began to see their world as a nicer place, where people were good and things were fun. No longer were they afraid to face new situations.

The second principle, and the one which has major implications for teaching methods, is based upon the concept of gradually leading the person to make the correct or desirable response by rewarding each improvement. Complex tasks are divided into parts and one part taught at a time. Initially, some persons were rewarded or reinforced for making a response which was only remotely related to that which we ultimately desired. How we break these tasks down into parts and the order in which we teach are extremely important, we have found.

Each task or skill was examined and studied carefully. We began our teaching with the easiest part. We work from the simple to the complex, often from the end back to the beginning, gradually increasing the difficulty of the task. Our approach is based on rewarding successes and every effort is made to keep the child from experiencing failure. When the children fail to learn or succeed, it most assuredly has a profound effect on the teacher as well as on the student.

Each child has an individual tolerance level for how long he will try and what he will do to get the reward. The key is to stretch this tolerance level, but not to exceed it.

Teaching New Steps and Skills

When teaching a new skill, always make sure the child understands what you want him to do. Show him what you want; then, help him do it and *reward* him even though you did the most. You might do this several times; then hold out for some effort on the child's part. *Teach the last step in completing a skill first.*

The standard procedure is based on ten steps:
1. Show him the reward.
2. Give the command and gesture.
3. Give the child time to respond.
4. If he doesn't follow through say "no" and take the reward out of sight. (Make sure he understands the request.)
5. After a short time lapse, repeat the above. (Do not repeat the command over and over.)
6. If the child doesn't respond, try and determine why. a. Reward not strong enough? b. Is he sick? c. Is he tired or frustrated?
7. When the child responds and while he is doing the request let him know what he is doing by saying it over. (When he is taking off his shirt say "off," "off.")
8. Make a big fuss over the child when he responds. Reward *immediately*.
9. Teach one skill at a time, by steps. When they have mastered one step, move to the next.
10. Reward the step you are teaching and the completion of the skill.

Examples of specific task sequences are presented below:

TAKING OFF PULL-OVER SHIRT:
Command: "Take off your shirt."
Gesture: Forward half-moon arch.
Steps: 1. Take shirt off arm.
2. Take shirt off head and one arm.

3. Over the head and both arms.
4. Off from chest high.
5. Take off completely.

TAKING PANTS OFF:
Command: "Take off your pants."
Gesture: A downward motion with palms down.
Steps: 1. Pants off except for feet. Have the child step out.
2. Pants up to the knees.
3. Over the knees.
4. From waist.
5. Completely off, thus completing the skill.

PUTTING ON PULL-OVER SHIRT:
Command: "Put on your shirt."
Gesture: A backward half-moon arch.
Steps: 1. Pull tail of shirt down (shirt is completely on except for pulling it down). Give gesture for down and say "down."
2. Put one arm in.
3. Put both arms in.
4. Pull down over head.
5. Hold shirt and put over head.
6. Pick up shirt and put it on.

PUTTING PANTS ON:
Command: "Put *on* your pants."
Gesture: A sweeping upward motion.
Steps: 1. Pull up from right below waist.
2. Pull up from above knees.
3. Pull up from above ankles.
4. Hold pants, put one foot in pants leg.
5. Put both feet in pants legs.
6. Pick up pants and put them on.

TAKING SHOES OFF:
Command: "Take *off* your shoes."
Steps: 1. Take shoe off foot (shoe is off heel).
2. Pull off heel.

PUTTING SHOES ON:
Command: "Put *on* your shoes."
Steps: 1. Push shoe on heel.
2. Hold shoe in palm of hand and put over toes.
Tennis Shoes:
1. Catch each side of shoe and pull over heel.
2. Catch shoe and put over toes.

PUTTING ON SOCKS:
Command: "Put *on* your socks."
Gesture: A sweeping upward motion.
Steps: 1. Pulling sock up from ankle and say "pull."
2. Pulling sock up over heel.
3. Putting sock on toes (place sock over thumbs and guide them over the toes).
4. Holding sock open by self.
5. Picking up sock and finding the top.
6. Complete skill.

TAKING OFF SOCKS:
Command: "Take off your socks."
Gesture: Short downward motion.
Steps: 1. Sock is halfway off. Put thumb inside sock and pull off.
2. Sock is completely on; have him take it off, completing skill.

PUTTING ON BUTTON-UP SHIRT OR JACKET:
Steps: 1. Start with the shirt on except for one arm; have child put last arm in and reward.
2. Catch and hold neck of shirt.
3. Putting first arm in sleeve.
4. Holding shirt over sleeve (show child where to hold).
5. Pick up folded shirt and put it on.

BUTTONING:
Command: "Button your shirt."
Steps: 1. Pull button (attendant puts button through buttonhole).
2. Hold side of shirt at buttonhole and pull button.
3. Grasp button.
4. Put button in hole.
5. Finding buttonhole and lining it up with the button.
6. Button completely by self.

UNBUTTONING:
Command: "Unbutton your shirt." (Sometimes if they are having difficulty distinguishing between buttoning and unbuttoning, we say "Unbutton and take off your shirt" and give the gesture for taking off a button-up shirt.)
Steps: Method I.
1. Hold button and push through.
2. Hold side of shirt and complete skill.
Method II.
1. Flip button (always start at bottom of shirt).
2. Pull button through.

PUTTING BELT ON:
Steps: 1. Last loop (attendant puts belt on except for the last loop).
2. Next loop.
3. Back loop (if this is too difficult and the child gets frustrated, have him bring belt around to side loop, eliminating this step for now).
4. Side loops.
5. Go to back loop.

LACING SHOES:
Steps: 1. Take string in hand and push through until they see the tip. They are learning to pull. Any effort toward reaching for the lace should be rewarded.
2. Put the lace into his hand and push it through. They now know how to catch and pull.

3. Put the lace into his hand. He should take it and push it through. He can and will pull it through. Hold the string in palm, "Get the string, Roger." If two strings, hold both so they will see you make the choice. Hold his hand and help him make the choice later.

4. Child makes choice, pushes through the string, pulls it out with the other hand.

5. Completes process for all eyelets.

TYING A KNOT:

Steps: 1. Cross and drop each string.
2. Pick up strings where they are crossed, and hold.
3. Push string through, catch and pull.

Should you want to teach the last step first, just reverse the steps.

TYING A BOW:

Steps: 1. Pull finished bows tight.
2. Catch and pull string which is already through the opening. Tighten the bow.
3. Push string through the opening with the finger and finish bow.
4. Wrap string around, push through and complete.
5. Hold first bow, wrap string around and complete.
6. Make first loop of bow and complete.

Training Personnel

Who makes a good trainer or teacher? Our experience has shown that neither education nor intelligence is a crucial factor in making a good instructor. The most important factor seems to be that the person be able and willing to adjust to new things. Many persons through long experience in "handling" retarded children have closed their minds to any but their own method. Nothing will change their minds. Such people not only are unable to shape behavior but frequently fight actively against it. A second characteristic necessary for an instructor is the ability to stay on a schedule. Many of the procedures in behavior shaping will not work unless done exactly as they are taught. Third, the instructor must be consistent and even in temperament. The profoundly retarded child cannot adjust to an instructor who is kind and gentle today and irate and irascible tomorrow. Indeed, frequently a loud voice disturbs the children. Fourth, the good instructor can get along with other people. This approach requires teamwork and the instructor who remains aloof cannot function. Fifth, the instructor must speak clearly and distinctly and he must be adept at using gestures along with his spoken commands. Finally, the instructor must be able to keep an objective attitude toward the child. The instructor who lets the child "get his goat" is worthless. So too is the instructor who becomes so emotionally involved with helping the child that he does for him things he should do for himself.

This method of teaching works and works rapidly. We feel it offers much promise for all levels of retardates; however it does not replace sound principles of supervision and administration. Of equal importance, it does not replace effort and dedication.

Summary

This paper has described briefly a successful program for teaching the profoundly retarded at Pinecrest State School, Pineville, Louisiana. The method utilizes a combination of operant and classical conditioning techniques here referred to as behavior shaping. Major principles involved in this teaching method and necessary qualities of a good instructor were discussed.

Reprinted by permission of the author from *Mental Retardation*, selected conference papers edited by R.C. Scheerenberger, Illinois Dept. of Mental Health, Springfield, Ill.

REFERENCES

Allyon, T., and Michael, J. The psychiatric nurse as a behavioral engineer. *Journal of Experimental Analysis of Behavior*, 2: 323-334, 1959.

Bensberg, Gerard J., Colwell, Cecil N., and Cassel, Robert H. Teaching the profoundly retarded self-help activities by behavior shaping techniques. *American Journal of Mental Deficiency*, 69 (5): 674-679, 1965.

Cassel, R.H. and Colwell, C.N. Teaching the profoundly retarded self-help activities by behavior shaping techniques. In Bensberg, G.J., ed., *Teaching the Mentally Retarded*. Atlanta, Southern Regional Education Board, 1965.

Colwell, Cecil N. Attendant training project—Southern Regional Education Board. Paper read at the 89th annual meeting of the American Association on Mental Deficiency, Miami, Florida, May 1965.

Colwell, C.N. Administrative considerations in establishing a training program, in Bensberg, G.J., ed., *Teaching the Mentally Retarded*. Atlanta, Southern Regional Education Board, 1965.

Colwell, C.N. Teaching in a cottage setting, in Bensberg, G.J., ed., *Teaching the Mentally Retarded*. Atlanta, Southern Regional Education Board, 1965.

Dayan, Maurice. Toilet training retarded children in a state residential institution. *Mental Retardation*, 2 (2): 116-117, 1964.

Ellis, N. Toilet training the severely defective patient, an S-R reinforcement model. *American Journal of Mental Deficiency*. 68: 98-103, 1963.

Girardeau, Frederic L., and Spradlin, Joseph E. Token rewards in a cottage program. *Mental Retardation*, 2 (6): 345-351, 1964.

Horowitz, Francis. Partial and continuous reinforcement of vocal responses, using candy, vocal, and smiling reinforcers among retardates. *Journal of Speech and Hearing Disorders*. Monograph Supplement No. 10, 55-69.

Zigler, E., and Williams, T. Institutionalization and the effectiveness of social reinforcement. *Journal of Abnormal Social Psychology*, 66: 197-205, 1963.

19. PHYSICAL EDUCATION AND PLAY

*Health is the vital principle of bliss;
And exercise, of health.*
—James Thomson

An understanding of the physical growth patterns of young children and their socially acceptable play interests is basic to planning a profitable program for physical education and play activities for retarded children.

Large muscle activities must precede those activities requiring finer coordination of smaller muscles.

As the retarded child needs a long period of time to graduate from large to small muscle activities, a wide variety of materials is needed to hold interest and to reinforce each small gain in motor control.

Emphasis must be placed upon improving body mechanics.

Social games—such as shuffleboard, hopscotch, croquet—that will be useful outside of the school situation should be stressed.

The same basic principles for a good physical education program for normal children apply to a program for retarded children.

The program should provide activities that are physically stimulating, socially constructive, and aesthetically acceptable. A program planned with these criteria in mind contributes to the child's growth in all areas—motor, social, emotional, intellectual, and aesthetic.

Careful planning is necessary. The gym or playground must never be regarded as a refuge from the classroom.

Formal gymnastics have the same place in a physical education program for retarded teen-agers as for normal children. However, the number of physically able teenagers is usually too small to justify allocating time for a program of limited scope. An interesting project has been carried out with our teen-age boys, to demonstrate the value of formal gymnastics. The results of this project indicate that formal gymnastics are profitable to trainable teen-age boys.

Care should be taken that "free play" does not become an unorganized, overly permissive opportunity. Free play is valuable in learning to share, but requires structuring and careful supervision; it is probably the most difficult supervising that a teacher will undertake, either in the gym or in the playground. It is usually quite misunderstood and therefore loses its value.

From about 4 years of age until almost 8 years of age children participate most successfully in circle activities. As trainable children seldom pass the 8-year level in mental development, circle games hold interest throughout their school careers.

Simple team play such as a relay is enjoyed by many trainable children, but it is complicated for some of the children.

Rank or file formation games are well within the ability of trainable children.

Teaching Games

Teacher preparation for play or physical education period:

1. Plan play or physical education period carefully.
2. Select games suited to the development and interests of the children in the group.
3. Know the game thoroughly.
4. Be sure of the rules. Do not change them during the game. Before the play period modify the rules to assure the greatest possible success for the participating group.
5. Assemble all necessary material in an accessible place so that a child can procure it successfully.
6. Be sure adequate space is available and is free from any hazards such as equipment not put away, chairs, piano bench, doors ajar, etc. Check ventilation. Playground blacktop should be free of twigs, loose sand, broken glass, or trash of any kind.
7. Each gym period should start without delay, with marching or running, in order to blow off steam and ready the children to listen to instructions for the first activity.
8. An active organized game should be the first activity. A quiet game should follow. The last activity should always be a quiet game.
9. If all children in the group are unable to participate in a game, alternate the selected game with another game suitable for those not in the first game.
10. Do not play a game for too long a time. Change to another game before interest lags.
11. Include some rhythm activity in each play period—either with or without music.
12. Insist upon fair play and courtesy. The social values of group play are as important as the physical activity.

13. Announce the name of the game; do not explain too much or talk too long; answer any questions about it; show the children how it is played; start playing as soon as possible; urge them to participate actively.
14. Help the lagger.
15. Insist that children return all equipment to proper place.
16. Repeat the old favorite games but introduce new games frequently.

Coordination, rhythm, self-control, and self-evaluation are basic components of growth in locomotion, body mechanics, and manual dexterity:

Locomotion

1. *Walking*: Should be rhythmic, with heel touching floor first, the weight shifted via lateral side of planter surface to transverse arch, toes extending for thrust forward.

Many retarded children have neurological involvements causing a slapping gait. Direct therapy is of questionable value. Rhythmic exercise in a group will help to improve the gait without directing the child's attention to the problem he is actually unable to correct voluntarily.

Many mongoloid children lack some ligaments in their feet. This accounts for the badly pronated feet so often observed in mongoloids. Usually the gait is almost normal until the body weight reaches about fifty pounds, causing a breakdown in the longitudinal arches. To date, no experiments have been reported in the literature concerning the possible prevention of this breakdown. Corrective exercises such as those used for any pronation problem—if begun early enough before any breakdown occurs—might possibly minimize such a breakdown.

2. *Tiptoeing*: Walking on tiptoe should be taught and stressed for its muscle strengthening, coordination, and value in gaining a concept of "quiet."

3. *Running*: Should be rhythmic, with transverse arch touching floor first, toes extending for thrust forward.

4. *Jumping and hopping:* Jumping with both feet; later hopping on one foot, and alternating feet.

5. *Sliding*: Sideways "step-together-step."

6. *Skipping*: Skipping is very difficult for most trainable children. It is taught as a *hopsa*, a "step-hop, step-hop." A skip is actually a syncopated hopsa. When the hopsa is well-established, a change in beat and rhythm should shift the pattern from hopsa to skip. Many European folk dances are variations and patterns, using a hopsa. A polka, "hop—step-together-step," the Scandinavian hambo or schottische, are quite difficult to teach to trainable children, as the shifts of weight to syncopation are too rapid for the ultimate diadochokinetic development achieved by them.

Most folk dances and singing games can be modified to walk, slide, gavotte, slow waltzing, and balance steps, and still preserve their patterns, rhythms, and social values.

7. *Walking on balance beams*: Allow the child to walk the 6" beam any way by which he can succeed. After a few successful games are played and the child is comfortably walking the 6" beam in a way of his own choosing, begin to guide him toward a heel-toe walk. Start this by allowing ample space between foot placement, for easy balance. Teach heel-toe walking on a straight line on the floor before trying it on the 6" beam. Progress to a 4" beam, then a 2" beam.

Body Mechanics

Good posture in walking, standing, or sitting is essential for maximum physical well-being. Distribution of body weight, good ventilation, proper leverage in maintaining balance while lifting and lowering the body or walking result in a feeling of well-being and a minimum of fatigue.

Physical defects may preclude the achievement of good body mechanics. In the absence of actual physical defect, good posture should be stressed. The teacher must set a good example by maintaining good posture. Chairs and desks must be the proper height for each child. Adequate lighting helps to prevent slumping over desks. Games and exercises requiring reaching and stretching are good for posture improvement.

Mirror correction will give a child an opportunity for self-evaluation. This should be done by the teacher or nurse with the child alone. A record should be made of the self-evaluation and referred to when reminding (instead of nagging) the child to stand or sit tall.

Throwing and catching: Balls are the principal tools for most active games. Early training leading to the ability to handle balls is essential.

Many retarded children are afraid of balls because of sad experiences of being hit in the face when trying to learn to catch long before they were able to do so.

The target should not be a child as catcher until some skill in handling bean bags and balls is gained.

A rough textured 8" or 9" rubber ball is desirable.

Start ball-handling by rolling a ball with the children seated on the floor, legs apart. This can be done with music.

When control of the direction of a rolling ball is gained, it is time to start to use bean bags. Be sure to use a soft bean bag. Throw the bean bag into a large carton or wastebasket. Start with the carton on the floor, gradually placing it a little higher, to learn to aim at a good catching height.

A child's first attempt to toss a bean bag to another child should be very carefully guided. The teacher should be beside the catcher to protect the child and to assure success.

When the children have learned to toss and catch bean bags, progress to rough-textured balls about 8" or 9" in diameter.

If a child is very fearful of catching a ball, work alone with that child for short periods. Have the child sit on a chair with arms. Draw a circle about 20" in diameter, about one normal stride in front of the seated child. The teacher should stand about 10' away from the child. Throw the ball at the circle; it will bounce gently into the child's lap so the child can get the ball into his hands. A few sessions will usually overcome this fear.

Throwing activities, various bean bag and ball games, and bowling provide a wide variety of interest and motivation.

Bouncing: Bouncing a ball is a good coordination activity. It is difficult for many trainable children, as it demands fast and close visual-motor coordination. It should not be urged to the point of frustration.

Crawling: Crawling involves total body coordination. Playground barrels, anchored tires, and large cartons provide good opportunities for purposeful crawling.

Pulling and pushing: Use wagons, carts, and a variety of large push toys.

Climbing: Stair climbing must be taught to many trainable children. Sturdy practice stairs with firm side rails are used. The risers should not be open, as that can be frightening.

The child should hold onto a side rail with one hand, and the teacher should take the child's other hand during all practice on the stairs until confidence is established.

The single step—with an ample pause to regain balance and to shift weight—should be allowed until the child has acquired confidence in ascending and descending the practice stairs. As speed is acquired and good balance is obvious, the child should be urged to alternate feet.

Walking *upstairs* with alternate feet will be learned first. The child may require the single step to descend stairs for a much longer time than needed for ascending. Do not pressure. Real fear exists and must be alleviated.

Stall-bar climbing: Children love to climb stall bars. They will start with a single step. Retarded children may always climb in this manner.

Jungle gym: This is an excellent climbing apparatus, but great care should be maintained if children with convulsions are permitted to use it. It is almost wiser not to have a jungle gym than to have an attractive piece of equipment and restrict its use to a part of the group.

Overhead ladders: Simple hanging by hands or hand-over-hand progress on overhead ladders is good for posture and coordination.

Pedaling: Tricycles, toy tractors, etc. require good coordination. A stirrup arrangement can be placed on the pedals to hold the child's feet in place while the child is pushed along on the bike. Pushing the child along with his feet being gently forced into the alternating push-and-pull necessary to pedal a tricycle will gradually convey the idea of how to propel via pedaling.

Teaching the Children to Form a Circle

Circle games are desirable and extremely valuable to all children. Circle activity allows each child the opportunity to be the focal point of interest, if only momentarily, during some part of any circle game.

Two concentric circles, preferably 12' and 14' in diameter, painted or taped on the floor or playground blacktop, are excellent props for learning how to form a circle. These circles provide the structure for many games. They also provide a good "track" for tricycles and carts.

Placing chairs in a circle for young children to march around is helpful.

Sitting in a circle on the floor provides a very substantial start for circle games.

All children will distort a circle formation and crowd in toward the center during the excitement of a game. Sitting cross-legged—or with legs extended, feet slightly apart—will keep a circle fairly intact.

Placing four painted blocks or inset tiles at equal intervals around the painted circle will save much time in teaching square dancing.

These markers are useful in playing games to reinforce ideas about the clock; "quarter past," or "quarter of" (or "to" or "before").

Do not hesitate to modify a game to make it appropriate to a group. Success in accomplishing the object of the game must be assured. It is less confusing, however, if the *new* game thus modified takes a new name. The new name and modification should be carefully noted in the game card index. The teacher might forget the changed rules, but some of the children won't forget!

An up-to-date file card index, with necessary modification, is a help to the next teacher as new groups come along.

Each of our classrooms is equipped with a set of balance beams (Creative Playthings #NP 157). A modification of Kephardt's sequence is used. Each classroom runs its own competition. A token reward system is used.

The play or physical education period should be fun; it must be disciplined and it should end with a feeling of happy accomplishment for the children and the teacher.

20. HANDWRITING

The pen is the tongue of the mind.
—Miguel de Cervantes

This is a guide for teaching retarded children to write legibly. The level of functioning of a moderately retarded child does not indicate success in the spontaneous production of a free-flowing, spontaneous type of handwriting.

It is hoped that some of these children can progress sufficiently to write their names, addresses, and words needed in everyday chores in the home or in a workshop situation with supervision—namely in school, a sheltered workshop, or an institution.

Writing will also serve as a helper in word recognition and in learning to read through the levels of reading for protection and—as far as possible—into the level of reading for information.

The writing of Arabic numerals is included in this writing sequence.

There is always skepticism about the value of teaching a moderately retarded child to write. The justification of teaching a moderately retarded child to write is presented in these observations:

1. Writing is a purposeful and meaningful activity. The achievement in just writing one's own name is a source of tremendous personal satisfaction. Saying "I can't write" is a very frustrating and embarrassing experience and one the child will face over and over again.

2. Learning to write is not simply a means to an end. Eye-hand coordination can improve through this activity because it can hold a meaning for the child. He has a goal within his reach each day.

3. Writing reinforces the recognition of words and numbers that the retarded child must accomplish for his own safety and usefulness.

Several factors must be considered before starting this program:

1. Is dominance definitely established?
2. Is the neuromuscular development adequate to start such a program?
3. Is there evidence of a visuomotor perception disturbance?
4. Is an emotional component present?

To provide the answers to these questions the following battery is presented. You can gather some of these answers from samples of work already in the child's folder. The other items can be presented through play situations. Better results will be gained if you do not set up a formal testing situation and the child remains unaware that he is being tested.

1. *Determining dominance*
   a. *Obtain history* from parents on child's hand preference. (Ask mother to show you how she sat beside the highchair to feed the child. If the history shows any prolonged illness requiring long bed care, ask which side of the child was on the approachable side of the bed.)
   b. *Observe child* in play, eating, reaching for articles. You will have to make a project of doing this, setting aside a time for this observation, and keeping a checklist. Five trials for each action is a good sample.
   c. *Test handedness* using crayons, handling a spoon, and turning pages. When studying handedness be very sure that each item—pencil, spoon, or book— is placed directly in front of the child, perpendicular to the child. This is essential so that free choice of hand is allowed.
   d. *Test footedness* kicking a large rubber ball and stepping over a barricade. If child can go up and/ or down steps, note foot preference for first step.
   e. *Test eyedness* by having child peek through a small hole in the middle of a sheet of paper or by gun sighting.

2. *Neuromuscular development and visuomotor perception*
   a. *Check grasp.* The child should have a scissors or pincer grasp.
   b. *Study samples* of free scribbling to determine level of gross motor control. Determine whether the child is in the push-pull, scribbling, or full-circle stage of development.
   c. *Have the child hold* a crayon or large soft pencil and follow a moving light beam as it is tracked along a writing surface. Use a pen-type flashlight. Hold the light beam away from the child and toward the eleven o'clock position if the child is left-handed. This will enable the child to see the beam readily. Tap the beam with your fingernail to direct attention to it, if necessary. Guide the child's hand in following the beam with his pencil a few times, to be sure he knows what is expected. Use very few words. "Catch me—here" should be

enough to capture interest.

After a few successful trips toward the beam in a straight, pushing-away direction, move the beam in a variety of directions to observe the child's ability to shift directions with this compelling stimulus.

d. *Use the green clock game.* (See Appendix IV)
e. *Use the red clock game.* (See Appendix IV)
f. *Ask the child to copy a circle* (use same technique you would use in administering this item on the Stanford-Binet Form L test).
g. *Ask the child to copy a simple cross* (use same technique you would use in administering this item on the Stanford-Binet, Form L-M).
h. *Ask the child to copy a square* (ditto above parenthesis).
i. *Ask the child to copy a triangle* (ditto above).
j. *Ask the child to copy a diamond* (ditto above).
k. *Ask the child to write his name*, unaided, three times, presenting a heavy black line for a base line. *Accept anything the child offers as his "name."* He may present only a few scribbles, but if he feels that this is his name and smiles as he presents it to you, accept it cheerfully and go on to another task.

(Items c through j are in order of increasing difficulty. Stop testing procedure after two items are failed.)

3. *Emotional components*
   a. *Note mother's reactions* to your questions about early feeding.
   b. *Study case history* for notes on emotional overlays.
   c. *Observe tension* in gripping writing tool.
   d. *Check hands* for dampness.
   e. *Examine reverse sides of all paper* used for excessive pressures.

Implications from Findings

1. *Dominance* If dominance is mixed and the parent interview conveys evidence to strengthen the possibility that early habit has tended to pull the child toward left-hand preference, you are justified in encouraging the child to use right hand. However, when presenting a crayon or pencil to the child with mixed dominance, always offer the pencil in the mid line. If he shows no choice in hand selection, touch his right hand. If he vacillates, possibly more study of dominance is indicated before the teacher may conclude that she should encourage the use of the right hand.

2. *Neuromuscular development and visual-motor perception*
   a. **Note grasp.**
   b. **The level of motor functioning as indicated by the stage in which the child is functioning—scribble, push-pull, or circling—designates a starting point.**
   c. Failure or poor performance in following the light beam indicate the need for more basic eye-hand-coordination training before starting this sequence.

d. and e.
Use of the green and red clocks is diagnostic as well as therapeutic. Weak areas are noted. Practice should be planned using the clock games to improve the ability to direct a writing instrument in any specified or needed direction. Use the light-beam technique and guide the child's hand to get him started. Diminish the use of these helps when he gets the idea of what is expected of him.

f, g, h, i, and j.
The sequence of copying *geometric figures* is based upon development observations and clinical evidence. It is a valid indicator for establishing the maturation and the functioning level of visual-motor perception. Success in copying the geometric figures indicates the starting point for help through a carefully structured readiness sequence in visual-motor perception.

It is assumed that the retarded child is older than the age assigned to the production of these graded figures in the Binet Form L test. The child who is able to copy a diamond will be likely to progress through the writing sequence very rapidly.

k. The result of having a child write his own name, or attempt to write his own name—no matter how he does it—is highly indicative. The approach to the task, the correctness, legibility and spelling assist in establishing a maturation level. If the "writing" is bizarre, but consistently so, a visual-motor-perception problem cannot be ignored. Consistent bizarreness may be a form of perseveration. It may be some configuration upon which the teacher may capitalize, as this configuration may hold meaning for the child.

3. *Emotional overlays*
Tension in gripping a pencil, damp palms, and heavy pressure observed are indicative of emotional overlays. When findings substantiate the existence of emotional overlays, success must be insured definitely and cheerful encouragement offered at each step of the way. Verbalization during the sequence item task will often help the child to be more relaxed and comfortable while working with writing tools. Possibly the parents began pressuring the child to write his name long before he was able to do so. This possibility should be explored and the cooperation of the parents enlisted.

Materials

As you will use a great deal of paper for each child, newsprint is recommended. It is inexpensive and available in desirable large sheets. Newsprint should always be well anchored at each corner with Scotch tape or masking tape.

Shirt boards are very good and are also "inexpensive."

Use felt pens or crayons—color to be selected by the child—or beginners' soft lead pencils. Wrap the pencil-gripping surface with a rubber band or a small collar of modeling clay to keep fingers from sliding too far down toward the point.

You will need *bound* tracing paper. It is less apt to slip and is easily kept in dated order. This facilitates self-evaluation. If bound tracing paper is not available, make a tablet of *dull-finish* tracing paper by fastening strong staples through three holes in a half-inch stack. Cover this with hinged tagboard covers. This kind of binding will allow a tagboard pattern card to slip under the tracing sheet and be held quite firmly.

When a child is ready for tracing, he should have his *own* bound "writing book" which is *his* tracing tablet. Each page should be dated as it is used. Self-evaluation is the strongest motivation. A tiny star placed in the lower right-hand corner of the page the child selects as "best" of each week's work is a source of great satisfaction.

For reproducing, as the child begins to graduate from tracing, use a dull-finish white typing paper and draw the necessary spaced lines with black crayon or colored crayon if perseveration is a problem.

Small counting sticks in four colors, to match the colors appearing in the sequence designs, may be needed.

Clay for "tracing" should be rolled into "snakes" in advance—using four colors selected to match those appearing in the sequence designs—and presented in a handy small tray. These clay snakes may not be needed, but if the child is having serious difficulty in tracing, they will be of tremendous value.

Modeling clay rolled to cover a small cookie sheet about 3/8″ thick will be helpful for the child experiencing difficulty in shifting from one configuration to the next in the tracing sequence. A butcher's skewer may be used as a stylus in place of a pencil.

Paper for actual writing should be lined at 1″ and interlined as both lower- and upper-case letters are employed. One-inch-square lined primary writing paper should be available.

White paper is preferable; colors are being reserved for foreground stimulation.

A pen-type flashlight such as doctors use will produce the light beam required by some children as a guide.

Techniques

Sit close beside the child on his dominant side. This enables the teacher to hold the light beam and to guide the child's hand, or to verbalize very quietly for his benefit only.

On all circle exercises be sure the motion is counterclockwise, regardless of dominance.

On confined circle exercises be sure to start at the "one-o'clock" point and go counterclockwise.

Verbalize as ingeniously as possible. Use jingles, either sung or singsonged, whenever appropriate in scribbling or making circular motions.

In using the clock games do not allow the paper to be moved. Place the paper squarely in front of the child and anchor it firmly. Shifting the paper destroys the purpose of the task.

When letters are being produced do not add extraneous cartoons and characters holding these new symbols. The direct approach, plus appropriate but sparse verbalization is most practical when letters are being formed.

Always sound the letters or words as they appear in writing practice.

Use self-evaluation as soon as any gain has been made.

Always start with success. Be sure that the first task of each session is something the child can do. You must know the child thoroughly to do this.

The Sequence

1. *Large muscle activity*

   a. Encourage the child to do free scribbling with full-arm motion.

   b. The child should be urged to make a push-pull stroke with his pencil or crayon. He will probably do better if he loops into the reverse action rather than lifting his pencil and attempting to repeat the action.

   This push-pull stroking can be encouraged by placing a turnaround at the ends of his own set course. Use the small discs from a wooden-block cone, or two large, bright flat beads or buttons. He can play "Go get the paper for Daddy, and bring it into the house—Go get it again," etc. As quite a bit of practice is needed to gain control of this action, a shift in color of crayon can alleviate possible boredom. A change in verbalization will appeal to the child's interest. The teacher can actually help with color awareness by saying: "Red goes out—*Red* comes home," etc. Be careful to use one color only in addition to black at each session. Avoid possible confusion. The color is secondary to the objective of intrinsic hand control.

   Playing "You chase me" is fun, and an early step toward controlling direction. Using a large sheet of newsprint, the teacher places a brightly colored block—the plain, 1″ Bradley cubes are good—on the paper. The child is supposed to push his crayon to the block. The teacher then moves the block to another spot and the child pushes the crayon to that spot. This continues in the same manner. It can be lots of fun as the teacher speeds up the game. If the child's name is simple or short, it's fun to end up with the name "written" in very large letters.

   c. Inscribing large circles may emerge from scribbling or from the push-pull activities. Making large circles should be directed, with the teacher guiding the child's hand. As the child begins to guide his own hand he should be encouraged to inscribe large circles—first in the air, then on paper.

2. *Progressing to more controlled direction*

   a. The large, sweeping circles will begin to trace themselves. When the child shows that he is gaining control of the production of large circles, it is time to start helping him to make smaller ones. Use smaller paper to urge smaller circles. If the child has difficulty confining his circles to a smaller area, the teacher should place her hand at the top of the paper and say pleasantly: "Don't touch me!" The teacher can almost verbalize the child into making a smaller circle.

   b. Vertical crosses should be mastered, followed by oblique crosses. Do not mix these tasks. One definitely comes before the other. Use large newspaper, well anchored, and a soft primary pencil or black crayon. Sit beside the child on his dominant side.

   Draw a horizontal line, from left to right, about two inches long. Then cross it with a vertical line of the same length, drawn from top to bottom.

Indicate that the child should do it too. If he does not proceed, the teacher should cover his hand, holding the pencil with him, and draw the crisscross saying: "Like this" (rising inflection in voice) "and like that" (falling inflection in voice). Make a few crosses, guiding his hand; then wait to see if he will try it. If not, draw the horizontal line, wait, and then urge the child to draw the vertical line. If he does not proceed, guide his hand a few times. If he continues to be unable to do it, go back to some of the easier games where success is assured. Proceed with the oblique crosses in the same manner. However, the oblique crosses should not be attempted until the child has good control of the square or vertical crosses.

 c. Learning to confine lines within specified limits is started with the "railroad-track" game. Two black parallel horizontal lines—the tracks—are made by the teacher. Start from left to right. Have the child use a small toy engine and chug along the tracks as you draw the ties. Trains just can't run without ties, so ties are drawn on the tracks from top to bottom as the train progresses. This compels a left-to-right progression. The child is urged to draw ties for the train as the teacher moves the train from left to right. If the child tends to perseverate and stack the ties one upon the other, have him change crayons after drawing each tie and say "Here we *go*! Here we *go*!"

 d. As control in drawing "ties" improves and spacing is notable, the next step is toward more confined direction and the ability to draw the lines (ties) either up or down. To accomplish this, draw two "tracks"—one green on top and the other red at the bottom—about two inches apart. Always start on the green track and go to the red, where you must stop. These tracks can be reversed to change the direction. This can also be used as an independent task.

 e. Large circles can be confined within a series of narrowing lines until they can be well done at a 1½" diameter. The narrowing of circles and confining of lines may take several months of daily practice. The eye-hand control gained is profitable in all areas requiring careful manipulation.

In both line and circle confining it may be necessary to have the child trace directly upon a sample until he perceives the confined space. Use a color to trace the black sample so the child can evaluate his success.

If difficulty is experienced in getting the child to start his circles at "one o'clock" and proceed counterclockwise, a large green GO sign placed at this one-o'clock spot will often assure success. It may be necessary to use light beam or actually to guide the child's hand to get him started.

If this step does not come easily, it can be a very rough course for a while, and can tax every bit of ingenuity the teacher can muster.

 f. Learning to guide a pencil purposefully in any direction

The red and green clocks used diagnostically are now used for training and later serve as an independent work activity.

Using a green crayon and moving counterclockwise, inscribe a circle approximately 8" in diameter—with the child watching. Say "Green means go"; then make a big 1" red spot in the center of the circle and say, "Red means stop." Pick up a pencil and say, "Now here is where we go" (making a big X at twelve o'clock). Guide the child to draw a line from the X in the green circle to the red spot in the center. Structure the situation; guide his hand; he must succeed as the teacher says "Go" and holds onto the O sound until his pencil reaches the STOP sign and she actually says, abruptly, "Stop!"

Without moving the paper, place another "Go" at the three-o'clock position and proceed to the six and nine-o'clock marks. Never shift the paper. The purpose of this activity is to make the child move his hand, directed by his eyes from or to any point in a 360° angle of his foveal vision. Always have the child watch the teacher inscribe the circle.

After a few successful days with this task present the process in reverse. Draw a red circle with a green spot in the center. *Start* on the green and *Go* to the stop marks on the outer circle.

As this is mastered, two circles are inscribed, side by side, on one sheet of paper—one with the green on the outside and one with the red on the outside. The necessary marks of twelve, three, six, and nine o'clock are made with Xs on the outer circles. Let the child proceed, but watch carefully to see that he always starts on green and stops on red. Allow him to verbalize, even when he has progressed to proceeding alone with these tasks. Be sure that his paper is taped down so it cannot be shifted.

Proceed by directing the child to fill in "lots of spokes, like a wheel," using a red or green wheel as the weaknesses in his control are shown.

Let the child evaluate his progress. Let the child decide where he may be having trouble and anticipate it by saying: "Now watch carefully—this is the hard part—let's look—and be very sure where we want to go—put your finger on where you want to go and . . ."

The difficult area is usually in the three to six-o'clock sector in either direction. A full view of the route is blocked off by the child's hand. Help will probably be needed, but patience and careful structuring will be rewarded.

 3. *Using visual motor control to produce a configuration with a definite meaning*

It is assumed that the child is having daily experience with three-dimensional materials which give him the opportunity to perceive shape, pattern, and space. Now the abstract lines and circles he is able to produce will begin to take a definite shape, and will become a pattern with a name and will occupy a space meaningfully.

Set patterns for tracing have been designed to give the child every opportunity to use visual-motor control. These patterns are presented in a definite sequence.

Constant self-evaluation in working with the prescribed pattern is of the utmost importance.

The patterns for tracing are made with felt pens on tagboard, cut to fit the tracing tablet.

The patterns for reproduction are made on tagboard, with colored felt pens. Be sure the color is bold, using red, bright blue, bright green, purple, and orange. The patterns are identical for tracing and for reproduction, except for color. The color shifts with each pair of lines. When the child starts to reproduce these patterns he will need guidelines drawn for him to help him organize his space. The shifting of colors will slow him down and prevent any tendency to perseverate.

The patterns for tracing are numbered in difficulty. The first two patterns are very simple to trace, so the child is assured of success. The child must be well able to confine vertical lines in a set space and be able to do well in drawing the spokes in both red and green clocks.

A new pattern is presented only when a good tracing and a good reproduction are produced on several successive days.

The patterns are designed to guide the child to inscribe lines and to shift in all directions. The lines are presented in pairs or in threes to help the child see that two or three lines may belong together.

The geometric patterns are presented to guide the child in shifting direction of the pencil to create a unit—one complete thing that has a name, a very special name. Naming the circle, square, or triangle is the beginning of symbolic production.

Starting to trace and reproduce in his very own writing book is a happy occasion and should be approached as an event of real importance. Present the first tracing card, and guide the child's hand, verbalizing if necessary when failure seems imminent. A few pages with help will usually suffice to start the child to trace independently. Four to six sheets per day should be ample. Be sure that the pages are dated and that the one the child likes best is starred.

When the child seems able to do a good tracing for a few days in a row, shift the tracing to reproducing without tracing. Paper the same size as the tracing paper is necessary, as mentioned above.

If the child has difficulty reproducing the patterns without tracing, use the colored clay or the colored counting sticks. Use these three-dimensional aids by laying them directly on the pattern card a few times. Then help the child to do the same on a clean sheet of paper, without the aid of the pattern. The teacher should then draw the colored lines for him where he put the sticks or the clay, so that the child has a record for his own evaluation.

If this additional aid is necessary, considerable additional help will very likely be needed. Patience and encouragement will eventually get the desired results.

If the child has difficulty finding the starting point for any tracing pattern, place a tiny, bright-green gummed circle (Dennison's) at the starting point. This can be felt through the tracing paper.

Frequent practice with the red and green clocks is suggested intermittently during the sequence of tracing.

By the time the tracing patterns are finished and each pattern can be satisfactorily reproduced, work on the child's own name should proceed.

Naming the geometric figures as he traces and reproduces them, the child has learned that certain configurations have names. He is "writing" something that means something. He can recognize his own printed name long before he is introduced to the process of learning to write. He is probably naming common objects in pictures and using many words in communicating.

Every child happily anticipates the day when he can write his own name.

As early as possible, without risking frustrations through trying to produce such difficult letters as *s*, *e*, or *r*, the teacher should make a tracing card with the first letter of the child's name in capital. Inscribe three of these letters to a line, repeating the line three times. Use this for a tracing exercise as soon as you feel the child is able to do it (can shift direction, control length of lines and size of circles). Use the shortest or most easily written nickname. "Bob" is surely much easier to write than "Robert." *Do not write the child's name in capital printing. Write it correctly*, with the capital letter, and correct Kittle small-letter manuscript. It is just as easy to do it correctly.

Make a special new tracing card with the child's own name printed with a felt pen in manuscript 1½" to 2" high. If the name is too long, turn the card and tracing tablet sideways.

Provide heavy, black base lines with a lighter top line. Inscribe a mid line to limit the lower-case letters. Allow ample space between sets of lines.

The child traces his name and then reproduces it, placing each letter directly below the traced pattern letter. If he has trouble, he may move up and retrace as often as he wants to.

Never hesitate to go back to an easier step to assure success at the end of a lesson if failure seems imminent.

As the child is working on writing his name, writing numbers and words useful in a school day comprise the subject matter for practice. Practice for writing his own name is an individual task when the child is ready. Help for this should be planned for in the daily program.

It is very easy to write "9 A.M. Hi!" This is the beginning of the school day. Writing this is in the realm of possibility and is a gratifying experience. All the letter configurations in this expression are the least complicated.

"OK" is rather easy to write. The child enjoys writing it as a sign of approval when the teacher gives him the word that his writing lesson has been done well.

All letters produced with straight lines are, of course, the easiest to produce.

We use the Kittle handwriting system consistently; the straight lines seem easier for our children to master. However, all the current systems—Palmer, Steck, Zaner-Blauser—are usable. The important point is that consistency be maintained. If a child is taught to write the letter "q" with a "circle and stick," he should not be confused by being confronted with the same letter being presented "g", a "circle and hook." I have seen experience charts in classrooms with the first letter of the alphabet written a, *a*, a, all in the same story. This is very confusing to a child with a learning disability. Mixing capital block printing (except when appropriate) with manuscript small letters should be avoided. A, E, F, H, I, K, L, M, N, T, V, W, X, Y, Z, are straight-line capital letters in the Kittle system.

i, k, l, t, v, x, z are the only straight-line small letters, unfortunately.

The "ball-stick-" letters are the next in ease of production; a, b, d, g, o, p, q. It is actually distressing that five of these seven letters differ only in the placing or limiting of these straight lines. Because of this easily confusing problem, the teacher should avoid presenting more than one of this group at any one time. As one of these letters is recognized, named, and reproduced readily, another of the group may be added. It is essential to proceed very slowly. Confusion among these seven letters is natural and devastating.

"Go" is a good starter. It can be used in connection with "9" A.M., Hi; 3 — go." "Three" is rather difficult to write. Being able to write and read these words that hold definite experiential meaning is a happy achievement.

Progress in letter production as the words are needed and useful. The day's schedule can be written and read, with a little ingenuity on the part of the teacher.

Small e, r, and s seem to give the most difficulty.

Writing all the words used in "reading" serves as a reinforcement and as strong motivation. These known words have definite meaning, as they are used in everyday life around school. The following are suggested words for writing:

Suggested Words:

own name	GIRLS	bleach	plates	Numbers (in order of usefulness in school)
address	MEN	detergent	trays	9, 10, 11, 12, 1, 2, 3, 4, 0, 5, 6, 7, 8
telephone number	WOMEN	(use name	brushes	large
name of school	LADIES	in caps)	combs	small
teacher's name	GENTLEMEN	flag	dry	pt.
driver's name	OUT	games	bathroom	pint
gym	IN	books	WAX	qt.
Nursery	PUSH	toilet	POLISH	quart
OFFICE	PULL	clean up	blankets	1/2 gal.
KITCHEN	UP	wash hands	cot covers	half gallon
SHOP	DOWN	wash dishes	cot parts	1 lb.
STOREROOM	towels	put away	ROPE	pound
BOILER ROOM	napkins	milk	rake	doz.
Playground	tissue	coffee	SUGAR	dozen
Music	soap	tea	FLOUR	1/2 doz.
Art	cups	glasses	BUTTER	1/4 doz.
BOYS	cleanser			

---

4. Shifting to cursive writing

Very few moderately retarded children gain much proficiency in cursive writing. The older children like to learn to write their names "like Mommy." Fernald's system, applied to writing the child's name only, will usually be successful.

The brain-injured child may develop a very good mastery of handwriting. This does not necessarily mean that he will succeed accordingly in productive writing. When a definite diagnosis of brain injury is made and the child progresses well through the course of eye-hand training directed at writing, it might be well not to attempt to teach manuscript but to proceed to Strauss techniques immediately.

Give the children plenty of opportunities to use what ability they have in handwriting. Some children can read the list of room numbers on a "milk-check" card and can make a check mark (√) in the correct places. Some can write the number of children present on the daily milk card or attendance report. Some can write the correct check-off on a bus rider's report.

A list of playground equipment on a card may be checked daily as things are properly put away and accounted for. These activities involve reading, writing, counting, and they are challenging and cherished jobs in the school complex.

The diaries kept by the older children are interesting and eagerly brought forth each day for the new entries and conversation.

The Frostig materials are extremely helpful and are used almost as soon as a child can hold a pencil or crayon in a scissors or pincer grasp. The tracing sequence (see above) is started first. When the child shows evidence of being able to control his tracings, shifting directions as required on the first few cards, the Frostig materials should be introduced. We have a shelved file of sheets of the Frostig sequence for easy access. As with the tracing sequence, the child must be able to evaluate, to judge for himself, how good his efforts are. Unless he is aware of exactly what is expected of him, and aware of how close he is to doing what is expected, the same errors will prevail. Self-evaluation is very important.

The programmed handwriting materials are magic for some children and very confusing to others. It will be interesting to learn what is involved in this procedure so that trial-and-error can be avoided in deciding whether to use workbooks and which ones to use.

EMOTIONAL GROWTH

21. BEHAVIOR

*The whole worth of a kind deed
lies in the love that inspires it.*
The Talmud

Behavior can be accounted for partly on the basis of outer environmental events, and partly on the basis of inner organic events.

What Are the Events and Experiences in a Child's Life that Can Lead to Behavior Problems?

Anticipated wants can easily keep a child from talking or becoming toilet-trained—if everything is done for him, why should he bother to try to talk or to do things for himself. When a parent knows his child has been labeled "retarded" it is easy to become indulgent, to let him get away with anything "because he doesn't know any better," and to supply all needs and wants before the child is ever aware of them.

All too often parents will expect brothers and sisters to give in to the retarded child instead of letting him learn about sharing and the give and take of everyday life. Then when the child doesn't get his own way, he throws a tantrum or retaliates very roughly. He is genuinely frustrated because he has been given every reason to expect to have the world turn just for him.

Frustration generates unacceptable behavior. A child who is brain-injured very often lives in a world that is all mixed up. He can't sort out sounds or what he sees to get real meaning. This child may be blessed with parents who are not too indulgent and who try hard to discipline or channel behavior but since the words he hears have no meaning he cannot obey them. His parents may feel he is guilty of "not minding" and punish him because of their own frustration, in which case he in turn will be frustrated because he can't understand why he is being punished.

Catastrophic episodes have been described by Kurt Goldstein as bizarre over-reactions to frustration when a brain-injured person tries futilely to do something. This sort of tantrum (it really isn't a tantrum because the child has no control of his behavior at the time) is a rough experience. It can be avoided if a parent or teacher is aware of its possibility and is able to intervene in the frustrating activity, and quickly change the focus and the pace.

There are times, however, when a quick change of pace is undesirable. Downs Syndrome (mongoloid) children are often described with the words, "He has stubborn spells—you can't budge him." This is very true if the child is expected to stop or start an activity too quickly. If you change the pace of a mongoloid child too quickly you will run into a complete balk. If you give the mongoloid child time to do something or warn him that time is running out the stubborn spells are avoided. If the young mongoloid is engrossed with a fascinating game or with getting a button through a buttonhole, and he is told to "hurry up now" or "put that away now," stubbornness is very apt to follow. This seems to be a mongoloid's way of showing the world that he will not be hurried or deprived of time to finish what his own plan of action calls for.

How Do We Encourage Acceptable Behavior in School?

First by knowing as much as possible about the child before trying to work with him. The teacher should know about seizure possibilities. Parents should freely discuss behavior observed at home. (Parents are prone to withhold information for fear the child won't be accepted in the school.) It is not unusual for the child to have a very different set of behaviors at school. The old saying that "home is where you act the worst and are treated the best" is too often true. Parents are frequently surprised to learn how good a child is in school—and sometimes we are surprised to learn how good a child is at home.

The school should present a picture of contentment and "wantedness." We set the pace for being pleasant with the first and last contact each day. The bus drivers are a part of our team. They meet with the principal and social worker on alternate Thursday mornings after the last run, and over coffee talk about how things are going.

During the day, we schedule time for free exploration with only a few books or toys around. The teacher takes time to listen to whatever the child is trying to convey and helps pleasantly with wraps, but only when needed. When free time is almost over, a gentle warning such as "almost time for school" or singing "Are you ready?" usually sends the children to their places in the circle or to an activity area. Good use of attention getters, such as gadgets or playing the game, "Is Tommy here?" provide the fascination that holds the child.

Lessons must be carefully planned so the program runs smoothly. Structured learning situation techniques avoid frustrations by assuring success. Each set of tasks or experiences must start and end with success. The teacher can manage such a program only if she is aware of the children's unique differences, has her objectives clearly in mind, and takes sufficient time. She must know what she is doing and why she is doing it. She must have many approaches and resources at her command. She must be quiet, pleasant, and firm. She must be very careful in the words she uses; too many words confuse our children, particularly the younger ones.

Through planned experiences (the teacher must be creative and resourceful) inroads can be made in the behavior dictated by the history. Careful record and journal-keeping and conferring with parents frequently are of utmost importance. So far a preventive management has been described. Frustrating situations are avoided. Usually behavior can be modified via this management.

Behavior Modification and Behavior Shaping

Behavior modification and behavior shaping are systems to enhance desired behavior by reinforcing it. This is often referred to as "reward training." For the practical application of these techniques, our thanks go to Cecil Colwell and Maurice Dayan, Pinecrest State School, Pineville, Louisiana. Reward training is a way of getting someone to do something successfully, so that he will eventually do the desired activity or behavior on his own. The way a person behaves, no matter who or under what circumstances, depends upon what happens to him as a result of that behavior. The result of the behavior, what happens to him, is called *reinforcement*. We learn only as a result of something happening to us. Reward training means that what happens is pleasant, is enjoyed, so we continue to behave in ways that earn us rewards. A contract exists that if you do something a certain way, you will be rewarded. The contract or *contingency* promises a reward or pleasure if you do your part. The effect of the reward (the reinforcer or reinforcement) is to strengthen or increase the desired behavior or activity that has just occurred.

Contingent reinforcement is a powerful tool. This technique can be used to teach a new behavior to a retarded child. To teach a new behavior the contract must be kept—the child is rewarded every time he does the desired behavior. This is called "*continuous reinforcement.*"

As soon as the desired behavior is learned, or the child acts as if he understands the contract or contingency, it is necessary to change from continuous reinforcement to *intermittent reinforcement* in order to keep or maintain the desired behavior. When the child does something just for the reward, he will become easily satisfied and may lose his desire—so we reward intermittently after several successful behavior responses.

There are two kinds of reinforcers—primary and secondary. Primary reinforcers are direct tangible rewards such as food and are received immediately upon doing, or even in some cases starting to do, what is the target behavior. Secondary reinforcers are smiles, hugs, pats, or tokens. Tokens are pennies, or bottle caps or color chips that can be exchanged for something desired when enough are earned.

Behavior shaping is taking a present behavior and molding it into a complex desired behavior. This is done in very small steps. For example, if you are using behavior shaping techniques to teach a child to take off a sock, you would pull the sock almost off, help the child to "pull it off" (he can't miss) and reward him immediately. The next time the sock is "less-off," and so on until he is doing the whole complex business of pulling a sock off entirely by himself before he gets a reward.

Sometimes shaping techniques are needed to teach the difference between two different situations involving the same behavior. It's all right to take off shoes at nap time or to change to gym shoes, but it isn't all right to take shoes off in the bus and throw them out the window. The set of conditions tells when behavior is desirable and a reward is forthcoming, and when behavior is undesirable and no reward is forthcoming.

Rewards should be forthcoming for each new behavior but only intermittently for established behavior. As new steps are completed you chain events together for a reward and fade out or increase the waiting time for rewards as desired behavior is established.

Before the shaping techniques can be used, the child must be attending to you or to the materials involved. This means he listens and turns his head to you or comes to you when you say "come to me" or moves toward you on command for the reward you represent. It is important to know what the child likes and what he will work for. All of us receive reinforcement for our behavior. Our rewards range from an M & M through smiles and words to Cadillacs, mink coats, and trips to Hawaii. Behavior shaping can only be done in a one-to-one situation. Behavior modification in some circumstances requires a one-to-one situation but can go on readily in a group.

A time-out room is a wonderful help for our children. It is a small, comfortable adjacent room, with no toys or books, where a child can take time out from the impact of his group or his tasks. It must never be regarded as punishment. The teacher gently suggests, when she notes behavior is escalating, "How would you like to (or let's) go in the other room for a while where it's quiet. You may come back when you want to (or when the little timer rings)." An oven timer can be set for any given number of minutes—never more than five—and when it buzzes, the teacher opens the door, smiles, offers her hand and maybe a reward.

A change of pace or activity will usually prevent acting out behavior if the teacher is alert to the points of frustration. Self-evaluation helps. When a child has learned from experience what is desirable behavior and what is not desirable the teacher can ask the child, "What do you think about that?" or "How do you feel about that?" or "Tell me how you feel about it."

Involving the Parents

A conference with the parents can be very profitable in clarifying a behavior problem. When talking to parents about their child's behavior, try to put yourself in their place. How would you like to hear about it? What understanding do you need and seek? You will learn more from the parents by simply admitting that Tommy's behavior has you baffled and that you need their help. Follow this with, "Tell me how you manage Tommy at home." Be very careful not to insinuate that what they are doing is wrong. You don't really know (though you might suspect—and you might be right). If you can guide the conversation to enable the parents to talk it over between themselves, clues might be forthcoming. If it is obvious that the parents need help in understanding and controlling their child, you can provide them with things to read. Two excellent books written especially for parents bewildered by their child's behavior are: (1) Lewis, Richard S., *The Other Child*, published by Grune and Stratton, New York; and (2) Patterson, Gerald R., and Gullion, M. Elizabeth, *Living With Children*, published by Research Press, P.O. Box 2459, Station A, Champaign, Illinois, 61820.

Should undesirable behavior persist despite all efforts to condition and modify, the physician should be consulted. Drug therapy has made good citizens out of unmanageable children.

Involving the Physician

The question is asked frequently, "How do you gain the cooperation of the physician?" If a school nurse is on the staff, she should be able to communicate with the attending physician. She should talk to the parents before contacting the physician unless it has been definitely established that the parents are unable to convey the problem and understand the discussion. Parents find it very difficult to describe disturbing behavior and tend to either minimize the situation or exaggerate it beyond credibility. Most doctors thank us for our observation and interest. A few seem to resent any intrusion and this is regrettable.

The teacher's daily journal should record behavior that draws attention to itself. Careful and frequent review of the journal can help the teacher keep things in perspective. We are all prone to react to the worst behavior and forget the good days. What happened on the good days? What was going on? What happened on the bad days and what was going on? Sometimes the answer can be found in such a review plus some soul-searching. I would not point the finger at the teacher and say, "It's your fault" any more than I would tell the parents, "It's your fault." Some children are hyperactive and as uncontrollable as a loose fire hose for no apparent reason. These are the children for whom medication has been a godsend.

Parents keep us informed of their children's medication needs. And when we know a doctor is trying to find the appropriate controlling medication, we are vigilant in spotting behavior changes. If it becomes apparent that no inroads are being made, we ask the parents to contact their physician or we make the contact ourselves.

Seizure management is completely dependent upon good communication among parents, physician, and school. The children themselves seldom recognize the aura, the signals that a seizure is about to take place, so we keep a record readily available describing the aura. Our teachers know the signs in their children and we have very few seizures that are not anticipated. In some cases, when prescribed, the nurse has appropriate remediation available. Should the seizure pattern change, it is reported immediately to the parents and the physician.

What Is Unacceptable and/or Inappropriate Behavior?

Persistent disruption of group activity or behavior that is dangerous or threatening includes attacking another child, exhibitionism, destruction of things in the environment, whacking the bus driver on the head. Such behavior is unacceptable and inappropriate in a school situation.

A teacher cannot manage to contain a class when such behavior exists without the help of another adult. Behavior modification techniques on a one-to-one basis have been successful in many instances. Medication has been very successful. A combination of behavior modification and medication has worked out very well, the rationale being that the medication quiets the child so he can comply; then via behavior modification he can perform and respond appropriately. The good behavior is rewarded, and a chain of happy events can take place. The medication then can be discontinued.

In the event that none of these remedies is effective, the school has no choice but to excuse the child.

Nothing is sadder in a school situation than the repentent "I'm sorry" aftermath of an incident that the child truly regrets but was helpless to avoid. A teacher must do some quick soul-searching to be able to comfort the child rather than punish him—and punishment in such cases is a sheer waste of time. Its only purpose is to provide an outlet for the teacher's—or, if it happened at home, the parents'—frustration. What the situation calls for is wise understanding as well as management.

The truly psychotic child cannot be served profitably in a school for children with retarded development. However, inadequate diagnostic procedures frequently refer a psychotic child to a facility for children with retarded development. If a child *is* retarded *and* psychotic, management is very difficult and services are very sparse. Prevention of the development of a psychotic overlay is a challenge to both school and parent. A social worker can help if the signs are recognized in the early stages. Unfortunately this is not often the case. Parents are often reluctant to use the medications prescribed by doctors. They say, "It makes him groggy" or "He's no good with that stuff" or "He'll be an addict." We must look to the physician for help in these cases.

All in all, working together; good record-keeping; staying in close communication with the parents, the physician, and the school, are the productive ways toward behavior management. A conforming child is usually a happy child, particularly if he feels that he is conforming of his own volition and that conforming yields reinforcement activities from those upon whom he must depend. The smile of approval is indeed magic.

SOCIAL GROWTH

22. LANGUAGE AND COMMUNICATION

*Hearts, like doors, will open with ease to
very, very little keys,
And don't forget that two of these are
"I thank you" and "if you please."*
Oxford Nursery Rhyme Book
edited by Iona and Peter Opie

The Language of the Teacher

The words uttered by each of us are winged, gone forever yet leaving their mark upon our listeners. Tone of voice, melody, and choice of words, linked with facial expression, gesture, and stance, convey more than the symbolic content of the words; they betray the entire depth of feelings, the real *you*.

Your greeting each morning to colleagues and children creates an atmosphere of expectancy and anticipation. If the bus driver has greeted the children in good cheer, the chances are that your children will arrive happy and eager. Don't let them down with a snappish, "Take your coat off."

Choose your words well. Don't overwhelm the children with so many words they can't be sorted out—but don't be gruff and ping out orders. Non-verbal communication is an art and a very effective technique. A smile and a gesture will gain appropriate response amid confusion and tend to quiet a situation.

A six-year-old, making her first unaccompanied trip to the girls' room, was located after a rather frantic search, comfortably enthroned in the boys' room. The relieved but amused teacher said, "Miss Robin, do you know you are in the boys' bathroom?" Whereupon Miss Robin slammed shut her Little Golden book and said, "Holy Smoke!" and departed full speed. And she never made the mistake again. How much better the teacher's calm approach was than fussing and threatening a punishment.

Never belittle a child in any way. Our children know all too often that they do not gain approval easily. Just remember the slogan, "We may be retarded, but we aren't stupid."

Be consistent. Let the child know just what he can depend upon. "Don't touch" must mean just that in relation to a designated thing. Don't you change your mind. Be consistent in the terms you use. "Slow up" and "slow down" might mean the same thing to you but if up and down are opposites—why?? If you say "Close the door," don't shift to "shut the door." Our little children have enough trouble learning about words. They can wait until they are older to learn what a mixed-up language we speak. Our language is loaded with double and even triple meanings. We shut our eyes, shut the door, shut up, shut out the noise or draft; we open our eyes, open the door, open a can. We say "open up," and "open your mouth," and we hear about "open heart surgery." It's very confusing.

Only recently have we become aware of the importance of exerting great care in the selection of the words we use in telling our older children to do something or how to do something. One day I was observing Sandy, a 17-year-old girl on assignment in Child Care, walking a nursery child in the hall toward a therapy room. Suddenly she jerked the child quite roughly. I quickly said, "Be kind, Sandy, be gentle." "I be kind, Mrs. 'Loy, I be kind." So she went along another few feet and jerked the little one again. This time I said, "Sandy, you said you would be kind." "I be kind, Mrs. 'Loy, I be kind."

By sheer inspiration I asked, "What does *kind* mean, Sandy?" Her answer was, "Well, what kinda ice cream do you want?" So I sought refuge in some graded word lists and learned that *kind* as an attitude is a fifth or sixth grade comprehension level word—and Sandy was functioning at a low second-grade level.

This was discussed with our social worker, and we realized we were imposing words and expecting appropriate behavior responses far beyond realistic possibilites. The Child Care Training program is described in Chapter 23.

We are now trying to establish criteria for verbal demands made by adults. Our children want so much to comply, to please us, to do a job well that they are prone to smile and say "ok" when they actually do not understand the direction sufficiently to follow through. Don't leave fulfillment of a task to chance. Be very sure your words are understandable and meaningful.

Communication with Parents

Involve the parents by asking them to keep a checklist on some development status. You confirm *their* findings. This way parents are helped to think more about their *child's* problem than about their own problems.

Refer to the child in warm friendly terms: "you little fellow," "you scamp," "you pretty little charmer."

Use words parents can understand. If you use the

word *conceptualize*, be very sure you can explain it in words that have meaning for the parents. Remember that even the word "sibling" is a trade word. Don't talk down or be patronizing to parents. Put yourself in their place and ask yourself how you would like to hear it. Emphasize that *we* work together—you, the parents, and we, the teachers, therapists, and administration.

Share gems and goodies, laughs and good thoughts. Be careful—avoid anything that could be interpreted as ridicule. Keep in touch with parents. Don't wait for trouble to send a note home or make a phone call.

The scheduled parent conference should be a comfortable dialogue concerning the child. Initiating discussion of serious trouble should take place before conference time and at a specially requested appointment. Parents should be able to look forward to their routine teacher conference as a pleasant opportunity to review the child's school experiences with the teacher.

The Goals of Language Therapy

Language development is delayed in most retarded children.

Useful and constructive communication is essential to the social, emotional, intellectual, and aesthetic growth of any child.

The maturation process itself cannot be accelerated. However, circumstances which will stimulate the need for communication can be structured and manipulated to capitalize upon every asset available in the retarded child.

Concomitant with the process of maturation is the observed sequence of language development. Basically, the problem is to structure readiness for producing speech by perceptual training and to proceed to induce speech on a conceptual level.

The structured perceptual training progresses through four stages:

1. Learning to listen through attention-compelling stimulations
2. Listening and reacting to sound
3. Listening and responding to sound
4. Listening and producing an appropriate response

As the child's language evolves through his broadening perception in orderly sequence from concern with self, to things, to people, it is essential to select materials to conform:

1. Within this orderly sequence—the child's social concern for himself, for things, for people
2. Within the limits of his motor, kinesthetic, visual, and auditory development
3. Within the realm of the child's own possible experience
4. With his implicit needs for self-protection

Strazzulla and Karlin (1952) urged the understanding of a basic concept for language therapy with retarded children:

> "In working with these children it must be borne in mind that the aim is not to attain perfect speech, but to assist them in developing usable everyday language to the maximum of their ability."

It must also be basic to any therapy for language development for retarded children to assure the understanding of the parents, to enlist their cooperation and willingness to accept the fact that the onset of speech does not uncover a normal child but produces a better-functioning child within the limits of his impairments.

The goal of everyday language precludes the use of the term "speech correction," per se, with retarded children. Speech correction is indicated and desirable *only* when language functioning is adequate and when directing attention to articulation, phonation, etc. will not distract attention from or lessen control of the content of the verbal output.

The philosophy advocated by Strazzulla and Karlin has served us well. Much attention has been directed to speech and language development since 1952.

Early intervention, the use of behavior shaping techniques, the application of basic linguistic principles, methods developed from using the Illinois Test of Psycholinguistic Abilities, the structure of the Peabody Language Development materials—all these have brightened the outlook for the future.

Good syntax, and use of all the parts of speech have been achieved by many of our children, and we feel we are only beginning to tap the potential for developing good communication skills.

With good usable speech, the trainable child should learn to:

1. Say his name
2. Make his wants known
3. Communicate his ideas and listen courteously when others talk
4. Say "Please," "Thank you," "You're welcome," "Excuse me," "Good-bye"
5. Participate in conversation
6. Accept and give a compliment
7. Take leave of a party hostess
8. Greet and say good-bye to guests
9. Make a phone call:
   To the doctor
   To the fire department
   To the police department
   To a friend and *get to the point*
10. Accept and deliver a message
11. Listen to stories and short poems—and respond within a suitable context
12. Whisper
13. Take part in some dramatic play, especially with puppets
14. Give directions gently and clearly. The child can be a very good helper, but must learn not to bark orders, but to speak gently when in authority. This is especially important when an older child is called upon to help with younger children in school.

Not all retarded children will succeed in all of these goals for useful speech. Each step is a real achievement. The degree of success varies with the individual child, with his own speech problems and other abilities at each period of his development. These achievements serve as guideposts to the steps a retarded child must travel to communicate with people usefully.

How Language Develops

When a child is admitted to a nursery-school group in a school for retarded children, it is assumed that he is ready to participate in small, well-structured group activity. Probably he is nonverbal, but has been observed to be functioning with inner speech and is now in the receptive level of language development.

The failure to develop inner speech must be explored by a skilled pathologist. If a central aphasia is present, plus established retardation, the child is more than likely not amenable to a school situation. Prognosis under these cirumstances is extremely poor.

These 3½ to 4-year-old nursery children are functioning arbitrarily from 35 to 65 per cent of normal. This actually means that their mental ages are from 14 months to 30 months. The normal child of 14 months is starting to say words. He is well into his expressive stage of language development. He has spent four to six months in the receptive stage and is graduating to produce his own symbolic expressions vocally.

In the nonverbal retarded children of 3 to 4 years, expressive language is long overdue, and parents become frantic for the child to talk. Those working in the field of retardation are well aware of the very difficult task confronting them in leading parents to a realization that their child is truly retarded. Acceptance of this fact is absolutely necessary for realistic planning, yet many parents never do accept the situation. Many are always certain that a normal child is hidden behind the inability to talk.

It is equally difficult to guide the parents toward accepting the fact that talking must wait until the child is actually ready and has gone through the receptive stage successfully. Teachers, as well as parents, are frequently guilty of misunderstanding this.

The genetic order of language development demands an orderly progression in planning a program for retarded children. *Receptive language must be acquired before expressive language can be expected.*

All adults working with retarded children must understand that receptive language comes first. The normal infant requires four to six months to progress through this receptive stage. Acquiring a working control of receptive language may take a retarded child one or two years—or more. He may not start his course of receptive training until he is placed in a controlled, structured situation.

One or two years devoted to receptive language training seems like a long, arduous course. It is essential and productive. This "listening" skill cannot be achieved without the cooperation of the parents. They must be led to understand what the teacher is doing and why she is doing it. They must be taught not to demand words. Most important of all, the parents must learn to lessen their verbal torrents and speak to the child in single words or very simple sentences and do it in a pleasant manner.

Tremendous confusions are heaped upon the retarded child from the time he says his first (and frequently only) word, "Mama," until the desperate presentation of the child to a speech clinic or if he is lucky, to a clinic for retarded children in a medical center where a team of experts is available.

Receptive Language for Protection

Living in a social structure beyond his social maturity, the retarded child must be trained to respond to certain auditory stimulation for his own protection. He must learn to respond to "No," "Wait," "Don't touch," "Sit down," "Come here," long before these responses would be expected in a progression of appropriate responses. These responses must be learned early and therefore are induced by a conditioned response technique. This can be truly called "training."

In using the single word "No," you do not need to bark or to sound gruff. The word must be emphatic, but can be said in such a manner that the child feels that he is expected to comply satisfactorily. Parents can learn this technique. Sometimes it requires more ingenuity on the part of the teacher to train both parents in this technique than it requires to teach the child to respond to "No."

The sequence of language development parallels the process of maturation. Basically the problem is to prepare the child for language use by perceptual training and to proceed to a conceptual level of functioning.

Much valuable time is lost in urging a retarded child to produce sounds or "say" words that he is not ready to say.

This is a carefully structured program, integrating language throughout the total program, with an adequate supportive background for planning.

Planning the Program

The teacher must know the particular problem and program for each child in order to give consideration and guidance accordingly in group situations. We are concerned first with what kind of a child has the language problem and later with what kind of a language problem each child has.

An evaluation of a child's level of language functioning should be made by a language pathologist, preferably in a clinic. The language pathologist will consider the factors listed here, summarize the findings, and indicate the implications for teaching. The report from the language pathologist will give the starting point for planning a program for each child.

1. The report from the language pathologist will consider the following areas:
    a. Is the auditory capacity adequate for the reception of spoken words? For the production of speech? Does the child use his hearing projectively?
    b. Is language development compatible with mental development?
    c. Is there an emotional overlay which affects the language development?
    d. Is the structure and control of the speaking

mechanism adequate for the production of usable speech?
    e. Is there evidence of symbolic disfunction?
 2. The teacher must understand that language evolves through three levels:
    a. Inner language
    b. Receptive language
    c. Expressive language
 3. The teacher should be aware of the possibility of a bizarre progression, deviating markedly from the morphogenetic expectancy.
 4. The time required for auditory training is not in proportion to the expected delay; i.e., a child operating on 50 per cent of normal intellectual ability may require much more than twice as long a period to develop usable auditory functioning ability in readiness for speech production. This is not a neatly stratified progression.

    Each step requires a broad horizontal extension, rigidly structured—as controlled and reinforced as an espaliered tree. No further structuring can be attempted until a broad supporting base is well established and controlled.
 5. No one learning theory can be employed. It is essential for the teacher to understand all approaches to learning and employ whatever methods are indicated. The child desperately needs ego status. He needs success. Therefore success must accompany each task, whether it be genuine or guided for reinforcement, hoping for genuine success next time. The role of the teacher must be that of *Security and Consistency*.
 6. Behavior must be channeled through consistent control, imparting a definite attitude of security and love.
 7. The parents must be instructed and counseled to assure their cooperation and understanding. This is not a one-time conference but a reoccurring, reevaluating contact.
 8. The environment must be structured and the climate controlled to assure a minimum of distractibility.
 9. Motor maturity must be considered in the selection of materials. This means developmental progressions must be reconciled. Do not give material to a child for language stimulation that he cannot handle motorically. (See the Performance Goals Record.)
 10. Specific words must be taught (trained) as early as possible for the child's own protection. An appropriate response to the word "No" is imperative. This is accomplished rather simply, but is possible only with the cooperation of the parents.

The Steps for Teaching the Meaning of "No"

The steps are:
 1. Immediacy. The punishment must meet the crime immediately upon the infraction.
 2. Capture the child's attention by taking his hands or shoulders and "squaring" him directly in front of the "executioner."
 3. Take child's chin in hand to guide him (gently; never, never jerk or pull, sort of "ooze" him into position) to look squarely into the teacher's face; holding his chin with one hand, move a finger of the other hand in front of the child's face to draw attention.
 4. Shake a finger of other hand—one good, determined shake, precariously close to his nose—and say,
 5. "No" firmly and authoritatively, not loudly, but with a stern frown.
 6. Hold your finger there and frown for five seconds,
 7. then smile and administer a hug. This means, "I like you—but I don't like what you are doing," and you hope to convey to the child the feeling that you like him and really expect him to mind.

The teacher must teach the parents this technique, to assure consistency.

The Four Stages for the Language Program

For convenience in planning and recording the perceptual training program for language development, it is broken down into four stages. The first three stages are definitely *nonverbal* and must be considered as belonging to the area of receptive language. The fourth stage marks the entrance into expressive language:

 I. *Learning to listen through attention-compelling stimulations* (stimuli that merely arrest activity)
 II. *Listening and reacting to sound* (total body reaction and/or large muscle activities)
 III. *Listening and responding to sound* (facial expressions, head shaking for "Yes" or "No," responding to one's name, etc.)
 IV. *Listening and producing an appropriate vocal response* (true beginning of speech).

The ability to produce this appropriate response is the actual shift into conceptualization.

The actual vocalized attempt to give an appropriate response must not be tried until the therapist is confident that the child has progressed to the fourth stage. Upon the accomplishment of meaningful vocalization, refinements of vowel differentiation and articulation develop in association with word production.

It is necessary to structure situations in progressive order. Steps are listed in numbered sequence for convenience in reference. While the order is in approximate sequence, it must be understood that the wide variations in types of ability will necessarily cause some children to succeed in developing their language skills in an erratic pattern. It should be emphasized that each type of activity may continue over long periods of gradual development.

In summary, the sequence is as follows:

I. Learning to listen through attention-compelling stimulations (stimuli that merely arrest activity)

II. Listening and reacting to sound (total body reaction, and/or large muscle activities)

III. Listening and responding to sound (facial expressions, head shaking for "yes" or "no," responding to one's name, etc.)

1. The first arrested activity upon introduction of a planned stimulation, such as calling a child's name, can be considered response to auditory stimulation.

2. Listening and reacting with large muscle activity such as rocking a doll to music, rolling or throwing large balls with music, marching, skipping, running, tapping, hand clapping, "patty-cake."

3. Listening and reacting with large muscle activity on command; learning to react to "Stop" and "Wait"; progressing to "Look," "Sit down," "Come here," "Don't touch," "Close the door," "Open the door," "Hot."

4. Various noisemakers are used, jingle bells, maracas. The teacher shakes the jingle bells in full view of the child. A second set of bells is placed in front of the child. He is expected to pick up the set in front of him and shake it, mimicking the teacher. This activity can progress to a more complex level. Three pairs of noisemakers are used ultimately, the child being expected to select the correct noisemaker in front of him to match what he hears, without seeing the teacher's selection.

5. Listening and responding, such as shaking head "Yes" or "No" by entire group during roll call. "Is Tommy here?" "Yes, Tommy is here." "No, Tommy is not here." "Tommy is sick, too bad"—responding with a sad expression.

6. Raising hand or standing up when teacher calls name in morning circle, then acknowledging by raising hand, shaking hands, or standing up.

7. This is the time to incorporate the meaning of the words "down" and "up," "little" and "big," "slow" and "fast."

8. Listening and responding to name by taking turns.

9. Listening and responding by indications: parts of the body; own possessions; identifying boys and girls. ("Is Tommy a girl?")

10. Listening and responding to simple directions. *This is a slow progression.* Direct the child, "Show me—" or "Put your finger on—" the named item of three represented. Common objects within the child's own experience are used as stimuli.

The direction "Show me" frequently will not evoke the desired response from a retarded child. The teacher, therefore, puts her hand on the object named, then moves it toward the child, taking the child's hand and placing it on the object at the same time that she is saying "Put your finger on—." A short period of practice using this technique usually enables the child to relate to the object indicated, and he eventually will respond to "Show me." If he does not shift to the direction "Show me," but continues to succeed to the more tangible approach, "Put your finger on—," it is not important to attempt to gain this conformance. He is responding satisfactorily and that is the objective. As the objects are mastered, progress to true pictures.

The next step is to direct the child to, "Give me—." This requires a more organized response.

A more highly organized response is demanded next. The child is directed to, "Put the ball in the box." This involves selection of the object and follow-up with direct action.

IV. Listening and producing an appropriate vocal response (true beginning of speech)

11. Listening to familiar sounds and finding the source—such as a bell, a drum, a triangle, the squeak of a familiar toy, the voice of a friend.

12. Listening to familiar animal or mechanical sounds and vocalizing in repetition.

13. Listening and mimicking words to name common objects, presented first in three dimensions only.

The retarded child requires every sensory stimulation that can be made available to him. He must have the opportunity to see the stimulation (the object to be named), to hear its name, to feel its contours, and to "see" and "feel" the mechanics of its vocalized symbol. The child can see the teacher's lips form a "b" and can feel them move into position for producing the "b" sound. He can feel his own lips mimicking the teacher. Lastly, he can feel the airstream escape from the teacher's lips as she holds his hand in front of her lips and exaggerates a "b" sound, then returning his hand to his own mouth so he can do likewise. This is, of course, common practice with the deaf or hard-of-hearing child.

Fortunately the collection of words with visible initial consonants (b, p, m, ch, j) is available in common objects well within the realm of experience of most retarded children. The simple vowel content in the majority of these words are back vowels and can be produced readily. In approximate order of difficulty these words are:

ball	book	pan
boat	bunny	potty
boots	bathtub	pop
bus	bell	puppy
baby	bed	chain
box	banana	choo-choo
bottle	bird	chin
bottom	birthday cake	jello
buggy	pipe	church

Reproduction beyond the first syllable is not expected during early attempts, but very frequently the teacher is happily surprised to hear all three syllables of "banana" and a reasonable facsimile of "birthday cake." In a group situation, present objects fastened to a wall pegboard. Small shelves and hooks are available at hardware stores. This step may require months of patient guidance.

Progress from objects to tactile pictures (with flocking or bits of textured materials added to the flat surface), to colored pictures, to black-and-white outline pictures. It is helpful to use a table easel to hold pictures when starting to direct attention to a picture. Mongoloid children, particularly, require an easel, as they experience difficulty focusing their eyes upon material lying flat upon a table.

A pocket chart is used for pictures. It should be hung at one side of the pegboard. The familiar objects already successfully named can be in view as the picture is placed in the pocket chart.

14. *Conceptualization*—practical use by recall of the association of things and activities employing the words (symbols) which represent them. Training in conceptualiztion is started with simple directions that involve relating two objects. (Perceptualization is the association of the meaning of stimuli with the stimuli themselves.)

In guiding a child to relate two familiar objects, no verbal response is expected at first.

This is a more complicated task than is demanded in step 10 where two objects are involved, but one—the receptacle (box or basket)—is always the same.

At this level a choice of the second objective is offered for appropriate response.

A sturdy wooden dollhouse, with a stock of wooden furniture and properly sized rubber people, is indispensable. Plastic furniture is less expensive, but breaks very easily and is seldom the proper color.

Show the furnished dollhouse to the child, naming the bathroom and the kitchen. Take the bathtub from its place and say, "Bathtub." Tell the child to "Put it there," pointing to the bathroom, and again say "Bathroom." Go through the same procedure with the kitchen and the stove.

Take the stove and the bathtub out of the house, placing them in front of the child. Indicate that he is to put them back in their proper places.

This can progress to a variety of tasks relating objects. It is a good group activity after each child has been introduced to the project.

Very easy or quite complicated requests can involve all the children in a group from "Put the stove in the kitchen" to "Put the baby to bed and put Daddy on the sofa."

Observing dramatic play with the dollhouse can be very enlightening.

(The child should now be *using* words instead of just *saying* words)

15. Naming objects, without mimicking upon presentation of an object. (If a child experiences difficulty in adding new words and exhibits signs of frustration, present three objects—one of which he can successfully name—and allow him to select one; immediately following his successful response, urge him to select another. Continue this until a large collection of successes is available for easy recall.

16. Rhythmic responses to tom-tom; walking, stopping, running, etc.; climbing up and down stall bars to scale played on piano or with bells.

17. Recognition of "boys" and "girls." Use children, "Jane is a girl," "Tommy is a boy"; progress to pictures and printed words.

18. Recognition of "Keep out" through dramatic play. Progress to printed word.

19. Naming the members of the family. Use snapshots of family. Progress to recognizing parents of other children.

20. Naming people who help us: the milkman, policeman, fireman.

21. Naming common foods. Progress to which foods are good for us.

22. Furniture and rooms in a house. Use dollhouse.

23. Appropriate action words introduced with all these words, such as "Mama *cooks*," "Baby *sleeps*," "Daddy *works*."

24. Articles of clothing.

25. Rote counting by the teacher, to ten, has been going on whenever the opportunity presented itself. Now the child should be urged to verbalize carefully. (See the section on numbers, below.) It is important to observe the level of a child's number concepts. Do not expect more than the child is ready to use meaningfully.

26. Color naming. This goes on whenever the opportunity presents itself and should be introduced as early

as possible. Except for the color-blind child, perceiving color differences, matching and sorting, are usually accomplished before the child can name the colors he is handling.

27. Appropriate response to more complex auditory stimulations. Having learned to respond to, "Put the ball in the box," etc., the child must progress to responding to more complex auditory stimulation. Direct the child to, "Bring me the ball." The article called for is in view but not directly in front of the child. This type of experience progresses to, "Bring me the *picture* of the ball." The child is expected to select the correct picture from a pocket chart displaying three pictures. The highest level of this activity is to direct the child to "Bring me the ball [or picture of a ball]" with the ball out of sight, in a drawer or cupboard. This is a long sequence and will take several weeks.

28. Selects own name card with color clues. Selects own name card without color clues. Selects name cards of other children with color clues. Selects name cards of other children without color clues. (This progression takes time and each step must be mastered before the next is taken.)

29. Names of other children to be used in taking turns.

30. Begins to express self-wants: "water" to "drink of water." A little child usually asks for something by simply naming it, such as "water." He should be urged to expand his questions to full sentences. *Be emphatic in demanding appropriate language for bathroom chores.*

31. Getting necessary supplies upon command.

32. Responding to facial expression. The little children, having learned to mimic the teacher's expression, now learn to produce a sad or happy face in games.

33. Dramatic play in finger games or playing train should be used to gain meaningful responses either with or without verbalization.

34. Listening and carrying out simple directions, such as delivering a written message to another room.

35. Single-word production through planned stimuli is expanded to include words appropriate to the child's environment: food, clothing, furniture, sports, seasons, holidays.

36. Qualify nouns using objects—then pictures. "The little boy—the big boy"; "the little box—the big box," etc.

37. Prepositions are added, using small objects. "Put the box on the table," or "*under* the table," asking immediately, "Where did you put it?" expecting the prepositional phrase in response.

The use of prepositions is increased to include "in front of," "beside," "behind." Within this area of direction the children learn the meaning of top shelf, bottom shelf. Note: avoid using the word "before" as a directive. It is a very difficult word to understand and leads to frustration. Use the expression "in front of" in its place. All comparative forms, such as "higher" and "lower," rarely hold meaning for the young retarded child.

38. Abstract propositions are now made. The child is to select from assembled objects upon being questioned, "What do you eat with?" "What do you lock the door with?" etc. (Or, "Show me what you eat with.")

39. Expand listening ability, using colors: "Give me the big, red ball," "Give me the little blue button.."

40. Progress to two commissions: "Get the big button and put it in the pan." "Get the little ball and put it in the box."

41. Capitalize on echolalia and jargon—use nonsense syllables with music, picking up used phonemes, adding a sounded final consonant.

42. Name unseen objects through tactile stimuli only (objects in a cloth bag).

43. Auditory training progresses to selecting and naming sounds we hear; use games, such as "Magic Music," "I'm thinking—of a girl with a blue sweater."

44. The words necessary for "protection" or for safe conduct at home or in the community are expanded. "Keep out," "Private," "Exit," "Men," "Women," "Ladies," "Gentlemen," "Wet paint," "Fire escape," "Hot," "Cold," etc.

45. Action pictures are used to elicit responses in good sentences. Q. "What is the boy doing?" A. "The boy is painting." Q. "What is the boy painting?" A. "His house." Q. "Who is painting his house?" A. "The boy is painting his house."

46. Using pictures, elicit sentences by asking "How do we know it is winter?" etc.

47. Expanding vocabulary, using single stimulus such as an apple with the question "What do you do with it?" The expected response is "You eat it"; a coat, a key, a pencil, etc. This is a more complicated step than 38.

48. Telephone numbers. Use the Tele-Trainer in dramatic play. Start the youngest children by answering the phone by saying only, "Hello, Mommy's coming," and going to seek whoever is playing the role of mother. Progress to answering, "Hello, this is Sharon [or I am Sharon]. I'm fine, thank you, I'll call Mommy."

49. Expand telephone conversation to social niceties, learning to terminate a conversation after completing mission: "My daddy will pick you up at eight." It is very difficult for a retarded child to

come to the point and conclude a conversation via telephone.

50. Learn to make emergency calls.

51. Practice good manners, greeting guests, saying goodbye, accepting a gift, acknowledging and giving a compliment, making introductions and requests at mealtimes or at parties, etc.

52. Practice telling "what happened," progressing from close to remote experiences. Use television programs as an entree to gain a concept of yesterday, today, and tomorrow.

53. Practice whispering.

Remember, this is an approximate sequence. Your strongest guide as to what comes next is the child's successes.

General Suggestions

1. Materials should be selected to supplement activity being stressed during a word unit. These supplementary materials may not always be in suggested sequence. However, the interest factor and variety might possibly bring forth that unexpected gain in adding a new word and phrase.

2. Any spontaneous speech should be recorded and used as an index for expanding vocabularies. The child with dysarthria may well be able to say words beginning with a "d" or "k" and be unable to sound an initial "b." Always capitalize on every possible success.

3. Use carefully selected music whenever possible.

4. Use Fitzgerald technique consistently for stimulating responses. ("Who?" "What?" "Where?" and "Why?")

Consistently patterned formulation of questions is essential in working with retarded children.

5. Final consonants are frequently omitted by retarded children. It seems that their auditory memory just does not carry them to the final touch in delivery. Clinical experience has demonstrated a technique that has proven successful. The teacher sits close beside the child, so that she can whisper directly in his ear. With the appropriate material in front of the child, the teacher strokes with a large paintbrush or a dab of finger paint and whispers the word "painting" with a strong emphasis on "t." The vowel sounds drop out, the child hears the "t," habitually dropping the unstressed "—ing," and returns a whispered word "paint" stressing the "t."

6. This same procedure can be followed with scissors and paper, saying the word "cutting." It can also be done with the word "pasting." After a few successes, "ing" can be omitted and the child will follow through. Words ending with ch, t, and p, are usually the first successes. (Pitch, catch, touch, lunch, punch, church, stretch, paste, paint, cut, put, pat, pop, pup, cat, coat, cup, hat, hot, hit.)

The whispering technique will usually produce a final consonant. The child's response may also be whispered for quite a while, but the pride of success is a wonderful stimulation for further effort, and a full vocalized response will follow.

7. When the Language Master is used with an individual child—with or without the mirror or headphone—the card is placed to the left of the child; the child says what he thinks it is (a response to a picture). He then runs the card through the machine, correcting the word if his response to the picture was wrong. He usually becomes aware of his errors and will self-correct. The teacher sits nearby and observes, without interfering with the child's self-correction. The child's growing awareness of his errors is vitally important.

8. Use the Language Master with a child with a volume problem. Use volume control to increase responding voice intensity. Decreasing volume is helpful in teaching voice control to a child who has explosive speech.

9. The printed words on the Language-Master cards are not used or referred to until the child reaches the intermediate level. If they are noticed and learned, it should be incidental to spoken language. The exception to this is the use of these specific words to be recognized as early as possible: "Boys," "Girls," "Keep out," "Men," "Women."

Conclusion

The language functioning of most retarded children can be improved by a structured developmental program in a social situation based upon a careful diagnosis of sensory and physical impairment and its implications for training residual pathways for usable communication.

Learning to follow directions is of utmost importance.

Basic Familiar Object List
For
Vocabulary Building
(Language Master Cards)

A

apple
arm

automobile

B

baby
bacon
ball
balloon
banana
band
barber
barn
bat
bath
bathroom
bathtub
bathrobe
beads
bed
bedroom
bell
belt
bike
billfold

birds
birthday cake
boat
bonanza
book
boots
bottle
boy
boys
bread
broom
buggy
bunny
bureau
bus
bus stop
butter
bush
button

C

cake
candle
candy
cap
car
cat
chair
check mark
cheese
chickens
chisel
church
cigarette

clock
closet
clouds
coat
coffee
collar
comb
cookies
cow
crayon
crying
cup
cupboard

D

danger
desk
dime
dining room
dishes
doctor
dog

dollar
door
down
dress
drum
drummer
duck

E

ears
egg
engine

entrance
eyes
exit

F

farm
farmer
father
feet
fell
fence
field
fingers
fire escape

fireman
first aid
fish
flag
flower
fly swatter
foot
fork
fruit

G

galoshes
gate
gentlemen
girl
girls
glass

glasses
gloves
go
goldfish
grass

H

hair
hammer
hand
handkerchief
hat

head
hen
horn
horse
house

I

ice cream
ice-cream cone

in
iron

J

jello
jelly

juice

K

keep off
keep out
kettle
key

kitchen
kite
kitty
knife

L

ladies
lamp
leaf
leg

letter
light bulb
(Abe) Lincoln
living room

M

mailbox
man
match
meat
men
milk

money
monkey
moon
mother
mouth

N

nails
nose

no trespassing
nurse

O

out

P

paint
paintbrush
pajamas
pan
paper
pen
pencil
piano
pie
plane

pliers
poison
policeman
popcorn
potato
private
pull
pumpkin
puppy
push

R

radio
railroad crossing
rain
rake
razor

road
roof
rope
rug

S

safety pin
sailor

salt
sandpaper

sandwich
Santa Claus
saw
school
scissors
screwdriver
shellac
shirt
shoes
shovel
show
skirt
sled
slide
slow
snowman
soap

socks
soldier
soup
spoon
squirrel
stain
stamp
steel wool
steps
stool
stop
store
stove
street
sugar
suit
sun

T

table
tacks
tea
telephone
television
TV
tie
toast

toaster
toothbrush
toothpaste
towel
train
tray
tree
turkey

U

underwear

V

vacuum cleaner
valentine

vegetables

W

wagon
walk
(George) Washington
waste basket
watch
water

wax
wet paint
window
women
woodpecker

Z

zipper

23. CHILD CARE TRAINING

by Marie Forman

He's not heavy, Father, he's my brother.

A child care training class was started at our school in February 1967 for the purpose of teaching young adult, trainable, mentally handicapped students to care for younger students.

The major emphasis of the program shifted so that the goal became preparing each student as thoroughly as possible to perform a useful service wherever he might be—in a contract workshop, in other work situations, in his home, in the larger community, or in a residential setting.

At first the students did not comprehend even such simple instructions as "be gentle," "be patient," "be kind," "speak in a quiet voice." Thus an important goal in the class was the development of a vocabulary to facilitate communication among student, teacher, and others.

Another aim of the class was to develop acceptable social behavior for whatever setting the trainable mentally handicapped student may find himself in.

Students

Originally, the students in the class ranged in age from 14 to 21 years. The minimum age was lowered to 13 years, and judging from our brief experience, even younger children could benefit from such a class. It now seems wise to start the program as early as possible in the child's school activities. Focused upon family living, the child care course can begin when a student enters school. Two prime objectives in the course of study at all levels are emotional growth and social growth. Material related to *Family Living* can logically be incorporated under these two divisions. The term family living here refers to the family in the broadest sense of the word—people in the student's environment—"The Family of Man."

Assignments

Several steps are followed to prepare the students for their assignments, which are created to fill staff needs. This involves several staff members.

One assignment for members of the child care class is to carry out play activities with younger children.

The music therapist, who is a former physical education teacher, trained the students to do the following:

I. Learn games

   The types of games suitable for play activities with younger children are

   A. Games that do not require too long a wait between turns
   B. Games that involve most of the children most of the time (not baseball)
   C. Games where the individual is opposed to the group
   D. Games where one group is opposed to another group
   E. Games that are active
   F. Games that are quiet

II. Learn to present games

   A. By practicing on each other
   B. By having peers criticize their presentation of the game

III. Present the game

   A. Three important rules need to be followed in presenting a game
      1. Explanation (tell about the game)
      2. Demonstration (show how the game is played)
      3. Participation (do or play the game)
   B. Don't talk too long on the above three points
   C. Try the game even if not everyone understands the rules; it is all right to make mistakes and go on from there
   D. Change games often (this is especially important where the students' attention span is short)
   E. Plan for the time assigned and be prepared with rules in mind and equipment at hand.

IV. Good examples of games are

   A. I Have a Little Dog; he won't bite you
   B. Squirrel in the Tree (scattered tag)
   C. I've Got It (a quiet game)
   D. Do This—Do That (a variation on Simon Says)

Another assignment given child care students is that of noon recreation helper. To prepare them for this a teacher presented the following objectives:

I. Learn individual games (some of the games were familiar to the child care students)
II. Learn how to show younger students to
   A. Form a circle
      1. Standing
      2. Sitting
   B. Form a straight line
   C. Set up equipment
III. Learn how to supervise
   A. Games
      1. Duck, Duck, Goose
      2. Doggy, Doggy
      3. Hot Potato
      4. Farmer in the Dell
      5. Simon Says
      6. Relay races
      7. Bean bag toss
      8. Musical chairs
      9. Hoop throw
      10. Follow the Leader
      11. Selected calesthenics
      12. Bowling
      13. Basketball: games involving shooting baskets
   B. Swings in the playground (emphasis on safety factors and taking turns)
   C. Slides in the playground (emphasis on safety factors and taking turns)
   D. Rainbow bars, climbing bars in the playground (emphasis on safety factors and taking turns)
   E. Sandbox
      1. Teach not to throw sand
      2. Teach to keep in our "territory"
      3. Teach to share toys

Learn to help children wherever they need help.

So child care students may learn useful duties to carry out with younger students the school nurse instructs them in:

I. Learning to wash other students' hands
II. Learning to help young students put on and take off outside wraps
III. Learning to tie shoes of young students
IV. Learning to toilet young students

The school nurse, in teaching the child care students to help the younger students, at the same time helps them to perfect their own ability to care for themselves.

Other assigned jobs are:

I. Bus helper
   A. Arranges the seat belts
   B. Places young students in seat belts
   C. Buckles seat belts
   D. Takes students out of seat belts
   E. Takes students to door of bus
   F. Sees that mother takes student
   G. Closes door of bus
II. Front door helper
   A. Opens the door for students getting off the bus
   B. Opens the door for others coming into the school at the same time
   C. Closes the door when no one is coming in or going out

The above process is repeated when the students leave for the buses at noon and again at the end of the school day.

III. Dish helper
   A. Learns to wash dishes
   B. Learns to wipe dishes
   C. Learns to load and put away the dish cart
   D. Learns to put dishes away
IV. Lunch time helper
   A. Learns to set up lunch bins
   B. Learns to get out the correct number of glasses for each room
   C. Learns to fill glass with milk
   D. Learns to place full glasses in the bin for each room
   E. Learns to count out correct number of napkins and place in each bin
   F. Learns to count out correct number of plates and place in each bin
   G. Learns to set up lunch tables
   H. Learns to get correct number of chairs and place them at each table.
   I. Learns to remove tables and chairs after lunch
V. Miscellaneous
   A. Learns to bring toys from the playground at the end of the day to a storage cabinet
   B. Learns to wash and dry floor mats used in therapy of physically disabled students

Depending on the needs of an individual facility, other tasks might be assigned.

Child care students have a homeroom. The homeroom teacher programs the tasks and assigns the students. This is in addition to programming academic work. The schedules are complex, as the students must be released and assigned according to a set schedule, which depends on other teachers' needs.

At the fall opening of school, teachers make formal requests for specific assignments of the child care class.

For example a teacher requests a student to come to her room at 10 A.M. to:

1. See how many students are present, and to
2. Bring the correct number of glasses of milk to serve with a morning snack

A description of the above example illustrates the many steps necessary to carry out a fairly simple task.

The student needs to know:

1. What room to go to
2. When to go to the room
3. What questions to ask
4. Where to find glasses
5. How to count the correct number
6. How to carry them to the room
7. What to do with them on arrival
8. How to complete the task

Each week the staff member who has a student helper from the child care class turns in a written report which includes:

1. Date of report
2. Name of staff member making the report
3. Days and hours of student's assignment
4. Record of attendance
5. Assignment
6. Performance on assignment
7. Strong points of student
8. Suggestions for better performance

Role of the Social Worker in the Child Care Class

Responsibility for the child care class rests with the social worker. The rationale for the class is explained to the students. They are consulted about the assignments available and, within limits, their preference for certain tasks is respected. Assignments are rotated periodically so that students can learn to function in a variety of situations.

Some of the reasons for changing jobs are:

1. Learning to work with and take orders from different staff members
2. Learning different tasks
3. Adjusting to changes in time of assignment

Since many of the students will go on to workshop settings, emphasis should be placed on getting along with others, coping with new and varying situations, learning to respond to the task at hand, and learning to express feelings about the task with all its complexities.

The social worker meets with the students three times a week for 45-minute sessions. One session is for boys alone, one for girls alone, and one for boys and girls together. The meetings for boys alone and girls alone are loosely structured discussion groups where students are free to reveal their feelings, ideas, thoughts, and job questions.

As might be expected, the boys react as most boys do. When asked where they went, they respond "out" and when asked what they did, the response is "nothing." The girls, like girls everywhere, discuss freely things that happen at home, how they think their parents treat them, whether or not they are liked, what makes them feel good, angry, nervous, or fearful. While what they say may not be absolutely factual, this is what comes through to them and it is of secondary importance to the social worker whether or not it is true. Feelings count—why should the retarded student feel less hurt by things than any other person? They have individual and unique personalities, likes and dislikes, good and bad days, dreams, hopes, and fears. We only fool ourselves if we think feelings don't get hurt or that slights are not felt.

The group session with boys and girls together is devoted to reading the weekly reports the staff has prepared. This meeting provides for a total group discussion. Students respond appropriately to the reports. Jobs well done are applauded. Where improvement is needed, the group offers suggestions or examples from their own experiences.

Role playing is used to demonstrate how to help younger students get on and off the bus, how to close a door quietly, how to be mannerly at a table.

In addition, it is used for demonstrating to a student who has grabbed a child by the arm, instead of holding his hand, how to "be more gentle" or "not to be rough." This not only shows a student how to act but offers an opportunity to find out if the words "gentle" and "rough" have meaning for the student.

As discussions continue more and more new words appear in staff reports. To involve the students in developing a better understanding of words, they learn to define them in their own terms. This class points up the need for careful use of words by adults from the time a student first enters school. This finding is incorporated in the parent education sessions.

Development of Social Behavior

The discussion group also helps students learn more desirable ways of reacting toward themselves, their peers, their teachers, and others. Annoying habits are pointed out by peers or staff. These are discussed; students are thoughtful about them and try to do something about them.

For example, one of the girl students was constantly nagged by peers and others to quit biting her nails. In discussion it was pointed out that the girl had to, by herself, stop or not stop and that it was up to her. Two years later, she came to school proudly showing her fingernails. A month before she had said she really wanted to stop biting them, and the social worker suggested she put hand cream on her hands and wear white cotton gloves to bed. This she did. Whether or not this brought about the change is of course unknown but it may have been a factor.

Child care students are identified by their clothing. The girls wearing special pink smocks and the boys wearing special blue jackets. Also a white stitching on the left-hand upper part of the garment says: M.E.C. Child Care. At the end of the school year on graduation day, each child care student is given a white star which is sewn on the smock or jacket to indicate a year in the class.

When a child care student graduates at age 21, the stars are removed from the garment and sewn on a red ribbon, which is given to the graduate on graduation day. In addition to the star, all child care students are given an achievement award and special merit awards are given to child care students who have perfect class attendance.

Development of Course of Study

The child care course was developed over a period of time. When the idea was in embryo older students sometimes helped the younger ones with wraps, sat with them, or walked a restless youngster. With the formation of a class it became necessary to develop a course of study.

The program is:

I. Instruction from staff members (See above)
II. Assignment of tasks
   A. A teacher must *need* and *want* a child care student.
   B. A teacher must explain in careful, minute

detail what the task consists of, and use language the student can understand.
III. Report on task performance
   A. Nothing can be left to chance. Each teacher must be very specific in saying exactly what she expects the child care student to do. So many steps are involved in each task it is difficult and tedious to list them all, but it is essential.
   B. The student must understand what to do, must be shown how to do it, and then be given a chance to do it.

As in conducting all classes, structure is needed, a lesson plan is worked out. Rigid adherence to it is not necessary but it is useful to have identified a target area.

Classroom Instruction

Prepare for each class. Regardless of the level of teaching, being prepared for a group session is essential for a comfortable smooth flow of events. Being prepared for this child care class enables one to approach problems in a variety of ways, and assures constant vigilance for the use of appropriate words (see vocabulary). Control of vocabulary is paramount if any communication is to take place.

Keep up in the field. Many areas are being researched. Often new ideas and findings can be at least partially incorporated in a child care training program.

If students are to be free to express their ideas and gain acceptance of their ideas, good planning must include flexibility. Spontaneous discussion is often the most valuable kind because it relates directly to what the student has in his mind at the time. The discussion leader, whether social worker or teacher, can readily judge whether the tangent is relevant or deliberately diverting.

Effective communication between students and leader is largely based on good planning. The establishment of rapport depends upon:
1. Flexibility
2. Respect for ideas a student presents
3. Creating and working in a learning climate
4. Emphasis upon positive contributions
5. Response to all contributions, whether or not they are appropriate. Positive reaction to all contributions is a strong reinforcer.

Each student is a unique person and individual differences in students must be recognized and considered in planning.

Competition must not be part of the activities of the child care class. Students should be measured only against their own individual performances with the expectation being improved performance as the class progresses.

Students in the child care class are taught to be aware of situations they have never experienced. These experiences are anticipated and leading questions presented. What would you do if you saw a young student fall down? What would you do if a young student was hitting another student? Do you only do things you are told to do or do you help when you see it is needed?

Lesson Planning

The following is an informal plan that is intended to give some structure to group discussions.

The objective of the child care training class is to learn to complete a given task in child care, assisting a teacher, performing with behavior appropriate to the task and the situation, within the limits of anticipated ability.

1. Discuss reports received from staff personnel. These reports are submitted weekly to help the student be aware of his need to improve in some areas and to know where and when he does his work well.

2. Review words used in the reports to assure complete understanding of what was expected and of any suggestions made for improving performance or attitudes.

3. Hold open and free discussion: The purpose of this discussion is to stimulate and effect awareness of the need to improve a task performance or an attitude, and to receive reinforcement for a job well done.

Again the need for flexibility is stressed, yet the material discussed should be relevant to the child care training program. Consistent failure to understand wherein the student has not performed to a teacher's satisfaction indicates a need to examine the teacher's own use of words in explaining the task analysis. Failure to do a job is usually failure on the part of the demander to convey the basics of what is being demanded.

24. VOCATIONAL TRAINING

*In works of labor, or of skill
I would be busy too;
For Satan finds some mischief still
For idle hands to do.*
—Isaac Watts

The vocation of most of our trainable children is living their lives in contentment—becoming socially aware and adequate and working at being useful and feeling worthwhile. This is the self-realization we work for, and should expect.

Very few children described as trainable become independent adults, able to compete in society and the job market and to manage their own affairs.

The few who do hold jobs in competitive society require supervision in making decisions that affect health and safety and in planning for life security.

Contract workshops offer daily opportunities to be productive and busy and to enjoy the companionship of peers. Financial independence is out of reach in the contract workshop structure however; in fact, in many cases the "tuition" exceeds the earnings. Such shops must be subsidized by grants, contributions, and tuition. The annual cost per capita in a well managed workshop is frequently double the per capita expenditure for a public school student.

Grants for vocational training, the lifeblood of contract shops, are intended to provide counseling, job training, and appropriate placement. The successful trainees (or clients) who move into competitive society are usually the "graduates" of school programs for educable, rather than trainable, retardates, who required more training than they availed themselves of in special high school programs.

When we talk about vocational training for trainable children we mean preparation for lifework.

We must prepare our children for their lifework—to be independent in caring for their own bodily needs, to get along with people, to use leisure time well, and to do some service that will contribute to the comfort and welfare of their families or of any community in which they reside. The performance of the service or work should yield feelings of worthwhileness, success, and being needed by someone.

Our curriculum has been planned to prepare children for this sort of lifework. Opportunities and experiences are presented in sequential order to inculcate the necessary skills for realizing vocational success within the limitations dictated by individual characteristics. The emphasis is always on a well coordinated and healthy body, good social adequacy, and the skills essential to usefulness.

Academics—reading, writing, and arithmetic—are presented as needed in life experiences within the obvious limitations. But for trainable children academics can be interpreted as those learning skills necessary to get along with contentment and pride; we achieve those skills to widespread levels of sophistication. Learning to listen, to follow directions, and to communicate are paramount goals. Our students can learn to follow directions by written word and many learn to read (not just call words) at primary levels. The right to learn to read should not be denied any child, but for our children the emphasis must be upon reading words essential to safety and to work. If potential is shown for progress in reading, time must be found to allow the child to learn.

Learning to write provides a source of pride as well as a helpful tool in work situations. Fine manipulation skill and eye-hand coordination are required for writing.

"How many" and "how much" are necessary concepts in work situations. It is true that various rigs and jigs are used in shops to obviate the need to count, but many household tasks require number recognition and some concepts of amount. Concepts of time, money, and quantity can be learned by trainable children.

Parents never give up hoping that tomorrow will bring a different picture of the future. They deserve consideration and assurance that we always strive for realization of potential. The preceding twenty years have brought us a long way from teaching children just to tie shoelaces, keep their noses clean, not bop their peers, heat canned soup, or make sandwiches. We still must teach our children to succeed in these basic tasks, but we must also teach them to realize their potentials and strive to produce adults who will be able to enjoy healthy, contented, and busy lives. All that goes into the production of these adults can be called vocational training. The product of our training must be an adult who feels worthwhile and who can look forward eagerly to each new day, for each new day is the first day of the rest of his life.

Intellectual Growth
25. OBSERVING THE WORLD AROUND US: SOCIAL STUDIES, SCIENCE AND THE BEAUTY OF THE EARTH

by Edna W. Eby

"Though we travel the world over to find the beautiful, we must carry it with us or we find it not."
—Ralph Waldo Emerson

Introduction

The goal of a science and social studies program for children with retarded development is to relate the physical and social world through general observation, identification of specific problems, and planned experiences.

Certain units continue throughout the school year. Others are important at specific times during the school year. Still other units of study can be inserted at any time during the year's program.

A logical pattern should be followed. We make general observations, identify certain problems, and, by means of experiments or experiences, come to conclusions. In addition, we keep records of progress and record our conclusions.

For certain units which are more related to social studies, the chief need is to become acquainted with the information presented and to learn how these facts relate to our daily lives as American citizens. A unit such as "safety" can be used at a certain time of year even though it needs to be discussed at regular intervals.

There are other suitable sources in addition to those listed in this outline. Most effective are materials devised, gathered, and organized by the teacher herself. A teacher's copy of various sources, like the science texts, is sufficient for information and for colorful pictures which illustrate a certain unit. A listing of source materials used at various levels is located at the end of the chapter. Authors, publishers, and addresses are in this section.

In this teacher's opinion, *My Weekly Reader* is the best single source of pictures, maps, poems, ideas, and experience stories for a science and social studies program related to a TMH class. It is wise to order a few extra copies in order to build up a file of pictures, information, poems, "read to" stories, and experience stories concerning the various units studied.

It should be noted that *Children's Activities* magazine is out of print. *Highlights for Children* is its successor. In many areas, back issues of *Children's Activities* have been kept. These magazines are valuable and worth looking for. They contain excellent stories, poems, and activities.

There are two excellent sources for beautiful colored pictures covering a variety of subjects. One is *The National Geographic* magazine. Pictures and information obtained from this source range from wild animals and moths, to the moon. The second source is state magazines. For example, the Arizona and Colorado magazines have provided a collection of pictures and information about mountains, plants, rocks, animals, and weather.

For the teen-age groups, the teacher writes short stories (manuscript) on the board related to the unit or part of the unit under study. The teacher first acquaints the children with the subject in various ways: by using pictures, a *My Weekly Reader*—either back or current issues—and any other related sources. She stimulates "talk" about the subject—asks questions, receives answers in sentences or phrases. Then, she writes the story on the board. Some children can read it and thus learn a few new words. Others can recognize certain words and learn a few more. Some may not be able to recognize or recall any words. Still, these children learn from the "talk" times and pictures involved.

This combined program—social studies, science, music, and art—is structured using the months of the year. Nonseasonal units are introduced at intervals. Experiences are planned to suit the social interest and the probable comprehensive ability at each grade level and to be useful in every stage.

The fascination of natural phenomena will be apparent when simplicity of presentation allows each child to feel he has successfully participated in a planned experience. The reinforcement offered by music and art enhances that precious feeling of success that leads to anticipation of more successes to come.

In addition to the list of sources, a list of nonseasonal units and a sample outline of one of these, a list of records and a list of films, filmstrips, and film loops appear at the end of the chapter.

Nursery

SEPTEMBER	ACTIVITIES	MATERIALS	SOURCES
I. *Summer Review* A. Weather 1. Clothing	Picture reading of summer Dress Peabody manikin in summer clothes and bathing suit	Pictures of children playing outdoors in summer clothes Peabody Manikin	Peabody Kit #P *The Happy Twins*—Rand McNally *Seasons*—Milton Bradley

B. Activities
  1. Family
  2. Trip to the beach
  3. Trip to a farm
		Mounted pictures (teacher's collection)
		
		Pictures of children playing in sand and water
		
		Rubber family
		
		Puzzle of the family
		
		Rubber farm animals
			My Family and I—Benefic Press
			
			Peabody Kit #P
			
			I Like the Farm—Whitman Pub. Co.
			
			Good Morning Farm—Whitman Pub. Co.
			
			The Farm Book—Golden Press
			
			Grandfather's Farm—Children's Record Guild

C. Nature 1. Group walks out of doors: look at grass, trees and flowers	Let children touch the grass and the trees and handle flowers	Pictures of grass, trees, flowers	*A Good, Good Morning*—Whitman Pub. Co. *I Am A Boy*—Golden Press

Nursery

	ACTIVITIES	MATERIALS	SOURCES
OCTOBER			

I. *Fall*
 A. Signs of fall
    1. Leaves
    2. Seeds
    3. Weather
	Dress Peabody manikin with jacket and hat	Mounted pictures (teacher's)
		
		 Pictures about fall
		
		 Pictures of children wearing jackets and hats
		
		 Peabody manikin
			Fall Is Here—Golden Press
			
			 Seasons—Milton Bradley
			
			 Peabody Kit #P

II. *Halloween* A. Time for fun	Finger games Songs	Pictures	*Our World of Color and Sound*—Rand McNally
NOVEMBER			

I. *Signs of Winter*
 A. Weather
    1. Clothing
	Talk time:
	  cold
	  need for mittens and boots
		Mounted pictures (teacher's)	*Seasons*—Milton Bradley
			
			 I Play in the Snow—Whitman Pub. Co.
			
			 What We Do Day by Day (poster and pictures)—National Dairy Council

B. Animals		Picture of squirrel Pictures of birds that stay all winter	*The Squirrel Book*—Golden Press *Our World of Color and Sound*—Rand McNally *Fall Is Here*—Golden Press *I Am A Bunny*—Golden Press *The Rabbit*—Wonder Books

Nursery

	ACTIVITIES	MATERIALS	SOURCES
NOVEMBER (cont.)			
II. Health Unit A. Foods We Need	Matching food pictures	Mounted pictures (teacher's)	Peabody Kit #P What We Do Day by Day—National Dairy Council
B. Teeth	Finger game: we brush our teeth up and down	Mounted pictures of dentist, nurse, teeth, and toothpaste	What We Do Day by Day—National Dairy Council Peabody Kit #P Mommy and Daddy—Wonder Books The Apple Book—Golden Press Food lotto games
III. Thanksgiving	Finger games: pumpkin turkey	Mounted pictures: pumpkin turkey Family sitting around table	Peabody Kit #P Fall Is Here—Golden Press
DECEMBER			
I. Winter Begins A. Weather		Mounted pictures: snowmen children ice skating children on sleds trees in the winter	Seasons—Milton Bradley I Play in the Snow—Whitman Pub. Co. Frosty, the Snowman—Golden Press The Snowman Book—Golden Press

Nursery

ACTIVITIES	MATERIALS	SOURCES
DECEMBER (cont.)		
II. *Holiday Time*		
A. Hanukkah		
Songs		
B. Christmas		
Songs	Christmas trees	*Santa's Toy Shop*—Golden Press
Children play with Christmas cards	Santa Claus	
	Toys	
	Reindeer	
	Used Christmas cards	
JANUARY		
I. *The Five Senses* (Suggested Unit)		
Game touching objects: without looking find another object that is the same	Mounted pictures: mouth hand and fingers ears eyes nose	Peabody Kit #P
II. *Wheels* (Suggested Unit)		
Finger game	Pictures	*Finger Play*—Schirmer Inc.
Bus	Puzzles	Peabody Kit #P
	Sounds of the city: milk truck garbage truck bus airplane taxi steam shovel train fire engine ice cream truck	Preschool Puzzles—Whitman Pub. Co. *All About*—Columbia Records

(January is an excellent time to bring in nonseasonal units.)

Nursery

FEBRUARY	ACTIVITIES	MATERIALS	SOURCES
I. *Sounds We Hear*	Listening activities	Pictures: birds telephone animals, wild and domestic rain wind	Peabody Kit #P *All About*—Columbia Records *Grandfather's Farm*—Children's Record Guild *The Choo Choo Train*—Wonder Books *Bow, Wow! Meow!*—Golden Press *Animal Talk*—Ottenheimer, Inc. *The Rooster Struts*—Golden Press *Train to the Zoo*—Children's Record Guild *Rainy Day*—Young People's Records *The Little Red Caboose*—Golden Press *A Good, Good Morning*—Whitman Pub. Co. *Baby Listens*—Golden Press

MARCH

I. *Signs of Spring* A. Plants	Songs about spring	Pictures of trees and the first flowers of spring	*Seasons*—Milton Bradley

135

Nursery

	ACTIVITIES	MATERIALS	SOURCES
MARCH (cont.)			
B. Animals		Pictures of robins and their nests Baby animals	*A Good, Good Morning*—Whitman Pub. Co. *Good Morning Farm*—Whitman Pub. Co.
APRIL			
I. Spring A. Weather	Talk about not needing to wear boots or mittens Dress Peabody manikin for rain	Mounted pictures (teacher's) Peabody manikin Puzzles: When It Rains—Playskool	Peabody Kit #P *Seasons*—Milton Bradley *A Good, Good Morning*—Whitman Pub. Co. *My Special Day*—Whitman Pub. Co. *Our World of Color and Sound*—Rand McNally
B. Plants C. Animals	Discuss need for rain for trees and flowers Discuss baby birds in their nests	Puzzles: The Robin—Judy Co. Colors I See—Playskool	
MAY			
I. Summer Is Coming A. Weather B. Plants C. Animals D. Activities	Discuss the need for less clothing as it gets warmer Go outdoors and look at all the flowers and talk about how green the leaves and grass are after the rain Walk to the park and see the squirrels	Mounted pictures (teacher's): things we do and see in spring and summer foods we eat in summer	*Seasons*—Milton Bradley *I Am A Bunny*—Golden Press *I Am A Boy*—Golden Press Peabody Kit #P *The Apple Book*—Golden Press *What We Do Day by Day*—National Dairy Council *The Little Red Bicycle*—Whitman Pub. Co.

Nursery

MAY (cont.)

ACTIVITIES	MATERIALS	SOURCES
II. *Transportation and Travel* Discuss objects that move: trucks cars trains airplanes	Means of Travel puzzle by Sifo Records Books Peabody pictures	Peabody Kit #P Sifo Puzzle *Grandfather's Farm*—Children's Record Guild *Train to the Zoo*—Children's Record Guild *Trucks and Cars*—Whitman Pub. Co. *Things That Go*—Whitman Pub. Co. *Let's Go for a Ride*—Whitman Pub. Co. *I Like the Farm*—Whitman Pub. Co. *Trucks*—Grosset & Dunlap Co. *My Flight Bag Book*—Golden Press *The Choo Choo Train*—Wonder Books *The Little Red Caboose*—Golden Press

JUNE

ACTIVITIES	MATERIALS	SOURCES
I. *Vacation Time* A. Family activities 1. Trips 2. Home-based	Trip to beach Trip to park Trip to zoo Pictures and stories of places to go	*Farm Animals*—Grosset & Dunlap *My Flight Bag Book*—Golden Press

Nursery

JUNE (cont.)

ACTIVITIES	MATERIALS	SOURCES
B. Sports Trip to farm Trip by car Trip by train Trip by airplane		*The Little Red Caboose*—Golden Press *Train to the Zoo*—Children's Record Guild *Animal Talk*—Ottenheimer, Inc. *I Walk To the Park*—Whitman Pub. Co. *My Friend the Cow*—National Dairy Council *Grandfather's Farm*—Children's Record Guild *I Like the Farm*—Whitman Pub. Co. *My Color Game*—Whitman Pub. Co. *The Happy Twins*—Rand McNally *The Little Red Bicycle*—Whitman Pub. Co. *Who's That in the Mirror*—Random House *The Yellow Boat*—Follett Pub. Co.

Kindergarten

SEPTEMBER	ACTIVITIES	MATERIALS	SOURCES
I. *Summer Review* A. Weather	Discuss weather very briefly in terms of warm days; differentiate warm and cold Touch water faucet	Pictures of iron, toaster, stove, refrigerator	Peabody Kit #P
II. *Dairy Farm* A. The farm	Sing songs about cows giving milk Recognize toy cow, pictures of cows Identify sound a cow makes	"Miss Mary Mac" "The cow says, 'Moo, I have milk for you'" Rubber cows Pictures Noisemaker cylinder	*Adventures in Rhythm* —Folkways
B. Distribution	Take turns sending milk truck to each child Talk about milkman	Milk truck and bottles—Fisher-Price Toys Milkman puzzle—Judy Co.	
C. Milk	Recognize pictures of cartons, bottles, and glasses of milk. Talk about foods that are good for you	Food cards—Ed-U-Cards Mfg. Corp. Lotto cards and game—Ed-U-Cards Mfg. Corp.	Peabody Kit #P

III. *Fall Begins*
A. Signs of fall
  1. Leaves
  2. Weather
    a. Clothing
	Show changing leaves briefly
	
	Dress dolls and manikins appropriately
		Dolls and doll clothes
		
		Manikin and clothes
		
		Clothing pictures
			Peabody Kit #P
			
			All About Fall—Bowmar

Kindergarten

	ACTIVITIES	MATERIALS	SOURCES
OCTOBER			
I. *Halloween* A. Time for fun	Songs Parties Identify pictures of pumpkins, jack-o-lanterns (miniatures also) Sing "Pumpkin Song" with actions: "Pumpkin, pumpkin, round and fat, turns into a jack-o-lantern just like that" Participate in school party, dressed in costumes	Pumpkin, jack-o-lantern pictures Plastic pumpkins	Traditional
NOVEMBER			
I. *Health Unit* A. Foods we need	Recognize foods that are good for us	Plastic fruits, vegetables Food stimulus cards	Peabody Kit #P
B. Teeth	Recognize materials used for brushing teeth Brush teeth daily	Household cards (sink, toothbrush, toothpaste)	Peabody Kit #P
II. *Thanksgiving*	Songs Parties Identify pictures of turkeys (miniatures also) Participate in school assembly	Miniature objects and pictures "Three Little Turkeys"—*Singing Fun*—Bowmar	

Kindergarten

ACTIVITIES	MATERIALS	SOURCES
DECEMBER		
I. *Winter Begins* A. Weather 1. Temperatures Discuss briefly in terms of *cold* weather; differentiate cold and warm Touch water faucet, heat vents, window pane Talk about snow	Pictures of iron, toaster, stove, refrigerator *The Snowman Book*	Peabody Kit #P *The Snowman Book—* Golden Press
2. Clothing Dress dolls and manikins appropriately	Dolls, doll clothing Manikin and clothes Clothing pictures (jacket, boots, hat, mittens)	Peabody Kit #P *All About Winter—* Bowmar
II. *Holiday Time* A. Christmas B. Hanukkah Identify Santa Claus, Christmas tree Menorah Parties Sing "Jingle Bells," etc. and play bells Participate in school program	Miniature objects Pictures Christmas songs	
JANUARY		
I. *Winter* A. Family activities Read story about winter activities		*The Snowman Book—* Golden Press

Kindergarten

	ACTIVITIES	MATERIALS	SOURCES
JANUARY (cont.)			
II. *The Five Senses* A. Identify body parts	Use bean bags for kinesthetic reinforcement Listen and respond to body part identification Assemble body parts to form a whole Identify body parts on others	Boy, girl Peabody manikins Boy, girl puzzle—Judy Co. Dolls Pictures of people Records	*Put Your Finger in the Air*—Columbia *Let's Plan a Musical Game* —Columbia *Where Are Your Eyes*— Pram Records Peabody Kit #P
III. *Transportation* (Suggested Unit)	Identify small car, truck, bus Progress to pictures	Toy school bus—Fisher-Price Toys Peabody transportation cards	Peabody Kit #P
FEBRUARY			
I. *The United States* A. Flag	Identify flag Put hand over heart during "pledge" Wave the flag Roll it up	"Flag Song"—*Special Needs #2*	*Songs for Children with Special Needs # 2*— Bowmar
MARCH			
I. *The Circus* A. Animals B. Clowns	Identify circus animals, rubber miniatures, and pictures Play with clown toys	Peabody animal cards Jack-in-the-box—Mattel Toys Toe-Joe swinging clown— Ohio Art Toys	Peabody Kit #P

Kindergarten

APRIL	ACTIVITIES	MATERIALS	SOURCES
I. *Spring* A. Weather 1. Kinds of weather	Discuss weather very briefly in terms of warm days Talk about rainy and sunshiny days	"Rain, rain, go away" song	Peabody Kit #P *All About Spring*—Bowmar Records
2. Clothing	Dress dolls and manikins for rainy and sunny days	Dolls and doll clothes Manikins and clothes Clothing pictures	

MAY			
I. *Summer Is Coming* A. Weather B. Plants C. Animals	Discuss warm weather Dress dolls appropriately Plant flower seeds in individual containers Identify wild animals, rubber miniatures, and pictures	Dolls and doll clothes Animal cards and miniatures	Peabody Kit #P

JUNE			
I. *Vacation Time* A. Weather	Discuss hot weather Dress dolls and manikins in summertime clothes	Dolls and doll clothes Manikin and clothes Clothing pictures	*All About Summer*—Bowmar Records Peabody Kit #P

Junior Intermediate

SEPTEMBER	ACTIVITIES	MATERIALS

I. *Summer Review*
  A. Weather
    1. Kinds of weather
    2. Clothing
    3. Temperature
  B. Activities
    1. Family
    2. Camp
  C. Nature
	Talk time: What did you do this summer?
	
	Picture reading: fishing, swimming, riding, picnicking, playground fun, car trips
	
	Guessing games (child imitates his activity and the others name it)
	
	Find pictures of thermometer and then discuss use of thermometer
	
	Walks to observe nature changing
		Pictures (teacher's collection)
		
		Magazines
		
		Books
		
		Catalogs
		
		Thermometer (real and artificial)

II. *Dairy Farm* A. The farm	Visit a farm Talk about what was seen Listen to records Films Stories	Pictures Magazines Newspapers Books Records

B. Distribution
    1. Stores
    2. Milkman
	Talk about community helper (the milkman)	Pictures

III. *Fall Begins*
  A. Signs of fall
    1. Leaves
    2. Weather
    3. Clothing
	Walks around school area to observe and collect leaves
	
	Picture reading
	
	Coloring leaves
	
	Fall poems
		Pictures
		
		Manila paper
		
		Watercolors
		
		Brushes
		
		Newspapers
		
		Books

SOURCES	MUSIC	ART
Peabody Kit #1 *Summer Is Here*—Harper & Row *My Weekly Reader Surprise* *Highlights for Children* *Summer*—Random House	"Good Morning Merry Sunshine—*Special Needs #1*—Bowmar *I'm Dressing Myself*—Young People's Records *Weather Watchers*—Bowmar	Draw pictures of summer fun with crayon; these will be mostly scribbles, but children should name parts of picture and tell story; do same for family. Some will have beginning schema of man Watercolor is fun for painting
Teacher's picture collection Peabody Kit #1 *My Weekly Reader*—Surprise *Highlights for Children* *Good Morning Farm*—Whitman Pub. Co. *The Farm Book*—Golden Press *Milk for You and Me*—National Dairy Council *My Friend the Cow*—National Dairy Council *Grandfather's Farm*—Children's Record Guild *Out of Doors*—Young People's Records	*Train to the Farm*—Children's Record Guild "Old McDonald Had A Farm" "Autumn Leaves"—*Singing Fun*—Bowmar	
Peabody Kit #1	*Men Who Come to Our House*—Young People's Records	
Peabody Kit #1 *Leaves*—David C. Cook Pub. Co. *My Weekly Reader*—Surprise *Highlights for Children* *A Child's Garden of Verses*—Robert Louis Stevenson		Paint pre-cut leaves—all fall colors of tempera; the more mixed up the colors, the prettier the leaves Crayon rubbing over leaves of all fall colors

Junior Intermediate

OCTOBER	ACTIVITIES	MATERIALS

I. *Fall*
   A. Harvest time
      1. What do the farmers do?
 	
   B. Plants
      1. Pumpkins
      2. Apples
 	
   C. Animals
      1. Store food for winter
 	
   D. Weather
      1. Colder
      2. Dark earlier
   E. Sports
      1. Football
	Discuss and show pictures of harvest time
	
	Trips to see pumpkins
	
	Trips to orchards
	
	Study fruits and vegetables
	
	Go for walks; observe squirrels, chipmunks, birds
	
	Daily weather observation and report
	
	Show pictures and discuss
		Pictures
		
		The window
		
		Pictures of football equipment

II. *Halloween*
   A. Time for fun
      1. Pictures
      2. Stories
      3. Costumes
      4. Parties
	Carve and decorate pumpkins
	
	Make masks
	
	Costume party
	
	Discuss and play Trick or Treat
	
	Discuss "please" and "thank you"
	
	Songs
		Pumpkin
		
		Pictures
		
		Costumes
		
		Paper bags
		
		Songs

NOVEMBER		

I. *Signs of Winter*
   A. Weather
      1. Temperature
      2. Clothing
      3. Kinds of weather
	Talk time: what winter means to us
	
	Picture reading
	
	Stories of winter fun
	
	Make snowballs, snowmen, angels in the snow
	
	Look about to see all the trees bare, flowers gone
		Pictures
		
		Magazines
		
		Newspapers

II. *Health Unit* A. Foods we need	Talk about 3 main meals of the day What we eat Snacks Play cafeteria, picking complete meals	Pictures

SOURCES	MUSIC	ART
My Weekly Reader—Surprise *Highlights for Children* *Seasons*—David C. Cook Pub. Co. Peabody Kit #1 Magazines Children's collections of records, books, etc. at home	"Weather Song"—*Singing Fun*—Bowmar "Paw Paw Patch"—*Treasury of Songs*—Hart Pub. Co. "Autumn Is Here"—*More Singing Fun #1*—Bowmar *All About Fall*—Bowmar	Color pumpkin shapes with crayon Decorate orange pumpkin shapes with pre-cut eyes, etc.
Holidays—David C. Cook Pub. Co.	Halloween songs: "Three Little Pumpkins"—*Singing Fun*—Bowmar "The Smallest Witch"—*More Singing Fun #1*—Bowmar "Three Green Goblins"—*Singing Fun*—Bowmar Rhythms—rhythm instruments "Ringing Doorbell," "Witches"—*Holiday Rhythms*—Bowmar	Make masks of paper plates or paper bags with tempera paint and pre-cut eyes, noses, etc.; yarn scraps can be used for hair and whiskers or beards Halloween noise makers—use 2 small paper plates stapled together and a tongue depressor for a handle (stapled between plates); insert beans or gravel between plates; decorate with crayon scribbles or scraps of tissue pasted on with full-strength liquid starch (from grocery store)
Teacher's picture collection Peabody Kit #1 *Seasons*—David C. Cook Pub. Co. *My Weekly Reader*—Surprise *Highlights for Children*	"Funny Little Snowman"—*Singing Fun*—Bowmar *All About Winter*—Bowmar	Use modeling dough to make snowmen
Teacher's picture collection Peabody Kit #1 *Our Food*—National Dairy Council National Dairy Council food pictures		

Junior Intermediate

NOVEMBER (cont.)	ACTIVITIES	MATERIALS
II. *Health Unit (cont.)* 　　B. Teeth	Play cleaning teeth Play going to the dentist Fun time when one loses a baby tooth Music	Tongue depressors Books Records
III. *Thanksgiving* 　　A. Family activities 　　B. Food 　　C. Meaning	Talk about the many things we are thankful for, the foods of the day, preparing the food Company manners Make turkeys and Indian feather hats	Pictures Books Records Filmstrips Newspapers Manila paper Crayons, scissors

DECEMBER

I. *Winter Begins* 　　A. Weather 　　　　1. Temperature 　　　　2. Kinds of Weather 　　　　3. Clothing 　　B. Animals	Talk about: 　Winter weather 　Snow, ice 　Warm clothing Sing winter songs	Pictures Newspapers Magazines Filmstrips
II. *Holiday Time* 　　A. Hanukkah 　　　　1. Decorations 　　　　2. Customs 　　B. Christmas 　　　　1. Decorations 　　　　2. Customs	Discuss the candle lighting and gift giving Talk about holidays and the party Make decorations Make gifts for parents Field trip to look at Christmas trees Practice for holiday program Songs	Pictures Magazines Newspapers Catalogs Art paper Crayons Songs Records

SOURCES	MUSIC	ART
A Trip to the Dentist—Golden Press	"Michael and the Dentist"—*After School Favorites*—Childcraft Records	
Teacher's picture collection Peabody Kit #1 *Holidays*—David C. Cook Pub. Co. *My Weekly Reader*—Surprise *Highlights for Children*	"Ten Little Indians"—*Treasury of Songs*—Hart Pub. Co. "Three Turkeys"—*Singing Fun*—Bowmar	Make bands for Indian hats decorated with crayon scribbles
Teacher's picture collection Peabody Kit #1 *Seasons*—David C. Cook Pub. Co. *My Weekly Reader*—Surprise *Highlights for Children* *Children's Activities*	*I'm Dressing Myself*—Young People's Records "Jingle Bells"—*Treasury of Songs*—Hart Pub. Co.	Cut simple snowflakes (teacher folds paper)
Teacher's picture collection *Holidays*—David C. Cook Pub. Co. *My Weekly Reader*—Surprise *Highlights for Children*	*The Merry Toy Shop*—Children's Record Guild "Mr. Santa Claus"—*More Singing Fun*—Bowmar	Gifts for parents; papier-mâché may be used; foil Christmas papers (instead of newspaper) to cover paper forms are attractive Paint cans (enamel) for pencil holders Sand and paint wooden articles; with vigilance, stain glass paints may be used for bottles, etc. Plaster of Paris soaked string, dropped on waxed paper makes pretty tree decorations; color plaster with tempera

Junior Intermediate

JANUARY	ACTIVITIES	MATERIALS

I. *Winter*
  A. Family Activities
    1. Indoors
      a. Stories
      b. Art
 	
    2. Outdoors
      a. Sledding
      b. Making snowmen
         and snowballs
      c. Games
  B. Sports
    1. Pushing, pulling and riding a sled
	Tell and pantomime
	
	Chalk drawing on black paper (snowflakes, snowmen, trees, etc.)
	
	Cut and mount winter shapes—snowflakes, mittens, sleds, snowballs, etc.
	
	Angels in the snow
	
	Tag
	
	Feel snow
	
	What happens to snow?
		Calendar—monthly and yearly
		
		Chalk, paper
		
		Scissors and white paper
		
		Paste
		
		Sled
		
		Books

II. *The Five Senses*
  A. Identify by "show me" eyes, nose, etc. on self
  B. "Show me" on peers or teacher
  C. "Show me" on pictures
  D. Use of parts, i.e.: we see with our eyes, we hear with our ears, we feel with our hands, we taste with our mouths, we smell with our noses
	Circle unit fun:
	  touch your eyes
	  touch your nose
	  songs
	  finding people in pictures
	
	Blindfold—remove
	
	Filmstrips
	
	Bag with familiar objects; each puts hand in and identifies
	
	Tasting: lemon—sour;
	        candy, sugar—sweet
	
	Flour—cooking
	
	Pleasant and unpleasant
		Catalogs
		
		Magazines
		
		Bag: block, pen, ball, peg
		
		Bag: fur, feather, stone
		
		Lemon
		
		Candy or sugar
		
		Flour

III. *Wheels*
  A. Modes of transportation
    1. Cars
    2. Trucks
    3. Buses
    4. Airplanes
    5. Trailers
    6. Vans
    7. Campers
  B. Kiddie transportation
    1. Bike
    2. Wagon
    3. Roller skates
	Talk time: Definite objects—similarities and/or differences
	
	Picture objects
	
	Ride on each where possible
		Miniature objects
		
		Teacher's pictures

SOURCES	MUSIC	ART

Judy Co.—calendar, 12-month calendar
 	
My Weekly Reader—Surprise
 	
Highlights for Children
 	
Little Brown Bear Stories—Child Training Assoc.
 	
How and Why Library—Childcraft-Field Enterprises Educational Corp.
 	
Look and Learn—Scott, Foresman
	Rhythm activities
	  Shovel snow
	  Make snowballs
	  Make snowman
	  Put on warm clothing
		Cut snowflakes
		
		Pictures of winter are made by pasting small white scraps of construction paper on grey or black background
		
		Use modeling dough to make snowmen and snowballs

Can You Guess?—Wonder Books	*Basic Songs for Exceptional Children*—#1 and #3—Concept Records *Basic Concepts Through Dance*—Activity Records "Touch Your Head"—*Special Needs #1*—Bowmar *Put Your Finger in the Air*—Columbia	Draw with crayon a circle for face and place eyes, nose, mouth in proper places Make collage of scraps of sandpaper, burlap, velvet, oilcloth, etc. for a "feeling picture"
	"The People on the Bus"—*Special Needs #1*—Bowmar "Little Red Caboose"—*Special Needs #2*—Bowmar "Down at the Station"—*Special Needs #2*—Bowmar *Trains and Planes*—Young People's Records	Unable to draw representational pictures

Junior Intermediate

FEBRUARY	ACTIVITIES	MATERIALS

I. *The United States*
   A. Map—*My Weekly Reader*
   B. Flag
      1. Stars
      2. Stripes
	Talk about the town and state we live in
	
	Recall own address
	
	Pledge allegiance with one child holding the flag and calling it by the name "The Flag of the United States of America"
	
	Songs
		Flash cards
		
		ID tags
		
		Flag

C. Famous Americans
      1. Lincoln
      2. Washington
	Talk about with pictures
	
	Show various pictures on money
		Pictures of the Presidents
		
		Mounted pictures
		
		Other pictures

II. *Light* A. Awareness of night and day	Talk time: what we do in the dark, what we do in the light Sources: sun, lamp, moon Poem, "Bed in Summer" by Robert Louis Stevenson	Books

III. *Water*
   A. Sources
      1. Rain
      2. Snow
      3. Ice
   B. Importance
      1. Drink
      2. Wash
      3. Swim and boat
	Experiment melting ice and freezing water
	
	Make steam
	
	Talk about how temperature changes water
		Kettle
		
		Water
		
		Pan

IV. *Valentine's Day*	Make Valentines Songs for the day Party	Paper Paste Scissors

SOURCES	MUSIC	ART
Teacher-made flash cards *Holidays*—David C. Cook Pub. Co. Teacher's picture collection "My Country 'Tis of Thee" "America the Beautiful" "Raise the Flag at Sunrise"	"America" *Music for Exceptional Children #1*—Summy Birchard "Flag Song"—*Special Needs #2*—Bowmar "Yankee Doodle"—*Holidays for USA*—Decca (sing, march, and use rhythm instruments)	
Teacher's picture collection *My Weekly Reader Surprise*		
A Child's Garden of Verses—Robert Louis Stevenson		
	"Roses are Red, Violets are Blue"—traditional tune Rhythms: Valentine dance—*Holiday Rhythms*—Bowmar	Make valentines and envelopes to hold individual valentines on *the* day, by folding a sheet of construction paper and stapling each side; paste on a paper doily and valentine stickers. Cut paper; some snowflakes may be used on valentines. Cover pre-cut valentine shape with bright foil paper; paste scraps on, and decorate with a lace paper doily

Junior Intermediate

MARCH	ACTIVITIES	MATERIALS

I. *The Circus*
    A. Clowns
    B. Other performers
    C. Animals
	Talk about the circus: the clowns—Who are they, what do they do? Pretend to be clowns
	
	Go to circus
	
	Pantomime clowns
	
	Show pictures of animals and circus people; listen to records
	
	Draw pictures
		Pictures
		
		Costumes and dolls
		
		Make-up
		
		Records
		
		Stories
		
		Children's newspapers
		
		Drawing paper
		
		Crayons, paint

II. *Magnets*
    (Suggested Unit)
    A. Function: attract
    B. Uses
	Talk and look at pictures
	
	Magnets can lift things and hold them
	
	Play fishing game
		Children's newspapers
		
		Magnet on string to lift clips, pins, etc.

III. *Signs of Spring*
    A. Temperature
    B. Weather
    C. Clothing
    D. Plants
    E. Animals
    F. Clean-up time
        1. Raking leaves
        2. Garden preparation
        3. Washing windows
        4. Painting
	Daily weather report
	
	Observe and discuss days getting longer
	
	Talk about change in clothing
	
	Start planting
	
	Make spring poster
	
	Look for signs of spring
		Children's newspapers
		
		Pictures of spring
		
		Seed, soil, pot
		
		Magazines
		
		Scissors
		
		Paste
		
		Pictures
		
		Colored paper

APRIL

I. *Spring*
    A. Weather
        1. Temperatures are higher
        2. Frequent rain
        3. Clothing
	Talk about warmer weather, spring rain, lighter clothing, rain clothing	Mounted pictures
		
		Teaching pictures
		
		Children's newspapers

SOURCES	MUSIC	ART
Teacher's picture collection *Bozo at the Circus*—Capitol *Bozo at the Party*—Capitol *My Weekly Reader*	*Circus Comes to Town*—Young People's Records "Circus Ponies"—*More Singing Fun #2*—Bowmar "Circus Clowns"—*Singing Fun*—Bowmar	Draw with crayon Paint with tempera; any picture with bright color may be called a circus picture; give only primary colors
My Weekly Reader		
My Weekly Reader—*Surprise* Teacher's picture collection *Seasons*—David C. Cook Pub. Co. *The Carrot Seed*—Children's Record Guild	"Five Little Kites"—*Singing Fun*—Bowmar *Swinging*—J. Barnett Record #3—Geo. Stanley Co. "Eensie Beensie Spider"—*Treasury of Songs*—Hart Pub. Co. *All About Spring*—Bowmar	Make flower pictures: Give 12″ x 18″ bright colored construction paper and a cut-out of a flower pot plus approximately 1″ squares of bright tissue paper; paste flower pot on large paper; then dot with library paste and press on tissue squares to resemble pot of flowers
Seasons—David C. Cook, Pub. Co. *My Weekly Reader*—*Surprise* *Highlights for Children* *Spring Is Here*—Golden Press *Look and Learn*—Scott, Foresman Peabody Kit #1 *Rainy Day*—Young People's Records *The Carrot Seed*—Children's Record Guild	"Rain, Rain Go Away"—*Treasury of Songs*—Hart Pub. Co. *Rainy Day*—Young People's Records "Lollypop Tree"—*Through Children's Eyes*—RCA	Draw rain pictures Learn that lots of crayon dots represent rain Tissue paper lamination: bright spring colors of tissue paper, cut or torn, placed on one sheet of waxed paper, covered with another, and pressed with a warm iron; very pretty to put in windows

Junior Intermediate

APRIL (cont.)	ACTIVITIES	MATERIALS
I. *Spring (cont.)* 　B. Plants 　　1. Growing things turning green 　　2. Spring blossoms 　　3. We plant seeds	Observe leaves, grass, flowers, etc. growing Look at pictures and filmstrips about spring Sing spring songs	Magazines Seed catalogs Thermometer Filmstrips Flower box, soil, seeds Record
C. Animals 　　1. Care and feeding of pets 　　2. Learning about wild animals and farm animals 　D. Sports 　　1. Outdoor tag 　　2. Catch	Discuss animals on the farm, at the zoo, at the circus Visit the zoo	
II. *Shadows* 　Look for shadows outdoors	Run to watch our own shadows Find other shadows—trees, buildings, etc. Jump on each other's shadows Recite poems	Book of poems
III. *Easter*		

MAY

	ACTIVITIES	MATERIALS
I. *Summer Is Coming* 　A. Weather 　　1. Temperature warmer 　　2. Days longer 　　3. Clothing lighter 　B. Plants 　　1. Flowers blooming 　　2. Trees filled out 　　3. Garden planting 　C. Animals 　　1. Birds	Daily weather observation and report Talk about longer days, clothing, nature Go for walks, observing trees, flowers, bushes, grass, birds, and animals	Pictures Newspapers Magazines Catalogs Filmstrips Poems, stories

SOURCES	MUSIC	ART
A Child's Garden of Verses—Robert Louis Stevenson: "The Rain" "My Shadow"		
	"Peter Cottontail"—Golden Records	Easter pictures featuring Easter bunny and Easter eggs
		Give a pre-cut basket shape to paste on larger paper; decorate pre-cut Easter eggs to fill basket using crayon scribbles
Science—David C. Cook Pub. Co.	*Out-of-Doors*—Young People's Records	Summer picture: use brown crayon to draw lines for a tree; paste on small bits of torn, green construction paper for tree leaves
Seasons—David C. Cook Pub. Co.		
Teacher's picture collection	*Let's Help Mommy*—Children's Record Guild	
Peabody Kit #1		
My Weekly Reader—Surprise	"Little White Duck"—*Burl Ives Sings*—Columbia	
Highlights for Children		
"How and Why Library" (poems and rhymes)—	*All About Summer*—Bowmar	
Childcraft, Field Enterprises Educational Corp.		
Look and Learn—Scott, Foresman		

Junior Intermediate

MAY (cont.)	ACTIVITIES	MATERIALS

II. Transporation and Travel
  A. Means of Transporation
      1. Land
      2. Air
      3. Water
	Talk about different means of transportation	Pictures
		
		Magazines
		
		Catalogs
		
		Toys

JUNE

I. Vacation Time A. Weather	Daily weather report Talk about summer Summer clothing	Show pictures Pantomime

B. Safety
 	
  C. Health
	Discuss safety:
	   playing outdoors
	   at the pool
	   at the beach
	   on vacation	

D. Family activities
      1. Trips
      2. Home-based
	Discuss:
	   summer vacation
	   day camp
	   sleep-away camp
	   visiting Grandma
	   trips with family	

E. Sports	Discuss:
	   swimming
	   boating
	   baseball	

SOURCES	MUSIC	ART
Peabody Kit #1	*Trains and Planes* —Young People's Records "I've Been Workin on the Railroad"— *Burl Ives Sings*—Columbia	
Teacher's picture collection Peabody Kit #1 *Seasons*—David C. Cook Pub. Co.		
	Songs of Safety—Decca	
My Community—David C. Cook Pub. Co.	Camp songs	
	"Take Me Out to the Ball Game"— *Songs of the Gay 90's*— Remick Music Corp.	

Intermediate

SEPTEMBER	ACTIVITIES	MATERIALS

I. *Summer Review*
   A. Weather
      1. What we wear
      2. What we might drink or eat in summer
      3. Temperature
   B. Activities
      1. At home
      2. At school (summer school)
      3. Trips
   C. Nature
      1. Month it is; when does fall begin?
      2. What do we look for outside
         a. Leaves change color
         b. Leaves fall
         c. Animals' habits
         d. Weather
         e. Halloween
	Circletime: What we did in summer
	
	What can we do in summer?
	  Swim, picnic, beach activities, go on trips to:
	    zoo
	    Grandma's
	    farm
	
	Pick out clothing we wear when it's hot
	
	Discuss in circle, use picture scenes and magnetic figures (playground)
	
	Playground: observe change in trees, etc.
	
	Walks to park; observe trees, color of leaves, squirrels storing food
	
	Collect and press leaves
		Thermometer
		
		Sounds and Patterns of Language—Holt, Rinehart & Winston
		
		Pictures of fall
		
		Pictures of clothing
		
		Poems about fall

II. *Dairy Farm* A. The farm	Identify farm animals as opposed to wild animals Listen to records	*Dairy Farm Trip to Hawthorne Melody*—Filmstrip and record—National Dairy Council Peabody Kit animal cards *Grandfather's Farm*—Children's Record Guild *Train to the Farm*—Children's Record Guild Dittos on farm animals to color *The Carrot Seed*—Children's Record Guild

III. *Fall Begins*
   A. Signs of fall
      1. Leaves
         a. Color changes
         b. Begin to fall
      2. Animals
         a. Squirrels and chipmunks hide food for winter
      3. Weather
         a. Cooler
         b. Days shorter
	Collect and press fall leaves
	
	Take a walk and observe animals carrying acorns and other nuts
		Pictures

SOURCES	MUSIC	ART
Peabody Kit #1 *My Weekly Reader* #1 *Highlights for Children* *Seasons*—David C. Cook Pub. Co.	Songs about summer Camp songs *Camping in the Mountains*—Bowmar *I'm Dressing Myself*—Young People's Records "Falling Leaves"—*Singing Fun*—Bowmar "Autumn Leaves"—*Singing Fun #1*—Bowmar *Weather Watchers*—Bowmar *The Zoo and the Circus*—Bowmar	Make pictures of summer fun Use crayons, tempera paint Make cut or torn paper pictures of falling leaves Laminate fall leaves between two sheets of waxed paper Paint cut-out fall leaves using tempera paints; all colors (no restrictions on keeping colors clear)
Peabody Kit #1 and #2	*Train to the Farm*—Children's Record Guild "Old McDonald Had a Farm"—*Children's Sing-a-Long*—Vocalion	
Seasons—David C. Cook Pub. Co.		

Intermediate

OCTOBER	ACTIVITIES	MATERIALS

I. *Fall*
  A. Harvest time
    1. What do the farmers do?
  B. Plants
    1. Pumpkins
    2. Apples
  C. Animals
    1. Storing food for winter
  D. Weather
    1. Getting dark earlier
    2. Colder
    3. Rain
  E. Sports
    1. Football
    2. Basketball
    3. Indoor gym
	Discuss pictures of harvest time
	
	Trip to pumpkin patch, apple orchard
	
	Go for walk and observe birds, squirrels, rabbits
	
	Observe weather
	
	Daily weather in circle
	
	Discuss current games
		Pictures
		
		Cardboard thermometer
		
		T.V.

II. *Halloween*
  A. Time for fun
    1. Pictures
    2. Trick or Treat
    3. Costumes
	Carving a pumpkin
	
	Making masks
	
	Costume party
	
	Discussion of Trick or Treat, please and thank you
		Pumpkin
		
		Pictures
		
		Costumes

NOVEMBER

I. *Signs of Winter*
  A. Weather
    1. Change of clothing
    2. Frost
  B. Animals
    1. Hibernation
    2. Migration
	Daily weather report
	
	Clothing: at circle time discuss appropriate clothing for winter
	
	Discuss hibernation and migration of
	  chipmunks
	  bears
	  birds
		Pictures of winter clothing
		
		Pictures of seasons
		
		Pictures of animals that hibernate and birds that migrate

II. *Thanksgiving*
  A. Origin
  B. Meaning
  C. Celebration
	Make turkeys out of pine-cones and paper
	
	Discuss what we eat at Thanksgiving
	
	Discuss the first Thanksgiving
	
	Make a list of what we are thankful for
		Thanksgiving with Peter and Carol—filmstrip and record—Society for Visual Education
		
		Pictures about Thanksgiving

SOURCES	MUSIC	ART
My Weekly Reader *Highlights for Children* *Seasons*—David C. Cook Pub. Co. Peabody Kit #1	*All About Fall*—Bowmar "Two Little Owls," "Mr. Rabbit"—*Burl Ives Sings*—Columbia	Draw crayon pictures of field trip activities
Holidays—David C. Cook Pub. Co.	*Halloween*—Bowmar Halloween songs: "In a Pumpkin Patch"—*Singing Fun*—Bowmar "Smallest Witch"—*More Singing Fun #1*—Bowmar "Three Green Goblins"—*More Singing Fun #2*—Bowmar	Make masks for Halloween using paper plates Decorate pumpkin shapes using cut paper Make paper-bag puppets Decorate Trick or Treat bags with crayon
Peabody Kit #1 and #2 *Seasons*—David C. Cook Pub. Co. Teacher's mounted pictures *Highlights for Children*, December 1969, page 19	"How Many Snowflakes"—*More Singing Fun*—Bowmar "Indians in a Teepee"—*Singing Fun*—Bowmar *Creepy Crawly Caterpillar*—Children's Record Guild *Autumn*—Bowmar	
Holidays—David C. Cook Pub. Co.	"Three Turkeys"—*Singing Fun*—Bowmar "Thank You Day"—*Children's Holidays*—Decca	

Intermediate

DECEMBER	ACTIVITIES	MATERIALS

I. *Winter Begins*
  A. Weather
    1. Snow
    2. Temperature
    3. Clothing
  B. Animals
    1. Birds that stay here
    2. Winter animals
	Daily weather report
	
	Select winter clothing pictures
	
	Discuss birds that remain, how we feed them, what animals we see in winter, where they get their food
		Cardboard thermometer
		
		Pictures
		
		Magazines
		
		Newspapers

II. *Holiday Time*
  A. Hanukkah
    1. Food
    2. Decorations
    3. Traditions
  B. Christmas
    1. Food
    2. Decorations
    3. Traditions
	Discuss gift giving and festival of lights
	
	Prepare for holiday program
	
	Make gifts
	
	Discuss celebration
	
	Make Christmas decorations
		Pictures
		
		Magazines
		
		Newspapers
		
		Christmas with Peter and Carol—Filmstrip and record—Society for Visual Education

JANUARY

I. *The Five Senses* (Suggested Unit)	Watching Listening Take a walk and discuss what you see and hear Identify and apply the different senses (i.e., Mary is wearing a red dress. How do I know?)	*Look About You*—filmstrip and record—American Guidance Assoc. *Listen, There Are Sounds Around You*—filmstrip and record—American Guidance Assoc. *Sounds I Can Hear*—Scott Foresman
II. *Wheels* (Suggested Unit)	Categorize and identify objects with wheels. Use things with wheels	Pictures Actual wheeled vehicles

(January is an excellent time to bring in nonseasonal units.)

SOURCES	MUSIC	ART
Seasons—David C. Cook Pub. Co. Peabody Kit #1, clothing cards *Highlights for Children* *My Weekly Reader*	*All About Winter*—Bowmar "Winter Wind"—*More Singing Fun #2*—Bowmar	
Holidays—David C. Cook, Elgin, Ill.	"Ten Little Angels"—*Treasury of Songs*—Hart Pub. Co. "Mr. Santa Claus"—*Singing Fun*—Bowmar "Jingles the Christmas Clown"—*Special Needs #3*—Bowmar *We Wish You A Merry Christmas*—Young People's Records *December Holidays*—Bowmar	Make Christmas gifts for parents: use papier-mâché (strip method) for many decorative effects and projects; use plastic granules for baking to make wind chimes Paint with stain glass paints: candle holders, ash trays, etc. Sand and paint wooden objects
	Basic Songs For Exceptional Children—#1 and #3—Concept Records *Winter Days*—Bowmar	Make collage of textures for a "feeling picture" (use small pieces of actual materials such as sandpaper, fur, leather, etc.)
Wheels That Work for Us—Tiny Tots Pub. House	*Who Wants a Ride*—Young People's Records	

Intermediate

FEBRUARY	ACTIVITIES	MATERIALS

I. *The United States*
   A. Flag
 	
   B. Famous Americans
	Daily pledge: discuss what it means
	
	Abraham Lincoln, George Washington, other well-known Presidents
		Flag
		
		Pictures

II. *Light*
   A. Sources
      1. Sun
      2. Moon
      3. Electricity
	Discuss sun and moon, day and night
	
	Show why we have day and night, cloudy weather, using flashlight
	
	Show how lightbulb works (simply)
		Pictures
		
		Globe
		
		Flashlight
		
		Lightbulb

III. *Water*
   A. Forms
      1. Ice
      2. Liquid
	Discuss two forms of water; relate to change of weather
	
	Experiment with ice cube melting
		Ice water

IV. *Valentine's Day*	Exchange cards at Valentine party	Pictures

MARCH

	ACTIVITIES	MATERIALS

I. *The Circus*
   A. Animals
 	
   B. Acts
	Visit circus
	
	Discuss circus animals
	
	Discuss circus acts
	
	Differentiate between zoo and circus animals
		Pictures

II. *Signs of Spring*
   A. Temperatures
 	
   B. Weather
 	
   C. Clothing
 	
   D. Plants
 	
   E. Animals
	Daily weather report; observe and discuss daily
	
	Talk about change in clothing
	
	Start individual plants; observe leaves coming out
	
	Trip to zoo; observe and talk about baby animals in the park
		Cardboard thermometer
		
		Pictures
		
		Seeds
		
		Animal and insect cards

SOURCES	MUSIC	ART
My Weekly Reader #1 *Holidays*—David C. Cook Pub. Co.	"Flag Song"—*Special Needs* #2 Bowmar "Washington's Birthday"—*Come to the Party*—Children's Record Guild	
Peabody Kit #2 Mounted pictures		
	"Snowflakes"—*Singing Fun*—Bowmar "Winter Wind"—*More Singing Fun #2*—Bowmar	Cut snowflakes (help with folding)

Holidays—David C. Cook Pub. Co.	"Won't You Be My Valentine"—*Children's Holidays*—Vocalian
	
	February Holidays—Bowmar
		Make Valentines
		    cut paper
		    paste

Mounted pictures Milk Foundation circus posters Peabody Kit #1 and #2	*Circus Comes to Town*—Young People's Records "Elephant Bells"—*More Singing Fun #2*—Bowmar "Circus Ponies"—*More Singing Fun #2*—Bowmar "Man on the Flying Trapeze"—*Songs of the Gay 90's*—Remick Music Corp.	Draw pictures of circus Use crayons Use tempera paints
Seasons—David C. Cook Pub. Co. *Train to the Zoo*—Children's Record Guild Peabody Kit #1 and #2	*My Playmate the Wind*—Young People's Records "Five Little Kites"—*Singing Fun*—Bowmar "Walking Weather"—*Singing Fun*—Bowmar *Scarf Dance*—J. Barnett Records—Geo. Stanley Co. *All About Spring*—Bowmar *A Springtime Walk*—Bowmar	

Intermediate

APRIL	ACTIVITIES	MATERIALS
I. *Spring* 　　A. Weather 　　B. Plants 　　C. Animals 　　D. Sports	Review previous month's activity	
II. *Shadows* 　　A. Look for shadows 　　B. When shadows occur 　　C. Definition 　　D. Useful information	Experiment with flashlight and children's hands Observe shadows outdoors	

MAY

	ACTIVITIES	MATERIALS
I. *Summer Is Coming* 　　A. Weather 　　B. Plants 　　C. Animals 　　D. Activities	Observe daily weather Discuss helping in the garden Observe what new animals are here now Discuss what tools we use during the summer	Cardboard thermometer Pictures
II. *Transportation and Travel* 　　A. Means of transportation 　　　　1. Water 　　　　2. Air 　　　　3. Land	Categorize and identify kinds of transportation	Pictures

JUNE

	ACTIVITIES	MATERIALS
I. *Vacation Time* 　　A. Weather 　　B. Safety 　　C. Family activities 　　　　1. Trips 　　　　2. Home-based 　　D. Sports	Daily weather report Change of clothing Water safety Talk about summer school Talk about vacation plans Discuss: 　baseball 　swimming 　boating	Cardboard thermometer Pictures

SOURCES	MUSIC	ART
	Rainy Day—Young People's Records *Indoors When it Rains*—Children's Record Guild *Let's Help Mommy*—Children's Record Guild "Lollypop Tree"—*Through Children's Eyes*—RCA Voctor "Little White Cloud"—*More Singing Fun #2*—Bowmar *The Easter Lady*—Bowmar	Make spring pictures; use cut paper, crayons, paints Make three-dimensional flowers using egg cartons
Seasons—David C. Cook Pub. Co.	*Out-of-Doors*—Young People's Records *Who Wants A Ride?*—Young People's Records "Eensie Beensie Spider"—*Treasury of Songs*—Hart Pub. Co. *Train to the Zoo*—Children's Record Guild *All About Summer*—Bowmar *A Spring Secret*—Bowmar	Make Mother's Day gifts
Peabody Kit #1 Magazine pictures		
Seasons—David C. Cook Pub. Co. Peabody Kit #1 and #2 Mounted pictures	*Songs of Safety*—Decca "Three Little Ducklings"—*Singing Fun*—Bowmar "Ten Little Frogs"—*Singing Fun*—Bowmar 'School's Out"—*Come to the Party*—Children's Record Guild *A Summer Day on the Farm*—Bowmar *The Harbor and the Sea*—Bowmar	Make Father's Day gifts

Senior

SEPTEMBER	ACTIVITIES	MATERIALS

I. *Summer Review*
  A. Weather
    1. Kinds of weather
    2. Temperature
    3. Clothing
  B. Activities
    1. Family
    2. Camp
  C. Nature
    1. Plants
    2. Animals
  D. Sports (follow-up)
    1. Baseball
    2. Golf, tennis, swimming
	Talk time: what did you do this summer?
	
	Pantomime: imitate an activity (teacher may need to help child)
	
	Picture reading (of summer)
	
	Read experience stories (first or second level)
	
	Copy stories (a few usually can do this)
	
	Summer activity scrapbook
	
	Story time (teacher)
		Mounted pictures (teacher's collection)
		Other pictures
		Chalkboard
		Chart stand and blank charts
		Felt-tip markers
		Magazines, catalogs, calendar pictures, etc.
		Thermometer (real and "teaching")
		Crayons, colored pencils
		Paste, paste brushes
		Water colors
		Manila paper
		Newsprint

II. *Dairy Farm*
  A. The farm
  B. The bottling plant
  C. Distribution
    1. Stores
    2. Milkman
	Visit dairy farm or visit bottling plant
	
	Talk about visit
	
	Picture reading
	
	Read about milk
	
	Read experience stories
	
	Write experience stories
	
	Recordings
	
	Films
		Dairy Farm Panorama Kit (wall panel)
		
		Photographs, record, study guide from Dairy Farm Panorama Kit
		
		Primer story—*Milk For You and Me*—The Milk Foundation
		
		Film—*Uncle Jim's Dairy Farm*—National Dairy Council
		
		Teacher's picture collection

III. *Fall Begins*
  A. Signs of fall
    1. Leaves
    2. Seeds
    3. Weather
      a. Daylight
      b. Temperatures
      c. Clothing
	Field trip to observe signs of fall
	
	Picture reading
	
	Talk about signs of fall (include clothing)
	
	Read experience stories
	
	Make scrapbooks of pictures about fall
	
	Story or poetry time
		Fall pictures (teacher's collection)
		Thermometers

SOURCES	MUSIC	ART
My Weekly Reader #1 and #2	"How Do You Do Everybody" (traditional tune)—greeting song.	Make pictures of summer activities using crayons; felt pens or tempera watercolors may be substituted
Thermometer (Ideal)	"Hello Song"—*Counting songs for Children*—Folkways	
Peabody Kit #2		Draw pictures of family and family activities; same media as above
Look and Learn—Scott, Foresman	*You'll Sing a Song and I'll Sing a Song*—Folkways	Draw pictures of home, flowers and trees; same media as above
All Around Us—Scott, Foresman	*Weather Watchers*—Bowmar	
Science Around You—Ginn and Co.	Review camp songs	Make collage of summer activities using magazine pictures
Science Near You—Ginn and Co.	"Take Me Out to the Ball Game"—Remick Music Corp.	
Science Around You—D. C. Heath	*Camping in the Mountains*—Bowmar	
Highlights for Children	*The Zoo and the Circus*—Bowmar	
Children's Activities		
	Train to the Farm—Children's Record Guild	
	The Milk's Journey—Children's Record Guild	
	Did You Feed My Cow—Folkways	
	"Autumn is Here"—*Singing Fun*—Bowmar	

Senior

OCTOBER	ACTIVITIES	MATERIALS

I. *Fall—Autumn*
  A. Harvest time
    1. Crops
      a. Grains, fruits, vegetables
    2. Processing food
      a. Fresh, frozen, canned, stored
    3. Related products
      a. Flour, jelly, soup, etc.
    4. Grocery store
      a. Each type of item stocked
	Simple definitions: fall, autumn, harvest, crops, grains
	
	Identify: grains, fruits, vegetables
	
	Talk, read, and write about harvest time
	
	Filmstrips
	
	Talk, read, write about food processing
	
	Collect pictures
	
	Visit grocery store
	Talk, read, and write about trip
	
	Scrapbook: paste pictures about grains, fruits, vegetables
	or
	fresh, frozen, dried foods
	
	Stories and poems
		Pictures
		
		Vocabulary cards
		
		Stories
		
		Chalkboard
		
		Charts
		
		Booklets
		
		Filmstrips
		
		My Weekly Reader #1 and #2
		
		Magazines
		Paper
		Scissors
		Paste

B. Plants
    1. Farm plants
    2. Trees and bushes
    3. Flowers
    4. Seed formation
 	
  C. Animals
    1. Migrate
    2. Hibernate
    3. Stay and are active
    4. Store food
	Talk about:
	  Growing season is over
	  Leaves change color and fall
	  Plants that bloom late
	
	Collect leaves at home and school
	
	Collect seeds and compare
	
	Make a fall scrapbook
	
	Read and write about fall plants
	
	Talk about:
	  Animals that hibernate (bears, turtles, frogs)
	  Animals the hibernate (bears, turtles, frogs)
	  Animals that stay and are active (cardinals, rabbits, squirrels)
	  Squirrels storing nuts, seeds, etc.
	
	Read and write about animals in fall
		Mounted pictures
		Vocabulary cards
		
		Display ripe farm plants: corn, pumpkin, apples, etc.
		
		Display seeds and leaves
		Leaves
		Outdoor thermometer
		Children's newspapers
		Children's magazines
		Adult newspapers
		Magazines (fall issues)
		Stories
		Poems
		Chalkboard
		Chart paper

SOURCES	MUSIC	ART
Teacher's picture collection	"Harvest"—*All About the Seasons* (fall section)—Decca	
Teacher's vocabulary cards		
"Our Food—Where It Comes From" (booklet)—National Dairy Council	"Paw, Paw, Patch"—*Treasury of Songs*—Hart Pub. Co.	
Peabody Kit #2	*All About Fall*—Bowmar	
Food Store—filmstrip 506—Education Center, Columbus, Ohio 43216	*Halloween*—Bowmar	
Food: 6 color filmstrips—Encyclopaedia Britannica Films		
A Food Chart for Children—National Dairy Council		
Seasons (chart)—School Supply Co.		
My Weekly Reader—old and new, levels 1 and 2		
Highlights for Children—October, old and new		
Children's Activities—October		
Look and Learn—Scott, Foresman *All Around Us*—Scott, Foresman *Science Is Fun*—Scott, Foresman		
Sounds I Can Hear—Scott, Foresman		
Basic Studies in Science—Scott, Foresman		
	"Many Pretty Trees"—*Rhythms of Childhood*—Folkways	Use collected and pressed leaves in a laminated picture, scatter shaved crayon chips (fall colors) over leaves

Senior

OCTOBER	ACTIVITIES	MATERIALS
D. Weather 　　1. Kinds 　　2. Temperature 　　3. Clothing	Talk about: warm days, cool days, shorter days, frost, warmer clothing Read and write about fall weather Listen to poems and stories	
E. Columbus Day	Listen to poems, stories Talk, read, and write about Columbus	Mounted pictures Vocabulary cards Children's newspapers Children's magazines Poems, stories Chalkboard Chart paper
F. Sports 　　1. Football 　　2. Other sports of local interest	Talk about the game Look at pictures, TV Read and write about football and other local sports	Mounted pictures Vocabulary cards Current weekend newspapers TV program listings
G. Halloween 　　A time for fun (Allot at least two full weeks for a Halloween project)	Talk about Halloween Read and write about Halloween fun Have a party Play games Listen to stories and poems	Mounted pictures Vocabulary cards Children's newspapers Children's magazines Adult magazines and newspapers (October issues) Chalkboard Chart paper

SOURCES	MUSIC	ART
	"Weather Song"—*Special Needs* #2—Bowmar "Upward Trail"—*Special Needs* #3—Bowmar	
Teacher's picture collection Teacher's vocabulary cards *My Weekly Reader*—old and new, levels 1 and 2 *Highlights for Children*—October, old and new *Children's Activities*—October	"Story of Columbus"—*Holidays for U.S.A.*—Decca "Three Little Ships"—*Children's Holidays*—Vocalion	
Teacher's picture collection Teacher's vocabulary cards	"Take Me Out to the Ball Game"—*Songs of the Gay 90's*—Remick Music Corp. Rhythms: imitate activities of football, baseball signals, etc.	
Teacher's picture collection Teacher's vocabulary cards *My Weekly Reader*—October, old and new, levels 1 and 2 *Highlights for Children*—October, old and new *Children's Activities*—October	"Trick or Treat Song"—*Children's Holidays*——Vocalion "Tonight Is Halloween"—*More Singing Fun* #1—Bowmar	Make masks, using paper-plates, paper bags, or strip papier-mâché over a balloon; decorate with scrap items. Make pumpkin-shaped Halloween candle holders of modeling material, such as flour and salt or corn starch and baking soda Make Trick or Treat bags by decorating shopping bags Make Halloween characters; use pop bottles as base, papier-mâché or styrofoam for heads, and dress in scrap material

Senior

NOVEMBER	ACTIVITIES	MATERIALS

I. *Signs of Winter*
  A. Weather
    1. Kinds of weather
    2. Temperatures
    3. Clothing
	Talk about:
	  signs of winter
	  weather can be cold
	  we see frost
	  it can snow
	  we wear warmer clothing
	
	Read and write about signs of winter
		Outdoor thermometer
		
		Teaching thermometer
		
		Mounted pictures
		
		Vocabulary cards
		
		Children's newspapers
		
		Children's magazines
		
		Films, filmstrips
		
		Chalkboard
		
		Chart paper

B. Plants
    1. Plants rest
    2. Seeds rest
	Talk about:
	  plants in winter
	  branches are bare
	  Evergreens keep their foliage	

C. Animals
    1. Some migrated
    2. Some are hibernating
	Talk about:
	  animals in winter
	  robins, butterflies, geese are absent
	  bears, turtles, frogs are hibernating
	  sparrows cardinals, squirrels, rabbits are active
	
	Read and write about animals in winter
	
	Listen to poems, stories about winter	

II. *Health Unit*
  A. Foods we need
    1. Four groups
      a. Meat, eggs
      b. Fruit, vegetables
      c. Milk, cheese
      d. Cereals, bread
  B. Teeth
	Make a scrapbook about four groups of food
	
	Talk, read and write about:
	  foods we need
	  parts of plants we eat
	  use and care of teeth
		Paper, scissors, paste
		
		Pictures
		
		Vocabulary cards
		
		Children's newspapers
		
		Magazines
		
		Booklets
		
		Chalkboard
		
		Chart paper

SOURCES	MUSIC	ART
Teacher's picture collection Teacher's vocabulary cards Peabody Kit #2 *My Weekly Reader*—November, old and new, levels 1 and 2 *Highlights for Children*—November, old and new *Children's Activities*—November Films and filmstrips *Science Is Fun*—Scott, Foresman *Look and Learn*—Scott, Foresman *All Around Us*—Scott, Foresman	*All About the Seasons*—Decca *All About Winter*—Bowmar *Autumn*—Bowmar	Continue fall projects—Painting pre-cut autumn leaves; only fall colors offered; no restrictions on mixing paints or keeping colors clear
Teacher's picture collection Teacher's vocabulary cards Peabody Kit #2 *My Weekly Reader*—Preschool Picture Series "Every Day, Eat the 1-2-3-4 Way"—A food chart for children—National Dairy Council "Our Food"—National Dairy Council (booklet) "How We Take Care of Our Teeth—National Dairy Council (Booklet and poster)	*Health Can Be Fun*—Decca "Michael and the Dentist"—*After School Favorites*—Childcraft Records	Introduce modeling clay or "sculpy"; use to model fruits, vegetables, or animals

Senior

NOVEMBER (cont.)	ACTIVITIES	MATERIALS

III. *Thanksgiving*
    A. First Thanksgiving
    B. Family activities
    C. Favorite foods
	Talk, read, and write about Thanksgiving
	
	Learn a poem
	
	Listen to stories and poems
		Pictures
		
		Vocabulary cards
		
		Children's newspapers
		
		Children's magazines
		
		Chalkboard
		
		Chart paper

IV. *Sports*
    A. Local interest
        1. Football
        2. Lacrosse
	Talk about sports
	
	Collect pictures
	
	Follow a favorite team or athlete
		Pictures
		
		Vocabulary cards
		
		TV program listings
		
		Daily newspapers

DECEMBER

I. *Winter Begins*
    A. Weather
        1. Kinds
        2. Temperatures
        3. Clothing
        4. Winter in the south
	Talk about:
	  winter weather
	  we expect snow and ice
	  temperatures can go below freezing
	  we wear warm clothing, mittens, boots
	  winter is warm in the south
	      a. Many people go south for vacations
	
	Read and write about winter weather
		Pictures
		
		Vocabualry cards
		
		Thermometers
		
		Children's newspapers
		
		Children's magazines
		
		Films and filmstrips
		
		Chalkboard
		
		Chart paper

SOURCES	MUSIC	ART
Teacher's picture collection Teacher's vocabulary cards Peabody Kit #2 *My Weekly Reader*—November, old and new, levels 1 and 2 *Highlights for Children*—November, old and new *Children's Activities*—November Films and filmstrips	"Thanksgiving"—*Holidays in the U.S.*—Decca "Thank You Day"—*Children's Holidays*—Vocalion "Over the River and Through the Woods"—*Singing Together*—Ginn and Co.	Draw Thanksgiving pictures, usually turkeys or family activities
Teacher's picture collection Teacher's vocabulary cards		
Teacher's picture collection Teacher's vocabulary cards Peabody Kit #2 *My Weekly Reader*—old and new, levels 1 and 2 *Highlights for Children*—December *Children's Activities*—December Films and filmstrips *Science Is Fun*—Scott, Foresman *Look and Learn*—Scott, Foresman *All Around Us*—Scott, Foresman *Basic Studies in Science*—Scott, Foresman	"Winter Wind"—*More Singing Fun #2*—Bowmar *December Holidays*—Bowmar	

Senior

DECEMBER (cont.)	ACTIVITIES	MATERIALS
I. *Winter Begins* 　B. Animals 　　1. Food for animals 　　2. Tracks	Talk about animals 　We put out food when ground is frozen or snow-covered Look for animal tracks Read and write about animals in winter See films and filmstrips about winter Listen to poems and stories about winter	
II. *Holiday Time* 　A. Hanukkah 　B. Christmas 　C. Local customs	Talk, read and write about Hanukkah and Christmas Have a holiday party Make bright decorations for classroom	Pictures Vocabulary cards Children's newspapers Children's magazines Chalkboard Chart paper Choose materials for room decorations
III. *The Home* 　(Suggested Unit) 　A. Rooms 　B. Furnishings 　C. Appliances	Talk, read and write about the home Gather pictures Make a scrapbook	Pictures Vocabulary cards Magazines Colored newspaper pictures

SOURCES	MUSIC	ART

Teacher's picture collection
 	
Teacher's vocabulary cards
 	
My Weekly Reader—winter, old and new, levels 1 and 2
 	
Highlights for Children—December
 	
Children's Activities—December
 	
Films and filmstrips
	"Deck the Halls"—*Treasury of Songs*—Hart Pub. Co.
	
	"We Wish You A Merry Christmas"—Young People's Records
	
	"Twelve Days of Christmas"—Young People's Records
		All available time is used in making a gift for parents; suggested media for gifts.
		    Papier-mâché, Christmas foil, papers torn in small scraps—used to cover wastebaskets or other forms
		    Sand casting—Christmas trees or stars of David
		    Stain glass paint—to decorate dishes, bottles, candle holders
		    Wood—sand and paint wood pieces to make plaques, decorate with antiqued artificial flowers.
		    Plastic granules (oven baked) or plastic resin—for plaques, wind chimes, etc.
		    Macaroni—decorate boxes or Christmas tree shapes
		    Driftwood and painted weeds—make wrapping paper, using string dipped in tempera and dropped or dragged on tissue paper

Teacher's picture collection Teacher's vocabulary cards Peabody Kit #2		

Senior

JANUARY	ACTIVITIES	MATERIALS

I. *Winter*
A. Family activities
   1. Indoors
      a. Reading and stories
      b. Games
      c. TV
      d. Other
	Talk about:
	 each child's activities in the home
	
	activities suggested by teacher
	
	TV programs that families share
	
	pictures which show family activities
	
	Read and write about winter activities in the home
	
	See films and filmstrips
		Pictures
		Vocabulary cards
		Children's magazines
		Other magazines (winter issues)
		TV program listings
		A list of children's games and activities (made up in class)
		Films, filmstrips
		Chalkboard
		Chart paper

2. Outdoors
      a. Sledding
      b. Skating
      c. Snow fun
	Talk about:
	outdoor family activities enjoyed by members of class
	
	activities suggested by teacher
	
	pictures which show family outdoor activities
	
	Read and write about family outdoor activities
	
	Listen to stories, poems
	
	See films, filmstrips, or TV programs involving outdoor winter activities	

B. Sports
   1. Outdoors
      a. Hockey
      b. Skating
      c. Skiing
	Talk about:
	   fundamentals of each sport
	   attendance at games or contests
	   watching them on TV
	   pictures involving each sport
	Read and write about outdoor sports
	See films or filmstrips
		Pictures
		Vocabulary cards
		Sports sections of newspapers
		Children's newspapers
		TV program listings
		Films, filmstrips
		Chalkboard
		Chart paper

2. Indoors
      a. Basketball (TV)
      b. Hockey (TV)
      c. Swimming (TV)
	Talk about:
	   fundamentals of game
	   attendance at games
	   watching basketball and hockey on TV
	   pictures involving the sports
	Read and write about basketball and hockey
	See films, filmstrips	

SOURCES	MUSIC	ART

Teacher's picture collection
 	
Teacher's vocabulary cards
 	
My Weekly Reader—old and new, levels 1 and 2
 	
Highlights for Children
 	
Children's Activities
 	
Games used in school
 	
Films and filmstrips
	Guidance in use of music equipment:
	   radio
	   record player
	   guitar
	   autoharp
	   flutophone
	   recorder
	
	"Skater's Waltz"—*Jingle Bells*—Young People's Records
	
	Winter Days—Bowmar
		Draw or paint pictures of holiday activities
		
		Cut snowflakes; this group folds own paper and does more intricate cutting

Teacher's picture collection Teacher's vocabulary cards *My Weekly Reader*—old and new, levels 1 and 2 Films and filmstrips	Rhythmic chants and cheers	

Senior

JANUARY (cont.)	ACTIVITIES	MATERIALS

II. *The Senses*
(Suggested Unit)
A. Name them
B. Show function of each
C. We learn through our senses
D. We experiment
	Name the senses
	
	Demonstrate use of each
	
	Collect pictures to illustrate what we hear, see, touch, taste, smell
	
	Collect pictures of eyes, ears, nose, tongue, hands
	
	Read and write about sound, sight, taste, smell, touch, weight, motion
		Vocabulary cards
		Mounted pictures
		Materials for experiments, for example:
		  Hear: drum (any kind)—loud, soft
		  See: pictures—fall, winter, spring, summer
		  Touch: sandpaper, velvet
		  Taste: sour lemon drops, sugar cubes
		  Smell: sliced orange, apple, banana
		Magazines
		Chalkboard
		Chart paper

III. *Wheels*
(Suggested Unit)
A. Describe
B. Uses
  1. Machinery
    a. Kinds
  2. Transportation
    a. Kinds
	Talk about:
	  what a wheel looks like
	  how wheels help people
	  wheels are used in machinery
	  wheels are used in transportation
	
	Look for objects that use wheels
	
	Discuss pictures showing wheels at work
	
	Collect pictures of wheels at work
	
	Make a scrapbook
	
	Read and write about wheels.
		Vocabulary cards
		
		Mounted pictures
		
		Objects at school that use wheels
		
		Magazines
		
		Chalkboard
		
		Chart paper
		
		Paper, paste, scissors
		
		Children's newspapers (back issues relating to subject)

FEBRUARY

I. *The United States*
A. Map
  1. 50 states
  2. Locate U.S. on globe
	Look for own state
	
	Look for neighboring states
	
	Look for U.S. on globe
	
	Look for Alaska and Hawaii on globe
	
	Read and write about the U.S.
		Simplified U.S. map
		
		Globe
		
		United States flag
		
		Vocabulary cards
		
		Mounted pictures
		
		News pictures and articles
		
		Filmstrips
		
		Chalkboard
		
		Chart paper
		
		Bulletin board or other suitable area for setting up display of unit including written work copied from experience stories on board or on charts
		
		Stories, poems

SOURCES	MUSIC	ART
Teacher's picture collection Teacher's vocabulary cards *My Weekly Reader*—old and new, levels 1 and 2 *Science Is Fun*—Scott, Foresman	*Put Your Finger in the Air*—Columbia; Basic Songs for Exceptional Children #1 and #3—Concept Records *Everyone Join in the Game*—Columbia	Use scrap materials of various textures to make a collage, a "feeling" picture; make a collage of magazine pictures showing texture Draw a scribble picture; fill shapes with different scribbles to denote texture Draw self-portrait; stress correct body proportions
Teacher's picture collection Teacher's vocabulary cards *My Weekly Reader*—old and new, levels 1 and 2 *Science Is Wondering*—Scott, Foresman *Science Is Fun*—Scott, Foresman *Look and Learn*—Scott, Foresman *Basic Studies in Science*—Scott, Foresman	*Trains and Planes*—Young People's Records	Learning to know a different wheel—make a color wheel, using one color plus black or white to show change of value by adding the black or white in gradual steps
United States map—*My Weekly Reader* level 1 A globe U.S. flag Teacher's vocabulary cards Teacher's mounted pictures Adult news articles and pictures *My Weekly Reader*—old and new, levels 1 and 2 Filmstrips *Children's Activities* *Highlights for Children*	"America" "America the Beautiful" "Star Spangled Banner" "This Land Is Your Land"—*Special Needs* #3—Bowmar	

Senior

FEBRUARY (cont.)	ACTIVITIES	MATERIALS

I. *The United States*
  B. Flag
    1. Stars—significance
    2. Stripes—significance
    3. Colors
	Observe flag
	
	Talk about meaning of stars, stripes
	
	Identify colors of flag
	
	Read and write about flag	

C. Capital of U.S.
    1. Name
    2. Location
    3. Important buildings
      a. White House
      b. Capitol
	Observe U.S. map
	
	Find capital on map
	
	Look at pictures
	
	Look at filmstrips
	
	Identify Capitol building and White House
	
	Talk about functions of each
	
	Read and write about capitol	

D. Famous Americans
    1. Lincoln
    2. Washington
    3. Others
    4. Monuments
	See pictures of famous Americans
	
	Talk about what they did
	
	See pictures of memorials
	
	Read and write about famous Americans
	
	Listen to stories, poems	

II. *Light*
  (Suggested Unit)
  A. Sources
    1. Natural
    2. Artificial
  B. Importance
    1. Illumination
    2. Plant growth
	Talk about:
	  the sun gives light in daytime
	  the clouds dim daylight
	  we use electric lights at night and on cloudy days
	  flashlights and candles give light
	  we need light to see—outside and inside
	
	Plants need light to grow
	
	Experiments:
	Observe daylight outside and inside on sunny and cloudy days
	Observe electric light in classroom on sunny and cloudy days
	Close drapes or shades; observe light from flashlight, candles
	
	Demonstrate:
	  Plants need light to grow; they grow toward light
	
	Read and write about light
		Vocabulary cards
		
		Pictures related to subject
		
		Classroom electric light
		
		Flashlight
		
		Large and small candles
		
		Materials for demonstrating how plants need light to grow: see p. 166 *Basic Science Handbook*; also p. 74, *All Around Us*; also, pp. 77-79, *Science Around You*
		
		Children's newspaper articles
		
		Chalkboard
		
		Chart paper

SOURCES	MUSIC	ART
	Flag drill—to the music of "Stars and Stripes Forever"	Make own flag; any design on tissue or tracing paper; attach to small dowel
	"Lincoln's Birthday," "Washington's Birthday"—*Holidays for U.S.*—Decca *February Holidays*—Bowmar	
Teacher's vocabulary cards Teacher's picture collection Flashlight, candles (available at dime stores, hardware stores) *Basic Science Handbook* K-3—Scott, Foresman *Look and Learn*—Scott, Foresman *All Around Us*—Scott, Foresman *Science Around You*—D.C. Heath *My Weekly Reader*—old, levels 1 and 2 *Basic Studies in Science*—Scott, Foresman		

Senior

FEBRUARY (cont.)	ACTIVITIES	MATERIALS

III. *Water*
    (Suggested Unit)
    A. Sources
        1. Lakes, rivers, oceans
        2. Rain
        3. Snow
        4. Ice
    B. Importance
        1. People and animals
        2. Plants
        3. Water animals
	Talk about water on the earth
	
	Look at U.S. map and globe; locate lakes, rivers, oceans
	
	Determine local source of water
	
	Talk about fresh water, salt water
	
	Talk about water from rain, snow, ice
	
	Look at pictures of rain, snow, ice
	
	Read and write about water
	
	Talk about:
	    People need water for drinking, bathing, washing, machines, transportation (boats)
	
	    Animals need water for drinking, bathing, finding food
	
	    Plants need water to grow
	
	    Fish get oxygen from water
	
	    Whales, dolphins must live in water
	
	    Some animals need fresh water; some need salt water
	
	Read and write about the need for water
	
	Experiment—seed germination
		Vocabulary cards
		Mounted pictures
		U.S. Map
		Globe
		Children's newspaper articles and pictures
		Chalkboard
		Chart paper
		2 water glasses, cotton, seeds, water. See *All Around Us* or another science text
		Ice cubes
		Snow

IV. *Valentine's Day*		

FEBRUARY (cont.) | ACTIVITIES | MATERIALS

SOURCES	MUSIC	ART
Teacher's vocabulary cards Teacher's picture collection Simplified U.S. Map—*My Weekly Reader* level 1 Globe *My Weekly Reader*—old, levels 1 and 2 *All Around Us*—Scott, Foresman *Science Near You*—Ginn and Co.	*What Makes Rain*—Decca	
	Valentine Songs: "Won't You Be My Valentine"—*Children's Holidays*—Decca "Let Me Call You sweetheart"	Valentine Day projects: Make valentine for parents using felt pens; snowflakes may be used for decoration; cover pre-cut heart shapes with papier-mâché, using foil or gift papers. Use small squares of paper as mosaics on pre-cut heart shapes Make a decorated construction-paper envelope; use as individual valentine container

Senior

MARCH	ACTIVITIES	MATERIALS

I. *Circus*
   A. Winter quarters
   B. People involved
   C. Animals involved
   D. Acts
	Talk about:
	  The circus in winter
	  The people involved—performers, workmen
	  The animals—lions, tigers, elephants, chimpanzes, etc.
	  Aerial acts, balancing acts, trained animal acts, etc.
	
	Look at films, filmstrips
	
	Read and write about the circus
	
	Visit the circus
		Vocabulary cards
		Mounted pictures
		Children's newspapers (articles and pictures)
		Adult newspapers (articles and pictures)
		Films, filmstrips
		Chalkboard
		Chart paper

II. *Magnets*
  (Suggested Unit)
   A. Function
     1. Magnets attract some things
     2. Magnets do not attract some things
   B. Uses
     1. Magnets attract iron and steel
     2. Magnets attract objects through glass, paper, plastic, wood
	Use magnets on various objects in classroom (thumbtacks, paper clips, scissors, wooden ruler, rubber ball, chalk, etc.)
	
	Use magnets to attract iron and steel through glass, paper, plastic, and wood
	
	Look at pictures
	
	Talk about, read and write about:
	  what magnets attract; how they attract through glass, paper, plastic and wood
		Vocabulary cards
		Mounted pictures
		Children's newspapers (articles and pictures)
		Objects to use with magnet as suggested
		Materials through which magnets attract
		Large and small magnets
		Chalkboard
		Chart paper

III. *Signs of Spring*
   A. Temperature
     1. May be like spring
     2. May be like winter
   B. Weather
     1. It can snow or rain
     2. It can be sunny
     3. It can be windy
   C. Clothing
     1. We may need winter wraps
     2. We may need spring wraps
   D. Plants
     1. Buds grow
     2. Grass shows green color
   E. Animals
     1. Migrating birds return
     2. Animals end hibernation
   F. Clean-up time
     1. Clean yard
     2. Clean house
	Talk about:
	  changes in temperature
	  weather changes
	  clothing changes
	  buds on trees, bushes; grass at home and at school
	  cleaning up the yard, garden, house
	
	Read and write about signs of spring
	
	Look at pictures, watch films and filmstrips
	
	Make a bulletin board about signs of spring
	
	Read and/or listen to poems about signs of spring
	
	Look for robins or other early birds
		Vocabulary cards
		Mounted pictures
		Children's newspapers (articles and pictures)
		Children's magazines
		Adult magazines
		Adult newspapers
		Pictures of tools, appliances (rake, vacuum cleaner)
		Films, filmstrips
		Stories, poems

SOURCES	MUSIC	ART
Teacher's vocabulary cards Teacher's picture collection *My Weekly Reader*—old and new, levels 1 and 2 Adult newspapers—pre-spring issues Films, filmstrips	*Circus Comes to Town*—Young People's Records "Man on the Flying Trapeze"—*Songs of the Gay 90's*—Remick Music Corp.	Make circus pictures before and after visit to circus, using crayons, paints, and felt pens
Teacher's vocabulary cards Teacher's picture collection *My Weekly Reader*, levels 1 and 2 *Science Is Fun*—Scott, Foresman *Science Near You*—Ginn and Co. *Science Around You*—D.C. Heath		
Teacher's vocabulary cards Teacher's picture collection *My Weekly Reader*—old and new, levels 1 and 2 *Children's Activities* *Highlights for Children* Adult magazines (March issues) Adult newspapers (early spring issues) *Look and Learn*—Scott, Foresman Peabody Kit #2 Film, filmstrips Teacher's poem collection	*My Playmate the Wind*—Young People's Records Rhythm activities Raking leaves Clean-up outdoors "Walking Weather"—*Singing Fun*—Bowmar *All About Spring*—Bowmar *A Springtime Walk*—Bowmar	Make small decorated kites Cut tulips from egg cartons, attach to pipe cleaner stem, paint and "plant" in a paper cup

Senior

APRIL	ACTIVITIES	MATERIALS

I. *Spring*
   A. Weather
      1. Temperatures are higher
      2. It rains frequently
      3. We wear lighter clothing
   B. Plants
      1. Leaves grow
      2. We see spring blossoms
      3. We plant seeds
   C. Animals
      1. Animals have babies
         a. Home area
         b. Farm area
         c. At the zoo
   D. Sports
      1. Baseball season opens
      2. Other sports begin
	Talk about:
	   warmer weather, spring rain, lighter clothing, rainwear
	   growth of grass and leaves, fruit tree blossoms, spring flowers (tulips etc.)
	   animal babies around home, farm, and zoo
	   baseball and other warm-weather sports
	
	Look at pictures, films, filmstrips about spring
	
	Read, write about spring
	
	Visit zoo or farm
	
	Plant flower seeds
		Vocabulary cards
		Mounted pictures
		Children's newspapers (articles and pictures)
		Children's magazines
		Adult newspapers
		Adult magazines
		Outdoor thermometer
		Films, filmstrips
		Seeds, jar, cotton
		Soil, flat, flower seeds
		Stories and poems

II. *Shadows*
   A. Look for shadows
      1. Indoors
      2. Outdoors
   B. When shadows occur
      1. Indoors
      2. Outdoors
   C. Definition:
      dark picture—light source cannot penetrate
   D. Useful information
      1. Determine time of day
      2. Direct light source to work area
      3. Make shadow puppets
	Turn off lights; with flashlight, make shadows against wall of child's silhouette or shapes formed with hands and fingers; this activity is fun as well as informative
	
	Point out shadows of trees, bushes, etc.
	
	Show how shadows occur when solid object blocks light source
	
	Observe outdoor shadows in morning, noon, and afternoon
	
	Demonstrate how work area is arranged to give best light
	
	Make simple shadow puppets or silhouettes of other familiar objects (chair, tree, etc.); set-up stage with piece of thin material with light source behind; demonstrate how puppets block light source and cast their shadows on screen
	
	Read and write about shadows
		Flashlight or lamp
		Table, simple wooden frame to stand near edge of table, thin material to thumbtack to frame
		Heavy cardboard, thin flat sticks (from ice cream bars, tongue depressors, etc.)
		Scotch tape or glue cardboard shapes to stick; allow space to grasp stick
		Children's newspapers
		Vocabulary cards
		Mounted pictures
		Chalkboard
		Chart paper

SOURCES	MUSIC	ART
Teacher's vocabulary cards Mounted pictures *My Weekly Reader*—old and new, levels 1 and 2 *Children's Activities* *Highlights for Children* Adult newspapers (spring issues) Adult magazines (spring issues) *Spring Is Here*—Golden Press *Look and Learn*—Scott, Foresman *All Around Us*—Scott, Foresman *Science Is Fun*—Scott, Foresman *Science Near You*—Ginn and Co. Peabody Kit #2	"Rain, Rain Go Away" "April Showers Bring May Flowers" "Little White Cloud"—*More Singing Fun #2*—Bowmar "Spring Is on Its Way"—*Singing Fun #2*—Bowmar "Take Me Out to the Ball Game" *Songs of the Gay 90's*—Remick Music Corp. *The Easter Lady*—Bowmar	Draw and paint spring pictures Laminate colored tissue paper—spring flower colors—between waxed paper sheets to represent spring flowers Make papier-mâché animals or puppets, using either "instant" or strip mâché (this project will take several weeks)
Teacher's vocabulary cards Teacher's picture collection *My Weekly Reader*—old issues dealing with shadows, levels 1 and 2 *All Around Us*—Scott, Foresman	Rhythms "Trees"—Joyce Kilmer (sheet music) G. Schirmer Inc. "Lollypop Tree"—*Through Children's Eyes*—RCA	

Senior

MAY	ACTIVITIES	MATERIALS

I. *Summer Is Coming*
  A. *Weather*
    1. Temperatures are higher
    2. Weather changes
    3. Days are longer
    4. Clothing is lighter
  B. *Plants*
    1. Trees have leaves
    2. Flower plants grow
    3. Crops are growing
    4. Weeds are growing
  C. *Animals*
    1. Baby animals grow
    2. Observe wild animals
  D. Summer plans
	Note temperatures on outdoor thermometer in morning and in afternoon
	
	Observe that rain replaces ice, snow, sleet
	
	Observe longer daylight hours
	
	Talk about:
	  clothing, plants growing
	  Note progress of flower seeds planted
	
	Look for baby animals in school area, home, zoo (field trip to zoo)
	
	Talk about trip—especially baby animals
	
	Talk about summer plans:
	  day camp
	  camp away from home
	  activities in home area
	  family trips
	
	Look at pictures, films, filmstrips
	
	Read and write about summer plans
	
	Listen to stories, poems
		Vocabulary cards
		Mounted pictures
		Chalkboard
		Chart paper
		Children's newspapers
		Children's magazines
		Adult newspapers and magazines
		Planted flower flats
		Films, filmstrips
		Stories, poems

II. *Transportation and Travel*
  A. Things are transported in different ways
  B. People travel in different ways
  C. People need maps
    1. U.S. map
    2. Road maps
	Talk about:
	  Things that are transported (cars, food, clothing, etc.)
	  Means of transportation (trains, trucks, airplanes, ships)
	  How people travel (cars, buses, trains, airplanes, ships)
	  Why people need maps (people need to know where states are, people need to plan travel with road maps)
	
	Read and write about transportation and travel
	
	Look at U.S. map, road maps
	
	Plan a simple trip from home city to another city in state
	
	Arrange a bulletin board with travel pictures, U.S. map, etc.
		Vocabulary cards
		Mounted pictures
		Travel folders
		Children's weekly newspapers (articles and pictures)
		Adult newspapers (especially weekend issues)
		Magazines—adult and children's
		U.S. maps, small and large
		Road maps (especially own state)
		Films, filmstrips

SOURCES	MUSIC	ART

Teacher's vocabulary cards
 	
Teacher's picture collection
 	
My Weekly Reader—old and new, levels 1 and 2
 	
Children's Activities
 	
Highlights for Children
 	
Adult newspapers (May issues)
 	
Films, filmstrips
 	
Science Around You—D.C. Heath
 	
Science Near You—Ginn and Co.
 	
Look and Learn—Scott, Foresman
 	
All Around Us—Scott, Foresman
	All About the Seasons—Decca
	
	All About Summer—Bowmar
	
	A Spring Secret—Bowmar
	
	"Memorial Day"—*Holidays for U.S.*—Decca
		Mother's Day project:
		make a gift suitable for mother:
		  recipe holder
		  papier-mâché jewelry
		  pin cushion

Teacher's vocabulary cards Teacher's mounted pictures Local travel agency *My Weekly Reader*: U.S. maps, large and small *My Weekly Reader*—levels 1 and 2 Adult newspapers *Children's Activities* *Highlights for Children* General magazines Road maps—local gas stations *Wheels That Work for Us*—Tiny Tots Pub. House *All Around Us*—Scott, Foresman *Science Around You*—D.C. Heath Films, filmstrips	*Trains and Planes*—Young People's Records "In Trinidad"—*Adventures in Rhythm*—Folkways	Make simple map of school and home area

JUNE	ACTIVITIES	MATERIALS

I. *Vacation Time*
  A. Weather changes
    1. Temperatures rise
    2. Kinds of weather change
    3. Kinds of clothing change
  B. Safety
    1. Look for safety signs
    2. Play in safe areas
    3. Follow safety rules
  C. Health
    1. People need regular meals
    2. People need planned exercise
    3. People need adequate rest
	Talk about:
	higher temperatures (observe outdoor thermometer)
	Warm sunny days, thunderstorms, tornados, wind
	lightweight clothing; few, if any, wraps
	safety signs (danger, stop, go, keep out, etc.)
	safe areas to play (park, yard, etc.)
	refusal to ride with strangers, avoiding too much sun, swimming in safe places, etc.
	regular meals; limit snacks
	planned exercise: swimming, hiking, ballgames
	adequate rest—at night, during day
	See films, filmstrips
	Read and write about vacation time (each category)
		Outdoor thermometer
		Vocabulary cards (safety signs)
		Mounted pictures
		Children's newspapers (late spring issues, back and current)
		Children's magazines
		Adult magazines (spring issues, back and current)
		Adult newspapers (especially weekend magazine sections)
		Food chart
		Booklet (health practice)
		Child feeding posters
		Pictures (personal health)
		Films, filmstrips
		Chalkboard
		Chart paper

II. *Family Activities*
  A. Families take trips
  B. Families stay home
    1. They swim
    2. They have picnics, cookouts
    3. They play outdoor games
    4. They visit museum, zoo, nature center
	Review family plans for trips
	Talk about family activities in home areas
	Review safety measures
	Look at pictures and maps
	See films, filmstrips
	Read and write about summer activities
		Vocabulary cards (safety signs)
		Mounted pictures
		U.S. map
		Road maps
		Children's newspapers
		Children's magazines
		TV program listings
		Films, filmstrips
		Chalk board
		Chart paper

III. *Sports*
  A. Summer sports include baseball, golf, swimming, tennis
  B. Some other sports have interest in certain areas
	Talk about summer sports in own area; performance of each sport
	Look at pictures
	Look at films, filmstrips, TV
	Read and write about summer sports	

SOURCES	MUSIC	ART
Thermometer Teacher's vocabulary cards Teacher's picture collection *My Weekly Reader*—late spring issues, old and new, levels 1 and 2 *Highlights for Children*—spring and summer *Children's Activities*—spring and summer Adult magazines—spring and summer Adult newspapers (especially weekend magazine sections) A food chart for children—National Dairy Council *Your Health* (booklet)—National Dairy Council Child feeding posters—National Dairy Council *My Weekly Reader* Preschool Picture Series on personal health Films, filmstrips	"In the Good Old Summertime"—*Songs of the Gay 90's*—Remick Music Corp. "Make New Friends"—*Special Needs #3*—Bowmar *Songs of Safety*—Decca *A Summer Day on the Farm*—Bowmar *The Harbor and the Sea*—Bowmar	Draw safety signs, can be used as designs for printing potato prints or mono-prints
Teacher's vocabulary cards Teacher's picture collection *My Weekly Reader*—late spring issues, old and new, levels 1 and 2 *Highlights for Children*—spring and summer *Children's Activities*—spring and summer Films, filmstrips TV program listings (local newspaper) *My Weekly Reader*—large and small maps Road maps—local service station		

NONSEASONAL UNITS

1. The City
2. Community Helpers: Occupations
3. Water
4. Light
5. Shadows
6. Magnets
7. Tools
8. Machines (including appliances)
9. Wheels
10. Transportation
11. Maps
12. Magnets
13. The Senses
14. The Dairy Farm
15. Animals
    Domestic
    Wild, Zoo
    Pets
    Insects
    Water Animals
16. Space (especially during space missions)
17. General Health
18. Safety
19. Sounds

Sample Outline for Nonseasonal Unit

Magnets

A. Magnets move things
   1. They pull iron and steel things
   2. Iron and steel things stick to magnets
   3. The ends of magnets are strongest

B. We use magnets (horseshoe, bar types)
   1. They pick up tacks, screws, paper clips, pins
   2. They do not pick up rubber bands, erasers, soap, pencils

C. Magnets work *through* things
   1. They work through **paper**
   2. They work through **glass**
   3. They work through **water**

D. Magnets are useful to us
   1. Teachers use magnet boards
   2. Magnets pick up spilled tacks, clips
   3. Magnets work in our homes in:
      a. Television sets
      b. Vacuum cleaners
      c. Electric trains

RESOURCES

I. BOOKS

Scott, Foresman and Company,
1900 East Lake Avenue,
Glenview, Ill. 60025.
Science Is Wondering
Science Is Fun
Look and Learn
All Around Us
Basic Science Handbook
Sounds I Can Hear
Basic Studies in Science

The Macmillan Company, 866 Third Avenue, New York, N.Y. 10022.
Science, Health, and Safety—book 1

Ginn and Company, Statler Building, Back Bay P.O. 191, Boston, Mass. 02117
Science Near You
Science Around You

D.C. Heath and Company, 125 Spring Street, Lexington, Mass. 02173.
Science Around You

Benefic Press, 1900 N. Narragansett, Chicago, Ill. 60639.
My Family and I

Remick Music Corporation, 488 Madison Avenue, New York, N.Y.
Songs of the Gay 90's

Holt, Rinehart & Winston, 383 Madison Avenue, New York, N.Y. 10017.
Sounds and Patterns of Language

Reader's Digest Association, Pleasantville, N.Y. 10570.
Marvels and Mysteries of Our Animal World

Field Enterprises Educational Corp., 510 Merchandise Mart Plaza, Chicago, Ill. 60654.
Childcraft: The How and Why Library

Golden Press, Inc., Education Division, 850 Third Avenue, New York, N.Y. 10022.
The Sign Book
Fall Is Here
Winter Is Here
Spring Is Here
Summer Is Here

Scholastic Book Services, 50 West 44 Street, New York, N.Y. 10036.
Magnets
Petunia's Christmas
The Snowy Day

Allyn & Bacon, Inc., 470 Atlantic Avenue, Boston, Mass. 02210.
Learning About Our Families

II. MAGAZINES

My Weekly Reader and *New Science Reading Adventures*—American Education Publications, Education Center, Columbus, O. 43216.

Highlights for Children—P.O. Box 269, Columbus, O. 43216.

Children's Digest Magazine elementary and *Humpty-Dumpty's Magazine* (primary)—Parents' Magazine Enterprises, Thompson Lane, Box 539, Nashville, Tenn.

World Traveler (adapted from *The National Geographic School Bulletin*)—Dept. RM, 1537 35th Street N.W., Washington, D. C. 20007.

III. INSTRUCTIONAL SYSTEMS

Science Research Associates, Inc., 259 East Erie Street, Chicago, Ill. 60611.
Distar Instructional System

Teaching Resources Corporation, 100 Boylston Street, Boston, Mass. 02116.
Vanguard School Program
Ruth Cheves Program
Dubnoff School Program 1 and 2

Educational Play Systems, Inc., 200 Ffith Avenue, New York, N.Y. 10010.
manipulative materials

Allied Education Council, P.O. Box 78, Galien, Mich. 49113.
Fitzhugh Plus Program
Mott Basic Language Skills

Educational Teaching Aids Division, A. Daigger & Co., Inc., 159 West Kinzie Street, Chicago, Ill. 60610.
Learning Aids for Early and Special Education

American Guidance Service, Inc., Publishers' Building, Circle Pines, Minn. 55014
    Peabody Language Development Kits
    Rebus Reading System

Follett Educational Corp., P.O. Box 5705, Chicago, Ill. 60680.
    Frostig Materials
    Developmental Program in Auditory Perception

Fearon Publishers, 2165 Park Boulevard, Palo Alto, Cal. 94306.
    Pacemaker Games Program

Developmental Learning Materials, 3505 North Ashland Avenue, Chicago, Ill. 60657.
    great variety of materials

Bowmar, 622 Rodier Drive, Glendale, Cal. 91201
    materials for exceptional children

McGraw-Hill, Webster Division, Manchester Road, Manchester, Mo. 63011.
    Sullivan Reading System

Creative Playthings, Princeton, New Jersey 08540

IV. FILMS, FILMSTRIPS AND FILM LOOPS

Educational Reading Service (catalog) East 64 Midland Ave., Paramus, N.J. 07652.

Adventures in the Wilderness—8 filmstrips
Americans Who Shaped History—6 filmstrips
Great Americans—Captain Columbus—filmstrip
People Who Help Our Community — 10 transparencies
Community Helpers—8 filmstrips
Children's World Series—6 filmstrips
Children Around the World—12 filmstrips
Holidays and Seasons—7 filmstrips
Signs of Spring, Signs of Autumn—transparencies for overhead projector—7 in each set
Weather and Climate—4 filmstrips
Learning About Our Fifty States—transparencies
Primary Grade Health Series —6 filmstrips
Safety Signs—2 sets transparencies
We Take A Trip—4 filmstrips
Wonders of Science—6 filmstrips
Learning About Our World: Time for Autumn and Winter; Time For Spring and Summer—filmstrips
Pictures Help Us Learn—9 packets

Kimberly-Clark Corp., Neenah, Wisc. 54956.
    film on care of colds (sound, color)

American Guidance Associates, Pleasantville, N.Y.
    Look About You (filmstrip and record)
    Listen, There Are Sounds Around You (filmstrips and record)

American Education Publications Education Center, Columbus, Ohio 43216.
    My Weekly Reader Preschool Filmstrips: *Health, Food Store, Transportation*

Society for Visual Education, Inc., 1345 West Diversey Parkway, Chicago, Ill. 60614
    Thanksgiving with Peter and Carol (filmstrips and record)
    Christmas with Peter and Carol (filmstrip and record)

Encyclopedia Britannica Educational Corporation, 425 N. Michigan Avenue, Chicago, Ill. 60611 (there are regional addresses)

Primary Filmstrips (k-3)

Exploring with Science (color)—Shortstrip Series No. 9900—Series of 12
Discovering Life Around Us—Filmstrip Series No. 11110
The Four Seasons (color)—Filmstrip Series No. 10660
Primary Science (color)—Filmstrip Series No. 8320
Different Kinds of Animals—Filmstrip Series No. 9410
Insects: How They Live and Grow (color) Filmstrip Series No. 9500
Learning about Animals (color)—Shortstrip Series No. 9940
Plants Around Us (color)—Shortstrip Series. No. 9960
Health Stories (color)—Filmstrip Series No. 7660
Safety Stories (color)—Filmstrip Series No. 7640
Learning About People (color)—Shortstrip Series No. 9920
Food (color)—Filmstrip Series No. 8420
The Home Community (color)—Filmstrip Series No. 7700
The School Community—Filmstrip Series No. 7720
The Neighborhood Community (color)—Filmstrip Series No. 7760
The City Community (color)—Filmstrip Series No. 7800

Each shortstrip series includes one plastic hand-viewer.

EALING, 1969 Cartridged Film Loops Elementary School Catalog, 2225 Massachusetts Ave., Cambridge, Mass. 02140

    Monarch Butterfly: Life History—Catalog No. 81-3444/1—Cartridged Super 8
    Common American Birds: Robin—Catalog No. 81-3584/1—Cartridged Super 8
    Seed Dispersal—Catalog No. 81-9631/1—Cartridged Super 8
    Beaver Dam and Lodge—Catalog No. 81-8104/1—Cartridged Super 8
    Bean Sprouts (Growing Seeds)—Catalog No. 81-4244/1—Cartridged Super 8
    Ground Squirrel—Catalog No. 81-8393/1—Cartridged Super 8

V. RECORDS

Folkways
Rhythms of Childhood
Adventures in Rhythm
Call and Response Rhythmic Group Singing
Counting Games and Rhythms for the Little Ones
This Is Rhythm
You'll Sing A Song and I'll Sing A Song

Children's Record Guild
The Merry Toy Shop
A Visit to My Little Friend
Come to the Party
Eensie Beensie Spider
Grandfather's Farm
Let's Help Mommy
My Playful Scarf
Strike Up the Band
Train to the Farm
Train to the Zoo
Creepy Crawly Caterpillar
Indoors When It Rains
The Milk's Journey

Childcraft Education Corp.
After School Favorites

Decca
Songs of Safety
All About the Seasons
Holidays for U.S.
What Makes Rain
Children's Holidays
Health Can Be Fun

Bowmar
Singing Fun
More Singing Fun—1 and 2
Weather Watchers
Holiday Rhythms
Songs for Children with Special Needs—1, 2, and 3
Rhythms to Reading: a child's calendar of action song-stories (with books)
All About Fall
All About Winter
All About Spring
All About Summer

Young People's Records
Building a City
Circus Comes to Town
Hooray! Today Is Your Birthday
Jingle Bells
Who Wants a Ride?
Out-of-Doors
Trains and Planes
Men Who Come to Our House
Rainy Day
My Playmate the Wind
When the Sun Shines

Young People's Records (cont.)
I'm Dressing Myself
We Wish You a Merry Christmas
Twelve Days of Chirstmas

Vocalion
Children's Holidays
Children's Sing-A-Long

RCA Victor
Bingo
Through Children's Eyes

Geo. Stanley Co.
Barnett Records, Jean Series

Capitol
Bozo at the Party
Bozo at the Circus
Learning to Listen (John Tracy Clinic)

Playwell Records
Sing a Song of Safety

Activity Records
Basic Concepts Through Dance

Summy-Birchard Co.
Music for Exceptional Children (with book)

Columbia
Burl Ives Sings
Put Your Finger in the Air
Let's Play a Musical Game
Everyone Join in the Game

Pram Records
Where Are Your Eyes

Golden Records
Peter Cottontail

Concept Records
Basic Songs for Exceptional Children, 3 volumes

Scott, Foresman
Farm in the Zoo (with pictures)
House (with pictures)
Neighborhood (with pictures)
School (with pictures)

VI. MISCELLANEOUS

David C. Cook Publishing Co., Elgin, Ill. 60120.
    Teaching Pictures: Seasons, Holidays, Children Around the World, My Community, Science

American Education Publications, Education Center, Columbus, O. 43216.
    My Weekly Reader Preschool Picture Series—Personal Health

Ideal School Supply Company, 11,000 S. Lavergne Avenue, Oak Lawn, Ill. 60453.
    teaching thermometer

National Dairy Council, 111 N. Canal Street, Chicago, Ill. 60606.
    Urban Panorama Kit
    Dairy Farm Panorama Kit
    Child Feeding Posters
    A Food Chart for Children
    How We Take Care of Our Teeth (booklet and poster)
    Your Health: How Can You Help? (booklet)
    Our Food: Where It Comes From (booklet)
    Milk for You and Me (primer booklet and posters)
    What We Do Day by Day

Ed-U-Cards Manufacturing Corp., 200 Fifth Avenue, New York, N.Y. 10010.
    lotto games

The Judy Co., 310 North 2nd Street, Minneapolis, Minn. 55401.
    puzzles

Ohio Art Toys, Bryan, O. 43506

26. NUMBERS IN EVERYDAY LIVING

Multiplication is vexation
Division is as bad;
The Rule of Three doth puzzle me
And practice drives me mad.
—Mother Goose

Our number system gives order to daily living. "How many" and "How much" are the bases for all arithmetic, and for learning where we are in relation to other people and things.

To learn "how many" and "how much," we count. The result of counting—the amount—has meaning. We learn to count first by simple notation, and progress through a tremendous sequence of involved mathematics in the quest for "how many" and "how much."

The levels for learning about numbers are clear:

I. Counting by notation
II. Counting by grouping and notation (partial counting)
III. Counting by grouping
IV. Multiplication and conversion (abstract reasoning)

For the moderately retarded child, mastery of the first two levels and some success in Level III is a *maximum* goal. Success through levels I and II is to be sought and is realistic for most trainable children. A firm working concept of the notation system—using simple amounts arrived at by notation, properly designated, named, and written by the appropriate symbol—is essential in useful everyday living at home or in a workshop.

Level I: Counting by Notation

Familiarity with the names of numbers can be gained by rote counting in games and songs. The actual names have no meaning during the rote-counting stage beyond a learned sequence system of sounds. There is some question concerning the value of rote counting because of the created invitation to perseverate. However, it is almost impossible to come across a verbal, retarded child who has not been exposed to rote counting at home. It does acquaint the child with sound symbols, and possibly this justifies the risk of aiding perseveration.

The child requires constant tactile, concrete stimulation to learn to count and to terminate. Each step should be reinforced through a total body activity.

Count by notation at every opportunity that presents itself. Always count from left to right. It is basic and essential in *all* counting opportunities at this level and later levels to count from left to right. It is a habit to be instilled.

So much of our counting in everyday living is from left to right; the calendar, the dials on washing machines, radios (TV dials are not consistently arranged, unfortunately), and many scales, card games, bowling scores, etc. The teacher should count the children from left to right, count everything passed out, and count, count, count, at every opportunity.

No matter what or who is being counted, the teacher should raise her voice emphatically at the terminal, drop her hand emphatically if she has been pointing, clap her hands or slap the table or do whatever is convenient to draw attention to the fact that *this* is the number on which we stop *this* counting *this* time.

STEP 1: *Counting and structured termination*

We have some ready-made "structured termination" for counting. One nose, one mouth, one head, one tummy, two eyes, two ears, two feet, two knees, two shoes, two socks, two boots, two mittens.

Cut up contoured egg cartons to contain two apertures; then three, four, five, six, etc. Paint each cut-out set a primary color. Talk about it—"We are painting this egg box that holds two eggs," etc. It helps to make the special container with the child helping or watching. You can then place pretend eggs (large beads or 1" cubes) in the correct amount. Each modified carton serves as a structured termination to break the tendency to rote count on and on.

The wooden trays used for 1" dowels (those you use for color matching) can be used the same way. Place beads, or dowels in the apertures and *count*.

Strips of cardboard can be made into good practice material for structured termination counting. Place gummed Denison 3/8" circles in a row with the written symbol at the right end. The child can feel the slight rise of the dots and then see the written symbol—3.

Cut the cards (tag board is good) about 3" x 8". Having the cards all the same size, regardless of the number of dots, seems to help the child to gain concepts of many-few, more-less: The card with ten dots has many dots; the card with two dots has a few dots. Vary colors, using different colors for each card. Later you can use the Language Master Number Cards.

Use Milton Bradley 1″ colored blocks (or any hard, wooden, clear, colored blocks). Assign a color to each number and do not vary color assignments until good progress in termination is obvious. Use red for one, yellow for two, purple for three, orange for four, green for five. Keep this set of blocks in a handy box.

Use corresponding cards of 8″ x 12″ colored construction paper with black 1″ squares of corresponding number. *Do not mention color.* The use of colors is to avoid perseveration and to assist in perceiving a difference. The name of the color is not essential at this point.

Place the red card on the table. Place the red block on the black square of the red card. Say, "one." Let each child take a turn placing the block and saying, "one." (You should be working with four children at the most.) Guide hands for success. Take two turns. Remove the red card and block.

Place the yellow card on the table and proceed the same way, placing the yellow blocks on the card. As the blocks are placed say, "one-two," saying "two" more loudly and with a higher pitched voice. Expect each child to mimic your voice. Do not progress to three until two is mastered. Proceed to four and then five. This should require at least a month.

Present only the correct number of blocks at this point. No attempt should be made, as yet, to attach the written symbol or to terminate counting independently.

Reinforce each number being worked on, by counting the children, chairs, books, cups, etc., using that particular number in any situation possible.

STEP 2: Counting without a visible structured termination

Toss three purple blocks on the table. Grasp each one progressively, tapping the block on the table as it is released, saying, "one - two - three" with increasing volume in your voice.

Now use two blocks in the same manner. This step must progress through:
   A. Grasping each block and counting
   B. Lifting each block and counting
   C. Touching each block and counting
   D. Looking at each block, without touching, and counting.

This progression will require a long term of daily sessions—probably months.

STEP 3: Concept of number symbol

When the child can "look and count," can see three or four blocks, and—without touching them—say the correct number, he is close to a symbolic concept.

Looking, thinking, and saying the number symbol "three" (and not counting either verbally or silently with eyes) is the true shift into a concept of three-ness. Practice in this can be obtained with a group of four sitting at one table with the teacher. It is better to work alone with any child who is experiencing difficulty with this step.

The teacher should keep the box of blocks out of sight. She grasps two blocks and drops them on the table saying, "two"—no other word at all. She puts these away and drops two more of another color and, shaping her mouth to say "two," expects the child to say, "two." Group only those children who are ready for this step.

When it is apparent that the child is able to say the number symbol without actually counting by notation with his eyes, when the teacher feels he actually thinks "three" when he sees three blocks, it is time to withdraw, gradually, the use of color as a prop and to shift to blocks of all one color. The teacher must feel that the concept is well established. Some confusion may arise from this shift. However, if each step has been learned, it should not be too difficult.

Allow the troubled child to go back to grasping, lifting, and touching, if necessary, to make the shift to counting without color props. The child must always have a feeling of success at the end of a lesson, even if he must go back to whatever prop he needs to succeed.

The children require repeated practice and reinforcement for good mastery of the skill of perceiving a group as a whole and attaching the appropriate number symbol. There are many games the teacher can devise to reinforce the acquisition of this step.

Note: For Step 3 do not start at the number one and progress to number five consecutively. Start with three or two. Number one will fit in easily. Go from four to two or three to one, etc.

STEP 4: Selection of proper groupings

Place blocks on the table—two in one group, three in another. Say, "Show me (or "give me," or "take") two blocks," etc. Proceed until children can indicate and select from three presented groups of one to five blocks. This can also be done later with specially selected pictures to reinforce this level. However, it is best to use the three-dimensional materials until the concept is well established.

STEP 5: Attaching the written number symbol to the concrete presentation

Use three-dimensional numbers about 4″ high and 1/4″ thick, of wood, plastic, or stacked cardboard, preferably black. Place these on the colored cards with the black squares. Review Step 1. Place the number symbol on the card as the terminal number is spoken. Have the child hold the number symbol and place it properly as that number is spoken. The children gain a tactile knowledge of the contours of each symbol.

The children are asked later to, "Show me three blocks; show me number three." The child now selects the number symbol from the lined-up group of symbols (one to five) on the table. When this step has been mastered, the number symbols can be presented at random for selection.

STEP 6: *Continuation and a reinforcement for Step 5*

Present a variety of objects in groups and ask the children to select the correct number of objects and the correct symbol. Blocks were used initially to avert the possible distraction of using toys, little cars, etc. Now the children should be able to tolerate these articles in a lesson situation. This step may also be reinforced by each child showing the correct number of fingers. (Use Language Master Cards.)

STEP 7: *Associating the seen or heard symbol with the terminal number*

The child must now stop counting, without help of any kind, *at the terminal indicated by the symbol only.* He has no pattern on a card, nor any groups from which to select the "answer amount." He must terminate counting only by the meaning of the symbol presented. *This is the actual act of counting by notation.*

STEP 8: *The converse of Step 7*

The number symbol is the stimulus to group the correct number of blocks or objects.

Each child has five blocks, all the same color. Show the cut-out symbol for three and have the child present three blocks from his own blocks. He should count them aloud to check himself. This step may also be reinforced by showing the correct number of fingers to match the shown symbol.

The use of fingers helps, if the child is slow in progressing with this step. The child puts the correct number of fingers on the edge of the table. The fingers not needed in the count being considered are thereby not visible. Later the child can hold up the proper number of fingers. Use the Language Master Cards to reinforce the mastery of this step.

Level II: Counting by Grouping and Notation

The children have learned to "see" a group and to give it the proper symbol name. Now it is time to learn to count with more speed and still be accurate. For example, when presented with seven objects, counting by notation will be accurate but slow.

Use five blocks of one color and two of another color. Place the five blocks on the table so that the child sees them all at once. As the child says, "five," perceiving five, toss the other two, and touching them one at a time, say, "six, seven." Proceed slowly with all the number combinations to ten, using five as a maximum for the initial group. Graduate to using all blocks of the same color. Success at this level will provide the foundation for simple addition and substraction. Proceed to new combinations only when a combination is definitely learned, reinforced, and can be used in a transferred situation.

Level III: Counting by Grouping

This level is not achieved by many severely retarded children. Some learn to "count" by twos or fives, but it is usually rote and not meaningful as perceived quantity.

Level IV: Multiplication and Conversion

This level is not to be considered as a possible achievement by severely retarded children.

The Vocabulary of Relationships
(in order of difficulty)

1. Nursery - Kindergarten

little	big
open	shut
down	up
one	more
slow	fast

2. Primary

small	large
short	tall
few	many
less	more
short	long
before	after (days of week only)
in front of	behind (people in line)
far	near
close	apart

3. Junior Intermediate

in	out
high	low
top	bottom
over	under
above	beneath
inside	outside
first	last
before	after

4. Senior Intermediate

beginning	end
before	after (numbers)
forward	back
empty	full
all	some
some	none
little	much
heavy	light
hard	easy

There are many other words denoting relationships which can be conceptualized for our children. The list presented has been the subject of rather intensive experimentation and is felt to be basic.

We have found that comparative forms are very confusing to the children who are still struggling to be comfortable with language. When it is established that the child does use the words "big" and "little," or any such pair, the comparative concept should be introduced.

Ordinals

Retarded children learn the meaning of "first" and "last" quite readily. Teaching "second," "third," etc. is not advisable until a good concept of the cardinal number is gained.

Time

The scheduled time to do things, the amount of time available, the amount of time actually needed to do certain chores, make it imperative to have some concept of time. The retarded child can learn to recognize the proper time to follow a set schedule. He must learn enough about the clock and the passing of time to estimate whether he has enough time to complete a familiar task—such as catch a bus or finish a portion of an assigned job—before another scheduled activity.

He must learn when to hurry, and have an idea of how much time must be allowed to complete certain tasks, such as weeding a given area or cleaning up for lunch.

Much confusion is apparent among teachers of the retarded as to what the "best" way is to teach the children how to tell time. The generally inconsistent use of "before," "after," "until," "past," "to," "of," etc. by various people is very confusing to a child struggling to learn about how people know what time it is. To date, no conclusive studies indicate the best ways to proceed or the most acceptable vocabulary to insist upon. However, within any one school all teachers should agree upon one set pattern and follow it consistently. We have agreed upon the use of "before" and "after," and have found that consistent use of these terms has produced a gratifying number of successful time-tellers. By successful time-tellers, we refer to those children who can tell time to five-minute intervals.

It is not too difficult to teach what time we do certain things. Using a real clock with a clear face—so that the hour and minute hands will move in proper relationship—the children can learn how and when the clock tells that, "We must hurry," "We have lots of time," "We are early or late," or "We must start to get ready," etc.

A retarded child must be helped to gain a concept of a minute and to understand about the actual passing of time. The maximum to be hoped for from a severely retarded child is that he will learn to tell time at five-minute intervals. Learning to judge the length of a minute is fun and teaches the concept of the passing of time. The object is to guide the children through a series of structured steps to "feel" the duration of a minute.

Using a clock with a sweep-second hand, have the children watch the sweep-second hand as you say aloud at the correct spots, "five seconds, ten seconds, fifteen seconds," etc. The child who can count by fives may join in calling the time as the hand moves.

After a few days of this, start saying, "five seconds, ten seconds, fifteen seconds—that's a quarter after!" (you must be quick!). Pick it up at the right spot and say, "That's half way"—"Now it's a quarter before"—and, at sixty seconds, say, "That's a minute."

Now try it just saying, "quarter after—half way—quarter before—that's a minute." Then the real fun begins. Have the children cover their eyes. Say, "now, quarter after," etc. Do it again, saying only, "Half way" and, "That's a minute." The next time, have the children call out, "Half way" with eyes covered when the full thirty seconds have passed. Immediately look and praise the right guess.

The last step is to cover eyes and guess a minute lapse. You can head off some mistakes by saying, "Quarter before," for a few trial runs. Our children love the game and eagerly talk about "time to hurry" when they gain the feeling of the passing of time.

Use a stopwatch and time how long it takes to go get a drink of water, or how long it takes to put a coat on, or how long it takes to put certain materials in their proper places. This activity seems to have more meaning for the intermediate grade children. All activities involving telling time should be reviewed regularly and reinforced by being incorporated verbally in daily activities.

Many children receive watches as gifts. You can help your children by letting parents know that watches should have clear faces, with all the numbers clearly showing. Avoid watches with only quarter-hour marks, or Roman numerals. A sweep-second hand is highly desirable.

A vocabulary related to concepts of time is listed for activities to be devised by the teacher.

now — later
soon — later
a long time
early — late
   (hours, time of day, season, week, or month)
night — day
morning — evening
noon
today
tomorrow
yesterday
long ago — quite a while
last week — next week
last month — next month
last summer — next summer, etc.
first — last
time for
days of the week
   (use color cues and special events as cues)
months of the year
seasons

Building a concept of these words into meaningful activities demands some awareness of verb tense. Children with retarded development have been allowed too long and too often to use any verb form in their daily communication. It is quite surprising how quickly an experimental group of young Downs Syndrome children developed competence in using correct verb forms via prescription teaching. The Peabody Kits are helpful. Total body activities reinforce time concepts. Questions such as, "What did you do?" or, "What are you doing?" should require a motor and a verbal response.

Special events, birthdays, holidays provide good content for talking about what will happen and later, what happened. The senior students (approximately ages 15 to 21) enjoy keeping diaries. Each student has his own diary, preferably a hard back book, with *one* page for each day. The school calendar and all birthdays can be entered during the first few days each January. The weather is entered each day, usually copied from the "weatherman's" report written on the blackboard. This diary serves many purposes. We can always find today, yesterday, tomorrow, next week, and on and on, gaining understanding of the vocabulary necessary to communicate about time.

Here is a general outline of the use of the calendar.

Calendar

1. Introduction: What the calendar tells us
    Circle time:
      Point to the day of the week
      Point to the month of the year
      Point to the year

2. Concept of today, yesterday, tomorrow
    Talk about activities pertinent to each day
    Talk about special personnel who are at school on certain days (volunteers)
    Relate events of past week, past month

3. Recognition of symbols
    Point out days of week
    Point out number symbols

4. Concept of this week, last week, next week
    a. holidays
    b. birthdays
    c. events

5. Concept of months, seasons
    a. holidays
    b. birthdays
    c. special events
    d. seasons and weather

Money—Learning to Recognize Coins

The meaning of "more" and "less" must be learned before retarded children can attach much meaning to the value of coins. This meaning can be carried over to learning about coins by confining the early lessons to the use of pennies. Five pennies are more than one penny. Ten pennies are more than five pennies. Learning the named value of the coins is comparable to learning number symbols, and should be taught the same way, pennies being the unit and a nickel or a dime the symbol.

Using money to pay a set amount or to count change requires mastery of Level II: *Counting by Grouping and Notation*. It is best to use real money in any project for teaching the value of coins.

When the children can recognize coins and have a concept of their value, playing store with real money, real candy bars, gum, packaged peanuts and pop, puts money in a useful perspective. However, teaching our children what a certain coin will buy is very precarious these days. Prices change overnight.

Trips to the various stores to buy definite (not random!) items previously talked about are essential to transfer the learned management of small coins to the community.

Collecting coins is fun and a lifetime leisure activity. It need not be an expensive hobby. The coin folders available from the Whitman Publishing Co., Racine, Wisconsin, are inexpensive and very practical. The interest in studying coins, learning about dates and issues can involve the student with parents (and relatives too) on some common ground—not too readily found for our young people.

Measurement

Measurement is essential in most jobs, in school, at home, or in a workshop: How many? How much? How long? How heavy? How warm or cold?

The meaning of these words is essential for good preparation: can-full, box-full, too full, cupful, half-cup, fourth-cup, third-cup, tablespoon, teaspoon, half-teaspoon, fourth-teaspoon, "pinch," pound, half-pound, quarter-pound ("stick," as of butter), dozen, gallon, half-gallon, quart, pint, half-pint. These are learned in practical experience.

Piaget's observations on *conservation*, the ways a child views and judges quantity presented in various forms, should be studied carefully. Many ideas are available that can be transferred into experimental teaching. Trainable children have been held at a concrete level traditionally. Many are capable of handling more abstract material.

Do not deny your children the opportunities to experiment with conservation phenomena. It is very exciting to learn by observation that two like pieces of bread, one broken into five pieces and one broken into three pieces, are the same quantity. Good social implications are offered here. You can plan many meaningful experiences from Piaget's observations.

Linear Measure

Gross measure of space is learned by pacing-off with strides. Rugs and marked off areas can be measured this way to gain some idea of what measuring means.

Baric Measurement

Some baric measurement is involved in food preparation. Learning about heavy and light (or not heavy) is fun using a variety of teacher-student-made gadgets.

Boxes and plastic containers holding varying amounts of pebbles or any available material are used. The materials developed at Laradan Hall in Denver are excellent for all measurement concepts. Children are interested in their own weight and the weight of their peers—and sometimes of their teacher. A height and weight chart, if explained with enthusiasm and understanding, can become a focal point in the classroom.

Thermal Measurement

How hot or cold something is, is a part of daily living as the weatherman on television becomes almost as fascinating as Superman. Daily weather reports bring practicality to the concept of measuring the temperature and translate the information into direct planning for clothing and activities.

Setting the oven at the right temperature is taught by practical experience after demonstration. Some of our children will not be able to handle gas stoves. Kerosene stoves are dangerous even for adults and cannot be handled by our children. Electric stoves seem to be the least dangerous.

Using Numbers for Own Protection

Every child should know his own age, birthday, address, telephone number, and how to use the telephone to dial in case of emergency.

Discriminating Shapes

The recognition of round, square, triangle, straight, curved, parallel, circle, is helpful in vocabulary building and necessary in crafts and work situations. The game approach to the practical use of numbers is profitable. A winning score is very meaningful. Counting various units to accumulate a score is a valuable activity. The use of games is a social approach to the acquisition of number skills.

Testing for Working Concepts of Quantity

Materials Needed:
ten red 1″ cubes in plain container
ten yellow 1″ cubes in plain container
ten blue 1″ cubes in plain container
If you have a sliding tray under the table, assemble the blocks in the tray.
Scoring Chart of Performance Goals Record
Comfortable table and chair and chair for tester low enough to be at same level with child.
A small bowl of wrapped candy and some M & M's.
Privacy
A smile of expectance and lots of praise. Try to keep the blocks out of sight when not in use. Palm the blocks you are going to drop on the table in front of the child.
Shift colors for each new number. This helps prevent any tendency to persecerate. We are not testing the child's ability to shift attention or his ability to verbalize the number symbols. We want only to know if he does know that each number is unique and has a definite meaning and meanings.

On the first item, a concept of one, when you say, "Now show me with your finger," if you put up one finger yourself to show how you want the child to respond, you have given it away by using the singular "finger," and don't assume that some children won't pick up that cue!

Should the child be unable to use his fingers to show "how many" because of some neurological problem or physical anomalies, use the Language Master Cards with the hands showing a matching quantity.

Ten is as far as you need to go and, of course, you will stop when it becomes obvious that the child's limit has been reached. When the limit has been reached, say, "That's very good—now would you like a piece of candy?" Pass the candy bowl and say, "You may have *one*—show me with your finger." Should the child be able to say the number, ask him, "How many do you have? Show me—that's fine."

To Start the Test:
One-ness

Pick up one block (keep the rest out of sight) and say, "Here is one block," as you place the block on the table with a slight tap. Then proceed as follows: "Give me one block." Extend your hand and say, "Put one block in may hand." *Reinforce!*

Put some identical blocks on the table. Say, "Give me one block—put one block in my hand."

Put two blocks on the table. Say, "I want one block—put one block in my hand; that's right; now show me with your finger."

Two-ness

"Here are two blocks"—place two blocks of another color on the table—"Put two blocks in my hand." Extend your hand and say, "I want two blocks." Reinforce! Pick up one block and hold it in your open hand. Say, "I want two blocks—I have one block, but I want two blocks." Extend your hand. Reward! "Good—I have two blocks in my hand, one, two."

Put several identical blocks, same size, same color, on the table. Say, "I want two blocks—put two blocks in my hand." Reward. Put three identical blocks on the table. Say, "I want two blocks—put two blocks in my hand; that's right; now show me with your fingers."

Three-ness

"Here are three blocks." Place three blocks of the same size and the same color on table. "Put three blocks in my hand." Extend your hand and say, "I want three blocks." Reward.

Pick up two blocks and hold them in your open hand. Say, "I want three blocks—I have two blocks—but I want three blocks." Extend your hand—"Good, I have three blocks in my hand, one, two, three."

Pick up one block and say, "I want three blocks—I

have one block, but I want three blocks." Extend your hand and say, "Good—I have three blocks in my hand, one, two, three."

Put several identical blocks on the table and say, "I want three blocks—put three blocks in my hand; that's right; now show me with your fingers." Put four identical blocks on the table and say, "I want three blocks—put three blocks in my hand."

Continue in this same pattern, noting successes on the Performance Goals Record.

The child does not need to verbalize to gain a concept of numbers, although using the verbal sound symbol is a strong reinforcer and is essential if the child is going to move along the Brownell sequence beyond practical notations. Many good studies have been made of the management of numbers, quantification skills by children with retarded development at the "educable" level. It is interesting to note that this very basic analysis of the task of enumeration has been effective in teaching quantification skills to young "educable" children. Too often the assumption is made that because a child can count and recognize number symbols, he is ready to manipulate numbers conceptually.

27. READING

*'Twas brillig, and the slithy toves
Did gyre and gimble in the wabe;
All mimsy were the borogaves,
And the mome raths outgrabe.*

"It seems very pretty--but it's rather hard to understand." (You see, she didn't like to confess, even to herself, that she couldn't make it out at all.) "Somehow it seems to fill my head with ideas—only I don't exactly know what they are!"

Lewis Carroll

Every parent must be apprised of the fact that "trainable" means that the three Rs, as generally understood, are not a major part of a realistic program. The trainable child will learn to read for protection and some useful information, to write his name and some other useful words, and to use numbers in a very limited but practical way.

We teach this reading of words for protection and information in devious ways. No one system has yet been demonstrated as the most effective.

Dramatic play, experience charts, color clues, initial-sound phonetic clues—all the devices used by primary-grade teachers—are employed to teach an appropriate reading vocabulary to trainable children.

Much has been written and many conclusions submitted about teaching reading to trainable children. It is said that if a child can learn to read beyond the words ascribed as protection words, he is not trainable, but educable.

Some questions hinder our complete acceptance of the edict not to teach reading to trainable children. These questions are:

Should a young retarded child—labeled "trainable" by his mental age—who shows a possibility of learning to read above the accepted level set as the goal in reading be allowed to go as far as he is able to go?

Should the group be sacrificed to allow this particular child some extra attention from the teacher?

Should the child transferred to a trainable group after a few years experience in an educable group receive no more help in reading because it is not in the curriculum?

During the past ten years very few of our children have failed to learn to read enough words, with comprehension, to be able to read *My Weekly Reader*, level 1, and some have learned to read level 2. This is a source of great satisfaction.

Supplementary stories of carefully graded word selection have been made on a 3/8" typewriter. This, of course, does not mean that these children are going to learn to read much beyond this level, but it is highly questionable whether they should be deprived of the privilege of learning to read this much.

Good instruments for measuring reading readiness are used in the schedule for each child in the kindergarten or the first grade. Using these evaluation materials to determine possible reading readiness in the ten-, eleven- or twelve-year-old trainable child has been revealing. It is of course true that very few score within the readiness range, but these few should be located.

Should a child show some aptitude in reading, this development must be communicated to the parents with extreme caution. Hopes soar with the slightest breeze of intimation.

Only when measurable gains can be demonstrated over a period of time should a parent be informed of the possibility of the child's learning to read more than is included in a program for trainable children.

Among the children declared no longer educable by the qualified psychological examiners and transferred to our training school, scores on the Gray-oral reading test range from 0.0 to 7.7.

Team teaching allows the children showing readiness—and those scoring reading ability in the usable range—to learn as much as they can absorb and to retain what they have already learned.

Repeated evaluation is essential to check progress, plateaux, or losses.

The justification for investigating the child's reading potential lies in the observed scattered abilities of most trainable children as revealed by psychometrics, observation, and implications of etiology.

Each child is entitled to an opportunity to develop any known potential for learning.

It must be emphasized that we are talking about reading, not parroting or rote memorizing.

Shifting from experience charts made in carefully inscribed manuscript to a pre-primer—where the printing is very different—confuses many normal children. It is devastating to a retarded child.

Few reading books are printed in manuscript type.

When a child is ready to have a pre-primer—such as the first book in the Dick and Jane series—type the legend for each page on the manuscript typewriter and paste it over the printed words.

Some comic strips employ manuscript. It is interesting to notice that older children will find these particular comic strips for their own enjoyment.

The transition to common print—such as found in newspapers and TV guides—will be made without much help when the older children have learned to recognize the names of their favorite programs or favorite sports heroes.

The words to be learned in reading are placed in the charted curriculum guide.

The "exchange student" from the educable mentally handicapped classes, with a Gray-oral score indicating ability to read simple material with comprehension, should have the opportunity to read carefully selected material to the younger children. This young person has probably experienced so much failure and has been the "low man" for so long that this opportunity to share his talent and be accepted and wanted will be a truly happy and gratifying experience to which he can look forward each school day.

28. COLOR

The colors live
Between black and white
In a land that we
Know best by sight.
But knowing best
Isn't everything,
For colors dance
And colors sing,
And colors laugh
And colors cry—
Turn off the light
And colors die,
And they make you feel
Every feeling there is
From the grumpiest grump
To the fizziest fizz.
And you and you and I
Know well
Each has a taste
And each has a smell
And each has a wonderful
story to tell.

(FROM HAILSTONES AND HALIBUT BONES by Mary O'Neill, copyright © 1961 by Mary LeDuc O'Neill. Reprinted by permission of Doubleday & Company, Inc.)

Color is excitement, and because it is excitement it is a powerful force in learning and a wondrous source of fun. Color is mysterious and ethereal and can transport us upon flights of fancy.

Color is a visual discriminating factor in learning about likes and differences. Gellner considered color as parallel in development with size and shape. Zeaman's studies confirm that size and shape usually precede the resort to color as a discriminator of visual stimuli. Therefore, it would seem expedient to ascertain if a child can differentiate sizes and shapes before emphasizing color as a discriminator.

Some of our children already are aware of color differences before we begin to teach the concepts of size and shape. Parents name colors in many experiences, as well as saying "big" and "little."

We introduce color as a discriminator as soon as the nursery child seems comfortably settled in his new surroundings. Confine the introduction to these colors: red, blue, yellow, green, orange, and purple. It is good that yellow and purple have two syllables. Orange usually gets just one rather slurry articulation. Color names are hard to say: "r" and blends of "bl" and "gr" are not easy.

Place three sheets of 9" x 12" construction paper on the table. Have the child select *his choice*. Name it. Do not expect him to say it. Just say, "*Blue*; Cindy's color is *blue*. Now I'll take my scissors and cut a pice of *blue* paper for Cindy. Here, Cindy, you may have this *blue* paper. Now I'll cut another piece of *blue* for Cindy's coat bin. We'll put your *blue* paper right here." Have a piece of tape ready nearby and as the paper is taped to the shelf edge, say, "*Blue*-Cindy-*blue*-Cindy's coat bin is *blue*." Then give Cindy your strip of paper to carry around with her.

After a few days, write "Cindy" in bold black manuscript on a matching blue strip, saying, "Cindy—Cindy's name is on *blue* paper." Make a duplicate of this blue strip. Place one on the bin shelf, replacing the plain blue strip, and reserve the other for daily roll call.

Hand the color name strip to each child as his name is called. This establishes that there are different colors, different children, and different names. Repeat the child's name and point to his own color strip at every opportunity.

It is a long time before naming colors is demanded. The children learn to match, sort, and find colors through a series of planned experiences. (See Performance Goals.)

When a child experiences difficulty in matching colors, confine the task to two colors, not complementary colors. Use red and blue, rather than red and green, or red and yellow rather than blue and yellow. The gross difference in the sounds of the words red and yellow seem to assist in making the necessary differentiation.

Using a metal tray on a small easel, a lotto game can be made. Divide one sheet of paper into quarters and color one red, one blue, one green, and one yellow. Then make small rectangles corresponding in size and color to the quarters on your sheet. Matching with the physical property of the magnet as an added dimension is reinforcing.

Should the difficulty persist, try painting a small container with tempera, getting a good messy bit on the hands. Repeat the word "red" with each dab of paint. Touch the paint on the child's hands, repeating the word "red." Have some colored beads or cubes on the table. As soon as the paint job is finished, using the messy hands, pick up a matching bead or cube, drop it in the container and say "red." If this activity has been necessary you should use shaping techniques and use a primary reward the instant the child reaches in the right direction to pick up a red cube. Structure the success a few times and reward, reward.

A wide variety of sorting and matching activities can be devised by the teacher. Try to sustain a game-like attitude for stimulation and sustained interest.

When sorting and matching are comfortably a part of behavior, naming should be expected. If the child can motorically decode the signal of a color word, he should be able to encode the name.

One young man, quite able in our weaving program, has a complete anomia for colors. He could sort and match. He could read and write all the color names. He could get the correct item from storage if I said, "Get four hanks of yellow filler #69." The order could be verbal or written. If you asked him, "Is this yellow?" (and it was) he would answer "yes." If you asked, "What color is this?" he would quietly try to find something yellow to touch and say "like this." If nothing was available, he would turn nearly purple with anguish and frustration and almost go into a catastrophic episode, a behavior he had long since outgrown.

Squares of carpet samples in primary and other solid colors (*no* patterns please) can be obtained through local stores. These can be used in many games and activities. A good supply of beanbags should be made of solid colors, good clear primary red, blue, yellow, green, orange, purple, brown, white, black. It is helpful to have at least four of each color in squares, circles, or triangles.

It is a mistake to assume that a child always perceives color differences. The route may be long and tedious for a child with severe learning disabilities.

Color and size often characterize the first words used in putting two and three words together. "A red ball" or a "big yellow ball" sometimes precede sentence production requiring a noun and an action word. Using colors in creative activities such as music and art is very exciting. A variety of experiences is presented in Chapter 22 and Chapter 29.

AESTHETIC GROWTH

29. ARTS AND CRAFTS

by Eleanor M. Healy

It is our basic philosophy to develop in every human being his uppermost potential creative ability, regardless of the degree of his handicap.

—Viktor Lowenfeld

Objectives

1. Develop creativity by providing a stimulating art program (using varied materials) which will achieve expression and success.
2. Develop manipulative skills by experience with many art processes and materials.
3. Help the child find joy and satisfaction in expressing himself.
4. Sustain and nurture an awareness of the beauty of the world about us.

Art and the Retarded Child

1. The child tends to follow a pattern of development in artistic expression similar to the normal child's, but at a much slower rate.
2. The child is limited in subject matter for his creative expressions by his limited personal experience, by his slowness and difficulty in gaining impressions from experiences.
3. The child requires challenging motivation to stir his imagination and gain identification with the theme. No creative expression is possible without self-identification and a feeling of relatedness with the final product. The child must feel "this is mine" with genuine satisfaction.

Child art has a distinct charm. The child does not draw things the way they look to adults. The child draws what is most important to him—not what he sees, but what is actively in his mind at the time of his drawing. This is true of retarded children as well as of normal children. The stages of creative activity that take place as all children grow and develop are well defined.

Viktor Lowenfeld in his book *Creative and Mental Growth* lists the Scribbling Stages as: (1) *disorderly scribblings* which the child at about two-years-of-age will make and over which he has very little motor control. The first control to be noticed will be (2) *longitudinal*, in up-and-down long strokes frequently continuously laid down in a pushaway, turn, pull back, turn again, etc. fashion. The lines tend to be slightly oblique and parallel. (3) *circular scribbling*, a different and more complex motion when the strokes and returning curves begin to curve outward from their former repetitive parallels.

As the child is scribbling he may start to name his scribbling—telling a story while going through his motions of scribbling though nothing he names is recognizable to anyone else. This important step is highly significant, for the child is now thinking imaginatively in terms of pictures. His scribbling has taken on meaning for him.

The teacher must share his enthusiasm with sincerity and credulity, no matter what importance he attaches to his scribbled picture. As he gains control over arm and hand motions and experiences with his eyes what he has done with his hands, he makes a vital step, for thus eye-hand control is growing.

Before any presentation of the progression of media may be considered, the teacher must ascertain what stage of the manipulative level the child has reached.

Level I—without visual guidance he can reach, grasp, carry, and release. A satisfactory experience especially for the older retardate with limited ability is a crayon or a confetti lamination prepared by the teacher. The teacher shaves different colored crayons into separate jars and places the jars in front of the child. She asks the child to drop different colored shavings onto a sheet of wax paper which the teacher covers with a second sheet and presses with a warm iron. Use same technique with colored confetti. Paint with water and a large brush outside on a sidewalk or blacktop area, or paint with a sponge and water on a blackboard.

Modeling dough and finger paint may be used for manipulation.

Level II—with visual guidance the child holds something with one hand, his other hand manipulating, and then he scribbles with crayon or chalk. Anything described in Level I may be used plus sponge and brush painting (one color), crayon drawing (scribbling).

Level III—manipulates with discrimination. Here begins size, shape, and color discrimination, and designs of set and free shapes may be made, pasting the set or free shapes to another paper. The set shapes are cut by the teacher; for free shapes use scraps of colored construction paper from other projects which may be torn or used as is. Only two or three shapes and sizes will be used at this level and fingers are used for the dab of paste. Two or three colors of poster paint or crayon may now be used. All other projects in Level I and II are applicable.

Level IV—construction level. Manipulating with discrimination to produce a whole from parts is the stage when picture making will begin and recognizable designs are made. All kinds of paper constructions may be used—folding, stapling, paper chains, etc. All colors of paint and crayons are appropriate and felt pens (the water color variety) are enthusiastically used. Papier-mâché, both strip and mashed (commercial instant papier-mâché) can be enjoyable and rewarding to work with because the project may be designed to produce a gift for parents or for use in the home. Any other art experiences mentioned previously may be used at this level.

Most retarded children in the "scribbling" stage will be classified as Level I or II and sloshing in finger paint can lead to the transition from a flat hand effort at manipulation to a more directed and controlled use of fingertips, with satisfying visible results before the child is able to handle a crayon or a piece of chalk. This "scribbling" in finger paint can, in time, be guided to the push-pull beginnings of control (Lowenfeld's second stage) and later to circular motion control (his third stage).

The ease with which this control can be transferred from finger paint to holding a crayon will vary with retarded children. Some children heartily dislike the whole finger-painting business (and so do some teachers). These children should be helped directly with crayons.

The teacher's own enthusiasm for the wonderful scribblings produced by young retarded children can do more to help the child to put real effort into using finger paint or crayons than any other tricks or techniques.

Lowenfeld's stage 2 (push-pull) and stage 3 (circular motions) will be seen emerging, as scribbling is done in planned sessions. The teacher should gently guide the child's hand and verbalize appropriately to assist him in gaining control during these scribbling sessions. This is, again, when the teacher must talk or sing an improvised tune while happily steering the child's hand into controlled action through these developmental stages.

It is very important to guide the child in making circular motions counterclockwise. Learning to write names and necessary work words will be greatly facilitated by the early establishment of the counterclockwise circular motion control.

Manipulation of scissors should be mastered before a child is asked to use scissors in some creative endeavor. Do not teach the manipulation of scissors during an art session. Directions for teaching the use of scissors will be found in Chapter 17.

Each scribbled picture produced with any satisfaction should be trimmed, to cut away blank or uninteresting areas. Let the child tell which part he likes best. The picture should be mounted on a piece of colored construction paper (the child's selection of color) and be displayed proudly for a short while. Be sure that the child's name and the date are inscribed.

At about four-and-a-half years of age a child enters the pre-schematic stage, making his first representational attempts: a very crude form of "man"—usually a circle with eyes and two lines drawn from the circle for legs. There will be an evident discrepancy between his intention and his execution. The older retarded child will recognize this discrepancy quite readily. This is the time to offer him pre-cut shapes and other similar media so that he can produce non-representational work which he will find satisfying.

As the child realizes that what he had intended to portray did not "come out that way," discouragement or greater effort can depend upon the teacher. All the encouragement the teacher can muster may not help a retarded child to do much better in representational attempts. Therefore, a shift in media is indicated. The child must have an opportunity to use the media through which he can succeed in producing something of his own that will yield satisfaction to him. The production of designs through media suited to his motor ability is a satisfying and gratifying experience.

At approximately five to seven years of age the child is in the schematic stage. Very few trainable children will go beyond this schematic stage. The concept of "man" (his "schema") is well established by now. It will appear and be repeated over and over again and will be as recognizable as handwriting.

After a child's schema has taken form, recognition and comprehension of space and a "baseline" appear. All things standing on the ground are now related to this symbol. Above the baseline is the sky with a sun and there is nothing in between. This is an indication that the child has grown beyond his own ego-centered ideas—beyond concern with just himself—and into a world of which he feels himself to be a part. Here again the retarded child may become discouraged with his poor presentation of what he wanted to "draw about." Again a shift in media can give satisfaction. Some retarded children do surprisingly well in telling a story in a picture of their own making.

No matter how poor the presentations may be, something good can be found for comment. This should not be overdone with older retarded children, as they know it isn't good and don't particularly care for being "kidded" or falsely encouraged. A child's self-evaluation can indicate the time to direct emphasis upon the elements of art and to direct creativity toward design through a variety of media.

Occasional representational projects should be attempted. A large mural can give each child an opportunity to create some contributing part that he is best able to do. The end result must be satisfying if the child is to gain any reinforcing strength through an art experience.

As the schematic stage progresses, the child realizes that there is a relationship between color and object. However, color may be chosen for its emotional appeal rather than for its resemblance to natural objects.

These various levels of the development of creativity indicate the variety of materials needed and the kinds of motivation necessary in working with retarded children.

Progression of Presentation

As eye-hand control is gained and the pre-schematic stage is entered, time must always be given to experimenting with and discovering the many ways of using each new medium.

Before attempting a representational crayon drawing from experience, the children must be familiar with the various ways to use a crayon: making a thin and a thick line, shading, using the long side, etc. Crayon drawings of familiar people, experiences, seasons, and events are suggested.

Tempera paints and water colors are introduced, while seasons, experiences, and people are continued as subjects. Keeping each color clear is stressed, and using a pleasant arrangement of lights and darks is suggested.

Working with paper may be carried on alternately with experiences with paint, and is frequently attempted before the children begin to experiment with tempera paint and water colors.

Working with paper proceeds from tearing and pasting free shapes, through cutting geometric shapes for practice, to cutting and pasting free shapes for a pleasant design. Designs of set shapes (pre-cut paper being provided) are attractive and interesting. Three-dimensional shapes made by cutting, folding, and manipulating to form a design, such as may be used for a mobile, are fascinating.

Experiments with what can be done with paper are conducted as a preliminary experience—curling, bending, fringing, etc.

The elements of art—line, shape, pattern, texture, and color—are presented and studied as a project in the older groups—with children about fourteen years of age and older. Making a variety of samples to reinforce a concept of each element provides a frame of reference for creative ideas which can be enjoyed when these elements are conceptualized.

The element of line may be reinforced by designs of straight lines, such as a plaid. A design of circular or wavy lines can be used in making pictures of flowers. Stick printing or printing with objects such as spools, forks, etc., provides a lesson in the elements of line and pattern. Designs with shapes, free or set, torn or cut, allow an infinite variety of creative experiences.

Experimenting with collage, using actual textures and patterns, leads the way to collage by picture textures and colors transposed into the child's own design. A picture of rough texture and smooth texture conveys a tactile experience and perception through a visual presentation.

Filling in areas created by a scribble picture, using felt pens (water-color type) to convey various textures or visual differences, is an interesting and sometimes revealing experience.

Printing with a brayer and with a variety of objects such as spool ends, cut carrots, tines of a fork, a piece of lettuce, a penny, a key, etc., is an interesting experience and especially good for developing manipulative skills.

Papier-mâché, both mashed ("instant") and in strips, is used for making puppets, masks, animals, and gifts. Clay or plasticine is used for manipulation, modeling human or animal figures, or making pottery by pinch-pot or coil methods. Sand casting has been done successfully.

Motivation

The subject must have meaning to the child, for no artistic endeavor will evolve if there is no personal involvement. The teacher must ask questions to establish a relationship between the subject and the child's experiences before work begins.

Motivation for the first experience in scribbling, paper tearing or finger painting, can be achieved by the simple introduction: "Let's have some fun with this," with accent on the "fun" because this is understandable to him.

When achievement indicates that the pre-schematic stage has been entered, the child is activated as his attention is attracted by a picture, a story, questions about the seasons of the year, what fun he has in that time of the year, or about the next holiday, etc. The guide for social studies (Chapter 25) includes all activities appropriate for the seasons, holidays, etc., and is the source of a variety of subjects which are familiar to the child.

Members of the family, pets, or the teacher are always interesting subjects, but no subject captures as much interest as a self-portrait. These will vary according to the developmental stage of the child (no matter how much detailed discussion of body parts and placement there has been, the pre-schematic child will put a head with legs where ears should be), but results are fascinating.

Discussion of a selected subject takes place to guide the introduction of ideas. Questions are asked to stir the imagination. No directions are given, only guidance when difficulties arise. *No drawing is done by the teacher*, but much encouragement and praise for sincere effort is offered.

A genuine effort is made to understand the child's picture—it is *his* picture and is different from that of any other child. *Never* laugh at a child's sincere effort and *never* ask, "What is it?" The teacher may suggest pleasantly and with genuine anticipation, "Tell me about your picture." Encourage him to talk about his picture. It develops his imagination to tell a story about it.

It may have no story that can be told, so we quickly call it a design, and discuss the bright and clear color, the light against the dark color, the strong lines or the good use of the space involved, etc. In evaluating a child's effort in this way, we make him aware of the fact that he did produce something of artistic value and design, something that is a success rather than a failure.

Practical Practices

Neatness must be stressed and motivated in all projects. Evaluating neat and tidy end results—and considering the labor involved in cleaning up after a project is finished or set aside temporarily—should provide sufficient motivation. The teacher should consistently direct attention to neatness (within realistic limits for each child) and demand that each child participate in cleaning up and putting away after each session.

Too much paste is hard to handle and contributes an untidy mess. Use small refillable jars, or a small dab on a piece of scrap paper for paste, and much vigilance. Require a child to cut with scissors for a creative project only when he can direct his attention to the project rather than to the process of cutting. Provide the child with shapes (pre-cut or free shapes—leftovers from the scrap box) so that he can enjoy an art experience with design. Work on his scissors technique alone and at a different time.

When tempera paint is used, provide plenty of individual paint pots and enough brushes to use one for each one color. This is a very small expenditure for a successful introduction to using these media.

When gadget, stick, or potato printing or sponge painting, give students pads of used material or paper and distribute paint to each pad as needed. This results in less clean-up and sharper prints.

A small amount of liquid starch (approximately one tablespoonful to a cup) added to tempera paints when mixing, keeps paint from flaking and makes it less likely to rub off after drying.

Smocks should be used for any messy projects. Dad's old shirt worn backwards can suffice. The teacher should have a collection of "scrap" on hand for gift projects, etc. or for use in collage, Halloween projects, and the like. Items to save include buttons, yarn, wire, feathers, glitter, beads, bottles, bright papers such as foil gift wraps, fur and leather scraps, lace and felt, burlap, string bags, and anything else with interesting shape or texture.

Wiping up any small paint spills with a damp sponge or paper towel and lifting up any dropped or stepped-on pieces of clay with a spatula soon result in very few dropped pieces.

Careful and attractive mounting of the children's pictures (as mentioned previously) for display in the classroom or school halls is fine motivation for better artistic endeavors.

Art is a social experience with many facets.

Media and Methods

1. Chalk
    a. On wet or dry paper
    b. Stencils

2. Clay
    a. Shapes and forms
    b. Human or animal figures
    c. Pinch-pot and coil-method pottery

3. Collage
    a. Using different textured materials for a tactile picture
    b. Cutting shapes from pictured textures in magazines for visual picture of texture
    c. Using cuts from magazine pictures to match background of colored construction paper selected by child

4. Construction
    a. Using toothpicks, reeds, match sticks, boxes for making three-dimensional shapes
    b. Popsicle sticks for picture frames, baskets, boxes, etc.
    c. Macaroni in many shapes, glued to background for wreaths, decorative plaques, or a variety of gifts

5. Crayon
    a. Scribbling with crayon giving one color at a time
    b. Drawing—representational (pre-schematic and schematic stages)—stories, seasons, familiar people, pictures of clay models
    c. Drawing to music—designs repeated and affected by what the music tells the child to do
    d. Crayon lamination—crayon shavings arranged on a sheet of waxed paper and covered with another sheet, then pressed with a warm iron
    e. Crayon etching
    f. Crayon rubbing—over cardboard shapes and textured materials
    g. Crayon resist

6. Felt pens (water-color type)
    a. For drawing or scribble pictures. A favorite media for all ages and levels

7. Paint
    a. Finger
    b. Tempera—on wet or dry paper (accidental designs resulting from paint running on wet paper are very exciting to the retarded child and delightful results are obtained)
    c. Detergent—whipped with small amount of water and colored with tempera laid on with a brush
    d. Water color—as a wash over crayon (crayon resist) or on wet paper, for accidental designs. Children seem to enjoy this medium more than tempera. There is no teaching of proper use of water colors (it's just for fun) Note: individual half-pans can be ordered to replace used colors in the paint boxes

8. Paper
    a. Tearing (freely, as scribbling) and pasting
    b. Pasting pre-cut shapes to a designated outline space. This is not an art experience, but a practice task to assist in gaining manipulative skill
    c. Creating a design by pasting free-cut shapes or pre-cut shapes on bright, contrasting paper
    d. Tissue-paper lamination. Tissue paper, torn or cut, arranged in a design on waxed paper covered with another sheet of waxed paper and pressed with a warm iron
    e. Cutting snowflakes from folded thin paper. Contribute assistance only in folding this paper. Cutting snowflakes is a timeless, delightful experience, repeated year after year, the children doing more of the task, unassisted, as they grow up
    f. Cutting, bending, curling, fringing, weaving, are some processes used to make interesting shapes

for a mobile. Staples are used to create three-dimensional shapes when cut paper is curled backwards or forwards

g. Tearing paper with directed definite purpose, such as making autumn leaves or material for a simple collage. Some retarded children who experience serious difficulty handling scissors can tear paper or tear on a sketched line with a happy result

9. Papier-mâché
   a. Torn or cut strips of paper are used to make models from molds, etc., for gifts, for making animals, masks, puppets, etc.
   b. Pulp or mashed (commercial "instant" papier-mâché is readily available and easy to use); also inexpensive-to-model puppet heads, animals, masks, etc.

10. Printing
    a. Creating designs of texture by rolling inked (water-soluble ink) brayer on paper placed over sand, screen, burlap, etc.
    b. Drawing on inked palette and taking off a monoprint (placing newsprint over drawing and rubbing gently with a hand or spoon; when newsprint is lifted drawing will be transferred to paper)
    c. Pressing paper on inked palette, then drawing on paper for a sharper print
    d. Blot printing
    e. Sponge printing or painting using small pieces of cut-up sponge
    f. Gadget printing—forks, spools, sticks, etc.
    g. Potato and vegetable printing
    h. Commercial stamps

11. Sand casting
    Wet sand is used as a mold. Plaster of Paris, colored with tempera paint if desired, is used to make casting. The most severely handicapped child can contribute something to this production

12. Theory
    Learning about the elements of art—color, line, shape, pattern or texture—is the basis for a program of creative activity
    a. A design of straight lines or circular lines; may be a repeat design. (This is hard for the retarded child but insist upon repetition of same colors and same lines. Fold paper or use small sheets of paper to give specific areas for repeats)
    b. Color—a visual demonstration of color mixing using food coloring in clear glasses filled with water. Use one color (tempera) plus black and white. Make color wheel showing how colors change by adding black or white gradually to original color.
    c. Shape—use cut-out shapes—circles, triangles, rectangles, squares, etc.; draw around shape, move and overlap until a larger design is made; find new shapes in the design and color as a scribble picture.
    d. Pattern—a repeat design of lines, as above.
    e. Texture—listed under Collage

13. Weaving
    Weaving with a two-harness loom is a practical and satisfying activity for the retarded. It is assumed that the child possesses the manipulative skill to handle a two-harness loom and understands the process when he begins to weave fabric. *The readiness program for weaving is not always a part of the arts and crafts program.*

Introduction to Weaving

1. The child draws parallel lines vertically with one color, and then draws parallel lines horizontally with another color. This creates a pattern drawing from which a child can see that interesting designs can be made with lines of different colors that cross each other with regular spacing. This should be done frequently and the results kept (dated, in a file) for the child's own re-evaluation of how his patterns satisfy him.

2. Motorically the child must be able to use both hands to grasp and pull, to control the strength output in his hands, to use fingers intrinsically, and to cut with scissors.

3. The weaver must know colors, and be able to measure—in that he must know when a certain limit has been reached. He must know the difference between thick and thin, heavy and fine, light and dark, etc.

4. The weaver must learn about warp and filler. He must know that the warp is set and not to be changed or handled. He must learn that the filler is what he must work with and that what happens depends on what he does with the filler.

5. The child's starting materials are semi-rigid materials; he will weave 1″ strips of oilcloth of one color through 1″ strips cut parallel in another colored oilcloth and held firm on an 18″ square of plywood or very heavy cardboard with slit-section.

The over-and-under technique can be learned in this way. The filler strips are fed along with fingers. No shuttles are used at this point. A variety of colors can be used in filler to hold attention until this skill is gained.

6. Allow the new weaver to watch the winding of a warp and the dressing of a loom. Respect for the labor required before weaving can start assures a more serious approach to the privilege of weaving.

7. A two-harness loom, dressed with carpet warp, about 5″ wide, set through an eight-dent reed, is set before the new weaver. Parts of the loom are talked about. The new weaver is shown a "shed," shifts the shed, and slips his hand into it. He feels the tension of the warp as it is "pulled up." He is directed to follow a warped thread from back beam, through a heddle, through the reed, and onto the front beam. He follows another warped thread and learns how heddles pull warped threads up and down to make a shed. Slipping his hand into the shed just as the shed is being changed directs the child's attention to the fact that another set of threads is coming up to form a new shed.

8. "Throw" an empty shuttle back and forth, alternating hands from right to left. Practice in passing the empty shuttle back and forth from hand to hand will help in avoiding snagging warp threads when the shuttle is carrying a thread. This should be practiced until the child can pass the shuttle back and forth with ease without snagging on any warp threads.

9. Show some finished fabric and explain about the making of a good edge.

10. Start with a wound shuttle of heavy roving, for a quick effect. The importance of a good edge must be stressed at the very beginning. Stand by, guiding the very first throw of the shuttle, and immediately explain the procedure of obtaining an even edge. Leaving the filler shot at approximately a 10° angle before beating assures a more even edge. At no time is the thread to be pulled tight enough to make a dent in the selvage.

11. Tell the weaver to "always beat the same." Let him beat too hard a few times, then too soft a few times, and discuss the results with him. Show the weaver samples of fabric, unevenly textured, and not salable because of poor beating. The importance of rhythmic beating must be stressed.

After this first sample begins to show the results of good beating and even edges, the practice loom can be set aside for the next beginner and a definite project can be started. Placemats of heavy cotton filler, in a color the weaver is "sure mother will like," make a stimulating beginning project.

Dressing a loom is a tedious and difficult job requiring patience, arithmetic, and practice. The weaver in a sheltered workshop will seldom be able to dress a loom. Some retardates can wind warp and can help in dressing a loom.

Advancing warp, maintaining tension, repairing broken or cut threads, measuring, and finishing require the help of the teacher or supervisor. It is the presence of this help that makes a workshop a sheltered workshop.

Planning a design for a weaving project is dictated by special orders, material on hand, ability of the weaver to follow a pattern, and cost.

The weaver must feel that he has had some part in planning what he shall weave, or anticipate the satisfaction of knowing that he is filling an order. This needed participation requires considerable guidance for him from the teacher.

Weaving is a highly stimulating and satisfying occupation for a person who must function in a noncompetitive situation. Weaving in a workshop provides social activity and an opportunity to be useful.

Note: Making looped potholders can be a very frustrating experience for some retarded children. This weaving does not help much in learning to use a two-harness loom, but it does afford an opportunity to practice over-and-under.

Be sure the potholders are designed—not just random outrages of horrible, mixed colors. Potholders can be made in very attractive patterns in pleasant color combinations. These can be made by the shop members for stock during free time or during waits for rewarping. Orders taken from mounted, attractive samples keep the young people in the shop busy in spare time. Filling an order for a special design and color scheme of potholders provides a real feeling of importance and usefulness.

Suggestions for Beginners' Art Program (listed in order of difficulty)

1. White chalk on blackboard
    a. Scribbling
2. Crayon—one color only
    a. Scribbling
    b. Scribbling "to music"
    c. Drawing
        1. Beginning of schema (circle with eyes and lines for legs)
        2. Names scribblings
3. Finger painting—one color only—using large muscles
4. Paper tearing
    a. Pasting and naming shapes
5. Construction
    a. Stick variety of objects into a ball of clay (stabile)
6. Painting-(tempera)
    a. To cover paper—one color
    b. Random brush strokes—often named
    c. Blot, on one side of paper, folding to reproduce blot
7. Clay—manipulation, forming balls, cakes or coils
8. Collage (paste-on) of simple textured materials
9. Paper—pasting pre-cut shapes to make designs
10. Painting—using string dipped in thin paint to decorate gift-wrapping papers
11. Cutting—snowflakes, geometric shapes, or pictures from magazines

Media for Artwork and Their Application to Various Age Groups

(Successive levels are dependent upon accomplishment of preceding level)

MEDIA	PRIMARY (approximately 6-8 years old)	INTERMEDIATE (approximately 8-14 years old)	SENIOR (approximately 14-21 years old)
Chalk—white and colored	Use white chalk, scribbling on blackboard	Same procedure used, but scribblings show beginning schema (a circle for head, with eyes, and lines attached for legs)	Colored chalks are used for drawing on wet or dry paper. Repeat designs are made by rubbing chalk into pre-cut stencils with soft tissues
Clay	Clay is used for manipulation and play. Some simple forms and shapes are made	Shapes of simple animals and the human form are made by the add-on method. (Few retarded children use the pull-out method.) A self-model is made, then a picture of the model is drawn. This is a very interesting experience	The pinch-pot and coil methods of pottery making are taught (some things are glazed and fired for gifts). Free modeling is a satisfactory experience
Collage	Simple paste-on of familiar textures; shiny, dull, scratchy, smooth, etc. are used	More categories are added, namely: dark, light, soft, hard, color, and "found" objects such as feathers, shells, corks, string, etc.	Collage is used several ways in these groups: 1. choosing materials and making a design for tactile stimulation; 2. pictures of texture are selected from magazines and a design is made; 3. the areas created in scribble pictures are filled with child's selection of texture symbols. Representations convey a tactile concept; 4. shapes cut from magazine pictures to match color of background paper

MEDIA	PRIMARY	INTERMEDIATE	SENIOR
Construction	Placing rigid objects only, such as twigs, wire, tongue depressors, etc. into ball of clay to make a stabile	More complex stabiles are made. Simple frames for pictures are constructed from craft sticks	Baskets are made with reeds in regular basketry weaves. Useful articles such as boxes and frames are made with craft sticks. Stabiles and designs are created. Wreaths for Christmas presents are made from various macaroni shapes, and gilded
Crayon	Scribbling with a black crayon is satisfactory for motor activity—many "pictures" will have stories and scribblings and will be named. Crayon laminations (teacher preparation)	Drawing pictures of familiar people or seasonal activities, or from a story read aloud, is very satisfying. Drawing may have little resemblance to what it is called by the child. Crayon rubbing, over cut cardboard shapes, objects or textures, is full of surprises to the group. "Black Magic"—crayon-resist— heavy scribbles covered by thinned tempera. Scribble pictures are enjoyed by the children. Eight colors are used for all crayon work	This group uses eight colors. The drawings are more representational with colors used correctly, as green for grass, etc. Crayon etching is difficult and results are not too satisfying. Crayon press or laminating (crayon shavings are pressed between waxed paper, with a warm iron) yield interesting designs which are enjoyed by the groups. These children enjoy drawing to music. A changing tempo is notable in resulting design
Felt pens (water-color type)	For "scribbling"	Scribble pictures and drawing	Scribble pictures, designs, representational drawing
Painting A. Finger paints; one color only is used for all groups	Especially good for big muscle manipulation. Finger painting at the primary	More finger manipulation and less full-arm swing is used in this group	Repeat designs and imaginative pictures are produced using fingers, side of

221

MEDIA	PRIMARY	INTERMEDIATE	SENIOR
Painting (cont.)	level is done with full-arm swing, usually using a flat hand		hand, fingernails, fists, or arms.
B. Poster or tempera	One color with a 1/2" brush can be used to color simple shapes. A paint-soaked string is dragged across paper to make designs. Blot paintings are made by folding paper and reproducing blot or blowing at blot through a soda straw to "make flowers"	This group uses all the primary colors plus green, orange and black—only three at one time, however. Designs, stories or experiences are used as subjects for painting. Paint dropped on wet paper and allowed to run makes exciting designs	Both groups enjoy and can handle all previously listed methods. Shapes made by dropping a wet starched string on cardboard (dried under pressure) are painted with as many colors as desired to form a design. More colors are used for wet-paper accidental designs. This technique holds almost endless fascination for the group
C. Water color	Not attempted	Paint for "fun"	Paint is used as a wash over a crayon pattern ("crayon-resist") or on wet paper for accidental results. Used for representational paintings with special emphasis on learning to keep color clear, waiting for color to dry before more painting, etc.
Paper (construction paper and newsprint)	Paper is torn in random shapes which the children will often identify and name. These torn shapes are then pasted upon paper of different colores. Pre-cut shapes, such as strips, squares, and dots, are used to make interesting designs, Some cutting, namely snowflakes, shapes, and pictures from magazines	Cutting and bending of a single sheet of construction paper is done to form a three-dimensional shape for a mobile. Designs are made with free shapes. a. Paper scraps or paper cuts as desired, pasted on a colored background b. Paper, cut or torn, laminated between waxed paper	New processes for paper, such as curling, fringing, weaving and pleating, are added to previous methods

223

MEDIA	PRIMARY	INTERMEDIATE	SENIOR
Papier-mâché	Not attempted	Strip method used to make models of bowls and shapes for gifts. Also used as coverings for animal forms, masks, Halloween projects, and puppet heads. Colored tissue paper (cut or torn shapes) adhered to form by brushing on liquid starch or polymer medium	Strip method. Pulp or mashed (using commercial "instant" papier-mâché for modeling puppet heads, etc.
Printing	Can use stamps from commercial printing sets. Potato printing (with teacher preparing potatoes)	"Gadget" printing, done by pressing objects, vegetables, etc. onto pads soaked with tempera paint and printing on newsprint. Sponge printing. Tongue depressors for stick printing	Printing is done by using brayer and water-soluble ink on glass palettes. Methods used: (a) designs of texture, by rolling inked brayer over paper placed on sand, burlap, screen, etc.; (b) monoprints—by drawing with sticks, etc. directly on inked palette. Paper is placed over drawing and rubbed with hand to "take off" the print; (c) sharper prints are made by placing paper over inked palette and drawing on top side
Sand casting	Not attempted	This medium not tried with this group, but simple bas-relief projects should be successful, with plenty of help in pouring plaster	To make decorated mold such as Christmas tree. For bas-relief, press objects, such as hands, shells, kitchen utensils, into wet sand
Sewing and creative stitchery	Not attempted	Not attempted	Learn to thread a needle, sew on buttons and make a hem. For creative stitch-

MEDIA	PRIMARY	INTERMEDIATE	SENIOR
			ery learn to do outline, running, button-hole and cross-stitches
Theory	Not attempted	To understand the use of light versus dark and to fill paper with drawing	The elements of art are discussed and samplers made to show line, shape, color, pattern or texture. Designs with repetition of lines and shapes are done
Weaving— two-harness and potholders	Not attempted	Learn principles of under-and-over by using oilcloth strips of one color to weave through a piece of slit oilcloth of another color or covering a heavy cardboard	*Senior Intermediate:* Learn weaving terms; such as shed, shuttle, loom, warp, weft, roving; plus the names of yarns, as carpet warp, chenille, etc. Progress to 6" practice looms, already warped with student's choice of colors—to make a belt *Senior:* Weave on pre-warped 12" and 14" two-harness looms, making articles for sale—following a pre-set pattern according to measure. Potholders are also made for sale

30. MUSIC AND DANCE

Eleanor Lesak

Music is love in search of a word.
Sidney Lanier

The use of music therapy in meeting the needs of the retarded in special education programs has made many people newly aware of the influence of music on body, mind, and spirit. Since therapy is defined as "that which attempts to change to an improved condition," the use of music to obtain this change can be called "music therapy."

In music therapy the emphasis is placed on what music can do for the person rather than on the development of musical skills. As a sub-verbal means of communication, music offers particular potential not present in other media.

Anyone who has observed a mother and child in the very beginning of interplay will remember the rhythmic patting and rocking; the semi-melodic and syllabic croon; the soft lullaby and the playful peek-a-boo. Mother's presence and attendance are felt and heard—to the infant she is "there." Gaston has said that music is closely related to tender feelings and that "the arousal of love is important and essential because it helps to provide feelings of security."

Hospitals and institutions where infants and small children are confined for extended periods of time affirm these findings. Children who are not fondled, patted, sung or crooned to tend to lag in physical and emotional development. Many volunteer organizations now send substitute "mothers and grandparents" who initiate just such activities when the natural mother is unavailable.

Family members of retarded infants and young children should be encouraged to begin these semi-rhythmic and melodic means of communication with their little ones. Parent education workshops should stress the importance of this activity. Musical sounds and rhythm are fundamental in their appeal. Fundamental also is the child's fright at loud, harsh, unmusical noises. Shouting or quarreling families should realize that even an infant can recognize the discordant emotion in a human voice. But a crooning lullabye gives assurance of love and security.

The young retarded child is often nonverbal. Music, because it offers a sub-verbal means of communication, can become a means of establishing the contact so necessary in developing an interpersonal relationship.

At the White House Conference on Children in Washington, D.C. in 1970, "The Sounds of Children" was the title given to a presentation on the impact of music. Thomas Willis commented in the January 3, 1971 issue of the Chicago *Tribune:*

Music for the child is neither singing, nor notes on paper. . . . Music is everything he hears which he does not put into words. A child listens to music—the tone of his mother's voice, the drip of a faucet—before he can talk.

"The Sounds of Children" are, after all, nothing more than the sounds of life.

The small child, newly separated from home and mother is comforted and reassured by hearing a familiar melody or nursery rhyme as he enters the strange new world of school. The youngster, greeted with regularity in this way, begins to feel secure in this structured and predictable situation.

Even the most limited children can profit greatly from a skillfully planned and presented music program. The goals of this program actually parallel the overall goals of all special education. The growth areas—physical, emotional, social, intellectual, and aesthetic—are each enhanced and hopefully accelerated by the use of music. In addition, music can be used to create a pleasant educational atmosphere or setting.

The ringing of a small school bell, accompanied by the teacher singing softly, "Time for school, time for school, ding-dong; it's time for school," soon becomes a pleasant signal that the "down to business time" of the day is about to begin. (A similar device may be used for lunch time, play time, nap time, and others.)

A happy classroom atmosphere can be created by the use of simple songs or chants to call a group to attention by initiating a call and response situation. Used in a pleasant manner such songs can serve a useful purpose in management as well as initiating a motor or an auditory response.

For example, the teacher sings (to the tune of "Frère Jacques" or some other song), "Are you ready, are you ready?" Class answers, "Yes, I am. Yes, I am." Teacher: "Come and do your work now, come and do your work now." Children: "Yes, I will. Yes, I will."

For the young child, brief and varied music activities such as finger plays, singing games, and action songs should be introduced into the regular learning session.

Abrupt changes in activities are difficult for young retarded children to accept. Brief songs or musical clues, because they take time and because they are stimulating, create an acceptable, understandable climate for change. Some examples are: "This is the way we do our work, do our work, do our work. This is the way we do our work, so early in the morning" (wash our hands, sit in our chairs, put on our coats, etc.—to the tune of "Mulberry Bush").

The success of the music program is dependent upon the skill and ability of the teacher or therapist in utilizing the many kinds of music activities moving toward these basic aims: to increase the ability to attend, to communicate, and to participate.

The very words "music," "sing," "dance," and "play" bring up an image of joyful activity. Even if the words are not completely understood by the child, the attitude of the teacher or therapist must convey the message. The therapist's participation and enjoyment in what he is doing must be obvious and sincere. His facil expression and body movements should be enthusiastic, encouraging, soothing, or stimulating as indicated by the material being presented.

Often this is an extension of the personality of the teacher-therapist, but it should also be considered as a deliberate device to obtain the desired results.

A well-rounded music program would ideally be a combination of:

1. Therapy sessions provided by a registered music therapist and based on prescriptive methodology as indicated by individual needs
2. Peer group music classes conducted by a therapist or specialist
3. Opportunity for participation in larger assembled groups composed of a variety of levels, depending on the ability to tolerate such sessions
4. The planned use of music in the classroom by the classroom teacher for a specific purpose.

The Role of the Music Therapist

"The music therapist in a public school special education program is often called upon to fulfill three roles. He must serve as a resource person for special education teachers, a music teacher-therapist working directly with the children, and a researcher developing new materials and techniques."

(*Music in Therapy*. E. Thayer Gaston)

The selection of basic equipment is usually done by the music therapist. Choosing among piano, organ, record players, and tape recorders is often his responsibility. As in most areas, the best quality that can be purchased with the funds available is recommended. While self-made or toy type rhythm instruments may offer some satisfaction, and certainly immediate financial saving, their long-term use is limited and the difference between toys and quality instruments is beyond compare. The more limited in ability the child, the more important the quality of the instrument becomes. Even the smallest effort can obtain a satisfying result with a fine instrument.

As a resource person, the music therapist makes available to the classroom teacher the rationale and techniques for the use of music. He researches, collects, and distributes recordings, tapes, music books, reference books, rhythm and simple musical instruments from a central area.

The modification of material is usually done by the therapist. Excerpts from recorded material or music played on the piano or other instrument can be taped at an adapted speed and then repeated several times to increase its usability and versatility. Taping is also an excellent method of reproducing a master recording which may not always be available. Recordings for children all too often do go out of print.

In working directly with the children, the therapist is able to provide the opportunity for many musical experiences. As with all teaching, these will vary according to his own abilities, interests, and training, but will fall within the framework of appropriate materials.

Ideally a special room for music therapy should be provided. It might be equipped with: piano, small chord organ, record player, tape recorder, and exercise bar, large wall mirror, floor mat, and movable seating. The room should be located away from the main arteries of traffic.

Cabinets with doors to contain books, pictures, records, tapes, and musical instruments should be provided with locks to keep the contents safe and out of sight. (Anyone provided with all of this treasure should regard himself as fortunate indeed.)

Soft colors in furnishings and wall colors plus an uncluttered atmosphere make attentiveness easier and provide no distractions. Coming to the music room for music class or therapy provides a change of pace and scene, which makes it a special and pleasurable experience.

Planning and programming for special events by the music therapist can make for continuity and avoid redundancy. The entire yearly program can be noted on the school calendar so that seasonal events and special holidays can be discussed and planned in the classroom for a specified time preceding the event. Art classes and other adjunctive sessions can be coordinated.

Assembly programs giving the children an opportunity to perform some of their classroom work or display art and individual skills should be provided. On very special occasions, parents and families are invited to attend but only after they have been carefully oriented as to the purpose of the program and the importance of their positive reaction.

Outside entertainment can be brought to the school assembly and the music therapist is responsible for screening it and preparing the children in advance so that the best possible response is obtained.

Puppet shows, and choral and musical groups are often available from local organizations such as the P.T.A., Junior League, or music organizations like Sigma Alpha Iota. Learning to be a good, attentive, and appreciative audience is a fine learning experience and can have great carry-over value for the children. It can also offer an opportunity for outsiders to observe the children under carefully supervised conditions. This can open new vistas to the observer as well as the observed.

Little or no cost is involved in this kind of experience and in addition to providing the double-edged learning—it's really fun.

Sometimes a once-a-year special "gala" is prepared as part of the music program. Such an event can be highly motivating and not too time consuming if it is done with the proper perspective.

One very good way is to select a theme such as: Around the Clock, Visits to Other Lands, Around the Seasons, Happy Holidays, etc., and then take the songs, dances, rhythm band, and other appropriate material already learned and adapt them to the theme. In this way the children have no special material to perform but merely take those day-to-day activities which they are learning and show them with the extra fillip of a gay headband, scarf, top hat or flowing tie—voilà! A performance!

Each child should be given an opportunity to participate—no matter what his limitations—but he should not be coerced in any way by teacher or family. This requires very careful planning and ingenuity.

Over the years, a collection of square dance skirts, drum major hats, Indian suits, and clown suits become a part of a "costume corner" that can be utilized from time to time with happy results (especially the smiling faces of the proud wearers).

As a researcher the music therapist will continually review the vast amount of fine new materials available through the National Association of Music Therapy as well as other professional associations that have published music material dealing with all areas of exceptionality. Catalogs containing especially prepared and modified material are available from many music companies. Workshops prepared and presented by the music departments of schools and colleges can offer refresher courses, new ideas, and techniques.

In addition the therapist should be prepared to participate in staffing and counseling and to assume an active role in the school management routine as indicated.

Music Therapy as an Aid to Goal Achievement

Physical Growth

Improved physical coordination, both manipulative and ambulatory, can be achieved through prescribed rhythmic and musical activities. Response to finger plays, such as "Open, Shut Them," "Two Little Blackbirds," "Ten Little Soldiers," are excellent for manipulative improvement in young children.

For example: with the teacher and children seated closely together around a low table, the teacher demonstrates first by placing both hands with palms up upon the table. She sings softly:

Open, shut them, open, shut them, give a little clap
Open, shut them, open, shut them, lay them in your lap.

As she sings she moves quietly and appropriately. Next, she smilingly suggests, "Let's all try it." An approving pat or glance to the acceding child is fine—but no attempt to insist that all comply is indicated. Daily repetition and an encouraging and expectant attitude usually guide the group into some degree of response.

Music which is matched to a particular activity is stimulating and in some instances actually aids concentration; marching, walking, walking on tiptoe, balancing, bending, stooping, stretching, reaching, pushing, swinging, and many other movements can be made easier by the use of appropriate music.

Dramatic music activities like the recording *A Visit to My Little Friend* are excellent. The story tells of a child who goes to see his little friend and every day he goes a different way. On Sunday he walks, on Monday he runs, on Tuesday he tiptoes, etc. Each movement is accompanied by an appropriate musical selection. The extra stimulus of the story is most persuasive and the narration is well done.

Active participation by the therapist is essential at this level. The young retarded child learns movement most easily by observation and imitation—simply implying movement or talking about it won't do.

Small groups or individual sessions are the most effective with children whose neurological and motor impairment are severe. Children with severe emotional problems should be seen alone or in small groups when possible.

With growth in age, interest and skills develop for which a variety of activities can be devised. Imitative and dramatized activities such as whirling leaves, rolling snowballs, flying kites, waving scarves, and bouncing balls or balloons to a variety of tempos are excellent for improving motor development.

The concepts and skills in the area of body image can be aided by the use of music. Songs containing lyrics that name body parts are available in books and on recordings. A few examples are: "Put Your Finger in the Air," "Two Little Hands," I Wiggle My Fingers." Using action songs makes the touching, naming, and using of body parts a pleasant musical experience.

At first the directions may be given with the teacher participating well in view and facing the class. When an individual session is indicated, it may be well to have the child face a mirror while touching and naming the body part in the song. Additional songs and their sources are listed in the reference area.

Simple folk and square dances can be modified and if carefully presented are helpful. Extreme caution should be used to see that the total body movement is directed. To say, "Circle right" is not enough if the child's feet are not "facing right." Say, "Let's turn right with our feet, our body, our arms and our eyes; now circle right." Use *large* well-known objects in the room as directional signals until the children know right and left—for example, "face the clock"; "use the foot near the door." These are easy-to-learn guideposts and accelerate the child's ability to take verbal directions, thus increasing his self-confidence.

Manipulative skills can be aided by the use of simple keyboard instruments which require some fingering. The chord organ is fine for this purpose because the sound continues to be heard as long as the child's finger is on the key and stops as soon as he takes it off.

The keyboard and "music" can be clued by the functioning level of the child. Numbers, letters, or colors can be used with great success. (Write them on music paper or below large musical notes. Sometimes this leads to note recognition.)

Have the child point to the "music" with one hand and play the note with the other hand. This permits the child to function independently and fosters self-confidence. Allow the child to use any finger which is comfortable for him at first; then show him that two or three fingers work better. The Richard Weber material called *Musicall* has some good instructional material (see references) for this purpose.

Emotional Growth

Both directed and spontaneous responses to music serve to create an appropriate emotional climate. The fearful or hyperactive child may be soothed or calmed when a quiet lullaby or softly played instrumental music is introduced. Conversely, a lively march, polka, or activity song tends to stimulate the lethargic child or to serve as an active release for tensions.

Great care should be used to see that these activities are properly channeled. The cliché of permitting the aggressive child to "bang out" his hostility on a drum is really teaching him to abuse a musical instrument instead of using it properly. Standing by and watching him do his worst tends to reinforce his behavior. Allow him a few healthy beats and then count, chant, or play music with a gradual reduction in volume and tempo. This way, we meet him at first on his terms and try to help him to adjust to acceptable ones which are pleasurable to him as well.

Similar techniques may be used to stimulate the slow-moving child by playing or singing rhythms at his functioning level and then gradually adjusting the music or rhythmic beat to the desired level.

The simple introduction of a lively tune to a lethargic child is rarely effective. He must be led through a series of graduated musical tempos and pitch changes which should help him modify his behavior. The strong desire to participate in such highly motivating activities as the rhythm band, community singing, square or folk dances engenders the self-control needed to respond to the verbal directions or physical clues.

Permitting the children to select one of their group as a "leader" is a rewarding experience for the leader and the group. It can be done after attention and decorum have been established.

Well-ordered and often repeated music activities which tend to recur with regularity help to establish a feeling of order, which in turn lessens turmoil and anxiety.

Social Growth

Communication with the young retarded child may occur first with music at the sub-verbal level. Learning to listen—the primary step in the language development program—is often accomplished with musical stimuli.

For example, the children can be seated in low chairs (feet touching the floor). The teacher, also seated on a low chair, faces the group. Active participation by the teacher is essential since observation and imitation initiate the activity at this point.

The teacher sings or chants:

Where are your eyes, show me your eyes.
Baby's eyes can see.
Where are your ears, show me your ears,
Touch each little ear.

Since any degree of participation is acceptable, even the minimal response of the most severely retarded has the effect of making him a participant in a group activity; socialization thus becomes a constant by-product of group music activities.

Musical group activities, such as singing, playing, dancing, or even listening are especially conducive to linking a group together. Often the child who isolates himself in other ways will take part in group singing or playing. He should not be pressured to participate but allowed to observe the pleasure which the teacher-therapist and other participants derive from the musical activity.

The child who is considered an outsider by his classmates can have his image improved if he has even a small amount of musical ability. A careful search of his strengths and needs may furnish some surprising results. Robert the thumb-sucker may become Robert the flute player, and Peter the foot jiggler may become Peter the tap dancer, thus adding greatly to his own self-esteem and producing more acceptable personality traits.

Social development of adolescent boys and girls is eased by alleviating some of the embarrassment at this age when physical contact is encountered. The taking of hands or linking arms comes easily when they are absorbed in following the directions of the square dance leader or caller.

Social or square dances provided by recreational centers can be attended while the pupil is still in school. Aiding him to acquire some of the skills necessary for participation will help to ease the transition from school to home and the community or a residential situation.

The young adult retardate who is living at home can be well served by a social club attached to a sheltered workshop. Here is a place where these young people can gather in social situations and share some of the social skills which they have learned. They can sing, dance, and serve refreshments with minimal supervision and enjoy the companionship of other young people at their own pace.

Intellectual Growth

As a tool for learning basic skills music therapy is

useful at many levels. Songs, singing games, and jingles can become a device for learning the names of family members, the names of animals and their sounds, the child's own name and the names of his classmates. The "Name Game" is a good example (see reference material). Little chants like "The cow says moo—I have milk for you," "Bow-wow doggie, eat your dinner, wag your tail and Bow-wow-wow" are fun for the little ones especially if a toy cow or dog is shown to them as the song is sung.

Large clean pictures which illustrate the sound or subject of the song should be sturdy enough to be touched and handled by the children at the appropriate time. Songs of family unity, community helpers, safety, and good manners are available on recordings and in song books. Some good ones are *Let's Help Mommy*, *Men Who Come to Our House*, *Building a City*, *Songs of Safety*, and many more. Songs of the seasons, love of country, and of God are more easily learned than more prosaic lessons. That they are long remembered and easily recalled can be attested to be all who refer regularly to "Thirty days hath September . . ." and singing television commercials that stay with us willy-nilly.

Counting songs, rounds, call and response, or echo songs require concentration and are highly motivating. "One, two, button my shoe," "Ten Little Indian Boys," "One, Two, Three, O'Leary," and other songs are all part of the child's life when he plays normally with other children. The retarded child must be taught to know them and to use them as a reinforcement of what he is learning elsewhere.

Spiritual and Aesthetic Growth

Spiritual and aesthetic growth in retarded children, an area not often explored, can be encouraged by familiarity with good music. The creative satisfaction of "making music" or of "dancing" brings an appreciation of beauty. For these children, their development can be measured best by their participation, happiness in achievement, and the glow of wonder seen in eyes too often dull and unattending.

Juliette Alvin of London, England, in her touching account of her "Musical Experiment with Retarded Children" (in *Music for the Handicapped Child*; see Music bibliography) has noted that "when a child's interest and curiosity is aroused, he is in the best condition to perceive and absorb . . . all children have a sense of beauty although it may not be an adult's sense of beauty . . . Music can open a new world of emotional and intellectual activity to those handicapped children whose lives are deprived of many fine experiences because of the innate poverty of their minds." Surely the point is well made.

No one could look at the glowing faces pictured so beautifully in Ferris and Jennet Robins' book *Educational Rhythmics for Mentally Handicapped Children* without recognizing the inner beauty present.

"Ballet class" at our school is a very special time. Special clothing and slippers are quickly donned and proper places are found with great eagerness. Ballet and rhythmic movements can be used to channel physical activity to enhance grace, balance, and harmonious movement. Increased willingness to follow a set pattern of motor techniques is notable when the word "dance" is used. A feeling of internal and external grace is instilled. The use of hands, arms, feet, legs, and entire body as an instrument can set up a pattern of emotional attitudes which in turn influence coordinated movement. Indeed, a skill which is socially acceptable and yet can be learned by observation and imitation can be a valuable asset to the person excluded from many other experiences.

The material and techniques are adapted, of course, but remain close enough to be recognized when the children see samples of their "art" performed by others. Their excited recognition is beautiful to see, and their appreciation of what they see and hear is certainly heightened. Many of our girls have become aware of their femininity through the dance group. Boyish behavior, often a refuge for clumsiness, tends to be reduced and sometimes disappears when girls are confronted with their own graceful image reflected in a full-length mirror. Posture particularly becomes improved and pride in feminine physical characteristics increases.

Ballet classes offer special training in auditory motor response. The teacher names a step, as *glissade*, and the class "dances" the step. Foot and arm positions from first to fifth position are performed from verbal directions.

Planning Music Time

Musical activities which are presented in brief interludes between other activities can provide release from tension, preparation for the next activity, or just fun. Let the children select something they know and enjoy unless something specific is indicated.

When a more formal, longer music time is scheduled, planning and organization are necessary. Each group will vary in abilities and needs as well as physical setting. The following suggestions will be useful:

1. Have seating arranged so that teacher and pupils can see each other (a semicircle with teacher at the front is ideal).
2. Have the proper height chairs so that feet touch the floor and "stand" or "sit" can be executed with ease.
3. Know the material—never try to teach something you are not familiar with.
4. Be sure the content is at the level of the ability of the group.
5. Demonstrate—sing or play the whole selection. (Don't try to play the piano and teach—use recordings, tapes, or a portable instrument such as a guitar or autoharp if an accompanist is not available.)
6. Have the group try a small section at a time; then let the group try the whole selection.
7. Don't be discouraged if you are doing all the singing or playing at first.

8. Review, but don't continue it too long; try something else and then come back to it.
9. Keep it fun!

Individual Therapy

If an opportunity for working with a pupil on an individual basis is indicated and possible, the following steps are suggested: an evaluation of the pupil's record as provided by a complete staffing; an analysis of the child's overall strengths and weaknesses; an assessment of the extent of the child's musical experience, interest, and/or ability. The selection of a musical activity that would offer the best chance for a successful experience should then be made. Then the teacher-therapist can present the activity in short sessions. These may be increased in length as the child's interest, attention span, and ability increase. Before undertaking each step, be sure that a good chance for success exists.

The autoharp, tonette, and recorder are easily played and can be modified to meet the child's ability level. Numbers, letters, or colors can be used instead of notes to simplify the scoring of well-known melodies.

Make it possible to place emphasis on his abilities and accomplishments rather than on his failures. Offer him an opportunity to display his skills when he wishes to do so. Even if he does not wish to perform for others, he has had a satisfying experience which will serve to bolster his self-esteem; hopefully the benefits may carry over into a variety of learning experiences.

Interesting Innovation

The use of some of the rhythmic and tonal patterns developed by the Carl Orff-Schulwerk can produce some interesting results. Dr. Dolores Nicosia, musical clinician, has provided fine material modified for use with retarded children. It offers an excellent means of producing rhythmic and tonal patterns.

Some activities which are usable are the roll call and rhymes and chants. Nothing is as interesting to the children as their own names. Place them so that chanting their names forms an interesting pattern; for example, Terry, Terry, Mary Lou, Mary Lou, Karen, Karen, Paul. Repeat many times; vary the pattern; allow them to create their own patterns; add a simple melodic tune—start softly; get louder; clap, stamp, or pat the rhythm.

Gesture broadly to help establish rhythm. Use inflection to add interest. Repeat the procedures with simple adages: "Keep calm," "Watch your step," "Look before you leap," "If at first you don't succeed—try, try, try, again." Television commercials are fun to use. Try "Dad's Old Fashioned Root Beer," which becomes (1 - 123-1-1).

The older girls and boys enjoy what is timely. Have them try these rhythms on percussion instruments; have them chant as an accompaniment. Divide them into groups; encourage them to develop their own patterns.

Call and response songs and echo songs and chants tend to improve diction and stimulate improved articulation. Ella Jenkins has recorded some splendid songs and chants at every level from the preschool child to the young adult. The children enjoy them thoroughly and respond with enthusiasm to her material.

Chromatic resonator bells offer a fine group experience for intermediate and senior groups at the trainable level. The necessity for complying with the directions for group participation and the motor coordination brought into play in using the mallet upon the tone bar are excellent activities.

Mrs. Lucretia Rogers, of Gillette State Hospital, St. Paul, Minn., has developed a method which has proved very successful in a group situation. Instead of placing notes on a staff, or even calling the notes by name, she suggests using various geometric patterns for common chords. The method has worked well for us.

In the key of C, the tone bars marked C, E, G, C, and E are marked with an X. The bars D, F, G, B, and D are marked with an O. The bars C, F, A, C, and F are marked with a #.

Give the group some practice in holding the tone bar and using the mallet. To indicate who should play, seat the groups according to the mark on their tone bar. The leader then indicates the symbol with the fingers or writes them on the chalkboard, using a pointer as an indicator.

Use a familiar tune and be sure that the group can sing the song before they attempt to play it. For example, "Mary Had a Little Lamb":

X O X O X X X (Mary had a little lamb)
O O O - X X X (Little Lamb, little lamb)
X O X O X X X (Mary had a little lamb)
X O O X O X (His fleece was white as snow)

"America":

X X O O X O (My country 'tis of thee)
X X # X O X (Sweet land of liberty)
O X O X (of thee I sing)
X X X X O X (Land where my fathers died)
O O O O X O (Land of the pilgrims' pride)
X O X O X X O X (From every mountain side)
X - O - X (Let freedom ring)

Try a Guitaro. It is made by Oscar Schmidt & Company and combines the push-button chord of the autoharp with the mobility of the guitar. As an accompaniment to singing, it is delightfully easy to play and can be used by the teacher or older girls and boys.

In summary, remember that a variety of music is usable and available at every level; that there is music for the feet, music for the heart, and music for the mind, and each kind can be adapted to enrich the lives of these children whose needs are so great. Most of all, remember that making music or listening to music should be a joyous experience, that indeed: "music is love in search of a word."

Some Favorite Recordings

Adventures in Rhythm Folkways

After School Favorites. Childcraft. Inclues "Peter Ponsil and His Tonsil," "Michael and the Dentist."

All About the Seasons. Decca. Good for older children.

A Visit to My Little Friend. Children's Record Guild. Rhythms; days of the week.

Barnett Records, Jean Series. Geo. Stanley Co. Excellent rhythms and dances with directions.

Basic Concepts through Dance for Exceptional Children. Bowmar. Each dance is recorded at three speeds: slow, moderate, and fast; piano accompaniment.

Building a City. Young People's Records. Tells about kinds of people who inhabit a city as well as kinds of workmen who build.

Call and Response. Folkways. Excellent for echo and response; uses percussion instruments; Ella Jenkins sings.

Children's Holidays. Vocalion. Tuneful melodies about many holidays.

Children's Sing-a-Long. Vocalion. Fine selection of songs for sing-a-long with Frank Luther.

Circus Comes to Town. Young People's Records. Many opportunities for dramatic play and imitative activities; peppy songs.

Come to the Party. Children's Record Guild. Short songs about holidays, including a birthday party.

Counting Games and Rhythms. Folkways. Live recording of Ella Jenkins and little people; includes "Hello Song" and others that are familiar and fun.

Eensie Beensie Spider. Children's Record Guild. Tells of the day's activities from morning until evening while the spider climbs.

Grandfather's Farm. Children's Record Guild. Taking a car ride to the farm; "Grandpa's Farm Song" tells about animals and their sounds.

Holiday Rhythms. Bowmar. Rhythms for holiday activities; well done.

Holidays for U.S. Decca. Excellent songs and stories of holidays sung by Frank Luther; recommended for older children.

Hooray! Today Is Your Birthday. Young People's Records. Songs and games appropriate for a birthday party.

Learning to Listen. Tracey Clinic. Recorded for the deaf, but fine for the young retarded child; variety of reflections, and use of male and female voices; rhythm activities included.

Let's Help Mommy. Children's Record Guild. Songs for helping Mother clean house and prepare for Daddy's birthday.

My Playful Scarf. Children's Record Guild. Dramatic play using a scarf as a prop to imitate butterfly, sailor, cowboy, and others.

My Playmate the Wind. Young People's Records. The wind in four seasons; good for dramatic play.

Sing a Song of Safety. Playwell Records. Includes songs about remembering your name and address, riding a bicycle, and many more.

Songs for Children with Special Needs. #1, #2, and #3. Bowmar. Well done. Rhythm and pitch are excellent.

Strike Up the Band. Children's Record Guild. Rhythm band melodies which include the names of the instruments.

This Is Rhythm. Folkways. Ella Jenkins tells the rhythm story as only she can; good for older children.

Through Children's Eyes. RCA. Live recording of children's voices singing many favorites; good for singing along.

Tom Glazer Concert. Wonderland. Live recording of children's voices; good for singing along.

Train to the Farm. Children's Record Guild. Songs about traveling and animals and their sounds.

Train to the Zoo. Children's Record Guild. Good rhythms for dramatic play—elephant, seal, monkey, and others.

When the Sun Shines. Young People's Records. Dramatic play and songs of the seasons sung by Tom Glazer.

You'll Sing a Song and I'll Sing a Song. Folkways. Live recording of call and response songs; easy to follow and fun to do; Ella Jenkins sings.

RECORD COMPANIES

Bowmar
622 Rodier Drive
Glendale, Cal. 91201

Children's Music Center
2858 West Pico Blvd.
Los Angeles, Cal.

Educational Record Sales
157 Chambers Street
New York, N. Y.

RECORD COMPANIES

Folkways Records
906 Sylvan Avenue
Englewood Cliffs, N. J. 07632

Little Golden Records
1230 Sixth Ave.
New York, N. Y.

RHYTHM INSTRUMENTS

Lyons Music Co.
688 Industrial Drive
Elmhurst, Ill. 60126

Rhythm Band, Inc.
P.O. Box 126
Fort Worth, Texas

Oscar Schmidt Instruments
19 Ferry St.
Jersey City, N.J.

The Grades

31. NURSERY

by Rochelle Weinstein

Washington Star Syndicate

Children grow as they learn to do things that have meaning and they learn to control themselves so that they can do these things on purpose. The program given here for nursery and kindergarten will likely take two full years. Some members of the group may require a longer time. During this school period, the children are in the listening stage. Listening is an important ingredient for each task encountered during the school day. Learning to receive the ideas of others, learning to follow directions, learning to respect other children, and learning to share and to take turns all require good listening.

Purpose of the Nursery School Program

The child who enters our nursery class at 2½ to 3 years of age is classically nonverbal, is not toilet-trained, exhibits a short attention span, and is poor in social skills. For this child, the first school experience is very important. A preschool experience for retarded children provides an opportunity to grow physically, socially, emotionally, and intellectually in a practical, planned environment, unhampered by emotional stress and family competitions.

The school situation will provide the young retarded child with experiences to develop behavior controls and a social awareness before frustrations and severe behavior problems develop. The preschool experience allows the teacher to gain insight on how each individual child learns; this provides invaluable resources in planning later school experiences. Combined with early and periodic contact evaluations with the child's parents, the preschool experience allows an opportunity to plan realistically for a practical and happier future for both the child and his family.

The Nursery Classroom

The ideal location for a preschool group activity for young retarded children is an undisturbed, bland, and quiet isolated place. The furniture should be suitable to the size of the children. It should not be brightly colored. A round table of suitable size for six people, or a hexagonal table with a beige or grey formica top, with no decorations whatsoever, is the best work surface for our children. The room for the preschool children should be large enough to enclose three sections, a work area, a play area, and a separate nursery bathroom.

The work area

This area should include low chairs with a grip in the back for easy handling by the children, a low table as described above, a record player on a movable cart, a rocking chair, and low windows covered with soft, solid-colored draperies. Under the windows, sturdy benches should be placed which allow the children to look outside when the draperies are opened. The benches are also helpful as a sitting place for the children while you are dressing them. Rolling bins for blocks, cars, or trucks can be built to fit under the benches.

Across one wall, a set of cupboards with sliding wooden doors should be located. Part of the cupboards should contain hooks for coats, with each child's name placed above his hook. On a shelf above the hook, plastic containers for socks, training pants, rubber pants, slacks, and an extra T-shirt should be stored. The other cupboard on the wall should contain low shelves to house puzzles, books, beads, doll furniture, and blocks. The beads and blocks can be stored in containers such as coffee cans with plastic lids, and can be covered with colorful contact paper. These lower shelves make it easier for the children to select their own materials and return them after use. The upper shelves may conveniently be used by the teacher for storing teaching materials.

The rocking chair is very useful for a child who becomes restless or frustrated. In such instances, the teacher may hold the child in her arms and gently rock him. The rocking chair will also become a part of the imitative play of the children.

The play area

A separate, carpeted area of the room should be reserved for play. Such materials as a low table and chair set, a small rocking chair, and wooden furniture consisting of a stove, refrigerator, sink, ironing board, doll buggy, and dolls will encourage parallel and imitative play. A large blackboard is beneficial for use in developing gross motor skills. A room divider can be used to separate this area from the work area.

The nursery bathroom

Adjoining the classroom should be a nursery bathroom, equipped with a juvenile-sized toilet and a low washbowl. If the bathroom is equipped with regulation-sized fixtures, they can easily be adapted for the preschool child. A well-constructed stepping stool can be placed in front of the toilet, and a training seat with back rest, arm rests, and safety belt are beneficial.

The Teacher

The teacher for the young retarded nursery group must love little children. She must be physically strong and good-natured. She must have a good sense of humor, a compassionate disposition, and a sense of dramatic presentation. She must be tidy and wear pretty, soft colors. She must be in accord with a non-permissive, structured program.

The Children

Four children with two adults should be the ideal limit for a class. The children must be ready for the nursery group experience. Their readiness is determined by the following criteria:
1. A report from a physician, indicating that the child is retarded, stating the cause, if possible, and declaring that the child is in good health, free from communicable disease, and has had routine immunizations. An established etiology will help to determine the potential of those children about whom there is question.
2. An evaluation by a competent psychologist, establishing the child's functioning ability to be above the custodial level and below that of a potentially educable child. Here it must be considered that the four-year-old Downs Syndrome child will likely score in the educable range, but will not remain in this category. He should be considered eligible.
3. A visit to the home to become acquainted with the parents and to observe the child in his familiar surroundings. From this visit, the teacher should gain some insight into the child's play habits and the parent's acceptence of the fact that the child is retarded. She must explain, and be as certain as possible that the parents understand, the child's limitations and the purpose and goals of the nursery-school program.
4. The child must be trained for the control of bowels and stay dry most of the time. The child who is not completely toilet-trained should not be refused admission upon this ground only. Many children who are not completely toilet-trained at this age need the nursery school to help them learn this control. The very fact that the parents have not been able to train this child completely indicates the need for another influence in the child's training program. Usually the toilet training is completed within a very short time after admission into the nursery-school program.
5. The child must be able to bear his own weight and walk with a minimum of help.
6. Vision and hearing must be functional.

The Philosophy of a Preschool Education

The first school experience is important for the young retarded child. To insure optimal support for the child, to give him a chance to explore his environment, to enable him to receive the teacher's individualized attention, and to assure the child's readiness level for nursery group experience, one child is admitted to the class at a time for a period of observation by the teacher.

During this observation period, the teacher studies which toys attract the child's interest, his visual-motor coordination, his toileting habits, and his personal needs. Often the teacher-child relationship will develop slowly, taking a few days, or as long as one week before the teacher is able to begin working with the child. The actual nursery school day may be too long for the young child beginning school. If this should be the case, the child's parent should wait in another room to take the child home if he becomes restless or upset. More time can be added gradually each day until the child feels comfortable with the full-day program.

After an adequate period of time, the teacher should be able to work with two children together. During this first group situation, social levels of the children should be evaluated. During the first group contact the teacher again strives to give both children support in the group situation, a chance to explore the environment, and her concentrated attention in the new experience. This group encounter may be difficult to structure, and much time may be spent trying to contain both children in the classroom.

The children should be allowed to explore the room and the toys, and the teacher should observe which toys each child favors. Parallel play will be nonexistent for some time, but as the children become more at ease in the room, more structure can be introduced.

The first group experience *must not be permissive.*

A closely structured and controlled program serves three purposes, offering security, safety, and directed effort.

Security

Beginning a routine and setting implicit behavior limitations provides comfortable security for the children. The new school surroundings are a big step away from the familiar surroundings of the home. The children are introduced to strange surroundings, to new adults, and to new demands and restrictions. They must gain a feeling that things are stable and dependable as early as possible. Absolute consistency in imposing limitations is essential. If one toy or drawer is off limits to the children and is used as an example of "Don't touch," it must stay that way for a long time. When a set of rules is learned, the sense of security and satisfaction gained are valuable in developing a more relaxed approach to the many new tasks and challenges ahead.

Safety

Early training in the appropriate response to "No," "Come here," "Don't touch," "Sit down" is essential for safety and for functioning in a group situation. Structuring a program for children with limited ability in making judgments helps to avoid hazards in play situations. A sandbox is a wonderful place to play; it is a place to experience how sand feels, how it moves through your fingers, how warm or how cold it is, how damp it is, and you can do so much with sand—but, *it is not for throwing.* An early experience in receiving a handful of sand in the face can create a fear that might take weeks to overcome.

Directed effort

Directing effort, or channeling attention for doing specific tasks, is essential in the guidance of young retarded children. They are all easily distracted and have a very hard time paying attention over a long time span.

The Structure of the Daily Program

A carefully structured program is built upon a foundation of realistic and desirable goals. A knowledge of the developmental progression in motor skills, in social interest and experiences, and in receptive and expressive functioning is basic. Knowing what the child actually is capable of doing motorically, knowing where his attention and interest can be captured, and knowing what he can receive from the meaning of sound and express appropriately—these three factors provide a firm basis for planning for each child's learning experiences.

After the initial observation period and initial group experience, the group of children should be working well together on a full nursery day program. Learning to listen with an adult's individualized attention is different from learning to listen in a group situation. Immediately sharing begins, and with it comes the importance of taking turns. As the daily program becomes more structured, the goals for the program are carried out in the activity periods: circle time, milk and cookie time, free play, and toilet training.

Circle time

The circle time is a very important part of the child's day. During this time, the children should be seated around the table with the teacher and aide spaced between the children. As they are ready to learn to pass objects, the word "turn" is introduced. The "attention getter" is put in front of one child, and the teacher guides his hands to touch the object. Having the child's hands on the object, the teacher helps him slowly move it to the next child. An example of this experience might be presenting the group with a toy hourglass. In presenting the object to the first child, the teacher says, "The sand is going down, down, down." Should one child attempt to grab the toy, the teacher says, "No, it's Tommy's turn." "No" must have meaning, but it must be followed by a definite indication that the child is loved; he needs to feel secure in the belief that the teacher knows he is going to comply. As the children gain inner control, they learn upon direction to pass toys to one another.

Once the children become accustomed to circle time, a more formal structure can be started. When all the children are seated around the table, the teacher begins the session by greeting each child—shaking his hand and saying "Good morning." After a few weeks, the teacher adds the child's name to the greeting. Next, "How are you this morning?" may be added. The child should learn to respond, "Fine, thank you." This verbal response should not be pushed.

Finger games using nursery rhymes like "Jack and Jill," "Open, Shut Them," "Ten Little Soldiers," "Little Miss Muffet," and "Hickory Dickory Dock" are fun for the children and encourage language development. First the hand motions are taught, followed by the ending word rhymes. When the children become familiar with the hand motions and word rhymes, the teacher is then able to ask each child which game he would like to play. The child does not need to be verbal to play the game. If a child puts both hands in front of him with his fingers up, the teacher knows he is asking to play "Ten Little Soldiers." If he rolls his hands in fists and proceeds to move them upward, he is asking to play "Jack and Jill."

Free play

Free play time is fun for the children. Again, the play must be structured and controlled. The children can use the books, build with blocks, set the table with the toy dishes, cook with the pots and pans, play with the trucks, or play with the dolls.

For the very young child, the teacher should select materials which will stimulate him and help lengthen his interest span. Examples include two-piece puzzles, beads and string, and building-block towers. When the child has completed the task, a smile, a handshake, or clapping of the hands is sufficient reward from the teacher. The child soon understands this to mean that someone is pleased with his accomplishment. Later, the teacher can share the child's work with the group, and when the group applauds, he is further reinforced by his peers.

It is most important that the children be given sufficient time to put their things away before the next activity begins. These children move slowly and work slowly. They must be told beforehand that they will have to put their things away soon, and what the next activity will be. Have the children help each other put the toys away. If one child is helping another, the teacher should say, "Jill is helping Tommy. Jill is a big helper." Soon the children will enjoy this verbal reward, and all will want this praise, and begin working together.

Milk and cookie time

Milk and cookie time is a good time to reinforce the learning of other activities, including taking turns. The children should be seated around the table. Each child should be assigned one job for a school week. One child may pass napkins, another the plastic glasses, another the cookies, and so forth. The teacher may begin the activity by standing at one side of the table and calling the child who will pass the napkins. Handing one napkin to the child, she says, "Please give this napkin to Tommy." If the child is not certain who Tommy is, the teacher directs the child by placing her hand on Tommy's head and saying, "Here's Tommy." When passing objects, it is best to name the children in succession as they are seated. When cookies are passed, the teacher says, "One cookie," and shows the children the symbol one finger.

It is not necessary to continue with only one learning experience until all children have succeeded. When two or three children have succeeded, it is possible to build on their accomplished tasks. For example, if some children can pass napkins and match child with name, by adding "thank you" you stimulate those children and yet keep repeating the same tasks every day for the other children. "Please" and "thank you" should be part of the normal vocabulary of the adults working with these children. For the very young child, the equivalent of "thank you" may be a smile or a nod.

As the children get older and the program lengthens, new tasks can be added to the job list. Some are bringing out lunch boxes, setting a stepping stool in front of the sink, passing out placemats and plates, and being a messenger who takes attendance to the office. This messenger should be escorted by an aide. After lunch each child can learn to put his plate and glass on a tray, wipe his face with the napkin, and then place it into the wastepaper basket.

Toilet Training

For the preschool child, the toilet schedule should be every twenty minutes. The child should be seated on the toilet or in the training seat described above. When the child's back and arms are comfortable and his feet rest on the stepping stool, he feels secure and is more able to perform. The teacher should sit on a low chair next to the child. Any conversation should be limited to the task. The teacher should softly say, "Let me hear," while pointing to her ear, or whispering descriptive sounds in the child's ears, or letting the water run in the sink.

If after two or three days on this schedule the child has not performed, it can be assumed that he is unaware of what he is to do. A small paper cup filled with lukewarm water may be slowly poured down his body starting from his navel. When the child has performed, he should be rewarded with a big hug; or you may help him applaud for himself.

Consistency is essential; therefore, the teacher should supervise the toilet-training program. It is most important that the child be handled the same way each time. The teacher should approach the child and say, "It's potty time," and gently take his hand. If the child is involved in play with a small object, allow him to carry it into the bathroom. If the toy is too large, tell him his toy will be waiting for him when he is finished.

As the child starts to train himself, the schedule should be lengthened to thirty minutes or to the transitional periods between activities. This way the child does not miss any of the activities. For those children who train faster than others, three times in a morning session are enough—upon arrival at school in the morning, before the outdoor activity or milk and cookie time, and before going home. At this stage in the training process, an aide may continue training the child, but she must understand the importance of consistency.

From the very beginning of toilet training, the child should be taught to help in pushing his pants down. The teacher puts the child's thumbs between the elastic of the training pants and his body, and slowly guides his hands saying, "Tommy is pushing his pants down, down, down." The same process should be used in pulling the pants up again.

After the training pants are down, the child should be helped onto the training seat, and the safety belt can be fastened. If the pants are already wet, the teacher touches his wet pants and, with the other hand, clasps the child's chin, pointing the child's face toward her own and saying in a normal tone, "Too bad, wet pants."

The wet pants can be removed and dry pants put on while saying, "Nice dry pants." Allow the child to touch the dry pants. As the child is guided in pulling up his pants, he should be told that he is being helpful to the teacher. In this way, the child begins to associate the teacher with her name, as he is learning to do with the other children and their names.

The child should be taught to flush the toilet early. To avoid a frightening experience, the toilet should not be flushed while the child is still seated.

The older children in school make very good child care workers. The teacher can use these children to help in removing outdoor clothes in the morning and dressing the children before they return home. The worker is most beneficial and effective when he is assigned to only one child in the classroom or on the playground.

Careful structuring and a nonpermissive approach must not result in gruffness or unwavering severity. Each child needs to feel that the teacher loves him and is confident that he is going to do his best.

DAILY PROGRAM FOR BEGINNERS' NURSERY GROUP

Program

9:15	Wraps—bathroom—quiet play to explore	10:30	Bathroom—wash—lights out for a few minutes of quiet time
9:30	Auditory training—common objects		
10:00	Playtime, purposeful—large muscle activities Outdoors, small gym (if available), or in classroom with tables moved to one side	10:45	Milk and cookies
		11:00	Music—rhythm instruments
		11:20	Wraps—dismissal
		11:30	Teacher records daily journal

CURRICULUM FOR YOUNG RETARDED CHILDREN
Nursery I (Beginners—first group experience)

OBJECTIVES	MANAGEMENT	MATERIALS
Physical Growth and Self-Help Outer clothing off	With help	
Stay dry	Take to toilet periodically	Toilet seat must be proper size and comfortable
Help with clothes in bathroom	By the time the child is staying dry, he should require a minimum of help	
Know hands must be washed after going to the toilet	Requires help; not yet ready to mix hot and cold or to rinse and dry thoroughly	Sink should be low enough to use comfortably
Eat food without help—not requiring a spoon Handle drinking cup or glass (1/3 full only)	Requires help. Some success should be achieved. Present very small amount at one time	Cookie or sandwich, cut in small pieces. Milk cup, not too big; use plastic cup or plastic drinking glass
Large muscle activity	Carefully supervise *all* activity. Do not overwhelm the group with more than one opportunity at a time	8" rough-finish rubber balls Playground barrels Large toys to push Floor mat to roll around on (Pescolite gym mat) A cart to pull, preferably a bin on wheels Rolling toys to ride on and push along with feet (no pedals at this time) Large blocks to carry Large boxes to crawl in and out of Rocking horse Rocking boat Sandbox (covered please—when not in use) Pots and pans and large spoons for sandbox Swinging gate
Social Growth Listen and respond appropriately to "No," "Come here," "Don't touch," "Sit down."	See sequence for Language Development	See sequence for Language Development
Listen and accept affirmative approval—"Yes" (with head nod from teacher) "Good boy," or, "Good girl."		
Understand "yours," "mine"	This will not be accomplished until many months of group experience have gone by	Accomplished with same approach as training appropriate response to "No," "Don't touch," etc.

OBJECTIVES	MANAGEMENT	MATERIALS
Learn to use one toy at a time	Careful structuring in selecting, presenting, and withdrawing teaching devices and toys. Sit at table with entire group, each with own toy, content or restrained, no grabbing or snatching for another's toy	
Take turns and share	Very consistent management and vigilance—not learned until a few months have gone by	During music time wait turn to use favorite instrument. Take turns being "first" in being served, helped, or selecting a toy Take turns on playground equipment
Carry out one simple order—such as, "Give it to me, please."		
Emotional Growth Self-control—control of biting, hitting, pushing	Immediate removal from activity; employ "No" technique	
Parallel play	Close supervision of each child, playing alone, with selected (by teacher) activity, in partial isolation	Sandbox, large muscle activity materials—all suitable manipulation materials Consult Performance Goals Record
Intellectual Growth Recognition of own wraps, mittens, etc. (labeled). Recognition of place for own wraps Handle materials (purposefully, without throwing)	With help—should learn this quickly Consistent control	Wardrobe and bin of proper size marked with child's first name on a colored card
Motor skills learned through structured programing	*Level I: manipulative level* a. Reach, grasp, release b. Thumb and finger grasp 1. *Without visual guidance* Sand; water; things to squeeze like clay, sponge, or rubber; textures; rattles; bells; musical blocks; humming tops 2. *With visual guidance* Large push toys; squeaky books c. Both arms reaching d. Both arms holding large object e. Finger use f. One hand holding, one hand manipulating g. Place objects in container with large opening h. Place 1″ dowels in board with 1″ apertures. Use round dowels first, then square dowels	sand water clay fabrics fleece sponge large balls blocks, 9″ construction bricks to 1″ cubes rattles bells musical blocks humming tops large push toys pegboards 1″ dowels four-piece puzzles
Direct attention to adult	Consistent direction. Bland environment and opportunity to function with minimum of distracting stimuli. One-adult-to-two-children ratio maintained until this skill is mastered	

32. KINDERGARTEN

by Anita Bank Manchik

> *Children are a bridge to Heaven.*
> —Persian Proverb

The goals, procedures, and materials used for trainable children at the kindergarten level are best described in the context in which they occur. This chapter begins with a detailed review of a typical morning and is followed by a more concise curriculum outline.

The beep of the bus as it arrives at school indicates the beginning of a busy morning. Each child steps off the bus and is greeted with a cheery, "Good morning!" as he proceeds to his room.

Encouragement is given to help each child remove his wrap and find his name in the closet. Name-tags are color cued for easy identification. An ideal closet for kindergarten children has individual cupboards with low hooks to hang coats and sweaters and a bin above for hats, mittens, and a change of underwear. A folding door helps to conceal the contents of the closet.

Graduates of the beginners' group or nursery level are included in this kindergarten group. Six children can be managed with the help of a teacher's aide or other adult assistance. An aide allows the teacher to spend more time in actual teaching, instead of on the necessary but less important tasks, such as unplanned toilet visits. An aide also provides the teacher with the opportunity to work with children individually. An enthusiastic, energetic, and supportive aide is a welcome addition to any kindergarten room.

Because many of the children ride on the bus for a long time, they are encouraged to move freely about the room for a few minutes. During this period, each child is allowed to select a favorite toy to play with. The bathroom is used by those children who require toileting before our usual 10:15 visit.

Exploring the surroundings and selecting activities of one's choice must be carried on with consistent limitations. The children must know just what they will and will not be allowed to play with or investigate. Experience teaches that a pretty spring rose in a paper cup may seem like an attractive room decoration, but a practical child who knows just what cups are for may toss the flower out and drink the water!

After this exploration period, each child sits in his chair around the hexagonal table. A definite place at the table is designated for each child. Knowing just where their individual places are and just what is expected of them helps the children develop a sense of security and belonging.

Throughout the day's activities an emphasis is placed on the importance of the individual child. Each child is expected to develop at his own rate and differ in capability. Individual differences are always taken into account when planning daily activities.

When the children are in their places around the table, we begin our circle time activities, starting with greeting songs and nursery rhymes. Children love the sing-song rhythms of these familiar tunes, and many soon learn to imitate the accompanying finger play movements and join in with a few words. Participation is heightened with the use of such attention-getting mechanisms as wind-up toys and wiggly play spiders. Hardly a morning goes by without one of the children asking to sing a favorite song, such as "Eensie Beensie Spider" or "Johnny Works with One Hammer." This activity is terminated with the expression, "Time to do our work."

References to activities we participate in are prefaced with the words, "Time for . . ." to provide our children with the security of knowing what they can anticipate next, and so they will learn to associate particular daily events with the times at which they occur.

Work time begins with roll call when the teacher takes out her attendance book and directs each child to put his finger on the book. She then asks one child to hand her the pencil. Attention is drawn to the materials to be used for roll call. As in all activities, only the materials for the specific task at hand are on the table or in view. All other materials are concealed until it's time for their use.

Roll call procedure is part of the continuous training in learning to listen and respond, which goes on throughout the morning and in daily routines at home. As the teacher asks, "Is Susan here?" each child responds to his own name by extending his hand or saying, "Here" or "Hi." Any absences are noted, and we often make a card to send to a child who has been gone for any length of time. The children like to "remind" the teacher to write an absence slip, for it is a special treat to be selected to bring the note to the office.

Next, flash cards with the child's name and color cue (as are used on the closet hooks) are placed in the pocket chart. Each child learns to identify his first name, then his last name, and then the names of the other children. Progression to name-cards without color cues follows. The children also learn to respond to the question, "What is your name?" by showing their identification tag, which must be worn at all times.

Use of smaller manipulative materials begins in the kindergarten program. The children progress at individual rates from the manipulative level of motor skills (see nursery program) to the discrimination level. Discrimination includes placing small objects in a small area, ½″ dowels in a pegboard, for example, and exact placement of small objects according to size, form, and color.

Size discrimination materials include stacking block trees, nesting boxes and cups, and graded cylinder boards.

Materials for practice in learning to discriminate according to form include familiar objects such as cups or small cars, and later geometric forms.

Color discrimination activities, including matching, sorting, and naming, are carried out with 1″ colored cubes (Milton Bradley assorted). These cubes are placed on colored construction paper, while the teacher states, "*Red* block on *red* paper." Once the child has learned to match colors, the blocks are given to him to sort for himself. Labeling the color with the correct name is the last step in color discrimination.

Work with manipulative materials is terminated by a welcome visit from "Mr. Alligator" (soap dish, Avon Products) who brings sugared cereal treats to the children. Knowing that Mr. Alligator is on the way helps many children through the more difficult or demanding tasks of circle time. Taking turns and sharing are emphasized as the children send Mr. Alligator to their classmates and anxiously await their own turns.

As the children's attention spans extend, so does the length of circle time. The rationale for having an extended work period for our young children is based upon social demands. The goals for our children emphasize socially acceptable behavior in the school setting, at home, and in the community. The necessity for this emphasis is clear when exemplified as follows: while the antics of a normal five year old may be regarded as "cute," the same behavior by a young retarded child is often looked upon with disdain. Social skills required of our children include learning to sit, attend, and follow simple directions as early as possible.

By maintaining a high interest level through continual stimulation, the teacher can make activities at circle time an exciting, anticipated part of the day. Time usually goes by so quickly that it is playtime before we know it! Playtime activities are either in the gym, outdoors, or in the classroom, depending upon the availability of space and the weather. Ideally, playtime should follow a period of seat-work activity, but it isn't always possible to get into the gym when other classes find that time ideal for them, too. As a result, we often find ourselves shuffling our schedule, the playtime activities, and frequently our classroom furniture accordingly!

We are fortunate to have once-a-week sessions in the gym with the occupational therapist. Interaction with the therapist at the kindergarten level is focused on individual work, but also involves the children with their initial experiences in group play. Again, the emphasis is on structured control of play periods so that they do not become disorganized "free play" time.

Activities and materials for playtime include bean bags for tossing into a large basket, and for kinesthetic reinforcement in identifying body parts. Hula hoops interlock the "cars" of our train while we play "Choo-Choo." Rocking boats, scooter dollies, balance beams, and stacking blocks are just a few of the materials used for large muscle development during this period.

Following playtime, each child takes his turn in the bathroom. The children should already be familiar with the bathroom routine, and many are capable of caring for themselves at the toilet with a minimum of help. The children learn that hands must be washed after going to the bathroom, and carry out the steps of the handwashing sequence with verbal reminders. When these steps are sung to the tune of "This is the way we wash our hands," even little boys can find handwashing an enjoyable task!

Preparations are then made for refreshment time, with the children helping to clean the table and put the napkins in the basket. Good manners are always stressed, but special emphasis is placed upon manners during milk and cookie time. Each child is expected to say, "Please" when asking for a cookie (or extending his hand if he is nonverbal), to take just one at a time, and to take small bites of his cookie. Most children are capable of handling a small plastic drinking glass without difficulty and drinking milk without gulping or spilling. Proper use and disposal of a napkin are also taught.

On special occasions, the children participate in party preparations. *Let's Help Mommy* (Children's Record Guild) is a record which we like to use for practicing such preparations.

The important steps of learning to listen and developing the ability to discriminate sounds in the environment are an integral part of the kindergarten curriculum. Music is one of the most effective methods used for such auditory training. At this stage in the development of learning to listen, the child is expected to listen and respond to sound. (See chapter 22, on language.) In addition to the auditory training exercises in the room, the half-hour visits with the music therapist once a week provide a highlight to the auditory training program.

Some activities employed during music time include the use of rhythm instruments. Children learn to start and stop playing various noisemakers upon command of the teacher, or when the music stops, or with changes in the tempo of the music. Playing their names on the drum or xylophone—i.e., two taps for "Dan-ny"—is another exercise used for auditory training.

Action songs, such as "Put Your Finger in the Air," *Let's Play a Musical Game* (Columbia Records), or *Where Are Your Eyes?*" (Pram Records) encourage body part identification with the use of full-length and hand mirrors. The children also listen and respond appropriately when the teacher reads a favorite book, such as *Whispering Sounds*, by Marie Frost (David C. Cook Publishing Company).

Before we know it, it's time to prepare for dismissal. Using the over-the-head method, the children learn to put their wraps on by themselves. The coat is placed on a low table with the lining facing upward and the collar near the edge of the table. The child faces the table, puts his arms into the sleeves of the coat, and then swings it over his head. Wraps are fastened, and mittens and hats are put on with help.

The drapes are opened so that we can look for the school bus. "The Bus" (Bowmar Records, *Songs for Children with Special Needs,* #1) is a favorite finger-play song to sing while we wait for the "Bus loading!" call over the intercom. A cheery "Goodbye!" ends another busy morning.

DAILY PROGRAM FOR KINDERGARTEN GROUP

8:30	Unload buses—wraps—bathroom—quiet play to explore and select own activity	10:15	Bathroom—wash
9:00	Circle time for greeting songs, roll call, work with pocket chart, manipulative materials	10:30	Milk and cookies
		10:45	Music—rhythm instruments—auditory training training
9:45	Playtime, purposeful—outdoors, gym, or classroom	11:10	Wraps, dismissal
		11:15	Teacher records daily journal

OBJECTIVES	MANAGEMENT—ACTIVITES	MATERIALS
Physical Growth; Self-Care Care for outer wraps with very little help	Take wraps off, put in proper place. Remove boots	Color cue name on individual hook in closet Bins for hats, mittens Clothespin to clip boots together
Put outer wraps on with some help	Use "over the head" method for coat Put boots on with help Fasten large buttons, zippers when put in the track, and hooks with help	Plastic bag over shoe for easier fit "All by Himself," "All by Herself"—Creative Playthings, Princeton, N.J. Button, zipper, and hook boards Dolls for dressing, undressing.
Care for footwear	Take shoes, stockings off—put them on with help—no lacing	
Go to bathroom routinely or without being reminded; care for self at toilet with very little help or reminding	Pull pants down, up Boys lift toilet seat, stand to urinate Use toilet tissue with verbal direction Flush toilet	
Wash hands after toileting with very little help or reminding	Follow handwashing sequence—wet hands, lather soap, rub both sides of hands, rinse, turn water off, dry hands, hang towel	"This is the way we wash our our hands" —*Songs for the Nursery*, McCartney Household cards—bathroom articles, Peabody Language Development Kit #2
Develop appropriate eating habits	Wash hands before eating (see handwashing sequence) Eat finger foods Handle cup or glass without spilling Use napkin on lap and to wipe mouth Handle spoon	*Let's Help Mommy*—Children's Record Guild Cookies, sugared cereal Easy to handle food such as ice cream, pudding
Continue development of large muscle activity	Handle smaller balls, blocks, etc. as management of larger materials is established.	5″ rough finish rubber balls Large cardboard blocks (like bricks) Tricycles for pedaling Balance beam—Creative Playthings Bean bags Wooden train—Creative Playthings
Begin development of small muscle activity	Handle smaller materials with help	½″ dowel pegboard Stringing beads—Playskool Hammering blocks—Playskool ¾″ paint brushes

OBJECTIVES	MANAGEMENT—ACTIVITIES	MATERIALS
Emotional Growth Display self-control	Accept routine and defined limitations	
Follow through on tasks of own choice	Urge completion of a task before beginning the next one Always insist materials be put in the proper place before next item is selected	
Accept changes in routine	Change routine occasionally, make it fun and capitalize on the opportunity to help children accept the change or possible disappointment	
Social Growth Listen and respond appropriately (nonverbal)	Respond to own name during roll call by smiling or extending hand to the teacher Identify name-card with color cue; progress to name-card without color cue. Participate in group finger play activity	Shirt cardboard and tag board with child's name printed on it and color cue below the name *Finger Play*—Golden Press, *Finger Play* (Kg-2) # 1—record and book—Educational Record Sales, New York
Start and stop activity on command or cues	Sit in a row of chairs far enough apart so that the children cannot touch each other. Clap hands, sway. Use rhythm instruments Hum or vocalize with music Run, march with music	Rhythm sticks, bells, drums with recorded music
Begin verbalization	Respond appropriately to "Put the— in my hand," "Show me," "Give me," and "Bring me"	Common familiar objects. Use actual object first, progress to miniatures, then pictures, unless otherwise indicated.
Use acceptable words for parts of the body and going to the toilet	Establish acceptance of appropriate terms with parent cooperation	
Take turns	Participate in daily activities with consistent management	
Begin to play together	Share an activity Share toys, materials, playground equipment Exchange toys	Balls for rolling, tossing Wagons for pulling each other Musical instruments Completed puzzles

OBJECTIVES	MANAGEMENT—ACTIVITIES	MATERIALS
Use appropriate manners	Say "Please" and "Thank you" or use a gesture. Shake hands with visitors	
Help to distribute supplies	Hand an article to each child as directed	Napkins (refreshment time) Musical instruments Art supplies, etc.
Intellectual Growth Increase attention span	Extend circle time activity gradually until maximum length of time is reached (structure activities carefully)	
Develop proprioceptive awareness		
Identify parts of the body	Use bean bags for kinesthetic reinforcement of body parts (i.e., "Put the bean bag on your knee," etc.)	Bean bags, full-length mirrors, hand mirrors, "Put Your Finger in the Air" — *Let's Play a Musical Game*— Columbia Records *Where Are Your Eyes?* Pram Records
	Assemble body parts to form a whole	Boy-girl manikins—Peabody Language Development Kit #P Boy-girl puzzles—The Judy Co., Minneapolis, Minn.
	Identify body parts on others	Dolls Pictures of people

Show respect for others
  Remain quiet
  Step aside
	Take own chair to proper place in circle or return chair to former place. Respond to "sh" gesture	

Begin to handle materials at the discriminative level	Manipulate with discrimination
	  a. Small object in small area
	  b. Exact placement of small objects.
	     By *size*—select, match, sort gradations in size
		½″ dowel pegboard; progress to 9/16″ dowel, then 3/16″ dowel pegboards
		
		Stacking block tree—Creative Playthings
		Nesting boxes—Walt Disney Productions
		Nesting cups—Building Beakers
		Graduated cylinder boards—Creative Playthings

	By *form*—select, match, sort	Begin with balls, plastic spoons, etc; progress to geometric solids (circles, squares, triangles) Form puzzle—Sifo Co. St. Paul, Minn. Shape sorting box—Creative Playthings

OBJECTIVES	MANAGEMENT—ACTIVITIES	MATERIALS
	By *color*—select, match, sort	Dowel and ball cap, small cars, etc. (enough to allow child to sort by colors—three each of four colors) 1″ colored cubes (Milton Bradley assorted) and colored construction paper.
Respond appropriately to "Slow—Fast" "Funny—Not funny" "Happy—Sad"	Walk, run to selected music Play musical instruments Use "Funny" to share a laugh, "Not funny" for unaccepted behavior, if child laughs about it Use "Happy" for good deeds, "Sad" for reprimands	Tom-tom, xylophone Facial expression stimulus cards, Peabody Language Development Kit # P
Recognize own first and last names and names of others in group	Select printed names, first with color cue and then without, from pocket chart	Shirt cardboard or tag board with child's name printed on it and color cue below the name Pocket chart—Beckly-Cardy Co.—Chicago
Graduate from the need for three-dimensional objects (actual size object and miniatures) to pictures with tactile textured surface to flat pictures	Give simple commands (e.g., "Give me the ball") with three-dimensional object; progress to simple commands with the picture of the object	Ball, cup, other familiar objects. Stimulus cards—Peabody Language Development Kit # P
Identify pictures according to name, then function—include food, clothing, toys, household articles, animals, people, transportation	Select one of two (gradually extend to one of four) pictures in the pocket chart according to name; e.g., "Give me the milk"; graduate to function; e.g., "Give me what we drink"	Stimulus cards—Peabody Language Development Kit # P
Discriminate tactile opposites Warm—cold Wet—dry	 Discuss weather very briefly, in terms of warm and cold days Touch "warm" and "cold" objects. Use "wet—dry" terminology in hand washing sequence Talk about rainy days and sunshiny days	 Water faucet, heat vent, window pane, pictures of iron, toaster, stove, refrigerator Sponges, facial tissues, sand and paper towels

OBJECTIVES	MANAGEMENT—ACTIVITIES	MATERIALS
Food Management Help to prepare table	Wash table, put napkin, plate, and glass at each place	*Let's Help Mommy*—Children's Record Guild Play housekeeping supplies—Creative Playthings
Develop appropriate eating habits and manners	Wash hands before eating Say "Please" and "Thank you" or use appropriate gesture Eat finger foods Handle cup or glass without spilling Use napkin on lap and to wipe mouth Handle spoon	"This is the way we wash our hands" —*Songs for the Nursery*—McCartney Cookies, sugared cereal Easy-to-handle food such as ice cream, pudding (*not* jello)
Help to clean up following a meal or snack	Place napkins in the basket Return supplies to proper place Pretend dishwashing Sweep floor Wipe table	 Wooden sink, cupboards Housecleaning set—Creative Playthings

33. PRIMARY

OBJECTIVES	MANAGEMENT	MATERIALS
Physical Growth Complete care of outer clothing, including boots	Jackets, coats, sweaters, etc. are provided with large tape loops (not elastic) as the easiest method of hanging in proper place Names are put on each child's locker on different colored paper (same color used for each child in any activity needing name selection) graduating to all in black and white. Same locker always used for each child For putting on wraps, coats are spread on a desk—linings up—child places both arms in respective sleeves and throws the coat over his head. Buttoning is started with the "all-purpose" book (single buttons sewed on strips of material in the book). Snowpants—slipped over buttocks—child sits on chair and removes one leg and then the other	
Shoes—lacing and tying	This is used constantly in daily activity—eye-hand time—each lace is a different color and is played as a game of crossing the road—tongue of shoe serves as the road	Colored shoelaces and wooden shoes
Get ready for bed alone at home and dress for school with help	Parent cooperation	
Complete self-care—except tying shoes—toileting	Assist only in emergency	(This does not include bathing, shampooing, care of fingernails)
Wash hands without help		
Brush teeth with supervision Brush hair		

OBJECTIVES	MANAGEMENT	MATERIALS
Climb	Assist with hand-over-hand ascent and descent, at the same time stressing one rung at a time	Stall bars Steps
Handle scissors purposefully	1. Experiment with tongs or forceps 2. Open, shut them 3. Finally scissors—first holding the paper for the child and then allowing him to hold the paper himself. With the narrow strips he is happy to see his efforts rewarded	Plastic forceps Cotton balls Small ball (ping-pong) Narrow strips of paper
Proprioceptive awareness should strengthen		
Social Growth Listen and respond to simple words	Name common objects Name common foods "Good morning" "Sit down"	
Qualify words to simple phrases, using appropriate language	Teacher goes to circle and requests each child in turn, "Come to circle," "Bring your chair," "Get me the book," "Bring me my pencil," "Go to the bathroom," "Wash your hands"	
Share; work together	Participate in group activities—e.g., music games—waiting turns in circle activity as well as games	
Respect adults	Respond to commands of adults	
Respect neighbor's property	Consistent management	
Answer telephone properly	Stress to say *only* "Hello, I'll call Mommy," and follow through	Telephones
Emotional Growth Self-control	Learn to conform to routine and sit in group activities for short periods	
Follow through on tasks of own choice	First, with assistance of adult complete task at hand and replace all materials; then with verbal assistance only; finally you present material to the child and completion is of his own volition	

OBJECTIVES	MANAGEMENT	MATERIALS
Accept change of routine	Explain to group ahead of time by saying, "When the hands of the clock say___we are going to___" allowing child time to absorb so change will not be too abrupt	
Intellectual Growth Lengthen attention spans	Circle time is increased slowly until the maximum is reached, and so with all the activities	
Begin writing readiness	Each child follows the teacher as a game, first in the air—round and round and round and round, then to the large cardboard When this is performed with assurance, progress to a series of circles confined to a defined area The circles accomplished, we go to the + An adult sits with child and makes the first mark:	and has the child cross over it: + Then this is produced by the child in a definite area Move on to the writing sequence	Chalkboard Shirt boards Black crayons Primary pencils Make circles Child makes circle and fills in features for a face, directed by teacher Fills boxes with circle Fills boxes with + + Fills boxes with x x
Select colors	Place colored block on same colored construction paper each time, repeating, "*Red* block on *red* paper"; adult then hands child the block and has him place on proper paper while naming the color; finally the blocks are given to the child to select for himself and make proper placement Note colors in room	Colored blocks Construction paper
Perceive gross differences	These objects are placed on a large table—children are grouped around; each in turn is called to come to the table, and teacher says, "Put your finger on the big doll; put your finger on the little ball; give me the little record; give me the little doll" Progress to pictures with the same object pictured big and little, and the same procedure: "Put your finger on the big bottle; put your finger on the little bottle" Gradually present pictures with very little difference	Familiar objects: Doll—big and little Ball—big and little Record—big and little Chair—big and little
Concept of little and big, short and tall, or short and long	Same procedure	

OBJECTIVES	MANAGEMENT	MATERIALS

Recognize words:
 	
    Stop   In   Wait
    Go   Out   Walk
    Boys   Push Danger
    Girls   Pull   Keep out
    Private Exit Men
    Poison   Women
		Electric stoplight
		Singing games
		Flash cards

Number concepts to five	See "Numbers in Everyday Living" (Chapter 26) Tangibles are used—e.g., when in circle ask each in turn how many girls are in the circle; how many boys in the circle, etc. Figures are placed on the board and children asked to place proper number with same number of figures and reverse the procedure	Magnetic figures Magnetic numbers
	Tell a number story Pictures are presented to child with the question, "How many shoes?"—here he touches as he counts Commands are then given as, "Bring me three blocks"	Finger plays Pictures Bradley cubes
Get supplies when directed and help distribute Begin awareness of weather, days, seasons, special days Learn to go to hall bathrooms and recognize signs on bathroom doors Orientation in family Orientation outside of family—people who help us.		

OBJECTIVES	ACTIVITIES	MATERIALS
Food Management Table manners—learn proper lunch routine (Objectives are same as activity)	Daily lunch routine Put napkin on lap Wait for everyone to be served Say thank you to person who serves Sit quietly Remain at table until excused Do not take other children's food Eat food in proper sequence Use napkin properly Use fork and spoon Use judgment in amount of food consumed Do not play with food Leave eating utensils and leftover food in front of you until collected Do not play with lunch boxes	Lunchroom utensils Lunches Lunch boxes
Table setting—learn how to set table properly	Assign lunch duty to different child each week Pass out plates Pass out napkins Pass out food at parties	Plates Napkins
Food preparation— Learn how to prepare simple foods Learn to pour liquids	Make peanut butter and jelly sandwiches Spread butter Make popcorn Make jello Make pudding Pour water in the pool	Peanut butter Jelly Butter Bread Popcorn Instant jello Shake-a-pudding Pool Plastic pitcher and cups
Clean-up— Learn how to clear table Learn how to dispose of garbage Learn where to put dirty dishes	Different child assigned each week to lunch duty Clear dishes when children are finished Wipe table Rinse out sponge Dispose of garbage in can Scrape or rinse dishes Put dishes in dish cart	Dish cart and bin Garbage can Sponge Sink

34. INTERMEDIATE

OBJECTIVES	MANAGEMENT	MATERIALS
Physical Growth Full self-care in school	A.M. and P.M. wraps	Use clothes hanger; begin with coat and hanger on a table
Dress and undress at home without help (except tying shoes)	Practice buttoning a very small button Use zippers in clothing Tie hats, scarves, shoes, etc.	Use activity books and mounted shoes, and proceed to managing own clothes (actually, lacing of shoes should have been mastered in primary group)
Bathe with little help	Nurse helps	Use teaching shower
Complete self-care in bathroom	Careful supervision	Children should flush toilet, wash and dry hands, leave washbowl and soap clean
Gain concept of need for cleanliness	Wash hands after going to toilet, before meals, and after playground activity Brush teeth after meals Comb hair and wash face after rest period	Discussion, pictures, making own workbook Use nailbrush Self-evaluation Care for own toothbrush, glass, and dentifrice Use washcloth
Acceptable manners	Lunchtime—chart activities to show each job assignment	Set tables; distribute lunch; pour milk; pass out milk Lead prayer "Thank you" and "You're welcome," with no exceptions Leader assigned to say when all are finished eating, they may leave table
Meet guests	Children take turns being guest and host Children evaluate performances	Use hats, purses, etc. for dressing up like grown-ups

OBJECTIVES	MANAGEMENT	MATERIALS
Social Growth Introductions Accept and give gifts Excuse self from room		
Speak in sentences	Roll call Speech time group activities See language development sequence (Chapter 10)	Child answers, "I am here" Recitation of short poems as child stands in front of teacher Language Master—short sentences (one idea) Lotto games requiring sentence responses Tape recorder
Carry messages	Carry written messages to office or rooms nearby Carry messages to rooms farther away	Child carries daily attendance report to office; no speech required except "Thank you" Later a short message may be added requesting a book (prearranged at first to assure success) At first, messages are notes requesting something to carry back, such as a book or jar or paint; later a verbal message is sent back with the requested item

Use telephone for most simple emergency calls	Practical situations:
	  Dial "O" for operator
	  Dial numbers as directed by teacher
	  Dial numbers from large printed numbers on card
		Use large black dial from Telephone Co. until "O" is located easily
		Use Teletrainer (Western Electric)
		Ask for assistance, naming problem and giving name and address
		Direct dialing to police and fire stations

Group participation	Assemble chairs for circle activity in orderly manner All circle activity Game participation other than circle activity	Children bring chairs to circle as names are called Children bring chairs to circle without being called, one at a time Lotto games "Bam" game
Team play	During physical education period, rank-and-file games Captain chooses team members Children take turns	Basketball toss Bean bag games Target games
Family orientation: grandparents, aunts, uncles, and cousins	Discussion and project scrapbook	Make scrapbook of snapshots of family and relations

OBJECTIVES	MANAGEMENT	MATERIALS
Emotional Growth Self-control Respect for property of others	Child is assigned own desk, chair, bin for clothing Child is expected to remain in his seat, leaving it only to perform a task upon request, or at a logical request of his own	Structure situation by placing desk and chair in corner or against wall to lessen temptation to wander "Don't talk" and "Don't hit" are replaced by "Close your lips" or "Fold your hands"
Accept change of routine	Any change in routines or schedules should be introduced and explained *before* carried out, if possible; these children thrive on routine and find security and comfort in it By the end of this level it should be possible to change the routine with a brief statement, without disturbance	Make slight changes in routine during the day Change seating arrangement for different activities Change "Housekeeping Chart" weekly at first, and later on make daily changes in one task at a time
Control of uninhibited behavior	Insist that children cross their feet and fold their hands in circle or close contact situations, to help them resist bothering others by hitting or kicking Substitute an acceptable activity for an unacceptable act Remove child from group if necessary	Remove toys or materials—completely out of sight
Deterring perseveration on a task, idea, or actions	Break in on activity by change of voice, change of pace, or removal from spot of activity; substitute an activity	
Follow through on tasks	Goal must be within reach and rewarding when complete As child progresses, goal increase is difficult, but must always be realistic Child must always understand what is expected of him	Pegboards, *completely* filled: first with various colors; then with rows of single colors—copied patterns Housekeeping task Sewing cards Stringing beads Any *set* and clearly understood realistic assignment
Intellectual Growth Write own name	See writing sequence (Chapter 20)	Pencils Tracing paper Red and green pencils for drawing lines Large newsprint paper 1″ lined primary paper
Vocabulary of arithmetic	Use list in "Numbers in Everyday Living" (Chapter 26)	

OBJECTIVES	MANAGEMENT	MATERIALS
Recognize all words for protection	Each word is placed (one at a time) on bulletin board, with color and picture clues Same picture is placed on white card in pocket chart Each child assembles his own "sign" project book; these books are used for "reading" and discussion	Words used: hot keep off telephone stop—go push—pull wait—walk (or don't walk) danger—poison wet paint boy—girl men—women ladies—gentlemen exit—entrance this way in—this way out first aid—police doctor, M.D., or physician Use the Language Master for reinforcement
Use *all* words for protection	Dramatic play	Use Stop-and-Go lights to act out traffic situations Assemble empty bottles for play medicine cabinet Play "push-and-pull" games with objects and in gym period Lotto games
Learn about days of the week	Associate a favorite activity with each day. For example: Monday, back to school Tuesday, movie day Wednesday, make-plans day Thursday, swim day Friday, square-dance day Saturday, home or temple Sunday, church; Daddy home	Use color cue and cards Arrange in order, black and white cards "Days of the week" lotto Reinforce with suitable singing games Make chart for days, showing favorite activities
Concept of yesterday and tomorrow	Discussion	Use same chart as for days of the week
Concept of seasons and their implication	Learn about current seasons Associate a favorite activity for each season Assemble project books Incorporate holidays	Use project books for discussion and "reading" about clothes we wear, sports, and activities Talk about months in each season
Number concepts	See "Numbers in Everyday Living" (Chapter 26); progress through Level II Notation counting, for number-symbol recognition, to ten	1″ colored cubes; collection of little cars, buses, or other common matching objects Language Master Hands showing numbers Later use cards for Level II, counting by grouping and rotation Magnetized cutouts Singing games "Bam," "Help your neighbor" A practice clock Milton Bradley calendar

OBJECTIVES	MANAGEMENT	MATERIALS
Count by fives Count by twos	Use "singsong" counting	Play clock game in gym Use practice clock with minutes at intervals of five, printed in large bold type from five to sixty
Recognize coins	Convert nickles and dimes to pennies to teach values (See "Numbers in Everyday Living"); be sure concept of "More—Less" has been achieved before starting this task	Songs Play store
Concept of relationships	Make workbooks for units: Rooms in home Kinds of stores Ways to travel	Doll house Lotto games Shopping games Dramatic play
Recognize written names of common foods and kitchen supplies	Experience charts of healthy menus Discussion of good menus	Play store
Orientation to "time"	Learn about time to do things Compare "lots of time" with "hurry" Learn to estimate one minute	Charts for daily schedules with clock settings Songs Dramatic play Watch sweep second hand on large clock. Children cover their eyes and listen while teacher taps each five seconds. Counting by fives, the children tap with her. Then they try to guess when a minute has passed
Language development	Telling a story from a picture	*We Read Pictures; We Read More Pictures*—Scott-Foresman) Selected pictures.
Direct careful attention and follow through on work directions	Attention must be captured and held. Teacher must demonstrate task, one step at a time. *Know how your children learn.* Some follow directions by being told, and some by being shown; some require both hearing and seeing what is to be done	Select tasks to assure success—give help to assure success. Most valuable "material" is teacher's own enthusiasm for task while presenting it Lessen assistance as work progresses
Doing chores *daily* Set and clear table	Set and clear table at school. Exchange starred "report" cards with home Send home a star for good help in school; have one sent from home when good help is given at home	Play restaurant Help at lunch time *Home cooperation*

OBJECTIVES	MANAGEMENT	MATERIALS
Dusting	Daily dusting and polishing	Assemble necessary things in marked basket
Scouring	Clean sinks and washbowls	Assemble necessary things in marked basket
Cleaning floors	Use single tool; graduate to broom and dustpan Demonstrate and use *much* verbal guidance; guide child's hands	Dry dust mop One child sweeps; another holds dustpan
Washing blackboards	Demonstration and guidance	Large sponge easily handled. Place newspapers on floor to catch drips until child learns how to manage
Straightening books, desks, and chairs		
Outside pickup: Rake tanbark Sweep up sand	Circle playground with two "teams"	Use large baskets or cartons to gather trash, twigs, papers, etc.

35. SENIOR

OBJECTIVES	MANAGEMENT	MATERIALS
Physical Growth Full self-care in school and at home, including bathing (except shampoo): Bathroom independence—care for self in bathroom with minimum of supervision Personal grooming—keep hair and nails in good order; select clothes tastefully; shine shoes; brush clothes Care of wraps—take off, hang up, put on coat, hat, gloves; also put on boots, remove and clip together Aware of good posture sitting or standing	Send to bathroom before lunch. Periodic checks on flushing toilet and washing hands Expected to ask if an extra trip to the bathroom is necessary Discussions and practice sessions on care of hair, nails, shoes, etc. Reminders when necessary This has become well established at this level. Each child takes his turn at coat closet and deposits or picks up own boots at appointed place in hall	Keeps own brushes or combs at school and keeps them clean Shoeshine kit Manicuring material Children have own bins to hang wraps Each child has a clip clothespin, with his name on, to clip boots together
Social Growth Social language: Say and use sentences when introduced to others Receive or offer a compliment Offer or accept invitation Speak on telephone Ask questions Leadership and responsibility: Follow directions, take orders willingly from leader, and follow through on assigned tasks. If chosen to be leader, he must be patient and pleasant with others	Practice sessions to discuss good manners in various situations and then actually practice introductions, etc. In our regular daily activities we stress speaking in sentences Each child is assigned a room duty for the week, to which he is expected to give his best efforts Each child has special chores on appointed days, such as chair and cot details, yardwork and lunch set-up and clean-up	Dramatic play Teletrainer Dust mitts Broom and dustpan Sponges for cleaning board, counters, and desks Placemats, large plates for sandwiches, etc.
Be a good winner and a good loser	Lunch set-up and clean-up Opportunities for delivering messages are offered regularly Gym periods offer opportunities for group effort, good sportsmanship, and leadership	Napkins, sponges for cleaning mats and tables Dishwasher, lawn tools (except mower) Basketball equipment Bean bags Rubber horseshoes Small hoops Volleyball

OBJECTIVES	MANAGEMENT	MATERIALS
Emotional Growth Self-control Control temper Avoid interrupting	A positive approach must be used. If child loses temper, isolation from group is best solution	Gentle but firm reminders
Follow through on an assigned task to completion	Proper guidance is imperative here. Task assigned must be at child's level of ability and he must be guided when choosing task for the same reason	
Accept discipline gracefully	Firm insistence on obedience, with use of fewest possible words. Reasons for restraint should be stated and be understandable	
Intellectual Growth Reading Each child should be able to recognize useful words, such as words for protection, work, days, months, seasons	Daily drill, also discussion Pictures illustrating works for scrapbooks Some children bring weather reports Some write well enough to keep a daily weather book	Language Master Safety signs Day by day calendar Scrapbooks Weather books Flash cards Experience charts
Some can learn to read through primary level	Individual instruction if imperative as each child is at individual reading level. Special materials and devices to aid concentration or comprehension. Progress is slow but definite, requiring regular reinforcement	Language Master Phonics cards Scott-Foresman readers and workbooks *My Weekly Reader*, levels 1 and 2 *My Weekly Reader* subscriber books
Writing When possible, child learns to write own name, address, telephone number	See handwriting sequence (Chapter 20)	
Number concept Progress through Level I, II, and III for those able	Drill in recognition of numbers in and out of sequence. Match number symbols with groups of objects concrete and abstract	Number cards Counting cubes Pictures with groups of objects to count and match with number symbols
Number concept to twenties Coins and playing store, understanding of money and numbers	Matching number symbol with number words Recognition of dates during calendar drill	Coins and store pictures

OBJECTIVES	MANAGEMENT	MATERIALS
Simple addition and subtraction (as seen in "Numbers in Everyday Living," Level II)	Some single column problems to do alone or with supervision as necessary	Counting cubes Flash cards
Tell time (see "Numbers in Everyday Living") Count minutes by fives Understand hour and minute hands	Constant practice in counting minutes by fives Drill in figuring time set on clock by teacher	Clock Clock with movable hands Clock stamp and pad
Eye-hand coordination: Handle buttons, zippers Tie own shoes Use scissors; cut on a line Use pencils and crayons	Much cutting, pasting, writing, and coloring Wooden puzzles from a few pieces to about twenty pieces	Wooden shoe Scissors Paste Large pencils Crayons Ruler Scrapbooks for mounting cut-out pictures
Improve muscle coordination	Daily practice	Wooden puzzles Large rubber balls Basketball hoop Bean bag Rubber horseshoe game 15" plastic hoop ring toss hoop ring toss Shuffleboard
Auditory and visual discrimination and memory	Daily practice	Rhyming game—rhythms Singing games Percussion instruments Copying seen forms Copying heard rhythms
Work progress: Assume more responsibility and independence in carrying out assigned routine tasks	Weekly assignments for cleaning chores Clean inside of cars Regular assignments for lunch tasks, cot detail, yard work, help in station wagon	Baskets and kits hold necessary supplies for each chore: Window and glass cleaning Woodwork Brightwork: silver Polishing furniture

36. YOUNG ADULTS - PREVOCATIONAL

OBJECTIVES	MANAGEMENT	CONSIDERATION FOR EVALUATION
Physical Growth: In planning for young adults, it is assumed that physical growth has been completed. The skills required to do a job become of prime concern.		
Work Progress To work alone or in a group, with consideration for others: dependably, cheerfully and generously Child care—work with younger children	Structure work schedules Proceed to more democratic planning of work schedules Discuss problems arising in group sessions Class instruction in toileting, cleaning up, undressing, dressing, play activities, behavior management	Attitude toward assigned job; cooperation with co-workers; ability to attack job from oral or written directions; ability to carry out assignment, to assemble needed materials and to report completion of job; cleanup skill; care for tools and materials; variety of abilities; cooperation with peer leadership; ability to assume leadership for (boss) a work crew (such as yard cleanup, weeding detail, setting up or putting away chairs in gym, window washing, emergency cleanup); ability to take an assignment not scheduled, such as emergency cleanups, nursery helper, fill-in for absentee, or any unscheduled chore), child care Ability to carry out any of the above tasks independently (note how much supervision is needed)
Emotional Growth Good self-control	Close supervision and self-evaluation	Self control; temper manifestations; ability to follow through on tasks of own choice and on tasks assigned; reaction to frustration; cooperation; reaction to confusion or change of routine
Social Growth Good social awareness; acceptable manners in all social contacts	Close supervision Self-evaluation Discussion groups Dramatic play Puppet shows	Sharing; respect for adults; respect for peers; manners, games, eating, telephoning, meeting people, compliments; sportsmanship; general language usage (consider any poor speech habits or unacceptable language); good subjects for conversation away from home; attention-getting mechanisms; acceptance of criticism; violation of

OBJECTIVES	MANAGEMENT	CONSIDERATIONS FOR EVALUATION
Social Growth (continued)		privacy (include interrupting, unbecoming curiosity, nosiness), repeating "home gossip"; playing role of peacemaker; unacceptable gestures and actions such as pulling at clothing; failing to keep hands to self
Intellectual Growth Reinforce all learned skills Most of this area is considered under *Work Progress*. However, in this category consider the following: ability to pay attention; curiosity; memory span; number concepts; concept of time; concept of money; use of tools; word recognition; ability to follow directions and to complete a task; planning for "leisure" time; accomplishment in production Chores: as listed in Evaluation of Motor Skills	Plan at least two hours each week for review of "reading" and number concepts	Each child keeps his own daily journal recording weather, temperature, special events, chore assignments, work completed.

GENERAL BIBLIOGRAPHY

Ayllon, T., and Azrin, N. *The Token Economy: A Motivational System for Therapy and Rehabilitation.* New York: Appleton-Century-Crofts, 1968.

Ayres, A. J. *Body Image.* Conference Proceedings, Cleveland, O.: American Occupational Therapy Association, April 1966.

Ayres, A. J. *Occupational Therapy for Motor Disorders Resulting from Impairment of the Central Nervous System.* Chicago: National Society for Crippled Children and Adults, 1963.

Bancroft, Jesse H. *Games.* New York: Macmillan, 1955.

Bandura, Albert, *Principles of Behavior Modification.* New York: Holt, Rinehart & Winston, 1970.

Bangs, Tina E., *Language and Learning Disorders of the Pre-Academic Child.* New York: Appleton-Century-Crofts, 1966.

Baumgartner, Bernice B. *Guiding the Retarded Child.* New York: John Day, 1965.

Bayley, N. *The Development of Motor Abilities During the First Three Years.* Monographs of the Society for Research in Child Development, no. 1, 1935.

Behrman, Polly. "Activities for Developing Visual Perception." *Academic Therapy*, 1970.

Bensberg, G. *Teaching the Mentally Retarded.* Atlanta, Ga.: Southern Regional Education Board, 1965.

Bernstein, Owen and Bebe. *Work for Independence: A Series of Special Education Photo-Stimuli Aids.* New York: John Day, 1971.

Bijou, S. W. *International Review of Research in Mental Retardation* vol. 1. Edited by N. Ellis. New York and London: Academic Press, 1966.

Bijou, S. W., and Baer, D. M. *A Systematic and Empirical Theory.* Child Development, vol. 1. New York: Appleton-Century-Crofts, 1961.

Bijou, S. W., and Baer, D. M. *Universal Stage of Infancy.* Child Development, vol. 2. New York: Appleton-Century-Crofts, 1965.

Brownell, William A. *Arithmetic in Grades I and II.* Durham, N. C.: Duke University Press, 1941.

Brownell, W. A, and Weaver, J. F. *Teaching Numbers We Need.* Boston: Ginn and Company, 1958.

Bush, Wilma Jo, and Giles, Marian Taylor. *Aids to Psycholinguistic Teaching.* Columbus, O.: Charles Merrill, 1969.

Cameron, W. M., and Pleasance, P. *Education in Movement.* Oxford, England: Basil Blackwell & Mott, 1965.

Carlson, Bernice, and Ginglend, David. *Play Activities for Retarded Children.* New York: Abingdon Press, 1961.

Castner, B. M. *The Development of Fine Prehension in Infancy.* Genetic Psychology Monographs vol. XII, no. 2. Worcester, Mass.: Clark University Press, 1932.

Cattell, Psyche. *The Measurement of Intelligence of Infants and Young Children.* New York: Psychological Corporation, 1940.

Cawley, J., and Matkin, N. *Visual and Auditory Defects Accompanying Mental Retardation.* Storrs, Conn.: University of Connecticut, 1967.

Cawley, John F. "Arithmetic for the Mentally Handicapped." *Focus on Exceptional Children*, September 1970.

Cawley, John F.; Goodstein, Henry A.; and Burrow, Will H. *Reading and Psychomotor Disability Among Mentally Retarded and Average Children.* Storrs, Conn.: University of Conn. School of Education, 1968.

Chomsky, N. *Aspects of the Theory of Syntax.* Cambridge, Mass.: M.I.T. Press, 1965.

Claus, Clavin K. "Verbs and Imperative Sentences as a Basis for Stating Educational Objectives." Paper presented at the National Council on Measurement in Education, 10 February 1968, in Chicago. Mimeographed.

Crawford, Caroline. *Dramatic Games and Dances for Little Ones.* Cranbury, N. J.: A. S. Barnes & Co., 1941.

Cruickshank, William M., et. al. *A Teaching Method for Brain-Injured and Hyperactive Children.* Syracuse, N.Y.: Syracuse University Press, 1961.

Diem. L., and Scholtzmethner, R. *Corrective Gymnastics and Special Exercise Classes in Schools.* Frankfurt am Main, Germany: Wilhelm Linpert-Verlag Gmb H., 1963.

Ellis, Norman. *Handbook of Mental Deficiency.* New York: McGraw-Hill, 1963.

Farber, Bernard. *Family Organization and Crisis: Maintenance of Integration in Families with a Severely Mentally Retarded Child.* Monographs of the Society for Research in Child Development, serial no. 75, vol. 25, no. 1. Urbana, Ill.: University of Illinois, 1960.

Farina, Albert M.; Furth, Sol H.; and Smith, Joseph M. *Growth through Play.* Englewood Cliffs, N. J.: Prentice-Hall, 1959.

Ferinden, William E., Jr., and Jacobson, Sherman. *Educational Interpretation of the Wechsler Intelligence Scale for Children.* Linden, N. J.: Remediation Assoc., 1969.

Friedlander, B. Z. "Automated Behavior Therapy for Prehension Disabilities in Retarded Children." Paper presented to the Department of Counseling and Behavioral Studies of the University of Wisconsin in Madison, Wisc. in September 1967.

Frostig, Marianne, and Horne, David. *The Frostig Program for the Development of Visual Perception.* Chicago: Follett, 1964.

Gearheart, B. and Willenberg, E. *Application of Pupil Assessment Information for the Special Education Teacher.* Denver, Colo.: Love Publishing Co., n. d.

Gellman, William. "An Attainable Occupational Goal." *Crippled Child Magazine*, 1956.

Gellman, William. *The Vocational Development of Mentally Handicapped Adolescents: An Experimental and Longitudinal Study.* Jewish Vocational Service Monograph no. 6. Chicago, 1967.

Gellner, Lisa. *A Neurophysiological Concept of Mental Retardation and Its Educational Implications*: five lectures. Chicago: Julian D. Levinson Research Foundation of Cook County Hospital, 1959.

Gesell, A., and Amatruda, C. S. *Developmental Diagnosis.* New York: Harper & Row, 1941-47.

Gesell, Arnold, et al. *The First Five Years of Life.* New York: Harper & Row, 1940.

Glaser, R. "Instructional Technology and the Measurement of Learning Outcomes: Some Questions." *American Psychologist* 18 (1963): 519-21.

Goldstein, K. *Language and Language Disturbances.* New York: Grune & Stratton, 1948.

Greenspoon, J., and Gersten, C. D. "A New Look at Psychological Testing: Psychological Testing from the Standpoint of a Behaviorist." *American Psychologist* 22 (1967): 848-53.

Growth and Development in the Normal Child and Deviations in the Emotional and Perceptual-motor Areas. Seminar proceedings. St. Louis, Mo.: Occupational Therapy Department of the Washington University School of Medicine, March 1966.

Halverson, H. M. "Studies of the Grasping Responses of Early Infancy." *Journal of Genetic Psychology*, December 1937.

Hatcher, C. C., and Mullin, H. *More than Words: Movement Activities for Children.* Pasadena, Calif.: Parents for Movement Publication, 1967.

Haeussermann, Else. *Development Potential of Pre-School Children: An Evaluation of Intellectual, Sensory and Emotional Functioning.* New York: Grune & Stratton, 1958.

Hebb, D. O. *The Organization of Behavior.* New York: John Wiley & Sons, 1966.

Heber, Rick F. "A Manual on Terminology and Classification in Mental Retardation." *American Journal of Mental Deficiency*, supplement, September 1961.

Homme, L. *How to Use Contingency Contracting in the Classroom.* Champaign, Ill.: Research Press, 1969.

Houton, W. F. *Movement Education for Infants.* London, England: Inner London Education Authority, 1966.

Hudson, Margaret. *An Exploration of Classroom Procedures for Teaching Trainable Mentally Retarded Children.* Arlington, Va.: Council for Exceptional Children Monograph no. 2, Series A., 1960.

Hunt, J. McV. *Intelligence and Experience.* New York: Ronald Press, 1961.

Jenkins, J., and Paterson, D., eds. *Studies in Individual Differences.* New York: Appleton-Century-Crofts, 1961.

Johnson, Doris, and Myklebust, H. R. *Learning Disabilities, Educational Principles and Practices.* New York: Grune & Stratton, 1967.

Johnson, W.; Darley, F. L.; and Spriesterbach, D. C. *Diagnostic Methods in Speech Pathology.* New York: Harper & Row, 1963.

Journal of Experimental Child Psychology.

Journal of Applied Behavior Analysis.

Kaliski, L. "The Brain-Injured Child: Learning by Living in a Structured Setting." *American Journal of Mental Deficiency* 63(1959): 688-96.

Kephart, Newell C. *Aids to Motoric and Perceptual Training.* Madison, Wisc.: State Department of Public Instruction, 1964.

Kephart, Newell C. *The Slow Learner in the Classroom.* Columbus, O.: Charles Merrill, 1971 edition.

Kirk, S. A. *The Diagnosis and Remediation of Psycholinguistic Disabilities.* Urbana, Ill.: Institute for Research on Exceptional Children of the University of Illinois, 1966.

Kirk, S. A.; Karnes, M. D.; and Kirk, W. D. *You and Your Retarded Child.* New York: Macmillan, 1955.

Kirk, S. A., and McCarthy, J. J. *The Construction, Standardization and Statistical Characteristics of the ITPA.* Urbana, Ill.: University of Illinois Press, 1963.

Kirk, S. A.; McCarthy, J. J.; and Kirk, W. D. *Examiner's Manual, ITPA.* Urbana, Ill.: University of Illinois Press, 1968.

Lee, L. L. "Developmental Sentence Types: A Method for Comparing Normal and Deviant Syntactic Development." *Journal of Speech and Hearing Disorders* 31 (1966): 311-30.

Levinson, Abraham. *The Mentally Retarded Child.* New York: John Day, 1965.

Lillywhite, H., and Bradley, D. *Communication Problems in Mental Retardation: Diagnosis and Management.* New York: Harper & Row, 1969.

Loritt, Tom; Schaff, Mary; and Sayre, Elizabeth. "Curriculum Development and Reading Evaluation." *Focus on Exceptional Children*, November 1970.

Lowenfeld, Viktor. *Creative and Mental Growth.* 4th ed. New York: Macmillan, 1964.

Luszki, Walter A. "Strictly for Parents: Controlling the Brain-damaged Hyperactive Child." *Journal of Learning Disabilities* 1 (1968).

Mager, Robert F. *Preparing Instructional Objectives.* Palo Alto, Calif.: Fearon, 1962.

Malott, Richard W., and Whaley, Donald L. *Elementary Principles of Behavior.* Kalamazoo, Mich.: Western Michigan University Dept. of Psychology, 1969.

Martin, Bill; Weil, Truda; and Kohan, Frances. *Sounds and Patterns of Language.* New York: Holt, Rinehart & Winston, 1969.

McCarthy, J. J., and Kirk, S. A. *The Illinois Test of Psycholinguistic Abilities Manual.* Urbana, Ill.: University of Illinois Press, 1963.

McCarthy, J. McR. "Patterns of Psycholinguistic Development of Mongoloid and Non-mongoloid Severely Retarded Children." Unpublished doctoral thesis, University of Illinois, 1966.

McCarthy, John L., ed. *A Guide to Curriculum Materials for Exceptional Children.* Mount Pleasant, Mich.: Central Michigan University, 1969.

McGavack, John Jr., and LaSalle, Donald P. *Guppies, Bubbles, and Vibrating Objects: A Creative Approach to the Teaching of Science to Very Young Children.* New York: John Day, 1969.

Mecham, M., et al. *Communication Training in Childhood Brain Damage.* Springfield, Ill.: Charles C. Thomas, 1966.

Menyuk, P. "Comparison of Grammar of Children with Functionally Deviant and Normal Speech." *Journal of Speech and Hearing Research* 7 (1964): 109-21.

Menyuk, P. *Sentences Children Use.* Research Monograph no. 52. Cambridge, Mass.: M.I.T. Press, 1969.

Meyen Edward L. "Evaluation and Effective Teaching." *Focus on Exceptional Children*, May 1969.

Molloy, Julia S. *Teaching the Retarded Child to Talk.* New York: John Day, 1961.

Molloy, Julia S. "Training Retarded Children to Enhance a Functioning Grasp Skill." Paper read at the International Congress for the Scientific Study of Mental Deficiency, September 1967, in Montpelier, France.

Moore, Josephine. "Principles of Neuroanatomy and Neurophysiology Underlying Current Treatment Techniques." Notes from seminar and lectures. Mimeographed. Chicago: University of Illinois, Curriculum in Occupational Therapy and Division of Services for Handicapped Children, May 1968.

Myklebust, H. R. "Aphasia in Children—Diagnosis and Training." In *Handbook of Speech Pathology*, edited by Lee Edward Travis. New York: Appleton-Century-Crofts, 1957.

Myklebust, H. R. *Auditory Disorders in Children: A Manual for Differential Diagnosis.* New York: Grune & Stratton, 1954.

Myklebust, H. R. *The Picture Story Language Test.* Development and Disorders of Written Language, vol. 1. New York: Grune & Stratton, 1965.

Myklebust, H. R. *Progress in Learning Disabilities*, vol. 1. New York: Grune & Stratton, 1968.

Myklebust H. R., and Boshes, B. "Minimal Brain Damage in Children." Final Report United States Public Health Service Contract 108-65-142, June 1969.

O'Connor, N., and Hermelin, B. *Speech and Thought in Severe Subnormality*. New York: Macmillan, 1963.

Orton, S. T. *Reading, Writing and Speech Problems in Children*. New York: W. W. Norton, 1937.

Patterson, G., and Gullion, M. Elizabeth. *Living with Children*. Champaign, Ill.: Research Press, 1968.

Perceptual-motor Dysfunction, Evaluation and Training. Seminar proceedings. Madison, Wisc.: School of Occupational Therapy, University of Wisconsin, June 1966.

Perry, Natalie. *Teaching the Mentally Retarded Child.* New York: Columbia University Press, 1960.

Peter, Lawrence J. *Prescriptive Teaching.* New York: McGraw-Hill, 1965.

Piaget, Jean. *A Child's Conception of Numbers.* London: Routledge Kegan Paul, 1964.

Piaget, Jean. *Play Dreams and Imitations in Childhood.* New York: W. W. Norton & Company, Inc., 1962.

Piaget, Jean. *The Origins of Intelligence in Children.* New York: International Universities Press, 1952.

Piaget, Jean. *The Language and Thought of the Child.* New York: Meridian, 1955.

Popham, W. J., and Husek, R. R. "Implications of Criterion-referenced Measurement." *Journal of Educational Measurement* 6 (1969): 1-9.

A Practical Guide for Teaching the Mentally Retarded to Swim. Washington, D. C.: American Association for Health, Physical Education and Recreation, 1969.

Robinson, Albert D. and Nancy M. *The Mentally Retarded Child: A Psychological Approach.* New York: McGraw-Hill, 1970.

Ross, Dorothea. "Incidental Learning of Number Concepts in Small Group Games." *American Journal of Mental Deficiency*, May 1970.

Ross, Dorothea. *Pacemaker Games for Mentally Retarded Children.* Palo Alto, Calif.: Fearon, 1968.

Rothstein, Jerome H., ed. *Mental Retardation: Readings and Resources.* New York: Holt, Rinehart & Winston, 1970.

Rupert, Harold A., Jr. "A Sequentially Compiled List of Instructional Materials for Use with the ITPA." Mimeographed, 1970. Available from the State of Colorado Dept. of Education, Denver, Colo.

Ruvin, Harold. "An Evaluation of Academics for the Trainable Mentally Retarded." Paper presented at Council for Exceptional Children Convention, 24 April 1970, in Chicago, Ill. Mimeographed.

Sanders, J. I. *The ABC's of Sign Language.* Tulsa, Okla.: Manca Press, 1968.

Schiefelbusch, Richard L.; Copeland, Ross H.; and Smith, James O. *Language and Mental Retardation.* New York: Holt, Rinehart & Winston, 1967.

"School Social Work in Illinois: Policies and Procedures." Mimeographed. Springfield, Ill.: State of Illinois, Office of the Superintendent of Public Instruction, 1969.

Simon, C. T. "The Development of Speech." In *Handbook of Speech Pathology*, edited by Lee Edward Travis. New York: Appleton-Century-Crofts, 1957.

Simon, Paul. "Commentary on Choice of Treatment Method in School Social Work." Paper presented to the northern division of the Council of Social Work in Schools, 21 May 1965, in Evanston, Ill. Mimeographed.

Skinner, B. F. "Verbal Behavior, II." *Encounter* November 1962.

Straus, Alfred, and Kephart, Newell C. *Progress in Theory and Clinic.* Psychopathology of the Brain-Injured Child, vol. II. New York: Grune & Stratton, 1955.

Straus, Alfred, and Lehtinen, L. *Fundamentals and Treatment.* Psychopathology of the Brain-Injured Child, vol. I. New York: Grune & Stratton, 1951.

Templin, Mildred C. *Certain Language Skills in Children: Their Development and Interrelationship.* Child Welfare Monograph Series no. 26. Minneapolis, Minn.: University of Minnesota Press, 1957.

Terman, L. M., and Merrill, M. A. *Measuring Intelligence.* Boston: Houghton Mifflin, 1937.

Travis, Lee Edward, ed. *Handbook of Speech Pathology.* New York: Appleton-Century-Crofts, 1957.

Tyler, Ralph. *Basic Principles of Curriculum and Instruction.* Chicago, University of Chicago Press, 1950.

Van Riper, C. *Speech Correction Principles and Methods.* New York: Prentice-Hall, 1941.

Van Riper, C. *Teaching Your Child to Talk.* New York: Harper & Row, 1950.

Voss, Donald. "Improvised Physical Education and Recreation Suitable for Use with the Mentally Retarded Child." Mimeographed. Elkhorn, Wisc.: Walworth County Special School, 1967.

Vygotsky, Lev Semenovich. *Thought and Language.* Translated by Eugenia Hanfmann and Gertrude Vakar. Cambridge, Mass.: M.I.T. Press, 1962.

Washington Guide to Promoting Development in the Young Child. Seattle: University of Washington, forthcoming.

Winitz, Harris. *Articulatory Acquisition and Behavior.* New York: Appleton-Century-Crofts, 1969.

Woodward, M. "The Application of Piaget's Theory to the Training of Subnormal Children." *Journal of Mental Subnormality* 8 (1962).

ART BIBLIOGRAPHY

Cole, Natalie Robinson. *The Arts in the Classroom.* New York: John Day, 1940.

D'Amico, Victor, and Wilson, Frances. *Art for the Family.* New York: Museum of Modern Art, 1956.

Emerson, Sybil. *Design, A Creative Approach.* Scranton, Pa.: International Textbook Co., 1953.

Gaitskell, Charles and Margaret. *Art Education for Slow Learners.* Peoria, Ill.: Chas. A. Bennet Co., 1953.

Hoover, Louis F. *Art Activities for the Very Young.* Worcester, Mass.: Davis Publications, 1961.

Knudsen, Estelle H., and Christensen, Ethel M. *Children's Art Education.* Peoria, Ill.: Chas. A. Bennet Co., 1957.

Linderman, Earl W., and Herberholz, Donald W. *Developing Artistic and Perceptual Awareness.* Dubuque, Ia.: William C. Brown Co., 1964.

Lowenfeld, Viktor. *Creative and Mental Growth.* 4th ed. New York: Macmillan, 1964.

Mattil, Edward L. *Meaning in Crafts.* Englewood Cliffs, N. J.: Prentice-Hall, 1962.

McIlvain, Dorothy S. *Art for Primary Grades.* New York: G. P. Putnam's Sons, 1961.

Saunders, Everett. *Painting I, Painting II, Painting III, Constructing I, Print Art I, Paper Art I.* ($1.00 each.) Racine, Wisc.: Whitman Publishing Co., 1966-1967. (Available in many grocery, variety, and discount stores.)

Schafer-Simmers, H. *The Unfolding of Artistic Activity.* Berkeley, Calif.: University of California Press, 1948.

Note: *Meaning in Crafts* by Mattil and the series by Everett Saunders are especially reccommended for regular classroom use to select art projects.
McCalls' Needlework and Crafts, McCalls' Summer Make-It, McCalls' Christmas Make-It, and *Better Homes & Gardens' Christmas Ideas* are excellent sources of gift projects which can be adapted for the retarded child.

MUSIC BIBLIOGRAPHY

Alvin, Juliette. *Music for the Handicapped Child.* New York: Oxford University Press, 1965.

Antey, John. *Sing and Learn.* New York: John Day, 1965.

Barnett, Jean. *Games, Rhythms and Dances.* Hallendale, Fla.: Jean Barnett Records, 1950.

Botwin, Ester. *Treasury of Children's Songs for Little Children.* New York: Hart Pub. Co., 1952.

Carlson, B., and Ginglend, D. *Play Activities for Retarded Children.* Nashville, Tenn.: Abingdon Press, 1961.

Cole, Francis, ed. *Music for Children with Special Needs.* Three accompanying records: *Songs for Children with Special Needs, #1, #2, #3.* Glendale, Calif.: Bowmar, 1965.

Coleman, J. L., et al. *Music for Exceptional Children.* Two accompanying records. Evanston, Ill.: Summy-Birchard Co., 1965.

Dobbs, J. P. B. *The Slow Learner and Music.* New York: Oxford University Press, 1966.

Elkan, B. *Songs for Today's Children.* New York: Clayton F. Summy and Co., 1961.

Gaston, E. Thayer. *Music in Therapy.* New York: Macmillan, 1968.

Ginglend, David B., and Stiles, Winifred E. *Music Activities for Retarded Children.* Nashville, Tenn.: Abingdon Press, 1965.

Jenkins, Ella. *Ella Jenkins' Song Book for Children.* New York: Oak Publications, 1966.

Journals of Music Therapy. Lawrence, Kan.: The Allen Press. Published quarterly by the National Association for Music Therapy.

Landeck, Beatrice. *Songs to Grow On.* New York: William Sloane Assoc., n.d.

Music for Living Series. 7 vols. Morristown. N. J.: Silver Burdett Co., 1960.

National Association for Music Therapy. *Proceedings: Music Therapy,* vols. I to XIII. Lawrence, Kan.: The Allen Press, 1951-1961.

Nordoff, Paul, and Robbins, Clive E. *Music Therapy for Handicapped Children.* Blauvelt, N. Y.: Rudolf Steiner Publications, 1965.

Nordoff, Paul, and Robbins, Clive E. *Music Therapy in Special Education.* New York: John Day, 1971.

Orff, Carl, and Keetman, Gunild. *Music for Children.* English adaptation by Doreen Hall and Arnold Walter. New York: Schott-Music Corp., 1950.

Robins, Ferris and Jennet. *Educational Rhythmics for Mentally Handicapped Children.* New York: Horizon Press, 1965.

Scott, Louise Binder, and Wood, Lucille. *More Singing Fun.* Two accompanying records. Glendale, Calif.: Bowmar, 1961.

Scott, Louise Binder, and Wood, Lucille, *Singing Fun.* One accompanying record. Glendale, Calif.: Bowmar, 1954.

Smith, Fowler, et al. *Songs We Sing.* Chicago: Woods, Hall & McCreary Co., 1941.

Songs of the Gay 90's. New York: Remick Music Corp., 1941.

Together We Sing Series. Chicago: Follett Pub. Co., 1960.

Weber, Richard. *Musicall.* New York: Musicall, Inc., 1964.

Winn, Marie, Miller, Allan, and Alcorn, John. *Fireside Book of Children's Songs.* New York: Simon & Schuster, 1966.

Appendixes

Appendix I:
Lesson Plans and Journals

The following lesson plan sheets are designed to keep the overall objectives of each group in constant view.

Details of current objectives are presented in the right-hand column.

Teachers should refer to monthly lesson plans filed from previous years, to check progress.

Details of planning for each individual and reporting daily behavior are kept in daily journals. The Spiral Plan Book # 4475 (obtainable from Educator's Paper and Supply Co., 3734 Oakton St., Skokie, Illinois) is very satisfactory for planning, keeping attendance records, and daily charting of behavior. A separate column can be allocated for each child.

Daily recording is essential, as little details of behavior will be forgotten if not noted. The accumulation of data can indicate pertinent information that can be very helpful in long-range planning for an individual child.

At the close of the school year, the monthly plan sheets and journals should be thoroughly reviewed. Failure to attain a goal may mean that this goal is unrealistic for that particular age group.

Failure to attain a goal can also indicate the need for reviewing techniques, climate, teacher-child attitudes, and suitability of materials.

How a child best learns a given task is not always indicated in psychological reports. Psychometry and neurological studies are very helpful, but the teacher's trial-and-error approach is still what she must resort to for ascertaining what method succeeds with an individual child. Neurology, psychology, and education must eventually work together toward the common goal of preparing the mentally deficient child for life.

Consistent and easy success may mean that the goals can be set higher.

In preparing material for parent conferences, consideration must be given to the behavior of the child as an individual, and to his behavior as a part of a group of peers.

His behavior as an individual may be studied from daily journal entries, from conferences with all other teachers and therapists having contact with the child and from the Performance Goals Record. The Performance Goals Record is designed to record goals in sequential order.

The report of a child's behavior as a part of a group is a comparison of his individual behavior with that of the expected behavior of the group to which he is assigned.

Each child's total functioning is reported in anecdotal form. Cover the five areas of growth—physical, emotional, social, intellectual, and aesthetic—using the gross objectives of his assigned group as criteria.

Molloy Education Center

Report of Lesson Plans and Current Activities

Nursery Group _____   _____ 19 ___   _____
                                  Month Ending   TEACHER

OBJECTIVE	PRESENT STATUS

PHYSICAL GROWTH

Gross Motor Activities

Remove outer clothing
Stay dry
Use tissues
Manage spoon and cup for feeding
Manage clothing for toileting
Wash hands with help
Some manipulative ability: stacking, pushing, rolling

BODY CONTROL

Movement: walk, run, crawl, climb, jump, recover, stretch, reach, roll, relax, control strength, grasp, carry, release, catch, throw

Use of Space: up, down, forward, backward, sideways, high-low

Time: quick, slow, sudden, sustained, rhythm

Flow: easy to stop
       difficulty in getting moving
       difficulty in stopping
       difficulty in stopping quickly or suddenly

Grasp: Should move from dagger grasp toward finger-thumb opposition. Grasp, carry, release, rotate
(Note Gellner Level and Grasp Level)

SOCIAL GROWTH

Understand "yours-mine"
Listen and respond appropriately to "no," "come here," "don't touch," "sit down"
Respect adults
Help self to cookies or other finger foods
Respond to own name, heard
Respond to own name, seen with color cue
Channel attention

EMOTIONAL GROWTH

Self control without pressure
Parallel play
Relate to adults other than own family or teacher

LESSON PLAN - continued
NURSERY GROUP

INTELLECTUAL GROWTH

Show ID tag when asked name
Identify body parts
Know own things: jackets, mittens, etc.
Handle materials, large shapes, and textures
Direct attention to adult
Match and sort primary colors, using cue color sheets or containers
Identify some common objects upon verbal cueing

PROJECTS: List specific tasks, games, etc. you are currently working on.

File in office on last day of month. Please keep notations current for quick reference. This will enable a substitute to proceed with better orientation to your objectives.

KEEP THIS INSIDE COVER OF DAILY JOURNAL

Molloy Education Center
Report of Lesson Plans and Current Activities

Kindergarten Group _____   _____19_____   _____
                             Month Ending   TEACHER

OBJECTIVE	PRESENT STATUS

PHYSICAL GROWTH
Outer clothing off and *on*
Keep nose clean
Go to bathroom with help
Wash hands
Large muscle activity
Use smaller manipulative materials; stacking, pushing, rolling
Pull wagon
Use feet to propel

BODY CONTROL

Movement: walk, run, crawl, climb, jump, recover, stretch, reach, roll, relax, control strength, grasp, carry, release, catch, throw

Use of Space: up, down, forward, backward, sideways, high-low, over-under

Time: quick, slow, sudden, sustained, rhythm

Flow: easy to stop
    difficulty in getting moving
    difficulty in stopping
    difficulty in stopping quickly or suddenly

Grasp: should move from dagger grasp toward finger-thumb opposition; grasp, carry, release, rotate
Concept of open—shut
(Note Gellner Level and Grasp Level)
Readiness activities for using scissors

SOCIAL GROWTH
Listen and respond appropriately
Select common objects on verbal cue
Follow simple commands on verbal cue
Progress to verbalization
Take turns
Play together
Respect adults and peers
Display good manners toward visitors
Respond to own name
Identify peers by spoken name
Respect closed doors, drawers, and cupboards
Pass napkins, spoons, or food to next child

EMOTIONAL GROWTH
Self-control
Follow through on tasks of own choice
Accept changes in routine
Relate to adults other than own family and teacher

LESSON PLANS—continued
KINDERGARTEN GROUP

OBJECTIVE	PRESENT STATUS
INTELLECTUAL GROWTH Longer attention span Sort colors; match colors Identify body parts Respond appropriately to slow-fast, happy-sad, funny-not funny Recognize own name and names of children in group Know foods that are good for us Begin transition from common objects to pictures for identifying and labeling Show ID tag when asked name.	

PROJECTS: List specific tasks, games, etc. you are currently working on.

File in office on last day of month. Please keep notations current for quick reference. This will enable a substitute to proceed with better orientation in your objectives.

KEEP THIS INSIDE COVER OF DAILY JOURNAL

Report of Lesson Plans and Current Activities

Primary Group _____   _____ 19 ____   _____
                                  Month Ending   TEACHER

OBJECTIVE	PRESENT STATUS

PHYSICAL GROWTH

Complete care of outer clothing, including boots
Get ready for bed alone at home and dress for school with help
Handle scissors purposefully

BODY CONTROL

Movement: walk, run, crawl, jump, recover, stretch, reach, roll, relax, control strength, grasp, carry, release, catch, throw

Use of Space: up, down, forward, backward, sideways, high-low, over-under

Time: quick, slow, sudden, sustained, rhythm

Flow: easy to stop
    difficulty in getting moving
    difficulty in stopping
    difficulty in stopping quickly or suddenly

Grasp: should move from dagger grasp toward finger-thumb oppositon. Grasp, carry, release, rotate.
Concept of open-shut
(Note Gellner Level and Grasp Level)

SOCIAL GROWTH

Listening and responding, using common objects, label without cue
Progress to pictures for labeling
State action when seen in pictures
Respond to Fitzgerald Key
Move from qualifying words to simple phrases
Share work together
Respect adults
Answer telephone by saying "Mommy's coming" and calling mother
Deliver a message
Complete a mission
Go to and from bus with lessening supervision
Be tidy at meal time; pass food carefully; help self to what is passed.

EMOTIONAL GROWTH

Self-control; follow through on tasks of own choice; on tasks assigned; accept change of routine with some warning

LESSON PLANS—continued
PRIMARY GROUP

OBJECTIVE	PRESENT STATUS

INTELLECTUAL GROWTH
Identify body parts
Increase attention span
Begin writing readiness sequence
Select colors on verbal cue
Find matching colors in environment
Recognize letters of alphabet for future cue recognition
Perceive gross differences in size
Recognize words
  stop boys men keep out in
  go girls women private out
Danger: recognize situations
 	
Recognize own name and names of all peers without color cues
Follow two commands
Categorize seasons, clothing, furniture, food, transportation, sports
 	
Concept of little and big, short and tall, or short and long
Number concepts to five
Show ID tag when asked name
Know address, telephone number, days of the week, months; some calendar recognition	

PROJECTS: List specific tasks, games, etc. you are currently working on.

File in office on last day of month. Please keep notations current for quick reference. This will enable a substitute to proceed with better orientation in your objectives.

KEEP THIS INSIDE COVER OF DAILY JOURNAL

Molloy Education Center
Report of Lesson Plans and Current Activities

Intermediate Group _____   _____ 19 _____   _____
                                 Month Ending   TEACHER

OBJECTIVE	PRESENT STATUS

PHYSICAL GROWTH

Full self-care in school
Dress and undress at home without help

BODY CONTROL

Movement: walk, run, crawl, jump recover, stretch, grasp, carry, release, catch, throw

BODY IMAGE

Use of Space: up, down, forward, backward, sideways, high-low, over-under

Time: quick, slow, sudden, sustained, rhythm

Flow: easy to stop
    difficulty in getting moving
    difficulty in stopping
    difficulty in stopping quickly or suddenly

Grasp: should move from dagger grasp toward finger-thumb opposition. Grasp, carry, release, rotate.
Concept of open-shut
(Note Gellner Level and Grasp Level)

SOCIAL GROWTH

Speak in sentences; use pronouns, articles, prepositions, and simple verb forms
Carry messages
Complete a mission
Self-concept
Use telephone for emergency; dial "O" for operator, state name, address, and phone number, use good manners on telephone
Share experiences
Team play
Participate in group activity
Use acceptable table manners
Meet guests; accept gifts; give gifts.

EMOTIONAL GROWTH

Self-control; wait for turn
Follow through on tasks of own choice or tasks assigned
Accept change of routine with minimal warning
Share willingly.

LESSON PLANS—continued
INTERMEDIATE GROUP

OBJECTIVE	PRESENT STATUS
INTELLECTUAL GROWTH Verbalize own name, address, and telephone number, or show ID tag Recognize words of protection and comprehend *in* and *outside* of school environment Read according to individual ability Count to ten; number concepts to five; count by fives using clock Recognize days of week; seasons and their implications Trace own name; write own name Categorize and conceptualize community resources (bakery, drugstore, etc.), animals, plants. Recognize and enjoy absurdities Set table; clear table; dust, tidy up	

PROJECTS: List specific tasks, games, etc. you are currently working on.

File in office on last day of month. Please keep notations current for quick reference. This will enable a substitute to proceed with better orientation in your objectives.

KEEP THIS INSIDE COVER OF DAILY JOURNAL

Molloy Education Center
Report of Lesson Plans and Current Activities

Senior Group _____   _____ 19 ___   _____
                                  Month Ending   TEACHER

OBJECTIVE	PRESENT STATUS

PHYSICAL GROWTH
 	
Full self-care in school to full self-care in school and at home, including bathing (except shampoo)
 	
BODY CONTROL
 	
Movement: walk, run, crawl, climb, jump, recover, stretch, reach, roll, relax, control strength, grasp, carry, release, catch, throw
 	
Use of Space: up, down, forward, backward, sideways, high-low
 	
Time: quick, slow, sudden, sustained, rhythm
 	
Flow: easy to stop
     difficulty in getting moving
     difficulty in stopping
     difficulty in stopping quickly or suddenly
 	
Grasp: should move from dagger grasp toward finger-thumb oppositon. Grasp, carry, release, rotate
Concept of open-shut
(Note Gellner Level and Grasp Level)
 	
SOCIAL GROWTH
 	
Speak in sentences; carry messages, use telephone in emergency
Social language: introductions, compliments, invitations, good manners on telephone
Accept messages, meet guests, accept gifts, give gifts
Accept simple directions for work; take orders from peer leader; team play
Participate in group activities
Assume leadership graciously
Begin child-care training
 	
EMOTIONAL GROWTH
 	
Self-control under pressure
Follow through on tasks of own choice or tasks assigned
Accept change in routine
Maintain good attention span	

LESSON PLANS—continued
SENIOR GROUP

INTELLECTUAL GROWTH

Write words and sentences as needed
Recognize useful words
Read according to individual ability
Recognize coins and know value
Measure: linear, solid, liquid, baric
Discriminate: visual, auditory, spatial
Define words

Write own name
Recognize and use *all* words for protection; days of week; seasons and their implications
Use number concepts to twelve; count by fives (using clock)
Use concept of relationship by categories, both concrete and abstract

Set table; clear table; dust; clean sink
Pick up on yard detail
Put away dishes
Put away play equipment

FOOD PREPARATION

Clean celery, lettuce; prepare tomatoes, onions, green peppers for salad; prepare canned fruits for salad or dessert; make and wrap sandwiches; peel potatoes and carrots

PROJECTS: List specific tasks, games, etc. you are currently working on.

File in office on last day of month. Please keep notations current for quick reference. This will enable a substitute to proceed with better orientation in your objectives.

KEEP THIS INSIDE COVER OF DAILY JOURNAL

Molloy Education Center

Report of Lesson Plans and Current Activities

Young Adults-Prevocational
Group _____ _____19_____ _____
                             Month Ending   TEACHER

OBJECTIVE	PRESENT STATUS
WORK PROGRESS Review and note: Attitude toward assigned job; cooperation with co-workers; ability to attack job from oral and written directions; ability to carry out assignment, to assemble needed materials, and to report completion of job Clean up skill; care for tools and materials Variety of abilities; cooperation with peer leadership; ability to assume leadership for (boss) a work crew, such as yard clean up, weeding detail, setting up or putting away chairs in gym, window washing detail, cleaning tables, sinks and counters Ability to take an assignment not scheduled, such as emergency cleanup, fill in for absentee, or any unscheduled chore Ability to carry out any of the above tasks independently (note how much supervision is needed) *CHILD CARE* Define and role-play: kind, gentle, firm, cheerful, cooperative, prompt, responsibility, consideration, willingness to learn *Skill*: in helping toileting, hand washing; assisting with clothing, feeding *Following directions*: knowledge of play activities; sandbox; assistance on playground equipment; getting materials ready; putting materials and toys (rolling stock) away; playing with little children *Attitude* toward group meetings *EMOTIONAL GROWTH* Self-control; temper manifestations; ability to follow through on tasks of own choice; on tasks assigned; reaction to frustration; cooperation; reaction to confusion or change of routine. *SOCIAL GROWTH* Sharing respect for adults; respect for peers Manners: games, telephone, meeting people, sportsmanship General language usage (consider any poor speech as unacceptable lanugage); good subjects for conversation away from home; attention-getting mechanisms; acceptance of criticism; violation of privacy, including interrupting, unbecoming curiosity (nosiness), repeating "home gossip"; keeping a trust, honesty, secrecy, promises, playing a role of peacemaker Unacceptable gestures and actions, such as pulling at clothing; failing to keep hands to self.	

LESSON PLANS—continued
YOUNG ADULTS—PRE-VOCATIONAL GROUP

OBJECTIVE	PRESENT STATUS

FOOD PREPARATION

Prepare canned foods (hot soups, baked beans, spaghetti, etc.)
Make salads
Prepare fresh fruits and vegetables (washing, cutting, and squeezing orange juice)
Prepare melons
Prepare mixes
(See Progress reports for full listing)

INTELLECTUAL GROWTH

Most of this area is considered under "Work Progress"; however, in this category, consider the following: ability to pay attention; curiosity; memory span; number concepts; concept of time; concept of money; use of tools; word recognition; ability to follow directions and to complete a task; planning for "free" time; accomplishment in production.

REVIEW ALL OBJECTIVES OF SENIOR GROUP
TO MAINTAIN ACHIEVEMENTS

PROJECTS: List specific tasks, games, etc. you are currently working on.

File in office on last day of month. Please keep notations current for quick reference. This will enable a substitute to proceed with better orientation in your objectives.

KEEP THIS INSIDE COVER OF DAILY JOURNAL

Molloy Education Center
Report of Lesson Plans and Current Activities

Multiply Handicapped
Group _____   _____19_____   _____
                                Month Ending   TEACHER
_____**OBJECTIVE**_____|_____**PRESENT STATUS**_____

I. *PHYSICAL GROWTH*

   A. Gross Motor—Body Control
      1. Movement: move total body, identify parts

         a. Lift and hold head up from prone positon

         b. Roll over in both directions

         c. Maintain sitting balance: with support; without support

         d. Use arms and hands to gain some change in positon; push to sitting or kneeling, side sitting, ring sitting, heel sitting

         e. Walk, crawl, run, jump (if ambulatory)

      2. Space: Move total body or body parts up, down, high, low, backward, forward, over, under, before, after, right, left, in front, in back

      3. Time, Flow: Move body parts as directed: fast, slow, alternating strength: "relax," stretch, loose, soft, curl, hold

   B. Grasp and Manipulation—arm and hand control

      1. Grasp, hold, push, pull, throw, stack, roll, pass (as a bean bag)

      2. Handle chalk, pencils, scissors, brushes purposefully

      3. Levels of manipulation:

         a. Touch and push

         b. Put hands to mouth

         c. Squeeze and release (small toys)

         d. Reach and push (ball)

         e. Grasp and shake

         f. Use both hands (large balls)

         g. Reach, grasp, and release

         h. Poke at small objects

LESSON PLANS— MULTIPLY HANDICAPPED GROUP —continued

OBJECTIVE	PRESENT STATUS
4. Manipulate smaller objects and place, as pegs and puzzles	
5. Use two hands for activities—one for support, one for manipulation	
C. Self-care	
1. Assist in undressing and dressing with outer clothing: hats, mittens, scarves, buttons on coats	
2. Remove shoes and socks while sitting on mats	
3. Feed self with fingers	
4. Hold cup with two hands	
5. Use straw for drinking	
6. Use spoon and fork	
7. Use napkin or tissue to wipe mouth and nose	
8. Assist in management of clothing for toileting	
9. Manipulate hot and cold watertaps to wash hands—with assistance; without assistance	
II. *SOCIAL GROWTH*	
A. Listen and attend to each other and to adults Respond to simple commands: "No," "Sit down," "Come here," "Give me," "Quiet," or "Shshshh"	
B. Share toys, games, and other material with each other	
C. Wait turn for attention and special activities	
D. Deliver a message; move to and from room with less supervision or assistance	
E. Show respect for adults and each other	
F. Answer questions politely; answer telephone briefly and politely	
G. Listen and respond to direction: choose and use common objects, pictures of objects, actions and pictures of actions; label objects and actions appropriately	

LESSON PLANS—MULTIPLY HANDICAPPED GROUP—continued

OBJECTIVE	PRESENT STATUS

    H. Help another child

    I. Participate willingly in room jobs

III. *EMOTIONAL GROWTH*

    A. Relate to other children in parallel work and play activities

    B. Use self-control; accept limitations on activities; laugh at appropriate times; control crying, pouting, and sulking

    C. Accept change in activities, routine, and adult supervision

    D. Follow through on tasks assigned or chosen

    E. Appreciate self-achievements and accomplishments of other children

    F. Accept self-limitations and function within them

    G. Accept and understand limitations of other children and differences among them

IV. *INTELLECTUAL GROWTH*

    A. Lower level functioning—multiply handicapped

        1. Attend to adults and other children around them

        2. Initiate some activity: reach for ball, block or doll; touch another individual; make sounds or words to gain attention

        3. Respond to own name

        4. Handle materials with different shapes, sizes and textures

        5. Respond to directions:

            a. Give me your hand

            b. Give me (an object, picture, color)

            c. Match primary colors

            d. Match pictures

        6. Recognize own first name and those of other children printed on cards

        7. Learn words of protection: stop, go, poison, danger, keep out, boys, girls, in, out

LESSON PLANS— MULTIPLY HANDICAPPED GROUP — continued

OBJECTIVE	PRESENT STATUS

8. Know gross differences: big, little; boy, girl; hot, cold; hard, soft

9. Scribble or draw lines with crayon, chalk, or pencil

10. Trace simple lines with assistance; without assistance but with verbal cues; without verbal cues

11. Count by rote to five; to ten

B. Upper level multiply handicapped

   1. Identify body parts and combine with movements

   2. Begin reading readiness work

      a. Recognize differences in shapes

         (1.) Name circles, squares, triangles, rectangles, ovals

         (2.) Identify likenesses and differences in pictures

         (3.) Identify likenesses and differences in configurations

      b. Categorize objects and pictures of objects

      c. Identify own name and those of classmates, first and last

      d. Match pictures on work sheets

      e. Match words

      f. Recognize letters of alphabet and use to form words; distinguish initial consonant sounds

      g. Recognize colors: match to clothing and other objects in environment; match color words to colors

      h. Start standard reading readiness workbooks

LESSON PLANS— MULTIPLY HANDICAPPED GROUP —continued

OBJECTIVE	PRESENT STATUS
3. Advance to beginning reading level: pre-primers and then primers; read simple story, answer questions, relate story	
4. Begin writing sequence:	
a. Trace lines and circles	
b. Work through curriculum tracing sequence	
c. Trace own name and letters and spelling, words and letters	
d. Write some letters freehand with guides for starting and stopping	
e. Write letters and words without guides	
5. Comprehend arithmetic concepts	
a. Count by rote to ten, twenty, one hundred	
b. Group objects and number them	
c. Combine groups to make number facts: to five and to ten; addition; subtraction	
d. Use calendar to find day, month, and year Know months of year Know days of week Relate changes of months to seasons of the year Identify written months of year and days of week	
e. Learn ordinal numbers: first, second, third . . . to tenth Know "first" and "last"	
f. Identify and relate number words to numbers: one to five; five to ten	
g. Develop time concepts with the clock: o'clock and half past the hour; count minutes in the hour; group minutes counting six by fives around clock; know number of hours in a day	

Appendix II
Forms Used in Various Procedures

INTAKE CONTROL

NAME _____ School Dist. No. _____
      Last   First   Middle

Address _____ Telephone _____

Mother _____ Father _____ Date moved to district _____

    Religion _____ Religion _____ Birthdate _____

Referred by _____ Date of inquiry _____

Reason for referral _____

Preliminary study _____

    APPLICATION _____ Completed _____

    LANGUAGE EVALUATION _____ Examiner _____

    MEDICAL: _____ Examiner _____

    _____ History _____ Examiner _____

    _____ Dept. Spec. Education _____ Examiner _____

    PSYCHOLOGICAL: _____ Examiner _____

    SOCIAL: __ Initial interview _____ History _____ Inventory _____ Home visit _____ By _____

PARENTS: _____

    Birth certificate rec'd _____ Brochure given _____

    Parent Assoc. membership rec'd _____ Information sheet signed _____

    School contract signed _____ Snapshot made _____

    Fee paid _____

RELATIVES: __ Name: _____ Address _____ Tele. _____

    Relationship: _____

    _____

AGENCIES AND INDIVIDUALS CONTACTED FOR INFORMATION:

    Name: _____ Address _____ Tel. _____ Date req. _____ Date rec'd. _____

    _____

    _____

INTAKE CONTROL - continued

Staff conference date: _____ Staff present _____

Decision _____ Date parents informed _____ By _____

Date of admission: _____

MEDICAL HISTORY

Name _____ Date _____

Address _____ Telephone _____

Sex _____ Race _____ Age _____ Date of birth _____

Referred by _____ Informant _____ History taken by _____

Father's name _____ Age _____ Health _____

    Place of birth _____ Education _____

    Second language _____ Occupation _____

Mother's name _____ Age _____ Health _____

    Place of birth _____ Education _____

    Second language _____ Occupation before marriage _____

                                                                                                                                    Present occupation _____

Siblings: *Name*   *Birthdate*   *Health*   *Grade in school*

1. _____

2. _____

3. _____

4. _____

5. _____

Other persons in home: *Name*   *Age*   *Health*   *Relationship*

1. _____

2. _____

3. _____

4. _____

5. _____

MEDICAL HISTORY - continued

Present complaint: (nature of the problem and onset) _____

_____

Mother's age at birth of child _____ General health before this pregnancy _____

Mother's health history: (list diseases and severity; accidents, surgery; TB; CA; VD;
                epilepsy; alcoholism; drugs; diabetes; mental illness)

Father's health history: (as above)

_____

Family health history: (paternal and maternal relatives; note consanguinity)
              (as above)

Mother's speech _____ Hearing _____ Handedness _____

Emotional stability _____

Previous marriage(s) _____ Children from previous marriage(s) _____

Father's age at birth of child _____

Father's speech _____ Hearing _____ Handedness _____

Emotional stability _____ Economic status _____

Previous marriage(s) _____ Children from previous marriage(s) _____

Birth history:
    Note excessive vomiting, diarrhea, spotting, exposure to X-ray, high temperature, rashes, illnesses,
    false labor, delivery, unusual happenings

Previous pregnancies: _____

Subsequent pregnancies: _____

This pregnancy: Spotting _____ Diarrhea _____ Excessive vomiting _____

              Exposure to X-ray _____ Accidents _____ High temperature _____

              Rashes _____ Surgery _____ Illnesses _____

              False labor _____ Delivery _____

              Any other untoward symptoms _____

Length of pregnancy _____ Duration of labor _____

MEDICAL HISTORY - continued

Type of delivery _____ Anesthesia used _____

Birth weight _____ Length _____ Did mother hear him cry soon after birth? _____

Did baby require resuscitation? _____ Any evidence of jaundice? _____

If so, when was it evident? _____ How long did it last? _____

Any transfusion given? _____ Was baby in an incubator? _____

How long? _____ Did the doctor tell you why? _____ Did the baby tremble or seem to shake? _____

Any convulsions? _____ When? _____

Any scars, deformities notable? _____

Length of hospital stay: Mother _____ Child _____

POSTNATAL HISTORY

Breast fed _____ How long? _____ Artificial _____

Any problem sucking? _____ Chewing _____ Swallowing _____

Feeding problem _____ Any drug sensitivity? _____

Allergies _____ Accidents _____

HOSPITALIZATIONS: Date _____ Reason _____

_____

DEVELOPMENTAL HISTORY

Head held up _____ Smile _____ Roll over _____ Sit up alone _____

Crawl _____ Stand alone _____ Walk alone _____

First tooth _____ First word _____ Put words together _____

Drink from glass or cup _____ Eat solid food with fingers _____

Use a spoon _____ Indicate need to go to toilet _____

Toilet-trained _____ Complete care of self at toilet _____

Present functioning:

    Ambulation (describe gait) (crawl, walk, run, hop, skip, climb, use a tricycle)

    Manipulative ability (grasp, hold, lift, carry, release, push, pull)

| IMMUNIZATIONS | DATES | REACTION (note temperature if any) |

Smallpox _____

Whooping cough _____

Diphtheria _____

Tetanus _____

Polio _____

Measles _____

Tuberculin test _____

HISTORY OF CONTAGIOUS DISEASES

Name	Date	Severity	Temperature

CONTRIBUTING LABORATORY FINDINGS

X-rays _____

Blood types: Mother _____ Child _____ Father _____

PKU test: Mother _____ Child _____ Father _____

NEUROLOGICAL FINDINGS:

Is the patient alert and responsive? _____

What is his approximate intelligence level? _____

Describe his memory, recent and remote? _____

Are there any cranial nerve involvements? _____

Is there any involvement of the motor system? _____

Is there any involvement of the sensory system? _____ Vision _____ Hearing _____

Are there any deep tendon reflex changes? _____

Are there any superficial reflex changes? _____

Are there any pathological reflexes? _____

What is the status of the vestibular-cerebellar system? _____

NEUROLOGICAL FINDINGS - continued

Is there asynergy, dysmetria, dysdiadkokinesia, and dysarthria? _____

Does he sway in the Romberg position? _____

Can he walk without assistance? _____

EEG   Yes _____ No _____ Date _____ Doctor _____

Results and recommendations _____

PREVIOUS EFFORTS TO OBTAIN A DIAGNOSIS:

PREVIOUS PSYCHOLOGICAL EVALUATIONS:
    Date   Examiner   Method   Results

PHYSICAL FINDINGS: Date _____ PKU _____

Ht. _____ Should be _____ Skull _____ Chest _____

Wt. _____ Should be _____ Speech _____

WORKING DIAGNOSIS: _____

_____

_____

_____

_____

_____

PROGNOSIS: _____

_____

_____

_____

RX _____   _____ MD

Date _____   Address _____

Phone _____   _____

M.D.: Please sign and date this history and Rx.

Consent Forms

This is to authorize ———————————————————
                                    (agency)

————————————————————————————————
                                    (address)

to release information concerning ——— ————————————————

TO: ————————————————————————————

                              (Signed) ————————————————

                              (relationship to above mentioned:
                               parent, guardian, etc.)

————————————————
      (Date)

I hereby give my consent ☐ do not give consent ☐ (check one box)

to have my child ——————————————————— photographed, both still and
                        (full name of child)

motion pictures, in any activity associated with school activities.

————————————   ————————————————————
      Date   Parent's signature

Invitation to Parent Education Study Group

date

Dear Mr. and Mrs. _____

For the past several years we have conducted a study-workshop series for parents of all our new children. Parents of infants and children recently diagnosed as falling short of expected achievement are welcome to attend.

Attendance is a *must* for the parents of children admitted to our school since the last series in May and children to be admitted in September. We also include parents who have not been able to attend in the past.

Working together, school and family, is essential and profitable for all involved in helping your child. The material discussed has been arranged to try to answer the questions parents have asked most frequently.

We have scheduled the series early this year to allow us all the opportunity to start the school term in September in mutual understanding. We hope you can arrange for sitters so both of you can come.

The time is set from 7 P.M. to 9 P.M. so you can get home early.

Coffee and a sweet will be served so you can enjoy your dessert and relax together. Please refer to the enclosed schedule and mark your personal calendar accordingly.

Sincerely,

PRINCIPAL

encl.

*Roundup of Parent Education Series 19*___

NAME: Mrs._____

          Mr._____ ADDRESS _____

Highest grade achieved: Mother _____ Father _____

Age of child when you learned development might be retarded

Who told you?

How did you react?

What did you do?

Did you approve of the way you were told?

How would you like to have been told?

What are the most important things you feel you need to learn about?
(This could be something we have talked about or something you feel needs to be talked about in future discussions)

In this series, what do you feel has helped you the most?

Social Security Information

To Whom it May Concern:

This is to certify that _____ born on _____ ,
                                      (name of child)
is a retarded child. The onset of this condition occurred at the age of _____ .

Type of retardation is _____ .

    This child is and will be dependent.

    Father's social security number is _____
under the name of _____ .

    Mother's social security number is _____
under the name of _____ .

List any other family social security holders who might be appointed guardians (List social security numbers).

_____

_____

_____

    This child has been examined by me on _____
                                                    (date)
                (Signed) _____ M.D.

                Address _____

                (Signed) _____ Parent or Guardian

                                                 _____ Notary

date

Dear Parents:

Discussion groups for parents have been meeting at the Molloy Education Center since February 1965. Many have found these groups helpful to them and have expressed a wish to continue in a group. Sharing of concerns helps one to cope with day-to-day problems.

These groups offer you an opportunity to express your concerns freely, discuss your feelings, and raise any questions you may have regarding your child who needs special education, yourself, or the school.

Individual counseling is also available by appointment. If both parents wish to come for interviews this too can be arranged.

So that we may plan for this school year, will you check the appropriate box below and mail the form or bring it with you on check-in morning?

I am interested in a group

Morning ☐   Afternoon ☐   Evening ☐

I am not interested in a group   ☐

I would like individual counseling

Morning ☐   Afternoon ☐   Evening ☐

If both parents wish counseling please sign both names.

(signed) _____
                        (your name)

Sincerely,

Social Worker

Emergency Information Sheet

Date _____   District No. _____

Date of birth _____ NAME _____

Home address _____ Telephone _____

Mother's first name _____ Religious pref. _____ Occupation _____

Father's first name _____ Religious pref. _____ Occupation _____

Mother's business telephone _____ Father's business telephone _____

Contact in absence of parents: NAME _____ Telephone _____
    (This person must be within fifteen minutes of the school and have agreed to help you in this way)
ADDRESS _____ Relationship _____

Private physician's name _____ Telephone _____

Hospital to be used for emergency _____ Telephone _____

    Skokie Valley Community Hospital   Resurrection Hospital
    Evanston Hospital   St. Francis Hospital
    Lutheran General Hospital   Bethesda Hospital

Will you assume financial responsibility for an ambulance, if public ambulance is not available? _____

List any known allergies _____

Date of last tetanus antitoxin _____ Booster _____

Contagious diseases, illnesses, accidents or surgery since the close of school last term

_____

_____

Any other information you feel we should have _____

Transportation—school service _____ Will drive own car _____

It is essential that our emergency information show up-to-date prescriptions. In case of any changes, *please let us know.*

MEDICATION	DOSAGE—TIME	DATE PRESCRIBED	PHYSICIAN

Signed _____ Relationship _____

TO: Attending physicians and dentists

The State of Illinois requires that our records contain annual reports of physical and dental examinations.

Under the paragraph "Medications now being used," PLEASE be very specific. In case of emergency, it is essential that we have this very necessary information.

If medication is to be given at school, specific RX, over your signature, is required. This includes permission to give aspirin, Bufferin, Anacin, etc. Absolutely *NO* medication, of any kind, will be given without your signed orders.

Your cooperation is appreciated.

_____ PRINCIPAL

_____ R.N.

ANNUAL MEDICAL REPORT

Please have your physician fill in this report and mail to

Molloy Education Center, 8701 N. Menard Ave., Morton Grove, Illinois 60053

Child's name _____ Date of birth _____

Address _____

Height _____ Should be _____

Weight _____ Should be _____ Gain or loss _____

Contagious diseases since last visit _____
_____

Immunizations since last visit _____
_____

Surgery, accidents, illnesses since last visit _____
_____
_____

Medications now being used _____
_____
_____

Remarks _____
_____
_____
_____

Date of examination _____ (Signed) _____ M.D.

Address _____

Phone _____

ANNUAL DENTAL EXAMINATION REPORT
(required by Illinois statutes)

TO: Molloy Education Center
     8701 N. Menard Ave.
     Morton Grove, Illinois 60053

This is to advise _____
                    (name of student)

Address _____

has been seen by me for dental check-up and corrective work on _____
                                                                                                             (date)

FINDINGS AND REMARKS:

(Signed) _____ D.D.S.

Address: _____

Telephone: _____

Date _____

(For new volunteers only)

DATE: _____

NAME: _____
           Last   First   Husband's

ADDRESS: _____ Zip Code: _____

Telephone: _____

Why do you want to become a Volunteer? _____
_____

Can you devote at least one day a week (except for emergencies)? _____

Do you have children? _____ How many? _____

Tell us about them: (name, age, grade in school, interests) _____
_____
_____

Have you ever worked with children besides your own? _____

Tell us about your experiences. _____
_____
_____

Educational background: _____
_____

Occupation prior to marriage: _____

Have you any special interest or hobbies—for instance:

    Piano   Arts and crafts   Sewing

    Sports (such as swimming)   Other

(Signed) _____

Dear Parents:

Conferences with all parents of children enrolled in our school are now being scheduled. These conferences are scheduled twice a year. Special conferences will be held whenever requested by either parents or teachers.

Parent conferences are being scheduled on:

in the evening, to enable BOTH parents to be present. It is most important to keep appointments promptly so full time can be profitably used.

Please detach, sign, and return the appointment sheet below so that we may complete our schedule with maximum convenience for all.

Sincerely,

Principal

DATE OF CONFERENCE:

TIME:

TEACHER:

(Keep this part)

(Detach and return this part to school office promptly)

PARENT-TEACHER CONFERENCE

DATE: _____   TIME: _____

TEACHER: _____

_____
Parent's Signature

FOLLOW-UP SURVEY

Dear Mr. and Mrs. _____

Molloy Education Center is interested in knowing about former pupils or children whose parents at one time made an application at the school, whether or not the child was ever enrolled here.

This information will be helpful to us in shaping our program.

Your help is needed to provide this information and we urge you to complete and return the enclosed questionnaire.

_____
Principal

Date: _____

Name of child: _____

Birthdate: _____

Birthplace: _____

Parents' names: _____
        (Father)   (Mother)

Parents' Address: _____
    Street number City State Zip

Parents' telephone number: _____

Brothers and sisters: Name Birthdate Grade in school or occupation

_____

_____

_____

Date child enrolled at Molloy Education Center: _____

Date child left Molloy Education Center: _____

Where did child go upon leaving Molloy Education Center? _____

_____

How long did he stay there? _____

Reason for leaving there: _____

List other places where child has been—such as residential center, state school, other school, vocational center—giving date of placement, length of time he stayed in each place, and reason for leaving: _____

_____

_____

Present whereabouts of child: _____

_____

Your plan for his future: _____

_____

_____

If child is new deceased, please give date and cause, if known: _____

_____

_____

_____

Additional remarks (include any information which might be pertinent but not covered in this questionnaire): _____

_____

_____

_____

_____

Thank you for your cooperation.

_____
Signed

Child Care Training Certificates

CERTIFICATE OF MERIT

THIS CERTIFIES _____

has been awarded this certificate for

_____

Given at _____ School

Date _____ _____

CERTIFICATE OF ACHIEVEMENT

THIS CERTIFIES _____

Has satisfactorily participated in

the _____ *with distinction and integrity and is therefore entitled to this testimonial*

Awarded at _____ this ___ day of _____ 19___

_____ _____ Teacher

Outline for writing anecdotal conference reports

Consider the level of your own group only. It is assumed that the child was ready for your group when placed there. Our overall picture, in summary, should be considered as a collection of concentric circles with the child as the center and concerned only with himself. The nearest circle is the family, then the group associations in the nursery, still playing alone, but being aware that others must be considered. The next circle is working and playing with peers. The larger community group (whole school) and then the outside community (beyond their families) follow.

The object of this evaluation is to consider these growth gradients at the level of your own group. Look carefully at the objectives for your group. Tell the story as you feel it from material in daily journals and in the Performance Goals Record.

I. *PHYSICAL AND MOTOR GROWTH*

    A. Ambulation (walk, run, skip, etc.)

    B. Handling large equipment (balls, swings, etc.)

    C. Handling smaller equipment

        1. Balls and toys, etc. with moving parts

        2. Manipulative materials

            a. Three dimensions (mailbox, pegs, puzzles, etc.)

            b. Scissors

            c. Pasting

            d. Crayons, pencils and paint brushes, etc. (at random, *purposefully*, profitably)

            e. Handling cleaning materials

    D. Self-care—bathroom and toilet habits

        1. Feeding

        2. Brushing teeth

        3. Toileting

        4. Hands

        5. Undressing

        6. Eating

        7. Nose and coughing

        8. Bathing and shampooing

        9. Personal hygiene

II. SOCIAL GROWTH

   A. Manners: appropriate table manners; respect for peers, adults, family; with familiar small group; with familiar large group; among strangers

   B. Communication

      1. Receptive

         a. Response to simple commands—"no," "don't touch," "come here," etc.

         b. Large body response to music, command, or other stimulation, such as "hurry," "stay there"

         c. Symbolic indications: selection of article by hearing name of article, qualifying "big ball," "little ball"

         d. Ability to follow directions

      2. Expressive

         a. Appropriate response to music

         b. Symbolic response: naming; qualifying (who, what, where, when, etc.); phrases; sentences; frames a question (by inflection or by actual interrogation)

         c. Social speech: introductions; carry message; answer phone; emergency calls; telephone manners; accept your invitation; accept your compliment; take a message (verbal)

      3. Use of leisure time

III. EMOTIONAL GROWTH

   A. Self-control

      1. Alone

      2. In a quiet group

      3. Under pressure of group

      4. Competition (team or individual)

      5. Among strangers

   B. Ability to share

   C. Good habits

   D. Unacceptable habits

IV. *INTELLECTUAL GROWTH*

    A. Perceptive

        1. Auditory

            a. Response to interpretation of auditory stimuli: selection of stimuli; responses; minding; following directions, etc. (limited)

        2. Visual tactile

            a. Likes and differences from gross three-dimensional to small flat surfaces without color (please note with or *without* tactile surfaces)

            b. Use of information gained from noting relationships (limited to familiar situations)

            c. Categorizing

            d. Colors—matching, sorting, selection by name, naming

        3. Word recognition: protection and information work words

        4. Number concepts: include vocabulary for arithmetic, such as "big," "little," etc.

            a. Awareness of time, telling time, etc.— in relation to school activities only

            b. Number facts (Brownell Sequence)

            counting by notation:

            * counting and structured termination

            * counting without a visible structured termination

            * concept of number symbol

            * selection of proper grouping

            * attaching the written number symbol to the concrete presentation

            * continuation and a reinforcement of the preceding step

            * associating the seen or heard symbol with the terminal number; the child must now stop counting, without help of any kind, at the terminal indicated by the symbol only. He has no pattern on a card, nor any groups from which to select the "answer amount." He must terminate counting by only the meaning of the symbol presented. This is the actual act of counting by notation

* this is the converse of the preceding step. The number symbol is the stimulus to group the correct number of blocks or objects

    c. Counting by grouping and notation

    d. Counting by grouping

    e. Multiplication and conversion

       vocabulary of relationships

       ordinals

       time

       money—learning to recognize coins

       measuring

       using numbers for own protection

       discriminating shapes

    f. Transfer to practical situations

5. Writing: use of writing tools, crayons, pencils

6. Orientation to surroundings

    a. Time: name days, months

    b. Seasons

    c. Weather

7. Job orientation—ability to plan, follow through, clean up; attitude toward chore; cooperation with co-workers

Always conclude your story on a positive note. Sincerely consider how you would like to hear this report if you were the parent of a child with retarded development

Appendix III
Balance Beam Exercises

1. Walk forward on beam, arms held sideward.
2. Walk backward on beam, arms held sideward.
3. Walk arms held sideward, walk to the middle, turn around, and walk backward.
4. Walk forward to the middle of the beam; then turn and walk the remaining distance sideward left with weight on the balls of the feet.
5. Walk to center of beam; then turn and continue sideward right.
6. Walk forward with left foot always in front of right.
7. Walk forward with right foot always in front of left.
8. Walk backward with left foot always in front of right.
9. Walk backward with right foot always in front of left.
10. Walk forward with hands on hips.
11. Walk backward with hands on hips.
12. Walk forward with bean bag balanced on top of the head.
13. Walk forward and pick up a bean bag from the middle of the beam.
14. Walk forward to center, kneel on one knee, rise, and continue to end of beam.
15. Walk backward with bean bag balanced on top of the head.
16. Place bean bag at center of beam. Walk to center, place bean bag on top of head, continue to end of beam.
17. Have partners hold a wand twelve inches above the center of the beam. Walk forward on beam and step over the wand.
18. Walk backward and step over wand.
19. Hold wand at height of three feet. Walk forward and pass under the wand.
20. Walk backward and pass under the wand.
21. Walk the beam backward with hands clasped behind the body.
22. Walk the beam forward, arms held sideward, palms down, with a bean bag on the back of each hand.
23. Walk the beam backward, arms held sideward, palms up, with a bean bag on back of each hand.
24. Hop on right foot, the full length of beam.
25. Hop on left foot, the full length of beam.
26. Hop on right foot, the full length of beam; then turn around and hop back.

27. Hop on left foot, the full length of beam; then turn around and hop back.

28. Walk to middle of beam, balance on one foot, turn around on this foot and walk backwards to end of beam.

29. Walk to middle of beam left sideward, turn around and walk to end of beam right sideward.

30. With arms clasped about the body in rear, walk the beam forward.

31. With arms clasped about the body in rear, walk forward to the middle, turn around once, walk backward the remaining distance.

32. Walk the beam backward with a bean bag balanced on the back of each hand.

33. Walk to middle of beam, do a balance stand on one foot, arms held sideward with trunk and free leg held horizontally.

34. Hold wand fifteen inches above beam. Balance bean bag on head, walk forward, stepping over wand.

35. Hold wand fifteen inches above beam. Balance bean bag on head, walk backward, stepping over wand.

36. Hold wand fifteen inches above beam. Balance bean bag on head, walk sideward right, stepping over wand.

37. Hold wand fifteen inches above beam. Balance bean bag on head, walk sideward left, stepping over wand.

38. Hold wand three feet high. Walk forward, hands on hips, and pass under the wand.

39. Hold wand three feet high. Walk backward, hands on hips, and pass under the wand.

40. Walk beam forward, eyes closed.

41. Walk beam sideward, eyes closed.

42. Walk beam backward, eyes closed.

43. Stand on beam, feet side by side and eyes closed, and record number of seconds balance is maintained.

44. Stand on beam, one foot in advance of the other, eyes closed, and record number of seconds balance is maintained.

45. Stand on right foot with eyes closed, and record number of seconds balance is maintained.

46. Stand on left foot with eyes closed, and record number of seconds balance is maintained.

47. Place hands on beam, have partner hold legs (as in wheelbarrow race) and walk to end of beam.

48. Same as 47, but partner walks with his feet on the beam, instead of the ground, straddling the beam.

49. "Cat Walk" on beam; walk on "all fours," hands and feet on beam.

Appendix IV
Patterns for Tracing in Teaching Handwriting

BLACK AND WHITE CHARTS

312

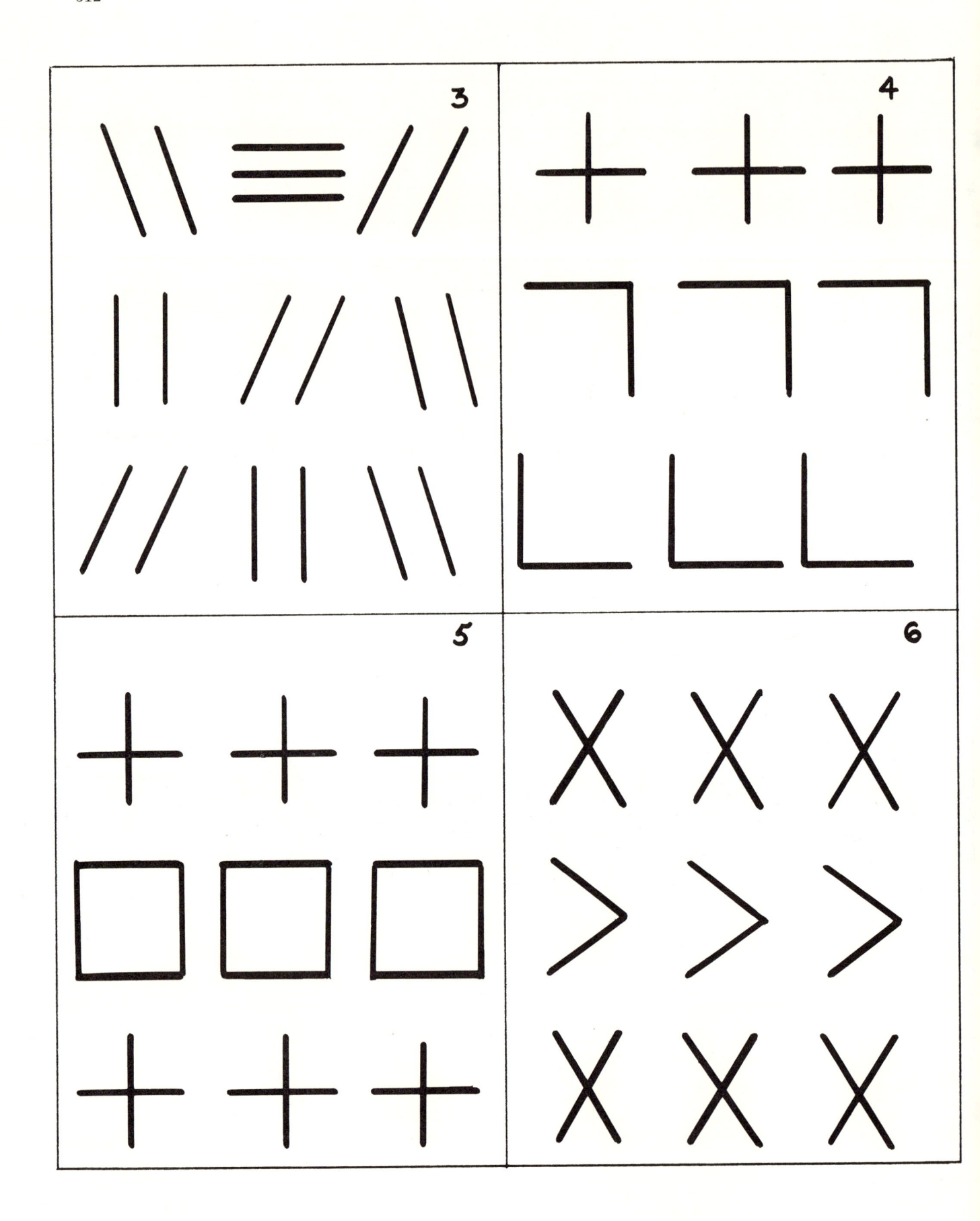

313

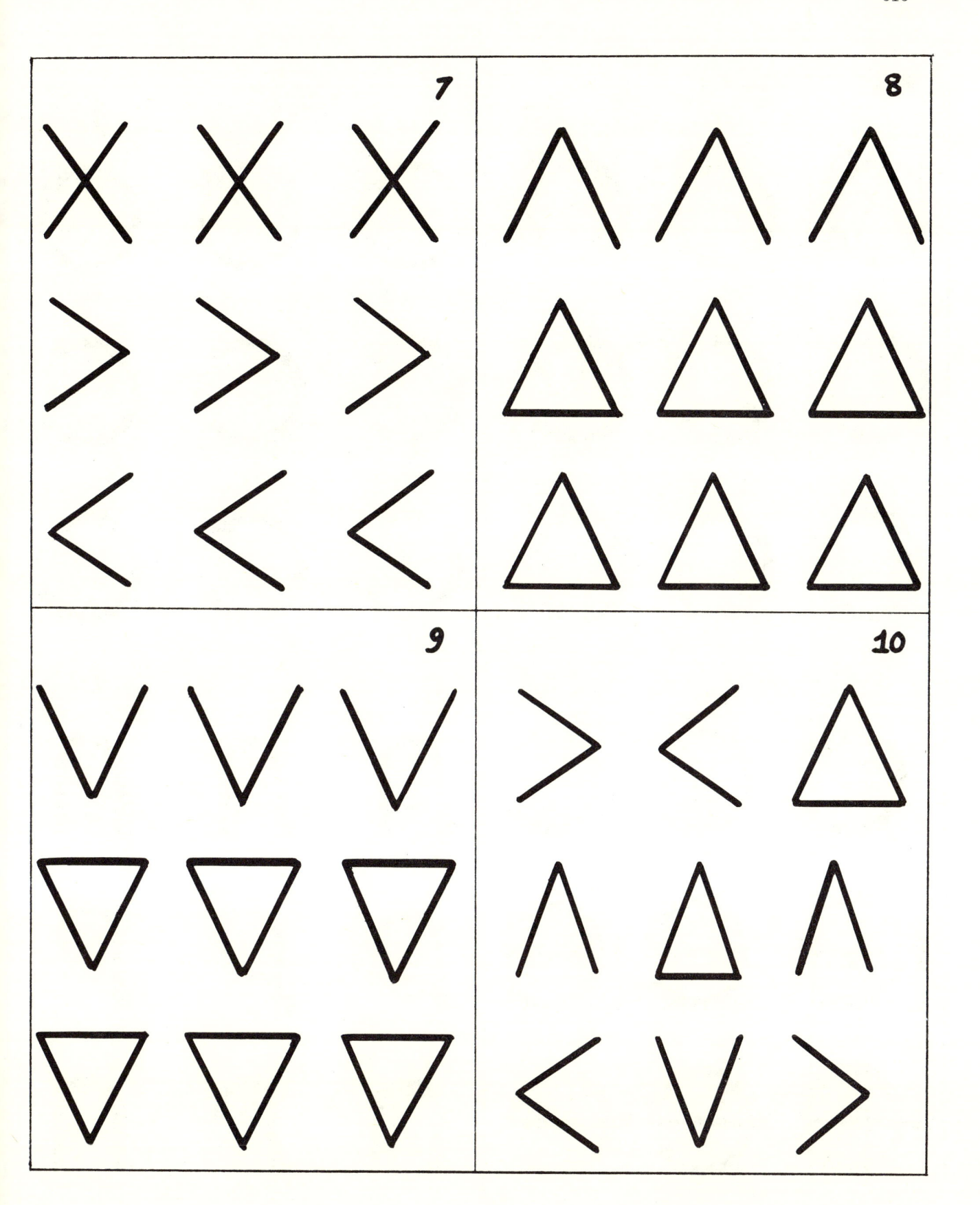

314

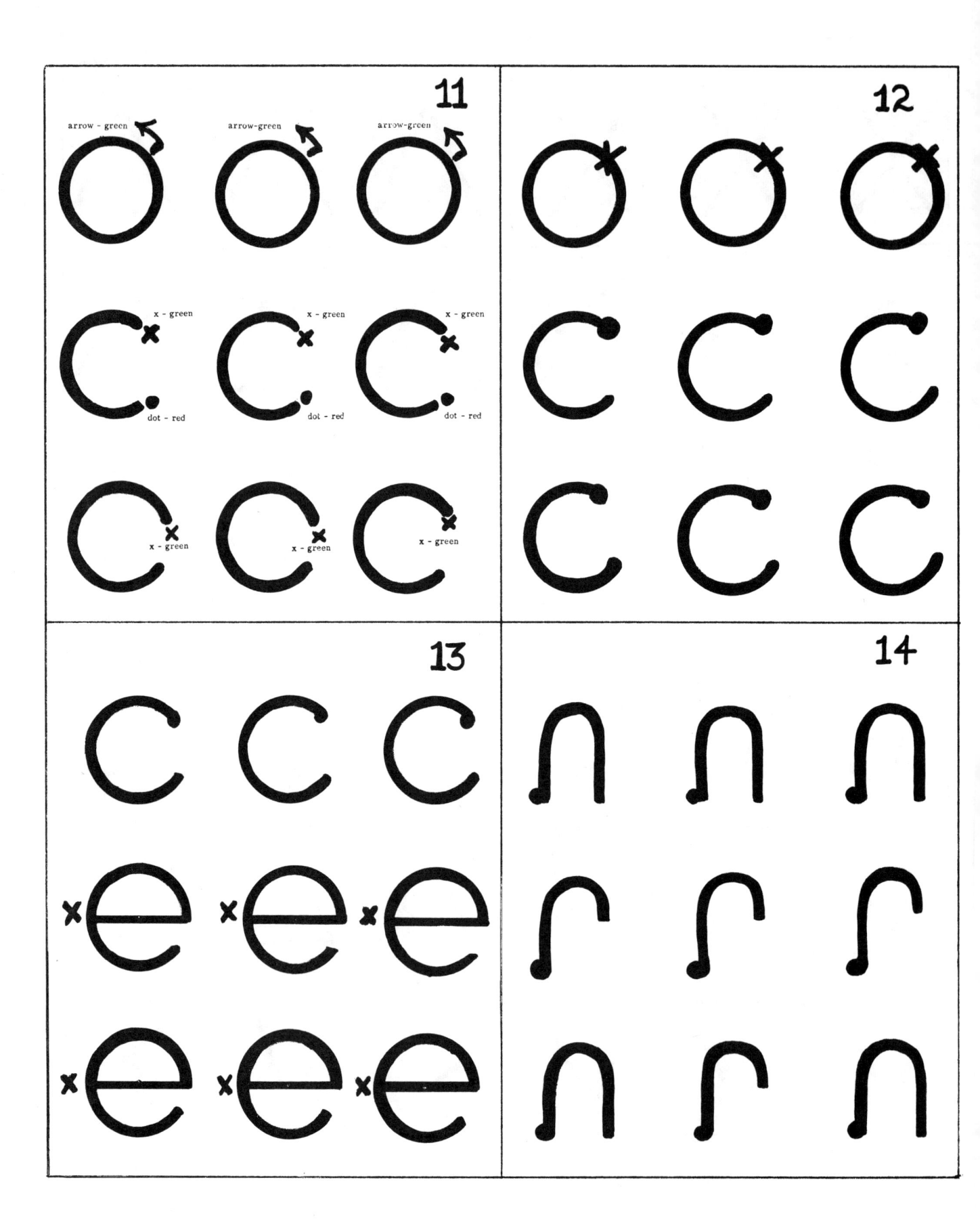

15	16
J J J Ŭ Ŭ Ŭ J U J	n n n m m m n m n

17	18
h h h n n n h n h	S S S c c c S S S

316

COLOR CHARTS

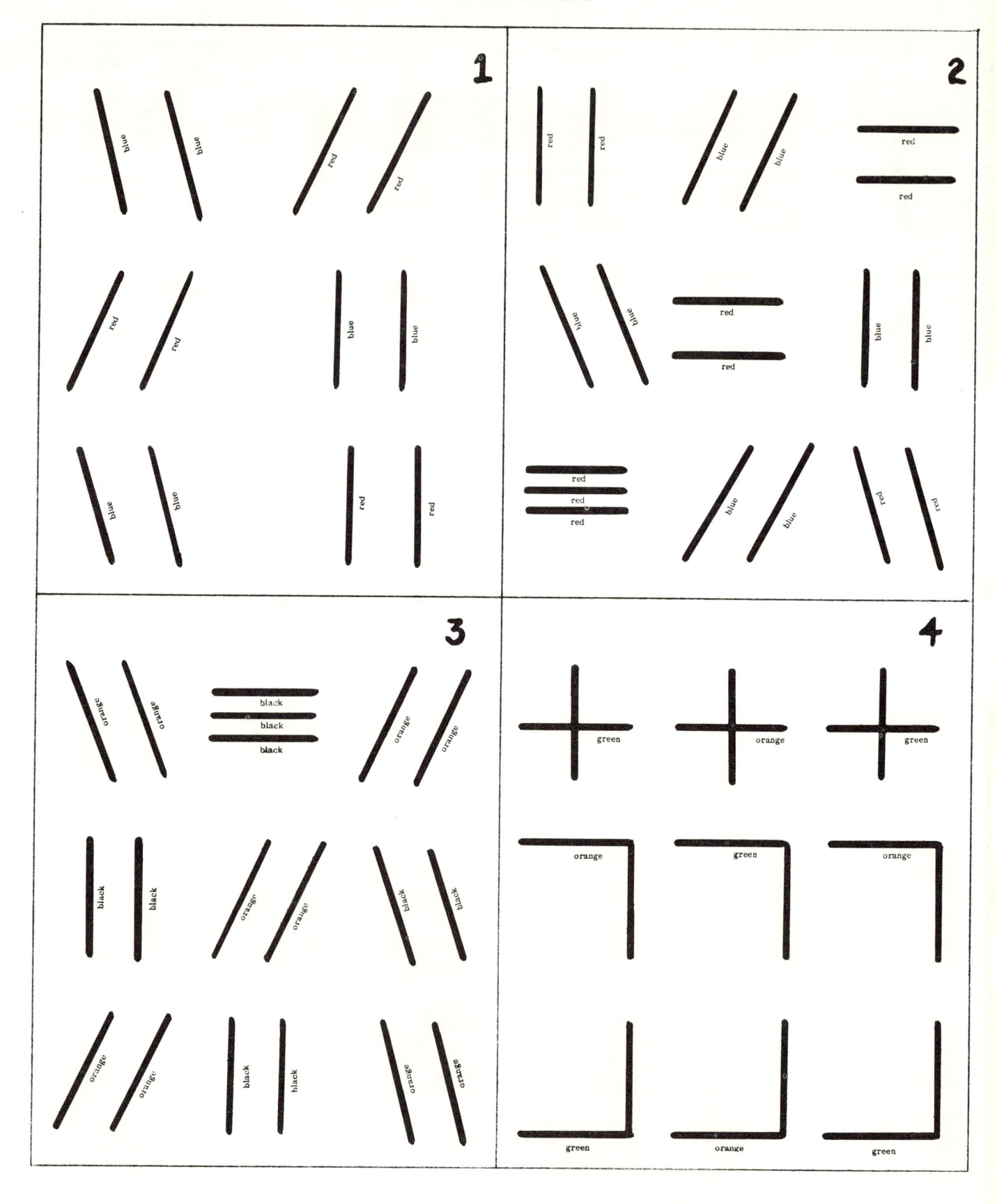

317

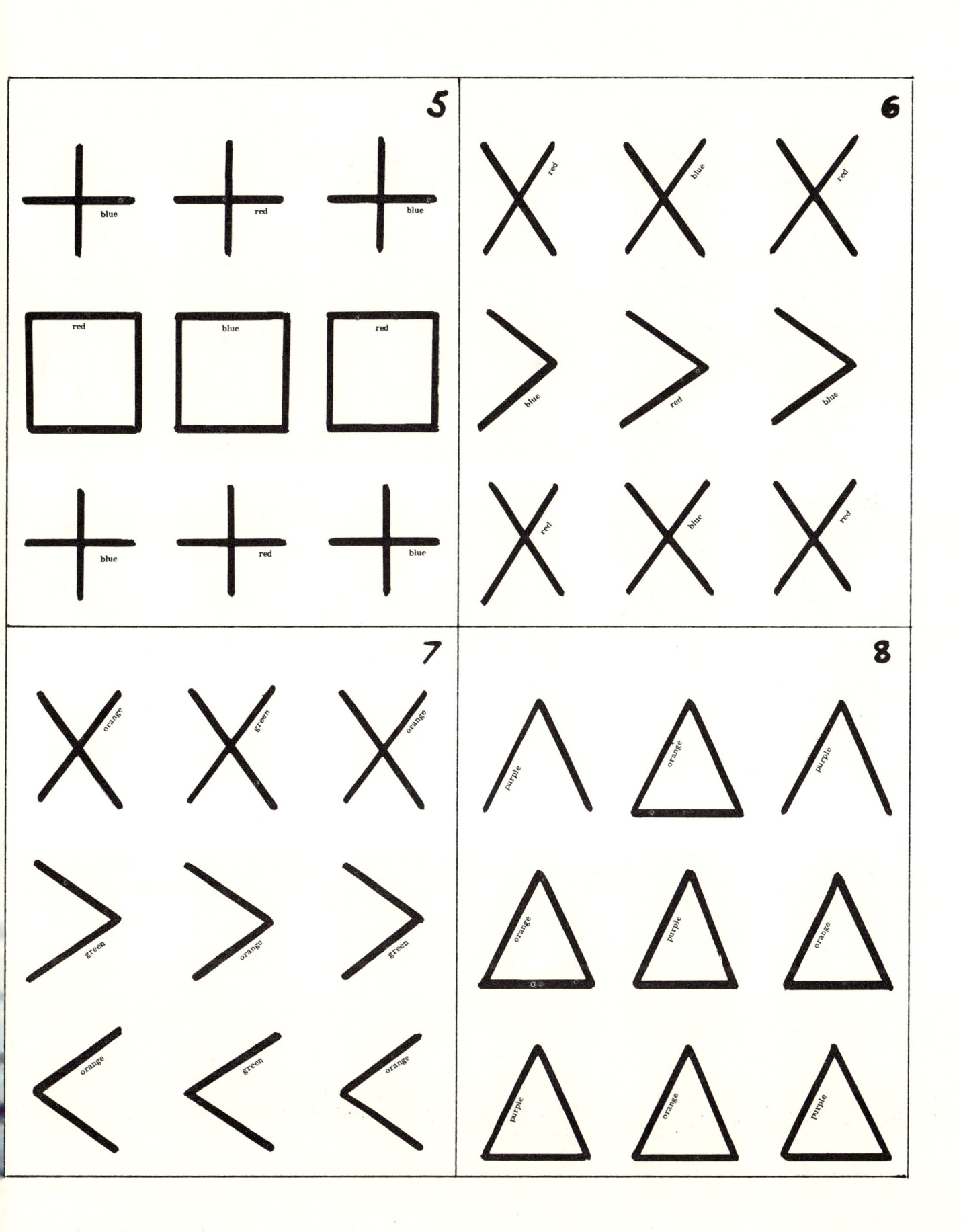

318

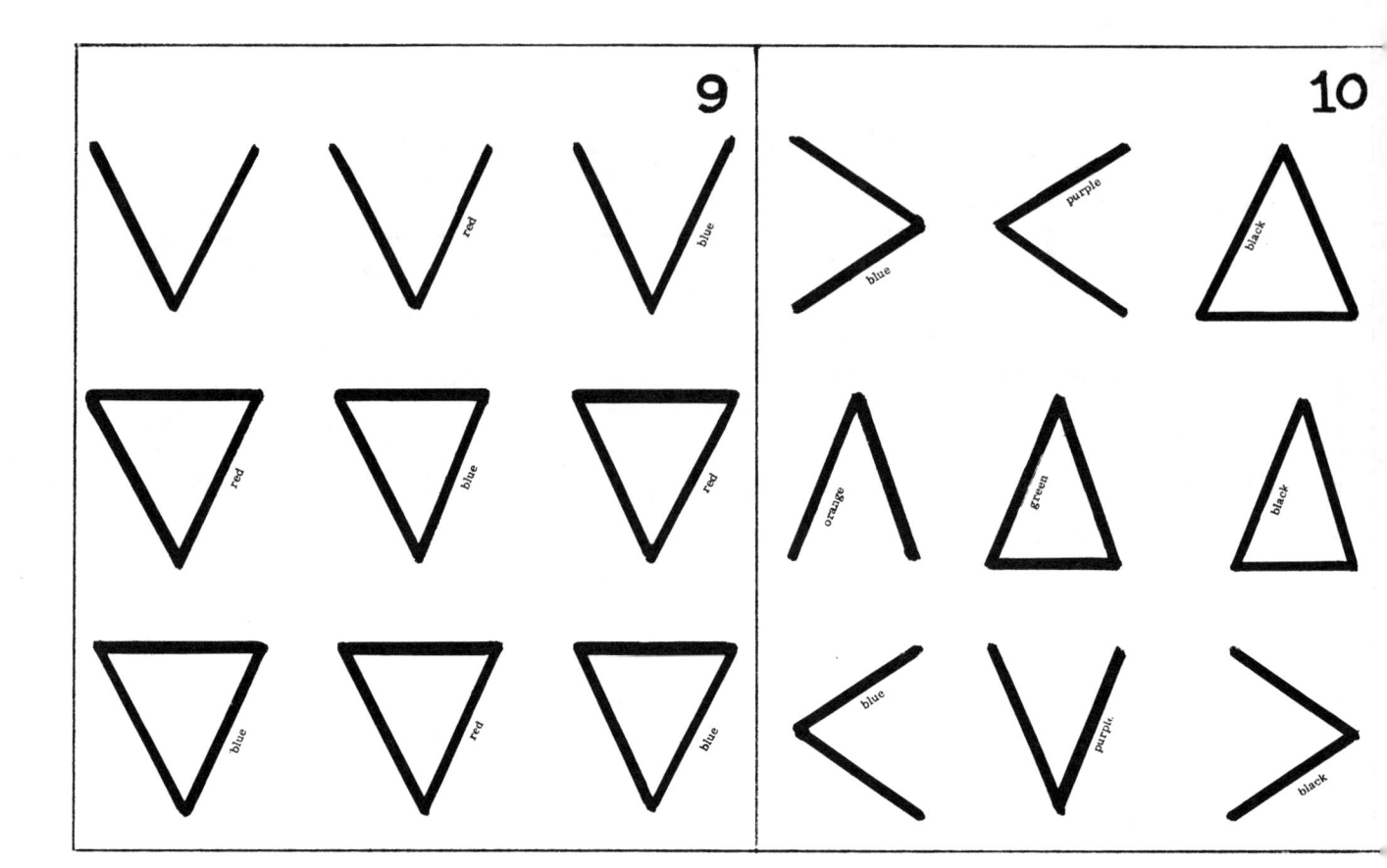

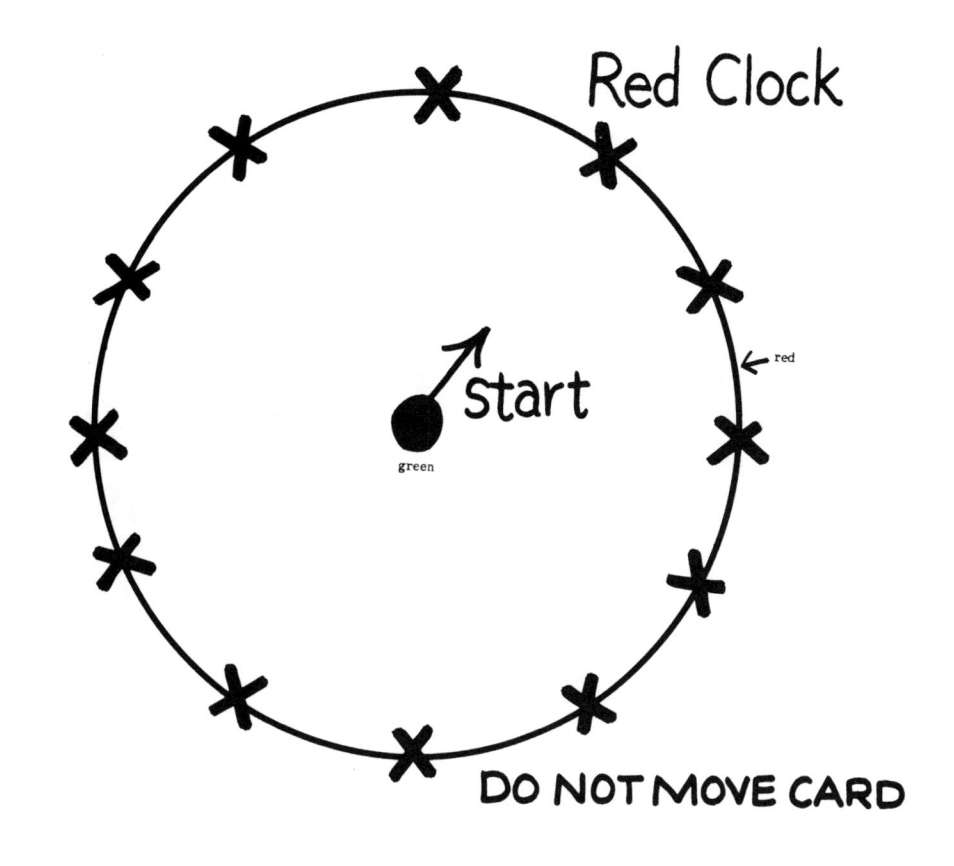

Red Clock

start
green
red

DO NOT MOVE CARD

Green Clock

start
red
green

DO NOT MOVE CARD

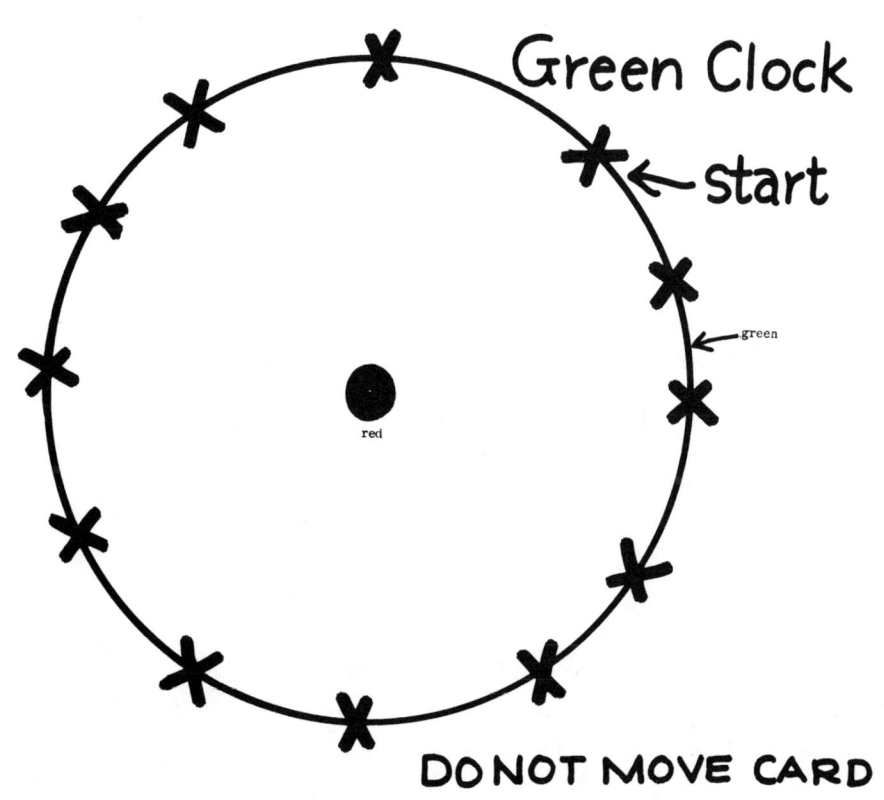

Performance Goals Record

The Developmental Progress

of _____
(Child's name)

by Julia S. Molloy

Principal, Julia S. Molloy Education Center

(Formerly Orchard School for Special Education)

and Calvin K. Claus, Chairman, Psychology Department, National College of Education

THE JOHN DAY COMPANY NEW YORK
An Intext Publisher

Copyright © 1972 by Julia S. Molloy

All rights reserved. No part of this book may be reprinted, or reproduced or utilized in any form or by any electronic, mechanical, or other means, now known or hereafter invented, including photocopying and recording, or in any information storage and retrieval system, without permission in writing from the publisher: The John Day Company, 257 Park Avenue South, New York, N.Y. 10010. Published on the same day in Canada by Longman Canada Limited.

Printed in the United States of America

Note: This *Performance Goals Record* may be purchased separately. Write to the Publisher for quantity prices.

Introduction to the Performance Goals Record

This system for recording the progress of handicapped children has been organized by Calvin K. Claus and Julia S. Molloy. To the staff of Orchard School, Skokie, Illinois (now Molloy Education Center, Morton Grove, Illinois), contributors to the 1972 edition of Trainable Children, *the authors extend sincere thanks for suggestions and hours of discussions.*

Evaluation is the process by which we judge and thereby learn what a thing or act is worth at the time the judgment is made.

We evaluate what students *can* do, so we may plan an appropriate placement and program.

We evaluate what students *do*, so we may record evidence of progress, plateauing or regression.

These remarks about evaluation have been emphasized by Tyler.

The Performance Goals Record is an attempt to put these ideas into practice. Evaluation provides a security to the school staff, to the parents, and to the community.

Five growth areas are used for organization. These growth areas or categories provide a construct for statements of terminal behavior objectives. The sequences are those presented by Gesell, Piaget, Castner, League, Lowenfeld, Kirk, and Van Riper.

The organization is such that it allows for materials to be presented in developmental sequence. The program is divided into performance steps. Skinner has suggested that hundreds or even thousands of steps may constitute the program. These steps are sufficiently close to insure the child success on nearly every response he makes. In this way, failure is almost completely removed from the child's experiences, and as he succeeds, so his attitude improves (Scagliotta).

The sequences in each area are continuous in the Performance Goals Record. The milestones for grade levels are purposely omitted as the record is intended to show progress for each individual child in competition with himself only, not in competition with a peer group.

The interim performance goals for peer groups, or grades, are stated in the teachers' monthly lesson plan reports. Grade levels in special education vary geographically and cannot be imposed upon a performance schedule intended for individualized recording of behavior changes.

This general procedure is what has been referred to as criterion-referenced measurement (Popham and Husek).

Criterion-referenced measures are used to compare an individual's status with respect to an established standard of performance (behavioral objective). Criterion-referenced measures, therefore, seem most appropriate to evaluation of special education with its emphasis on individualized instruction. Performance criteria are an inherent part of behavioral objectives and serve as the focal point for evaluation.

An accurate evaluation of regular or special education proceeds most effectively when based upon a list of major objectives of the program. Special education objectives form the initial and sound basis for an evaluation in special education (Ahr and Sims).

The progress of any child is measured in terms of his achievement of the goals (or objectives) specifically prescribed for him (Scagliotta).

Four systems of recording contribute information for summarizing a progress report for parents, permanent records, and curriculum effectiveness:

1. Teacher's daily journal: a short anecdotal sketch of daily observations of behavior.
2. Teacher's monthly lesson plan reports: review what was accomplished as a group toward realization of objectives for that particular class.
3. Standardized test data: psychometrics; language evaluation instruments; motor growth scales; Illinois Test of Psycholinguistic Abilities.
4. Performance Goals Record.

A review of information from all four systems is essential to writing a comprehensive progress report. A short guide for writing a progress report is presented. The teacher writes what she has observed about the child's behavior as an individual, and as a member of a peer group. By following the guide and referring to data, detailed coverage of the growth areas is recorded.

PHYSICAL GROWTH: Note gait, both walking and running; coordination on playground equipment (note adding new ventures); handling of manipulative material at own expected level; use of writing materials, crayons; use of scissors; self-care gains.

EMOTIONAL GROWTH: Self-control; temper manifestations; ability to follow through on tasks of own choice; on tasks assigned; reaction to frustration; cooperation.

SOCIAL GROWTH: Sharing; respect for adults; respect for peers; manners (conduct in all contacts, eating, playing games, on the telephone); sportsmanship; language development (note ability to listen, to talk, or to make wants known).

INTELLECTUAL GROWTH: Number concepts; orientation in group; ability to follow directions; word recognition; memory span, attention span; curiosity, ability to complete a task.

Always compare your findings with previous reports. Be sure you have talked to other teachers having contact with the child.

Using the Performance Goals Record

Recording behavior is merely saying that a child does do a specified task.

The first time a behavior is observed, enter the date in the cell in the I (Initial) column. That behavior may persist and remain a definite part of the child's repertory or it may not occur again for several days or weeks, or it may begin to occur frequently. When the teacher's professional judgment is that the behavior occurs appropriately and always, under usual circumstances, the date is entered in the cell in the B (Behavior) column.

Regressions, or erratic performance, should be recorded and dated in the C (Change) column.

The first time the Performance Goals Record is used is the most tedious as much information is required. It is suggested that the teacher, psychologist, or social worker be well acquainted with the content and proceed to gather information in very much the same way as the Vineland Scale of Social Maturity is administered.

Planning experiences will be necessary to observe the various behavior to be recorded. Actual testing can be done in some areas of physical growth and to record progress in quantification skills.

The effectiveness of the Performance Goals Record is directly related to the care taken by individual teachers in recording entries. With careful recording, the teacher, the child, the parent, and the next teacher can be shown a clear record of progress. This record should be shared with the student and with parents. This sharing serves to motivate all concerned. Since careless entries in the Performance Goals Record can be its undoing, it is absolutely essential to systematically account for each performance of each child. As this is an accumulative record, only gains are obvious. This alone is a reinforcement for all concerned about the progress of each individual child.

Two charts are provided for an accumulative account of behavior changes.

The *quarterly* account renders an accumulative recording of total behavior changes.

The *annual* account renders an accumulative recording of behavior changes in the five growth areas. After the initial entry, counts of behavior changes are entered at the end of the school year only.

Both accumulative accounts should balance at the end of the school year.

Count all entries in each of the three columns in the Performance Goals Record and record the totals in the Initial entry cell.

The maximum score would be:

Physical Growth	391
Emotional Growth	13
Social Growth	328
Intellectual Growth	462
Esthetic Growth	142
Task Total	1,336

Behavior established before your contact with this child should be designated by putting PRA (previously recorded activity) in the appropriate B cell.

After the initial entries have been made, these totals should be entered in the Initial entry cell of the *Quarterly Accumulative Account* (see sample chart). After the first entry has been made, to facilitate getting the totals for entries for each quarter, 2 cells are provided. To avoid recounting each quarter, place a tally mark in the upper cell as you note and record the behavior change. *Add* the tally score to the previous total for the quarterly score. *Bring forward* the quarterly score to the next column to serve as the new (initial) starting total for that quarter.

At the end of the school year, count the entries in each growth area and enter the totals on the *Annual Accumulative Account of Behavior Changes in the Five Growth Areas*.

The 1,336 tasks are sequenced and could be considered criterion-referenced measures.

References

Ahr, E., and Sims, H. "An Evaluation System for Special Education." Title III Project Report. Niles Township (Ill.) Department of Special Education.

Bzoch Kenneth R., and League, Richard. "Receptive-Expressive Emergent Language Scale." Computer Management Corporation, Gainesville, Fla., 1970.

Castner, B. M. "The Development of Fine Prehension in Infancy." *Genetic Psychology Monographs.* Volume XII, No. 2 (August, 1932).

Gesell, A., and Amatruda, C.S. *Developmental Diagnosis.* Harper & Row, 1941-1947.

Kirk, S. A. *Teaching Reading to Slow-Learning Children.* Riverside Press, 1940.

Lowenfeld, V. *Creative and Mental Growth.* Macmillan, 1957.

Piaget, J. *The Origins of Intelligence in Children.* International University Press, 1952.

Popham, W. James, and Husek, T. R. "Implications of Criterion-Referenced Measurement." *Journal of Educational Measurement* V. 6 (1967), 1-9.

Scagliotta, E.G. *Education Planning for the Disabled Learner.* The Mafex Press (newsletter, Vol. 2, No. 1.) 1971

Skinner, B. F. *The Technology of Teaching.* Appleton-Century-Crofts, 1968.

Tyler, R.W. "General Statement on Education." *Journal of Educational Research* XXXV (March, 1942).

SAMPLE CHARTS

Name **Tom Jones**
D.B. **3-3-64**

QUARTERLY ACCUMULATIVE ACCOUNT OF BEHAVIOR CHANGES

Date		C.A.	Sept.			Dec.			March			June		
			I	B	C	I	B	C	I	B	C	I	B	C
Initial Entry	9·6·70	6-6				⑭	⑱	0	㉖	⑳	0	⑪	⑲	0
Cum. Total			30	44	0	44	62	0	70	82	0	81	101	0
Tally						㉒	⑩	②	㉜	⑲	③	㊱	⑯	⑤
Cum. Total	9·8·71	7-6	81	101	0	103	121	2	135	189	3	171	157	5
Tally															
Cum. Total															

Name **Tom Jones**
D.B. **3·3·64**

ANNUAL ACCUMULATIVE ACCOUNT OF BEHAVIOR CHANGES IN THE FIVE GROWTH AREAS

Max. Total Date	C.A.	391 Physical			13 Emotional			328 Social			462 Intellectual			142 Esthetic			1336 Total		
		I	B	C	I	B	C	I	B	C	I	B	C	I	B	C	I	B	C
9/6/70 Initial Entry	6-6	30	45	0	0	2	0	24	26	0	17	20	0	10	8	0	81	101	0
9/8/71	7-6	55	60	0	2	4	0	44	40	2	47	35	3	22	18	0	170	157	5

PERFORMANCE GOALS RECORD OF _____

Date of Birth _____ Admitted _____ at _____ years of age

ETIOLOGY IF KNOWN _____

PREVIOUS SCHOOL EXPERIENCE:

IMPLICATIONS FOR TEACHING: (note source and date of Rx)

INSTRUCTIONS FOR USING THIS RECORD

This sequence of performance goals is intended to record evidence of changes in behavior in the five growth areas used for organizing our curriculum: physical, emotional, social, intellectual and aesthetic.

The goals require a series of performances, each of which is intended to enhance a desirable change in behavior. Tasks have been analyzed and sequenced in order of maturation and/or difficulty.

Sample

I	B	C
10-1-71 E.L.	10-20-71 E.L.	

The *INITIAL* performance, the *first time* a behavior is observed, enter the date, and the observer's initials, in the column headed I.

When the *BEHAVIOR* sought is a part of performance under usual circumstances, enter the date of this observation and the observer's initials in the column headed B.

After the initial entry, entries should be made quarterly: September, December, March, June. Should a child regress, enter the date in the column headed C, *CHANGES*. When the behavior is reinstated, enter the date in the B cell beside the earlier entry.

The accumulative account charts provide a system for:
1. viewing progress on a quarterly basis and,
2. viewing total progress in the five growth areas annually.

Upon receiving a child in your class, this record will assist in establishing a baseline. Some entries will have been made following the intake interview.

I. PHYSICAL GROWTH

Terminal Performance Objective: Control, intentionally, movement of the body for ambulation and performance of tasks involved in (1) caring for our body needs, (2) manipulating of tools and media productively, and (3) maintaining good health.

A. *Body Awareness*	I	B	C
1. Identify body parts by pointing or gesturing			
a. Identify facial features			
mouth			
teeth			
tongue			
nose			
eyes			
face			
head			
hair			
ears			
cheeks			
chin			
eyebrows			
eyelashes			
b. Identify extremities			
hands			
fingers			
arms			
legs			
toes			
thumbs			
c. Identify parts of trunk			
stomach			

	I	B	C
back			
"butt" or bottom			
neck			
d. Identify joints			
shoulders			
elbows			
wrists			
knees			
ankles			
hips			
2. Move body or body parts while supine (on back) on mat			
a. Move with verbal, visual, and tactual cues: arms sideways: in (to body); out (away from body)			
legs apart and together—in, out			
legs up (hips flexed); legs down (keep legs straight)			
lift head off mat—with hands behind neck			
b. Move with visual cues (imitative motion)			
arms sideways—in, out			
legs apart and together—in, out			
legs up; legs down			
lift head off mat—with hands behind neck			
c. Move with verbal direction			
arms sideways—in, out			
legs apart and together—in, out			
legs up; legs down			
lift head off mat—with hands behind neck			
3. Recognize own space, size, and shape as demonstrated with use of own body			
a. Move over and under obstacle			

	I	B	C
b. Move through tunnel, hoop, etc.			
c. Move around object			
d. Place object "in front of" self			
"in back of" self			
"at the side of" self			
e. Place self "in front of" (line up)			
"in back of"			
"at the side of"			
f. Curl up to make self small			
g. Bend or stoop to make self small			
h. Reach and stretch up			
i. Reach and stretch arms out			
j. Stretch arms out in front of self			
k. Stretch arms behind self			
l. Stretch arms sideways			
m. Reach and stretch up, on tiptoes to make self tall			
B. *Physical Development*			
1. Head raising			
a. Raise head from prone position 45°–90°			
b. Raise head and chest, support weight on arms and shoulders			
2. Roll over			
a. Turn self from stomach to back			
b. Turn self from back to stomach			
c. Roll over in either direction			
3. Sitting balance			
a. Maintain balance after being assisted to position			
sit with support on chair			

	I	B	C
sit on floor (mat)—side sitting			
sit on floor—ring sitting			
sit on floor—tailor sitting			
sit on floor—heel sitting			
sit on floor—legs extended in front			
b. Assume position and maintain balance			
side sitting			
ring sitting			
tailor sitting			
heel sitting			
legs extended in front			
approach chair, turn back toward chair and sit down			

C. Ambulation

1. Crawling

	I	B	C
a. Creep, amphibian fashion on stomach			
b. Crawl on hands and knees			
c. Scoot, in any other fashion			

2. Walking

	I	B	C
a. Walk with ataxia but gain objective			
b. Walk, rhythm absent, gait bizarre			
c. Walk with rhythm absent but touch heel to floor first, toes extending for thrust forward			
d. Walk rhythmically, but with slappage or steppage gait			
e. Walk with rhythmic gait, heel touching floor first, toes extending for thrust forward			
Elements of time: walk slowly with verbal direction and/or demonstration			
Elements of force: Walk quietly			
march			
stamp			

	I	B	C
Elements of flow: stop suddenly			
sustain rhythm			
start and stop on command			
3. Running			
a. Run, gain objective but gait ataxic			
b. "Run" as a hurried walk with heel touching floor first			
c. Run with difficulty stopping			
d. Run rhythmically with transverse arch touching floor first, toes extended for thrust forward; stop controlled with verbal direction and/or demonstration			
Elements of time: run slowly			
run fast			
Elements of force: run quietly or lightly			
run heavily			
Elements of flow: run and stop suddenly on command			
run and sustain rhythm			
4. Tiptoeing			
a. Tiptoe, rhythm absent			
b. Tiptoe rhythmically			
5. Sliding (sideways—step together style)			
a. Slide without rhythm			
b. Slide with rhythm			
D. *Skill Development*			
1. Jumping (see "Use of Equipment" next page)			
a. Jump down from object or height			
b. Jump up from floor with both feet			
c. Jump forward			
d. Jump forward over 2" height			

	I	B	C
e. Jump forward over 8″ height			
f. Jump backward with both feet			
g. Jump sideways with both feet			
2. Galloping			
a. Lead with either left or right foot at all times			
b. Lead with either foot, at will			
3. Hopping			
a. Hop on one foot, with assistance			
b. Hop on right foot—two or three hops			
c. Hop on left foot—two or three hops			
d. Hop on right foot for a distance of 10 feet			
e. Hop on left foot for a distance of 10 feet			
f. "Step-hop-step-hop" leading to skipping			
4. Skipping			
a. Skip to one side only, rhythm absent			
b. Skip to one side, rhythmically			
c. Skip with alternate feet, with rhythm, maintain balance, and terminate with control			
5. Climbing stairs			
a. Require help, crawl on hands and feet or knees			
b. Ascend with dominant foot leading with assistance of rail or adult hand			
c. Descend with dominant foot leading with assistance of rail or adult			
d. Ascend, alternating feet with assistance of rail or adult			
e. Descend, alternating feet with assistance of rail or adult			
f. Ascend, alternating feet without assistance			
g. Descend, alternating feet without assistance			
E. *Use of Equipment*			
1. Ride on rocking horse, rocking boats, etc.			

	I	B	C
2. Pedal toys such as tricycle, etc.			
a. Pedal, but require a start and guidance from another person			
b. Pedal, but need to be guided			
c. Pedal conveyance requiring circular pedaling but have difficulty steering			
d. Pedal and steer tricycle, or conveyance requiring circular pedaling			
3. Balance beam			
a. Stand on line			
b. Walk on line			
c. Walk on board placed on floor			
d. Step up on board			
e. Walk on wide base beam (4″ board or two 3″ boards placed together to make wide platform—Creative Playthings)			
f. Curb walk—one foot on, one foot off beam			
g. Stand on board with both feet			
h. Alternate feet, walking forward			
i. Walk forward on beam, arms held sideward			
j. Walk forward on beam, then turn and walk back			
k. Walk forward on beam, then walk backward from the end			
l. Walk forward to the middle of the beam, then turn and walk sideward left with weight on the balls of the feet			
m. Walk forward to the middle of the beam, then turn and walk sideward right with weight on the balls of the feet			
n. Walk forward, carrying bean bag (or other object) in one hand; alternate hand used next time			
o. Walk forward with left foot always in front of right.			
p. Walk forward with right foot always in front			
q. Walk forward with hands on hips			
r. Walk backward with hands on hips			

	I	B	C
s. Walk forward with bean bag balanced on top of head			
t. Walk forward and step over wand held 12″ above center of the beam			
4. Trampolet			
a. Jump down on trampolet and continue bounce with assistance			
b. Jump up and down on trampolet, starting bouncing action with assistance			
c. Jump up and down on trampolet; maintain control, balance, stopping with assistance			
d. Stop without assistance			
5. Stall bars			
a. Make a definite attempt to climb beyond second bar			
b. Climb a few bars and descend, any fashion			
c. Climb to top and descend, one hand and one foot leading			
d. Climb to top and descend, hand over hand, one foot leading			
e. Climb to top, descend, hand over hand, alternating feet			
6. Slide			
a. Climb to top with assistance; need much help in sitting self at top; need encouragement and help in coming down			
b. Climb to top; need help in sitting self at top; slide down once seated			
c. Climb to top; turn self and sit appropriately for sliding down by self			
7. Scooters			
a. Sit, with help, on scooter			
b. Sit self on scooter, move legs together in moving scooter around			
c. Sit self on scooter, alternate feet in moving scooter around			
d. Move around freely on scooter, changing direction and pace, controlling stopping action			
8. Roller skates			
a. Manage one skate			
b. Remain upright with help using both skates			
c. Skate independently			
9. Participate in parachute activities			

F. Development of Manipulative Abilities

1. Grasp

	Without visual guidance	With visual guidance imposed by adult	Spontaneous behavior with own visual pursuit	I	B	C
a. Grasp reflexively						
b. Watch own hands while supine in crib						
c. Touch, scratch at sheets, bumpers in crib						
d. Engage in finger play as both hands meet						
e. Grasp—whole hand closure (palmar)						
f. Squeeze and release (squeaky toys)						
g. Put hands or objects to mouth						
h. Slap, push against toys; slap, splash water						
i. Reach and explore by touching or pushing						
j. Grasp and shake a rattle or toy (no voluntary release)						
k. Bilaterally hold large toys						
l. Reach, grasp, hold, and voluntarily release						
m. Grasp and transfer toys from one hand to the other						
n. Play Pat-a-Cake with aid						
o. Reach with some approximation of direction						
p. Poke with forefinger						
q. Clap hands, holding fingers and hands in extended position						
r. Hold peg or pencil in scissor grasp						
s. Pick up and hold smaller object with pincer grasp						

	I	B	C
2. Discrimination by size, shape, color			
a. Place object in larger area (toy in drawer, large ball in larger box, etc.)			
b. Place small object in specified area 1″ dowel in pegboard; 9/16″ dowel in pegboard; 3/16″ dowel in pegboard; note size			
c. Stack block tree			
d. Fit pieces into 3-piece form board			
e. Stack circular block tree			
f. Nest 3 boxes			
g. Nest 5 boxes			
h. Sort and group objects of same size, selecting from two sizes of gross differences			
i. Sort two geometric solids (squares and circles)			
j. Sort and group three similar geometric solids, selecting from two kinds of objects			
k. Match dowel and ball cap (3 colors, naming not expected)			
l. Select and sort 3 or more objects by color (not naming; use small toy cars, etc.)			
m. Select and sort dowels by color (no naming)			
G. *Development of Construction Level; manipulating with discrimination to produce a whole from parts*			
1. Mark a paper with random scribbling			
2. Stack two cubes			
3. String large beads			
4. Stack 3 cubes			
5. String beads, copying pattern			
6. String beads, using own pattern			
7. Begin writing sequence (see "Intellectual Growth," below)			
8. Use large paint brushes			
9. Set friction wheels in motion			

	I	B	C
10. Put simple wooden puzzles together			
11. Build something with blocks and name results			
12. Paste paper on paper			
13. Make design in any medium			
14. Use scissors			
a. Open and shut tongs or forceps (use thumb and middle finger for support)			
b. Pick up small ball of cotton with tongs			
c. Cut narrow strips crosswise			
d. Cut with one hand holding paper			
e. Cut along straight black line			
f. Cut bold outline			
g. Cut curved lines or patterns			
h. Cut thread or string			
i. Cut cloth			
15. Wind up a spring-driven toy and release it			
16. Handle a ball			
a. Roll ball with direction and purpose			
b. Receive rolled ball and return it with direction and purpose			
c. Throw bean bag into large container			
d. Throw 9" ball randomly			
e. Throw 9" ball with some direction			
f. Throw 9" ball into large container			
g. Pass 9" ball from own hands to another's hands (emphasize "to my HANDS")			
h. Throw 9" ball "from your hands to my hands"			
i. Throw 9" ball with direction and purpose			
j. Catch 9" ball between chest and knees			
k. Catch bean bag between chest and knees			

	I	B	C
l. Bounce large ball once and catch it			
m. Bounce large ball three or more times			
17. Use swings on playground			
H. *Social Use of Construction Skill*			
1. Form a circle with other children with help			
2. Form a circle			
3. Walk with a partner			
4. Take a partner and proceed as directed			
5. Join in team play, relays, etc.			
6. Play shuffleboard, croquet, keep-away, hop-scotch, etc.			
I. *Haptic Discrimination*			
1. Wet			
2. Dry			
3. Damp			
4. Cold			
5. Hot			
6. Warm			
7. Soft			
8. Hard			
9. Smooth			
10. Scratchy			
11. Rough			
12. Slippery			
13. Squishy			
14. Sticky			
15. Stretchy			
16. Sharp			

	I	B	C
17. Dull			
18. Crisp			
19. Chewy			
J. *Self-Care*			
1. Toileting			
a. Remain dry			
urinate at regular time			
urinate when taken—not on schedule			
indicate need by gesture			
ask to be taken to toilet			
approach toilet alone			
b. Use toilet independently			
c. Arrange clothing			
pull outer pants—down-up			
pull under pants—down-up			
arrange shirt or dress			
d. Use toilet tissue with direction			
use tissue when directed			
unroll and tear off appropriate amount			
use and dispose of in toilet			
e. Use toilet tissue without direction			
use tissue when given			
unroll and tear off appropriate amount			
use and dispose of in toilet			
f. Flush toilet			
g. Wash hands after using toilet			
go to basin			

	I	B	C
complete task			
2. Washing hands			
a. Hold hands under running water			
b. Lather soap			
c. Rub both sides of hands			
d. Rinse hands			
e. Dry hands			
f. Dispose of paper towels			
g. Turn water—on-off			
h. Hang towel			
i. Mix hot and cold water			
j. Leave soap and basin clean			
3. Undressing			
a. Unfastening			
unzip			
unsnap			
untie			
unbutton			
unhook			
unbuckle			
b. Removing outer clothing			
mittens			
scarf			
cap			
jacket			
snowpants			
boots			
coat			

	I	B	C
c. Removing clothing to bathe or go to bed			
shoes			
socks			
pants			
shirt			
dress			
underwear			
d. Putting clothing in proper places			
outer clothing—hooks or hangers			
underclothing—hang or fold			
soiled clothing—in hamper			
4. Dressing			
a. Put on:			
underwear			
dress			
shirt			
pants			
socks			
shoes (know right and left shoe)			
b. Fasten			
zip			
snap			
button			
hook			
tie			
buckle			
c. Select clean clothing			

	I	B	C
d. Adjust and fasten lingerie			
hook bra			
adjust slip strap			
pull on girdle			
put on hose			
fasten garters			
wear pantyhose			
e. Change clothing for physical education or special events (costumes)			
5. Care of clothing			
a. Clean boots			
b. Shine shoes			
c. Hand-wash hosiery, socks, blouses, etc.			
d. Use clothes brush effectively			
6. Personal hygiene			
a. Wash own face			
b. Wipe nose			
c. Blow nose			
d. Brush teeth			
e. Comb hair in proper place			
f. Bathe self in tub or shower			
g. Use deodorant			
h. Clean nails			
i. File or clip nails			
j. Shampoo own hair			
k. Pin up own hair			
l. Care for self during menstruation			
m. Shave—with direction; independently—boys and girls			

	I	B	C
n. Clean comb and brush			
o. Use cosmetics			

7. Eating

	I	B	C
a. Suck			
b. Swallow consecutively			
c. Chew			
d. Lick			
e. Bite			

8. Eating habits

	I	B	C
a. Wash hands before eating			
b. Handle finger foods tidily			
c. Drink from a cup or glass without spilling			
half-filled cup or glass			
full cup or glass			
drinking fountain			
pop bottle or can			
d. Wipe mouth with napkin			
e. Use fork			
f. Use spoon			
g. Cut meat on plate			
h. Butter bread			
i. Leave silver on plate when finished			
j. Wait until others are served			
k. Stay at place until dismissed			
l. Put used dishes in proper place			
m. Wipe up spilled food			
n. Serve self properly			
o. Pass dry foods (cookies, etc.)			
p. Pass drinks			

II. EMOTIONAL GROWTH

Terminal Performance Objective: Control behavior, reacting to own self-generated needs, progress to appropriate reaction under increasing social pressures.

	I	B	C
A. *Control Behavior*			
1. Indicate needs by gesture or pointing			
2. Sit quietly in a small group			
3. Sit quietly in a large group			
4. In competition			
5. With a change of routine			
6. When confronted with strangers			
7. In public places			
a. With family			
b. With peers in small group			
8. Say what is wrong or bothering him			
B. *Share and take turns*			
1. Reluctantly and only when urged			
2. Willingly			
3. With classmates			
4. With other children in groups			

III. SOCIAL GROWTH

Terminal Performance Objective: Extend interest from self to other people, communicating ideas, and interacting appropriately in social situations.

	I	B	C
A. *Extend Interest to*			
1. Self			
2. Things			
3. Other people			
B. *Behavior in Social Situations*			
1. Differentiate "yours" and "mine"			
2. Parallel-play without disturbing others			
3. Play with other children under supervision			
4. Show respect for adults and peers			
5. Show acceptable behavior in presence of visitors			
6. Accept gifts			
7. Offer gifts			
8. Follow directions for doing a chore			
9. Take directions from peer leader			
10. Assume role of leadership graciously			
11. Select good subjects for conversation			
12. Accept criticism			
13. Permit others to talk without interruption			
14. Keep a promise			
15. Keep a secret			
16. Play role of peacemaker			
17. Show respect for parents and elders			
18. Observe privacy			
19. Show modesty			
20. Respect request for quiet time			

	I	B	C
21. Show acceptable behavior with familiar small groups in classroom			
22. Show acceptable behavior with familiar, large group			
23. Show acceptable behavior in public places			
24. Carry a message			
25. Answer telephone			
26. Use telephone in emergency			
27. Use telephone socially (with restraint!)			

C. *General Manners*

	I	B	C
1. Say "please" and "thank you"			
2. Make requests politely ("May I please have . . .")			
3. Greet guests			
4. Say "goodbye" to guests			
5. Leave a party			
6. Accept a compliment			
7. Give a compliment			
8. Pass food before helping self			
9. Pass food around table			
10. Stand up to greet elders or to be introduced			
11. Offer to take wraps for guests			
12. Walk to door with departing guests			
13. Share conversation			
14. Hold doors for strangers as well as family and friends			
15. Offer assistance appropriately			

D. *Communication*

	I	B	C
1. Auditory decoding (receptive)			
a. React attention compelling mechanism (stimulus that arrests activity)			
own name			

	I	B	C
"no"			
music			
environmental sounds (i.e., doorbell, telephone)			
television			
a sound toy			
2. Auditory association (receptive)			
a. React to sound (total body reaction or large muscle activities)			
respond to social approach by smiling			
turn when voice is heard			
locate source of sound			
carry out limited activities to music (rocking a doll, swaying to music)			
react to environmental sounds (go to door when bell rings)			
come when own name is called			
b. Respond to sound (through gestures and other meaningful motor movements)			
listen to familiar sounds and find source			
react to simple commands			
"come here" or "come to me"			
"don't touch"			
"stop"			
Select and/or match corresponding sound toys (teacher shakes bell within child's view, then the child is asked to shake a second set of bells in response to an auditory signal)			
respond to own name with a gesture			
respond to "no" or "yes" with a gesture (i.e., head shaking)			
pat a picture in a book			
give objects on command with a gesture			
obey simple commands ("sit here")			

	I	B	C
follow directions			
one commission			
two commissions			
three commissions			
identify own body parts (see "Motor Growth" area)			
identify body parts on			
others			
doll			
picture of a person			
select one of three large objects with a clue of "put your finger on," "show me," "give me"			
select one of six objects			
select one of ten objects			
match an object to its miniature			
three objects			
six objects			
ten objects			
match an object to its picture			
three objects			
six objects			
ten objects			
identify a picture of one of three common objects on the clue: "put your finger on" "show me," "give me"			
three objects			
six objects			
ten objects			
respond appropriately to the significance of grammar (semantics, syntax, morphology)			
nouns:			

	I	B	C
point to objects			
point to items of clothing			
point to objects in the room			
point to objects in a picture			
qualifiers			
size (big, little)			
select by			
shape			
color (red, yellow)			
verbs			
point to appropriate picture			
prepositions: place objects on command			
point to pictures demonstrating preposition			
pronouns			
Respond to "show me" clothing items for body parts for			
your			
my			
our			
with dolls—boy and girl—for			
he			
she			
his			
her			
him			
with pictures evaluate this level for *plural endings*			
demonstrate with objects			
identify through pictures			

	I	B	C
comparative adjectives—select from two			
big—little			
large—small			
soft—hard			
light—heavy			
adverbs—indicate yes or no to			
loud—soft			
fast—slow			
categorize nouns			
furniture in the room			
miniatures—doll house furniture			
pictures			
complete sentences			
abstract level with pictures, given clues			
no clues to complete sentence			
3. Auditory association (expressive)			
a. Produce an appropriate vocal response			
babble			
when playing with toys			
socially			
repeat same sound over a period of time			
say "dada," "papa," or "mama," during babbling, but not in relation to parents			
echo sounds			
imitate gesture associated with songs and words			
gesture with appropriate verbalization to			
bye-bye			
hi			
up			

	I	B	C
imitate sound of adults			
say "dada," "papa," or "mama" in relation to parents			
add sound to object or picture			
listen to and mimic words to name common objects presented in three dimensions only			
label			
ten objects			
fifteen objects			
twenty objects			
twenty-five objects			
b. Express needs, self-wants through			
gestures			
words			
c. Use verb appropriately			
d. Join two words together (may be a noun and verb or noun and qualifier)			
e. Refer to self by			
first name			
whole name			
f. Imitate sentence			
three-word sentence			
six-word sentence			
nine-word sentence			
g. Join three or more words together in sentences			
article before noun			
use verb tense correctly			
plural endings			
pronouns			
interrogative sentences			
comparative adjectives			

	I	B	C
h. Tell about a picture			
enumerate items			
describe picture			
interpret picture			
describe an object or person			
i. Tell spontaneous story			
enumerate events			
describe			
interpret			

E. *Home, School and Community Usefulness*
   (Pre-vocational)

1. Chores: Perform useful tasks

	I	B	C
a. Table setting and clearing			
set place			
serve and pass food			
clear table			
wipe table (crumbs off with a damp cloth)			
empty liquids and garbage in proper container			
stack dishes and silver in dish boxes			
rinse dishes			
stack dish machine			
unload dish machine			
stack dishes and sort silver			
put dishes and silver away in proper places			
clean sinks, counter and wipe up any spills and drips			
clean coffee pots and urns			
scour pots and pans with steel wool			
measure soap or detergent			
b. Food handling			

	I	B	C
wash hands before handling any food			
open packages			
put cookies in servers			
pour milk for self			
pour milk for milk trays			
clean fruits and vegetables (potatoes, salad greens, tomatoes, celery, grapes, plums, etc.)			
peel potatoes, carrots			
butter bread			
make sandwiches			
prepare Kool-Ade			
prepare salads			
prepare frozen orange juice			
make lemonade from frozen mix			
release ice cubes			
refill ice trays and return to refrigerator			
serve cake			
prepare food for refrigerator			

c. Cooking

	I	B	C
bake potatoes (set timer and check clock)			
open cans			
turn electric stove burners on and off			
turn gas burner on and off and regulate flame (with pilot light)			
heat food from can (baked beans, etc.)			
heat soup from can requiring addition of water or milk			
heat frozen food in double boiler (prepared hash, chicken à la king, etc.)			
heat TV dinners			
make dessert (uncooked) with packaged mix			
cut or drop cookies already prepared			

	I	B	C
prepare any other foods			
prepare tea, coffee, cocoa			
pop corn (packaged)			
clean up pots and pans			
leave stove clean			
leave sink clean			
leave counter clean			
put cooking utensils in place			
d. Laundry			
sort laundry for loads for washing machine—white, colored, linty (towels), nylons			
move load from washer to dryer			
hang laundry on clothes line			
sort dry laundry by ownership (swimsuits, towels, etc.)			
fold clean laundry			
iron flat work			
iron clothing			
press clothing (describe)			
hand wash single items			
e. Sewing			
sew on button using prethreaded needle			
use thimble			
thread needle			
knot thread			
baste			
pin and baste			
hem			
lay out pattern and pin			
cut pattern			

	I	B	C
use sewing machine			
f. Bed making			
make own bed			
change sheets and make bed			
fold blankets			
g. Household tasks			
empty ash trays			
dust furniture			
use dust mop and shake it before putting it away			
use carpet sweeper			
use vacuum cleaner			
empty vacuum cleaner			
handle broom and dust pan			
properly use sponge rubber mop, rinse, and store it			
clean wash basins, bath tub, soap dishes and all porcelain			
clean toilet (use bowl cleaner, brush, and bactine solution)			
clean wall around basin area			
clean bathroom wall and dividers			
scrub tile bathroom floor			
wet mop floor			
apply floor wax			
clean painted woodwork			
polish furniture			
clean window and glass shelving			
polish flat silver			
polish hollow silver			
clean inside of an automobile			
wash and dry an automobile			

	I	B	C
wrap a package			
h. Yard chores			
pick up trash			
sweep up sand around sandbox			
rake around playground equipment			
take playground toys outside, bring them in and put them away			
weed around plantings			
rake grass and dispose of it properly			
rake leaves and dispose of them properly			
shovel snow to make a path			
sprinkle de-icer on walks and driveway			
sweep blacktop on playground			
i. "Crew chores" (working together required)			
arrange cots for rest time			
stack cots after rest time			
"set up" for lunch (tables and chairs)			
clean classrooms after lunch			
empty wastebaskets			
check all paper supplies			
kleenex			
paper towels			
toilet tissue			
paper cups			
paper napkins			
shovel snow from driveway			
put up flag and take it down			
set up or stack chairs in assembly			

	Needs Supervision	B
2. Child care		
a. Play appropriate games		
b. Tell how a game is played		
c. Differentiate between an active and a quiet game		
d. Show others how to play a game		
e. Play the game		
f. Ask for help when needed		
g. Tell when to stop an activity		
h. Plan what will be played		
i. Prepare necessary equipment		
j. Form a circle		
standing		
sitting		
k. Form a straight line		
l. Follow safety rules for using swings		
m. Follow safety rules using slides		
n. Follow the rule for "taking turns"		
o. Show how and help child use overhead ladders		
p. Sandbox		
show how to fill and dump sand		
show how to make a hill		
play with sand appropriately		
permit "territorial rights" in sandbox		
q. Wash a child's hands		
r. Take off outer wraps and boots		
s. Put on outer wraps and boots		
t. Tie shoes of a young child		
u. Toilet young child		

	Needs Supervision	B
v. Bus helper		
escort child to bus		
arrange seat belts		
take child out of seat belt		
close door of bus		
open and hold school door for children arriving or leaving		
w. Food assistance		
set up lunch bins		
count correct number of items		
take milk count		
set up milk trays		
set up and take down lunch tables		
place correct number of chairs at tables		
put chairs away properly after lunch or assembly		
prepare dishes for dish machine		
load dish cart		
put dishes and silver in proper places		
x. General assistance		
wash toys and rinse in antiseptic solution		
wash and dry floor mats		
put rolling toys on blacktop area		
put rolling toys in storage area		
react appropriately to:		
be kind or gentle		
be responsible for		
be prompt		
set an example		
use a pleasant voice		

IV. INTELLECTUAL GROWTH

Terminal Performance Objective: Demonstrate maximum potential in job-related skills and basic academics.

	I	B	C
A. Attention			
1. Attend by intrigue or fascination only			
2. Attend when name is called accompanied by gesture			
3. Attend when name is called without a gesture			
4. Attend ten or more minutes to one activity			
B. Recognition of Words (Graphenes)			
1. Own first name			
2. Own last name			
3. Names of classmates			
4. Days of the week			
5. Months of the year			
6. Own address			
C. Read Pictures			
1. Point to items on verbal cue			
2. Name item indicated			
3. Name action			
4. Place two pictures in story sequence			
5. Place three items in story sequence			
6. Place two to four pictures in story sequence and tell story			
a. Naming only			
b. Construct sentence			
c. Construct correct syntax			
D. Alphabet			
1. Say, rotely			
2. Know order of letters			
E. Word Recognition			
1. Sight recognition			
a. Phonetic cues			

	I	B	C
F. *Read Group of Words or Sentences from*			
1. Daily weather report			
2. Experience chart			
3. "The Big Book" (Scott, Foresman)			
G. *Read for Information*			
H. *Read from "My Weekly Reader" for Pleasure*			
I. *Reading*			
1. Words for protection (can point out, act out, say, find place such as BOYS (bathroom)			
STOP—GO			
IN—OUT			
UP—DOWN			
DANGER			
FIRE ESCAPE			
EXIT—ENTRANCE			
RAILROAD CROSSING			
SLOW			
FIRST AID			
KEEP OUT			
BUS STOP			
POISON			
BOYS—GIRLS			
MEN—WOMEN			
NO TRESPASSING			
WALK			
GENTLEMEN—LADIES			
PUSH—PULL			
WET PAINT			
ENTRANCE			
REST ROOMS			
2. Read useful words			

	I	B	C
a. Job list			
with picture clue			
without picture clue			
b. Weather words			
with picture clue			
without picture clue			
c. Days of the week			
with picture clue			
without picture clue			
d. Months of the year			
with picture clue			
without picture clue			
e. Food labels			
with picture clue			
without picture clue			
f. Cleaning supplies			
with picture clue			
without picture clue			
g. Directives			
with picture clue			
without picture clue			
match directives			
with picture clue			
without picture clue			
J. Writing			
1. Scribble randomly			
2. Push-pull stroking			
3. Inscribe overlaying circles			
4. Attach name to scribbling			

5. Confine circle to limited area			
6. Confine lines to set boundaries			
7. Start circle at "1 o'clock position" and proceed counterclockwise			
8. Complete green clock game			
9. Complete red clock game			
10. Make vertical crosses in defined areas			
11. Make oblique crosses in defined areas			
12. Draw with schema appearing			
13. Trace writing sequence cards			
14. Copy writing sequence cards			
15. Trace and name			
a. Square			
b. Circle			
c. Triangle			
16. Copy and name			
a. Square			
b. Circle			
c. Triangle			
17. Trace own name			
18. Copy own name			
19. Reproduce own name			
20. Write own name spontaneously			
21. Write own address spontaneously			
22. Write ten words for protection			
23. Copy and read ten useful words			
24. Write and read ten useful words			
25. Copy and read weather records; special events			
26. Write and read weather records; special events			
K. *Number Concepts: Quantification Skills Scoring Chart*			
1. Demonstrate concept of			

	I	B	C
1 means 1 thing			
1 is less than 2			
Relate symbol 1 to quantity			
2. Demonstrate concept of			
2 means 2 things			
2 is 1 more than 1			
2 is 1 less than 3			
Relate symbol 2 to quantity			
3. Demonstrate concept of			
3 means 3 things			
3 is 1 more than 2			
3 is 2 more than 1			
3 is 1 less than 4			
Relate symbol 3 to quantity			
4. Demonstrate concept of			
4 means 4 things			
4 is 1 more than 3			
4 is 2 more than 2			
4 is 3 more than 1			
4 is 1 less than 5			
Relate symbol 4 to quantity			
5. Demonstrate concept of			
5 means 5 things			
5 is 1 more than 4			
5 is 2 more than 3			
5 is 3 more than 2			
5 is 4 more than 1			
5 is 1 less than 6			
Relate symbol 5 to quantity			

	I	B	C
6. Demonstrate concept of			
6 means 6 things			
6 is 1 more than 5			
6 is 2 more than 4			
6 is 3 more than 3			
6 is 4 more than 2			
6 is 5 more than 1			
6 is 1 less than 7			
Relate symbol 6 to quantity			
7. Demonstrate concept of			
7 means 7 things			
7 is 1 more than 6			
7 is 2 more than 5			
7 is 3 more than 4			
7 is 4 more than 3			
7 is 5 more than 2			
7 is 6 more than 1			
7 is 1 less than 8			
Relate symbol 7 to quantity			
8. Demonstrate concept of			
8 means 8 things			
8 is 1 more than 7			
8 is 2 more than 6			
8 is 3 more than 5			
8 is 4 more than 4			
8 is 5 more than 3			
8 is 6 more than 2			
8 is 7 more than 1			
8 is 1 less than 9			
Relate symbol 8 to quantity			

	I	B	C
9. Demonstrate concept of			
9 means 9 things			
9 is 1 more than 8			
9 is 2 more than 7			
9 is 3 more than 6			
9 is 4 more than 5			
9 is 5 more than 4			
9 is 6 more than 3			
9 is 7 more than 2			
9 is 8 more than 1			
9 is 1 less than 10			
Relate symbol 9 to quantity			
10. Demonstrate concept of			
10 means 10 things			
10 is 1 more than 9			
10 is 2 more than 8			
10 is 3 more than 7			
10 is 4 more than 6			
10 is 5 more than 5			
10 is 6 more than 4			
10 is 7 more than 3			
10 is 8 more than 2			
10 is 9 more than 1			
10 is 1 less than 11			
Relate symbol 10 to quantity			
11. Order			
a. Place numbered cards in proper sequence (nonverbal)			
1 to 5			

6 to 10			
11 to 15			
16 to 20			
b. Place numbered cards in correct place			
1 to 10			
11 to 20			
21 to 40			
41 to 60			
61 to 100			
12. Level I: Count by notation			
a. Step 1 count with structured termination			
b. Step 2 count three-dimensional objects without structured termination			
grasp and count			
lift and count			
touch and count			
look only and count			
name number symbol			
c. Step 3 Respond correctly to spoken number symbol to signify termination			
with clues			
without clues			
use number symbol from picture			
point to symbol named			
name symbol			
d. Step 4 symbol transfer: select correct group of blocks from spoken symbol only without touching or nodding			
with clues			
without clues			
transfer meaning of spoken symbol to properly selected picture without touching or nodding			

	I	B	C

e. Step 5 attach the visual number symbol to the concrete presentation

    select correct cut out number symbol to match presented group of blocks

    1

    2

    3

    4

    5

    6

    7

    8

    9

    10

    write the correct number symbol to match presented group of blocks

    1

    2

    3

    4

    5

    6

    7

    8

    9

    10

f. Step 6 transfer to practical situation

    select correct group of designated objects from mixed objects from heard number symbol only (auditory cue)

    show correct number of fingers from heard number symbol (auditory cue)

g. Step 7 select correct group of blocks to match seen number symbol (visual cue)

    select correct group of objects to match seen number symbol

h. Step 8 attach correct symbol to match group of blocks, objects, or pictures not presented or structured; say word, spontaneously, for "how many?"; look only and select correct symbol, pointing or placing it appropriately			
say correct symbol to match a given group			
respond verbally with number symbol to "how many?"			
use (say) number to ask question			
write correct symbol to match a given group			
write correct symbol from auditory cue			
i. Step 9 transfer to home situation			
arrange one place setting			
set table for given number			
count given number of			
chairs			
milk glasses			
spoons (or any table silver)			
paper napkins			
children in class			
children in bus			
13. Level II: counting by grouping and notation			
a. With color clues (contrast)			
1 to 5			
6 to 10			
b. Without color clues			
1 to 5			
6 to 10			
c. Add combinations to 10 by grouping and notation with color cues			
d. Add combinations to 10 by grouping and notation without color cues			
e. Subtract combinations to 10 by grouping and notation with color cues			
f. Subtract combinations to 10 by grouping and notation without color cues			

	I	B	C
g. Add and subtract to 100 without carrying or borrowing			
14. Level III: counting by grouping			
a. Count by 5s and terminate			
b. Count by 2s and terminate			
c. Add by grouping			
d. Subtract by grouping			
15. Ordinals: demonstrate meaning of			
a. First			
b. Last			
c. Second			
d. Third			
e. Fourth			
f. Fifth			
g. In front of (ahead of)			
h. In back of (behind)			
i. Next			
j. Next to last			
16. Vocabulary of relationships: demonstrate meaning of			
little—big			
open—shut			
down—up			
one—more			
slow—fast			
in—out			
over—under			
small—large			
short—tall			
few—many			
less—more			

short—long			
before—after (days of week only)			
in front of—behind (people in line)			
top—bottom			
high—low			
above—beneath			
inside—outside			
first—last			
before—after			
long—short			
far—near			
close—apart			
beside—away			
beginning—end			
forward—back			
all—some			
some—none			
little—much			
heavy—light			
hard—easy			

17. Concept of time

    a. Use of clock

identify number symbols to 12			
point out little hand (hour hand)			
point out big hand (minute hand)			
point out position of little and big hands ("show me")			
point out position of big hand for *before* and *after*			
point out lines indicating intervals of five to thirty minutes—for *before* and *after*			

    b. Relate clock to school schedule

    c. Estimate length of a minute

	I	B	C
d. Respond to "hurry," "wait"			
e. Tell time to			
half-hour			
quarter hour			
five—minute intervals			
f. Demonstrate meaning of			
now—later			
soon			
a long time			
early—late			
night—day			
morning			
noon			
afternoon			
yesterday			
today			
tomorrow			
time for (lunch)/(gym)			
before—after			
first—last			
days of the week			
seasons			
fall			
winter			
spring			
summer			
baby			
child			
youth			

age			
18. Money (always use real money)			
a. Name			
penny			
nickle			
dime			
quarter			
b. Tell value of			
penny			
nickle			
dime			
quarter			
half-dollar			
c. Compare			
penny—nickle			
penny—nickle—dime			
nickle—dime—quarter			
d. Count change from a quarter			
e. Show or demonstrate that money can buy			
5c—one package gum			
10c—one large candy bar			
10c—two small candy bars			
19. Measuring			
a. Count, pace off			
b. Stretch pre-set measure to define a limit in weaving			
c. Measure inches on a ruler			
d. Demonstrate meaning of			
can-full			
box-full			
too full			

	I	B	C
glassful			
bottle-full			
half-dozen			
cupful			
tablespoon			
teaspoon			
half-teaspoon			
half-cup			
pound			
pint			
quart			
half-gallon			
gallon			
dozen			
more—less			
20. State numbers used for personal identification			
a. Age			
b. Own address			
c. Telephone			
d. Birthdate			
21. Discriminate basic shapes			
a. Round			
b. Straight			
c. Parallel			
d. Square			
e. Curved			
f. Triangle			
g. Circle			
22. Thermal discrimination			

a. Know

    hot

    cold

    warm

b. Tactile discrimination

    warm—cold   food

    warm—cold   water

    warm—cold   sand

23. Baric discrimination

    a. Heavy

    b. Light

    c. Heavier

    d. Bulky

24. Linear discrimination

    a. Long

    b. Short

    c. Longer

    d. Shorter

    e. Far

    f. Near

    g. Close

L. *Color Concept*

1. Differentiate, using color clues

    a. Own locker

    b. Classmates' lockers

    c. Own name

    d. Classmates' names

2. Match colors

    a. 1″ dowels with matching caps

        red

	I	B	C
yellow			
blue			
green			
b. 1" cubes to given base			
red			
yellow			
blue			
green			
c. Magnetic color lotto			
d. Sit-upon carpet and bean bags			
e. Place pegs in board; match large pattern			
3. Sort colors; select color from group to match given base			
a. 1" cubes			
red			
yellow			
blue			
green			
b. Variety of sizes, same colors			
c. Variety of shapes, same colors			
d. Variety of colors, same shapes			
4. Name (label colors)			
a. Echoic			
b. Spontaneous			
5. Transfer to environment			
a. Match colors in classroom			
b. Match colors on playground			
c. Match colors in arts and crafts activities			
M. *Orientation to Environment*			
1. Say father's name when asked			

2. Say home address and telephone number or show where to find it on identification tag			
3. Identify members of family from pictures			
4. Identify school personnel and what they do			
a. Bus driver			
b. Teacher			
c. Principal			
d. Social worker			
e. Psychologist			
f. Occupational therapist			
g. Music therapist			
h. Speech therapist			
i. School nurse			
j. Custodian			
5. Demonstrate clothing appropriate for weather			
6. Identify days of the week			
7. Show indications of when we do things			
8. Demonstrate rules and regulations			
a. At home			
b. At school			
c. In community			
9. Walk between home and school			
10. Mail a letter			
11. Identify community workers and what they do			
a. Milkman			
b. Policeman			
c. Mailman			
d. Crossing guard			
e. Public health nurse			
12. Follow requirements for privacy			
a. Keeping a secret			

	I	B	C
b. Not repeating "home gossip"			
13. Buy something in a store			
a. With a note			
b. Independently			
14. Identify where to buy things			
a. Grocery store			
b. Drugstore			
c. Bakery			
d. Hardware, etc.			
15. Know how to transport self on public conveyance			
16. Follow basic health rules			
a. Tell about signs of illness			
b. Keep away from other children when told to			
c. Accept immunizations			
d. Cooperate with dentist			
e. Cooperate with doctor			
f. Cooperate for tests			
17. Follow procedures in emergency			
a. Fire drill			
b. Weather disaster			

V. AESTHETIC GROWTH: ARTS & CRAFTS

Terminal Performance Objective: Enjoy life via experiences observing the beauty of the earth and natural phenomena, art, music, dance, mores and goodness of leisure time.

A. *Paper: Construction, Newsprint, Tissue*			
1. Tear paper randomly			
2. Arrange torn paper on background			
3. Paste torn paper on background			
4. Name shapes of torn paper			
5. Paste torn paper on background to produce design or picture			
6. Produce design from pre-cut shapes (set shapes prepared by teacher)			

7. Create design from own cut shapes			
8. Laminate design from torn paper shapes			
9. Laminate design from cut paper shapes			
10. Staple to create paper strip sculpture			
11. Cut, twist, and staple paper to create mobile			
12. Curl, fringe, pleat, weave paper			

B. Printing

1. Use stamps and stamp pad			
2. Press objects (gadgets, potatoes, carrots, etc.) fingers, in tempera and print (teacher prepares design on gadgets)			
3. Print design with cut sponges			
4. Print representational picture with cut sponges			
5. Use brayer and water soluble printing ink on glass palette			
6. Make design on printing palette and take off print			

C. Chalk, Crayons, Felt Pens

1. Scribble on chalk board			
2. Scribble on paper			
3. Scribble, using push-pull motion			
4. Produce concentric circles in scribbling			
5. Name scribbling			
6. Produce obvious schema			
7. Tell story from own scribbling			
8. Laminate, using prepared crayon chips			
9. Use crayon on flat side			
10. Rub crayon over shapes or textures			
11. Use colors for representational drawing			
12. Use wet chalk on wet paper			
13. Stencil with dry chalk to make rubbings			
14. Use base line (ground and sky)			
15. Laminate, preparing own crayon chips			

	I	B	C
16. Repeat designs within set limits			
17. Copy designs or pictures			

D. *Clay*

	I	B	C
1. Squeeze, pound, roll clay to produce shapes and forms			
2. Name product			
3. Use add-on method to produce animal or human form			
4. Use "pinch-pot" for pottery			
5. Coil to create pottery			
6. Roll and cut clay for slab built pottery			
7. Use drape molds to produce pottery			
8. Use gadgets and tools for decoration and texture			
9. Glaze and underglaze for decoration			

E. *Painting*

	I	B	C
1. Finger paint			
a. Use one color only—flat hand			
b. Manipulate with fingers			
c. Use side of hand, fingernails, fist, arm			
2. Poster or tempera			
a. Use one color only, 1/2" brush			
b. Design with paint soaked string			
c. Use three colors			
d. Wipe excess paint from brush			
e. Drop paint on wet paper			
f. Use a subject for painting			
g. Use as many colors as desired			
h. Use brush for light or heavy lines and for dry brush technique			
i. Paint with sponge			
3. Watercolor			
a. Wet all paint pans before painting			

    b. Wash brush when changing colors

    c. Produce wet paper (accidental) designs

    d. Produce representational painting

F. *Collage*

    1. Paste or glue familiar textures on background

    2. Choose materials for design for tactile stimulation

    3. Select pictures of texture

    4. Fill in scribble picture to convey idea of texture

G. *Theory*

    1. Fill paper (use of space)

    2. Prepare background before making picture

    3. Use light versus dark

    4. Show variety of lines: thin, thick, wavy, zig-zag, circular, etc.

    5. Identify basic shapes and produce them

    6. Name colors

    7. Make other colors from primary colors

    8. Name textures

    9. Select pattern or design (repeat)

    10. Make repeat designs exactly as to line, color, and pattern

H. *Construction*

    1. Make stabile with rigid objects and ball of clay

    2. Make stabile for definite purpose

        a. Picture frame

        b. Holiday decoration

            with assistance

            with minimal assistance

            proceed independently

        c. Basketry

    3. Construct freely, for fun, with cardboard tubes, toothpicks, sticks, or wood scraps (using glue)

    4. Use papier mâché

	I	B	C
a. Use strip method over form to make containers, bowls, etc.			
b. Make animals by using strip method over armature of wire, newspaper, or boxes			
c. Make masks using either strip or "instant" papier mâché			
d. Use pulp or "instant" papier mâché to make puppet heads			

I. *Sewing and Creative Stitchery*

	I	B	C
1. Thread needle			
2. Move needle in and out of holes in rigid cards, boards, or mesh (screen)			
3. Do running stitch			
4. Sew on button			
5. Hem			
a. Pre-basted			
b. Baste and finish			
6. Outline stitch			
7. Cross stitch			
8. Button-hole stitch			
9. Outline stitch			
10. Sew on snap			
11. Sew on hook and eye			
12. Darn			
13. Gros point			
14. Knit			
15. Crochet			
16. Afghan			
17. Embroider			

J. *Weaving*

	I	B	C
1. Move rigid "shuttle" (flat stick) "over and under" slit fabric stretched on a frame			
2. Move filler over and under a rigid warp (pot holder)			
3. Define or identify weaving terms: loom, shuttle, warp, filler, shed, beater, roving			
4. Manipulate 6" loom (pre-warped)			

5. Manipulate 12″ or 14″ loom (pre-warped)			
6. Beat rhythmically			
7. Beat with uniform pressure			
8. Produce even edges (selvage)			
9. Use measure marks (on tape)			
10. Detect errors			
11. Follow pattern			
12. Advance warp			
13. Wind warp			
14. Assist warping			

AESTHETIC GROWTH: MUSIC

A. *Attend to Good Music*			
B. *Desire to Participate in Good Music*			
C. *Participate in Music Activity*			
1. Clap hands			
2. Respond to rhythms, using cues, starting and stopping			
3. Use one hand			
a. Shake bell, maracas			
b. Strike with one rhythm stick			
c. Strike xylophone			
4. Use both hands			
a. Strike two rhythm sticks			
b. Clash cymbals			
5. Hold instrument with one hand and play with other hand (percussion) triangle, gong, hollow block, single resonator, drums			
6. Use both hands to play			
a. Resonator bells			
b. Drums			
7. Play autoharp or guitar			

	I	B	C
8. Play tune on organ or piano			
D. *Sing Familiar Songs with Strong Support*			
E. *Sing or Hum a Tune without Accompaniment*			
F. *Express Pleasure Participating in Rhythmic Pattern and Melody*			

AESTHETIC GROWTH: DANCE
(movement to express and communicate emotionally and socially)

	I	B	C
A. *Use Basic Steps for Dancing (folk, square, social)*			
1. Walk—forward and backward			
2. Glide (step together)			
3. Step-together-step			
4. Stamp (rhythm)			
5. Hopsa: step-hop			
6. Skip: hop-step, hop-step			
7. Polka: hop-step-together-step			
B. *Rhythmic—Interpretive*			
1. Respond to music with total body movement			
2. Improvise			
3. Engage in directed activity			
C. *Basic Ballet—Demonstrate*			
1. Arm movements			
2. Body trunk movements			
3. Elementary footwork			

Name _____

D.B. _____

QUARTERLY ACCUMULATIVE ACCOUNT OF BEHAVIOR CHANGES

Date	C.A.	Sept.			Dec.			March			June		
		I	B	C	I	B	C	I	B	C	I	B	C
Initial Entry													
Cum. Total													
Tally													
Cum. Total													
Tally													
Cum. Total													
Tally													
Cum. Total													
Tally													
Cum. Total													
Tally													
Cum. Total													
Tally													
Cum. Total													
Tally													
Cum. Total													
Tally													
Cum. Total													
Tally													
Cum. Total													
Tally													
Cum. Total													

Name _____

D.B. _____

ANNUAL ACCUMULATIVE ACCOUNT OF BEHAVIOR CHANGES IN THE FIVE GROWTH AREAS

Date	Max. Total C.A.	391 Physical			13 Emotional			328 Social			462 Intellectual			142 Esthetic			1336 Total		
		I	B	C	I	B	C	I	B	C	I	B	C	I	B	C	I	B	C
Initial Entry																			